D0821746

W. B. Yeats:
The Writing of
The Player Queen

Manuscripts of W. B. Yeats
David R. Clark, *General Editor*

W. B. Yeats

The Writing of *The Player Queen*

Manuscripts of W. B. Yeats transcribed,

edited & with a commentary by

Curtis Baker Bradford,

Late Oakes Ames Professor of English Literature,

Grinnell College

Northern Illinois University Press

DeKalb

Library of Congress Cataloging in Publication Data

Yeats, William Butler, 1865–1939.
 W. B. Yeats: the writing of the Player Queen.

 (His Manuscripts of W. B. Yeats; v. 2)
 Bibliography: p.
 1. Yeats, William Butler, 1865–1939. The Player
Queen. 2. Yeats, William Butler, 1865–1939–
Manuscripts. I. Yeats, William Butler, 1865–1939. The
Player Queen. 1976. II. Bradford, Curtis Baker,
1911–1969. III. Title: The writing of The Player
Queen.

PR5904.P453Y4 1976   821'.8   73–18798
ISBN 0–87580–048–3

Dedication

Manuscripts of W. B. Yeats *is dedicated to the memory of George (Mrs. W. B.) Yeats who did pioneer work on the manuscripts of W. B. Yeats plays.*

The volume W. B. YEATS: THE WRITING OF The Player Queen *is dedicated to Maria Gerson Bradford.*

Contents

Illustrations

Tables

Preface

W. B. Yeats's *The Player Queen* was first produced by the
London Stage Society at the King's Hall, Covent Garden, on 25 May 1919.
On 9 December 1919 it was produced at the Abbey Theatre. It was published
3 November 1922 in *Plays in Prose and Verse* (London); again on 21 November
1922 in *The Player Queen* (London); and in *The Dial* for that same month.

Yeats had already commented, in "Anima Hominis," dated 25 February 1917,
on his long struggle to complete the play.

> Some years ago I began to believe that our culture, with its doctrine of
> sincerity and self-realisation, made us gentle and passive, and that the Mid-
> dle Ages and the Renaissance were right to found theirs upon the imitation
> of Christ or of some classic hero. Saint Francis and Caesar Borgia made them-
> selves overmastering, creative persons by turning from the mirror to medita-
> tion upon a mask. When I had this thought I could see nothing else in life.
> I could not write the play I had planned, for all became allegorical, and
> though I tore up hundreds of pages in my endeavour to escape from allegory,
> my imagination became sterile for nearly five years and I only escaped at
> last when I had mocked in a comedy my own thought. (*Mythologies,* pp.
> 333–34)

If Yeats really tore up hundreds of pages, hundreds more (over 1,100 folios)
remain, which, selected, arranged, transcribed, and edited here by Curtis Bradford,
show clearly the evolution of the play. That evolution is not quite what one would
expect upon reading the provocative accounts by Yeats which first led me to
suggest to Bradford that he do this book.

In his 1922 note to the play Yeats describes its first form as "verse tragedy"
and its published form as "farce."

> I began in, I think, 1907, a verse tragedy, but at that time the thought I
> have set forth in *Per Amica Silentia Lunae* was coming into my head, and I
> found examples of it everywhere. I wasted the best working months of several
> years in an attempt to write a poetical play where every character became an

example of the finding or not finding of what I have called the Antithetical Self; and because passion and not thought makes tragedy, what I made had neither simplicity nor life. I knew precisely what was wrong and yet could neither escape from thought nor give up my play. At last it came into my head all of a sudden that I could get rid of the play if I turned it into a farce; and never did I do anything so easily, for I think that I wrote the present play in about a month; and when it was performed at the Stage Society in 1919 I forgot that it was my own work, so completely that I discovered from the surprise of a neighbor, that, indignant with a house that seemed cold to my second act (since much reformed), I was applauding. If it could only have come into my head three years earlier. . . . [*Variorum Plays,* p. 761]

This comment agrees with that in the "Introduction" to "The Resurrection" in *Wheels and Butterflies* (London: Macmillan and Company, 1934):

Then after some years came the thought that a man always tried to become his opposite, to become what he would abhor if he did not desire it, and I wasted some three summers and some part of each winter before I had banished the ghost and turned what I had meant for tragedy into a farce: *The Player Queen.* [*Variorum Plays,* p. 933]

This myth of an unsuccessful verse tragedy reborn suddenly into a brilliant farce becomes even more attractive when one reads in Richard Ellmann's *Yeats the Man and the Masks,* p. 215, that it was Ezra Pound who performed, as he had done for Eliot's *The Waste Land* (also published in 1922), the necessary Caesarean operation: "It was Pound who, hearing that Yeats had spent six or seven years trying to write *The Player Queen* as a tragedy, suggested that it might be made into a comedy, with such effect that Yeats completely transformed the play at once."

It was the hope of being able to document this miraculous rebirth and to lay before the public what would amount to a new verse tragedy by Yeats—even if an unsuccessful or unfinished one—which motivated my eager inquiry to Bradford. I had hoped to find—as my coeditors and I had found in *The Shadowy Waters* manuscripts—a version of the play uniquely different from the final version and even perhaps worthy of study in its own right as a separate but related piece of literature (cf. *Druid Craft: The Writing of The Shadowy Waters,* ed. Michael J. Sidnell, George P. Mayhew, and David R. Clark [Amherst: University of Massachusetts Press, 1971; Dublin: The Dolmen Press, 1972], being the first volume of the series "Manuscripts of W. B. Yeats").

And Bradford has indeed shown that there *was* an earlier version of the play— a version that Yeats tried to perfect for many years—vastly different from the published version, and that there was a sudden change, a radical reorientation which resulted in the achievement of the play's present form. And he has shown also that "a tragic ending for *The Player Queen* . . . is found only in the scenarios" that Yeats wrote at various times up through 1910, preliminary to starting new prose or verse versions. Bradford distinguishes seventeen separate drafts written in this period. (After 1910, Yeats pretty much dropped the play until forming the new conception in 1915.) Many of the early drafts lack endings, but in none of them where there is an ending does the Player Queen die tragically. In five of them, including Draft 16, the best example of the play in its original form, the Player Queen, after enacting her role in real life, gives up her robes and crown cheerfully, is reunited with her estranged poet-playwright husband, and even chooses to play Noah's wife, although her distaste for that part has been the occasion of the play's action. The end itself would be suitable to a Shakespearian romantic comedy. To quote Bradford, "By the end of Draft 17 Yeats had written a full-length play, largely in verse, which is serious in tone though it has a comic ending —a 'drama' as Chekhov used the term" (cf. p. 6).

As for Ezra Pound's midwifery, Pound was indeed acting as Yeats's secretary "During the winters of 1913–14, 1914–15, and 1915–16" (Ellmann, *Yeats the Man and the Masks,* p. 215), and Yeats "saw a good deal of Pound" during 1915 (cf. K. L. Goodwin, *The Influence of Ezra Pound* [London: Oxford University Press, 1968], p. 95). Pound may have been close to Yeats when the great change occurred. But in none of the passages above does Yeats speak of the intervention of a friend. Yet he does so in a parallel instance: In the "Preface" of *The King of the Great Clock Tower, Commentaries and Poems* (1934) Yeats speaks of consulting a "poet not of my school who would, as he did some years ago, say what he thought." The poet was Ezra Pound, and the opinion "a single word 'Putrid' " (*Variorum Plays,* pp. 1309–10).

Whatever Pound may have said about *The Player Queen,* Bradford finds other reasons for Yeats's successful breakthrough. Not only was Yeats "in 1915 a greater artist than he had been in 1910" (p. 270 infra) but in the process of writing "Ego Dominus Tuus" (completed 5 December 1915, and worked on for some time before that) he had expressed "fully the doctrine of the self and anti-self, which he had been maturing for many years" (pp. 270 and 457). In other words, the breakthrough in his thought made way for the breakthrough in writing a play intimately involved with that thought. A third reason Bradford gives for success is what might be described in Mark Schorer's phrase "technique as discovery." For instance, in debating whether the Player Queen should be executed by the rebels, or take her own life, or be content to return to her role as Noah's wife, Yeats found that only the third solution worked; he discovered, in short, that what he had written was technically a comedy. He then turned with relief to the Comic Muse and wrote the play we know, with its new farcial end (p. 455 infra).

These facts are of great value to students of Yeats's work. Of even more value is the presentation in ordered fashion of manuscripts representative of the play's development. These show not only the growth of *The Player Queen* but also the inception of ideas, images, and actions which, although discarded from this play, matured and were used in other works of Yeats's.

There are incidental riches to which the reader will wish to return for special purposes. The introductory chapter traces Yeats's progress in writing the play, the state of the manuscripts, and the development of the text. The table of elements from various drafts which are retained in the finished play (p. 6) and the table of rejected elements (p. 9)—although bare and skeletal enough at first glance—are the parts of the book to which serious students of Yeats may refer most often—along with the table representing the parts of the play covered by each manuscript (p. 15). Appendix One: "The Dates of Letters" will be used by scholars to correct the dating of several letters in Wade's edition (p. 467).

In Part 1, chapters 2 through 11, summaries of transcriptions of all the scenarios and drafts (Drafts 1 through 17) pertaining to the original version of *The Player Queen*—what Bradford calls a "drama" in the Chekhovian sense—are presented. In Part 2, chapters 12 through 17, transcriptions of all the drafts (Drafts 18 through 31) that pertain to the published play are presented. After each presentation a commentary points out its significance.

In connection with certain drafts—very late ones, because Bradford wished to wait until all the evidence was in—extended comments on related subjects appear. In connection with Draft 29 (chapter 14) Bradford gives (pp. 396–99) the definitive answer to the vexed questions, What is symbolized by the names of the characters? Why do these names form the number sequence 7, 8, 9, 10: Septimus, Octema (not, of course, an actual character), Nona, and Decima? Bradford's conclusion—"there is no dark conceit" (p. 399)—will not put all curiosity at rest. Nevertheless, all future investigators must take account of Bradford's evidence and arguments.

In chapter 16, "The 1919 Productions and the 1922 Printings," Bradford gives information on the productions and presents a survey of the reviews of the first performances of the play in London (pp. 413–16) and Dublin (pp. 416–20). Although his purpose is to determine from the content of the reviews that Draft 31 was the text used in the Dublin production, nevertheless the reviews are of interest in themselves. It is convenient to have them gathered here and good to have Bradford's comments on them.

Having demonstrated from the reviews that Septimus's lines announcing the end of the Christian Era had probably not yet been added to the play by the time of the 1919 performances, Bradford goes on, in the same chapter, to detail the additions that appear in the Macmillan texts of 1922. A number of these additions "enlarge the myth of the unicorn" (p. 421). The unicorn motif being fully developed in the 1922 printings of *The Player Queen,* Bradford gives us a succinct and definitive treatment of the development of the unicorn symbol in Yeats and its meaning in this play (pp. 428–46). We have included reproductions of the fascinating examples of the unicorn in art which form part of Bradford's argument. In the words of Professor Marion Witt, a distinguished Yeats scholar, who read Bradford's manuscript, this study of the unicorn symbol is "new and important."

Curtis Bradford died on 1 October 1969. He had completed a final draft of his book, but the final typed copy had not been made. This was done after his death and the copy carefully checked against the final draft by Bradford's literary executor, Professor M. M. Liberman. I have gone over this fair copy and have found almost no errors. Bradford himself would undoubtedly have found things to change, cut, or add, if he had lived to see the book through the press. I suspect that he would have wished to tighten up the text here and there. We have thought it best, however—and this was the advice of Professor Witt—to print it just as Bradford left it, rather than to risk altering his meaning and emphasis. If there are mistakes which he might have caught—and which I, with less knowledge of the materials, have let slip by—I can only apologize to his memory.

Bradford had done work on this play and many other manuscripts in Dublin in 1954–1955, and in 1957 had sent me his notes on *The Player Queen* along with some on *The Resurrection* and *Purgatory.* When, in the spring of 1966, the series "Manuscripts of W. B. Yeats" was projected, it was natural to ask him to edit for it the manuscripts of *The Player Queen.* In fact the idea of a series of volumes each presenting manuscripts relating to a single work by Yeats was conceived from a statement in Bradford's *Yeats at Work* (Carbondale and Edwardsville: Southern Illinois University Press, 1965). Addressing himself to a problem "with which students, say, of Milton, do not have to deal," that for many of Yeats's works "a complex tangle of prepublication manuscripts survives," Bradford regretted (p. vii) that in order "to survey Yeats at work in all his varied genres" within the cover of a single volume he was forced to avoid "works whose manuscript development was so complex that a study of it would require a monograph or even a book (*On Baile's Strand* (1903), *Deirdre* (1907), *The Player Queen* (1922), *A Vision* (1937))." Other works which Bradford might have mentioned are *The Countess Cathleen* (1892) and *The Shadowy Waters* (1900). When, in 1971, the first volume, *Druid Craft: The Writing of The Shadowy Waters*, appeared, it was dedicated to Bradford's memory.

From 1966 on Bradford spent summers and part of a first semester 1968–1969 sabbatical leave in Ireland working on the book. The first draft was finished in February 1969 and the final draft early that summer. The hiatus between the submission of the manuscript in 1969 and its publication now is something about which I have feelings of guilt. Yet it was nobody's fault. It was caused by the financial difficulties experienced by university presses during that period. The original publisher, unable to continue the series without help, sought long for a subsidy, without success. The editors involved in the series are grateful for the foresight, courage, and sense of responsibility toward the scholarly knowledge of Yeats shown by Northern Illinois University Press in taking over the publication of this volume.

This book is the final fruit of Bradford's many years of Yeats scholarship. I thought it appropriate, therefore, to include in an appendix an account of Bradford's career and an appreciation of him as a man. Suffice it to say here that if —on the basis of *Yeats at Work* and such essays as his well-known account of the writing of Yeats's Byzantium poems (*PMLA* 75, no. 1 [March 1960]: 110–25)— Bradford was not already the leading scholar concerned with Yeats's manuscripts, he becomes so with the publication of this book. There is, moreover, his edition titled "The Unpublished Prose of W. B. Yeats," which Bradford called "my principal scholarly work" in a vita dated 27 April 1960 (*Yeats at Work* was finished in June 1959). A recent essay by James L. Allen and M. M. Liberman, "Transcriptions of Yeats's Unpublished Prose in the Bradford Papers at Grinnell College," *The Serif: Quarterly of the Kent State University Libraries* 10, no. 1 (Spring 1973): 13–27, has at last called attention to the existence of this monumental transcript (836 typed pages) of the most important unpublished work of Yeats: "1.) Yeats's unfinished novel *The Speckled Bird;* 2.) the first draft of *Autobiographies* ('a rough draft of *Memoirs* made in 1916–17'); 3.) 'Journals,' including 'A Journal: 1908–1914'; 4.) 'Works Completed but Never Published' [including, among many important items, the Leo Africanus papers]; 5.) 'Extracts from the Manuscript Books'; and 6.) 'Addresses' " (Allen and Liberman, p. 14). Detailed descriptions of the contents of these transcriptions are given in the essay. Permission was not granted Bradford to publish these papers, nor has it been given to his executor, but the papers may be seen in the Burling Library at Grinnell, Iowa. Anyone who has worked on Yeats's manuscripts will conclude that Bradford's unpublished work must have demanded the highest scholarly achievement and must represent the work of many years.

Bradford's introductory chapter shows how Yeats worked and reworked three books throughout his whole creative career: *The Shadowy Waters* from the 1880s to the acting version of 1906 and beyond, *The Player Queen* from 1907 to the first production of 1919 and beyond (to a final version published in 1934), and *A Vision* from the psychic experiences of 1917 to final publication in 1937. The reader will find the development of *The Player Queen* of particular interest, because the years when Yeats wrote it are the years when he was beginning to form his "system," and the developing play reflects the developing concepts of that system. Moreover, it is a brilliant prose play, the quality of which fully justifies this thoroughgoing investigation of its growth.

DAVID R. CLARK

Amherst, Massachusetts, 1975

Acknowledgments

GRATEFUL acknowledgment is made to Miss Anne Yeats and Senator Michael Butler Yeats for permission to publish manuscripts of W. B. Yeats. The courtesy of A. P. Watt and Son of London is appreciated. Thanks are due to the Director, Dr. Patrick Henchy, and to the Trustees of the National Library of Ireland, Dublin, for permission to consult and to use here MS8764, W. B. Yeats's *The Player Queen,* and to Dr. Henchy and Mr. Ailfrid MacLochlainn, Keeper of Printed Books, for their assistance and cooperation. The Trustees of Southern Illinois University are thanked for permission to consult and to quote from an unpublished letter of W. B. Yeats in the collection of the Southern Illinois University Library.

In addition to thanking the above, Professor Bradford would have gratefully honored the memory of Mrs. W. B. Yeats, who made Yeats's manuscripts available to him in 1954–1955, when he first worked with the manuscripts of *The Player Queen,* and again in the summer of 1960. He would have wished me to mention also his gratitude to the late Professor H. O. White of Trinity College, Dublin, and Dr. R. J. Hayes, former Director of the National Library.

A Ford Faculty Fellowship made possible Bradford's year in Dublin in 1954–1955; a grant from the Lilly Endowment enabled him to return to Dublin in the summer of 1960; a sabbatical leave from Grinnell College enabled him to work on *The Player Queen* in Ireland in 1968–1969.

Bradford would have wished to thank—in addition to the staff of the National Library—the staffs of the Burling Library, Grinnell College, of the Library of Trinity College, Dublin, and of the Houghton Library Reading Room, Harvard University.

Professor Marion Witt read the manuscript and made valuable suggestions by which the General Editor has gratefully profited. Brig. Gen. Russell K. Alspach has very carefully checked line numberings to indicate similarity or identity of various lines in Part 1 to those numbered in Draft 16 and of Part 2 to those numbered in *The Variorum Edition of the Plays of W. B. Yeats.* He has also made many helpful comments on other matters. The General Editor is very grateful to him for the improvements he has made.

The courtesy and help of Mrs. Leone Stein, Director of the University of Massachusetts Press, and of her staff, are gratefully acknowledged. I wish to acknowledge the long and patient cooperation of Curtis Bradford's literary executor, Professor M. M. Liberman, in expediting the publication of this book. Professor Arra M. Garab of Northern Illinois University has functioned as an on-the-spot Yeats consultant in DeKalb, and I wish to thank him. Professor Vincent DiMarco of the University of Massachusetts has helped in the search for illustrations. Professor Albrecht B. Strauss of the University of North Carolina and Professor R. J. Kaufmann, Stiles Professor of Humanities and Comparative Literature at the University of Texas, have graciously allowed the use of their letters to me about Bradford.

I wish to express grateful appreciation for permission to quote material copyrighted by the following or in some other sense belonging to them:

Autobiography (includes "Reveries Over Childhood and Youth") (Copyright 1916, 1935 by Macmillan Publishing Co., Inc., renewed 1944, 1963 by Bertha Georgie Yeats).

The Letters of W. B. Yeats, edited by Allan Wade (Copyright 1953, 1954 by Anne Butler Yeats).

Mythologies (© Mrs. W. B. Yeats, 1959).

The Variorum Edition of the Plays of W. B. Yeats, edited by Russell K. Alspach (Copyright © Russell K. Alspach and Bertha Georgie Yeats, 1966).

Early Poems and Stories (Copyright 1925 by Macmillan Publishing Co., Inc., renewed 1953 by Bertha Georgie Yeats).

A Note on the Transcriptions

CURTIS BRADFORD left no "Note on the Transcriptions" that I know of. I believe, however, that the following description of his practice is accurate.

There is no attempt to reproduce all of *The Player Queen* manuscripts that have survived. To have done so would have resulted in too huge a book. Although all known manuscripts are taken account of, scenarios and drafts that do not add to our understanding of the play's development are merely summarized. On the other hand, all those scenarios and drafts necessary to such an understanding are reproduced.

In the transcriptions, no attempt is made to produce a diplomatic copy of the manuscripts, even in the case of passages in verse. The attempt has rather been to produce a clean, readable text accurately representing Yeats's latest intention (without pointing out all the cancellations and insertions that establish that intention). Many canceled words and groups of words are silently omitted. Many insertions are silently brought down to the line. (However, when notes, additions, or alternate versions from left-hand pages are inserted in a draft, this fact is clearly indicated.) Words added by the editor are in square brackets, but uncanceled words which revision has made redundant are occasionally dropped. Undeciphered words are so indicated. Dubious readings are questioned [?]. Missing essential punctuation (mainly periods) has been silently supplied even in verse passages. Many trivial errors in spelling and punctuation have been silently corrected, as have been obvious typographical errors. Ambiguous capitalization has simply been normalized. Unimportant abbreviations have been expanded. Where the styling of stage directions and speaker indications has varied within a draft, this has been normalized. Where *Dectora* appears for *Decima,* this error has been corrected.

In *Druid Craft: The Writing of The Shadowy Waters,* the end of each of Yeats's manuscript pages was marked and each of his lines was printed separately, often even in prose passages. In *W. B. Yeats: The Writing of The Player Queen,* however, the pages run on without interruption, as do the lines, except when they are

W. B. Yeats:
The Writing of
The Player Queen

CHAPTER ONE

The Writing of
The Player Queen

WHATEVER HIS other productions, throughout the whole of his creative life Yeats worked and reworked three books: *The Shadowy Waters, The Player Queen,* and *A Vision.* He began to ponder the theme of *The Shadowy Waters*—man's longing for some romantically enhanced way of life—in the 1880s and brought the poem to one conclusion in 1900. The acting version of the play that grew out of it was produced at the Abbey in December 1906. It was in 1907—or so he tells us in the note he wrote to the play in 1922—that he began *The Player Queen.* Though this note was written long after the event, the date is not far wrong, if wrong at all. The play was produced in 1919, in London in May and at the Abbey in December. Yeats did not print the play until he had revised Scene ii; then, in November 1922, three printings appeared. At some later time, probably in 1927, Yeats revised three scenes: Decima's choice of another lover by staging a dancing contest, the players' praise of their former successes, and the end of the play. These revisions were first printed in *Collected Plays* (1934), 27 years after Yeats began to plan the play. Yeats started *A Vision* before *The Player Queen* was produced. The psychic experiences on which it is based began in October 1917, and Yeats worked on the book until 1937. Thus *The Player Queen,* like *The Shadowy Waters* and *A Vision,* will reward special study.

We can trace Yeats's progress with this play, though not in great detail, from various sources: Occasionally there are dates, or notes concerning other works in progress, in the manuscripts themselves; there are references to the play in Yeats's published letters and in other works by Yeats, published and unpublished. Some scholars think Yeats's 1907 date for the play's beginning to be incorrect. J. B. Saul cites *Letters,* p. 511, for a 1908 date, and indeed the earliest allusion to the play is by J. B. Yeats in a 1 July 1908 letter. However, there is other evidence. At the end of Draft 5, Yeats planned the table of contents for *The Collected Works,* published by Bullen in the fall of 1908. Since Draft 5 is not the earliest draft of the play Yeats made, a date late in 1907 or early in 1908 for his beginning seems about right. It is clear that Yeats did no concentrated work on the play until the many revisions made for the *Collected Works* were off his hands. These occupied him into the summer of 1908. Beginning in the summer of 1908 and continuing through 1909 Yeats worked on his play regularly.

There are frequent references to the play in Yeats's published letters, though several letters that refer to the play have been dated incorrectly. Dates that I have supplied are put in square brackets in the account following. (See Appendix One: "The Dates of Letters" for a summary of the evidence for changed dates.) When the correct dates are supplied, these references show that Yeats worked very hard on the play from midsummer of 1908 through 1909 and into 1910, that he then did little work on it again until late in 1915, when he began to shape the play that we know (Drafts 20 and 21), and that the play was virtually completed by May 1917. The earliest reference occurs in a letter to his father written 17 July [1908]: "I am working every day on *The Player Queen*, but will not for a long time yet get at the verse writing. It is still all scenario" (*Letters*, p. 532). In October he writes John Quinn, "I have finished the prose version of what is to be a new verse play, *The Player Queen*, and Mrs. Patrick Campbell talks of producing it" (p. 512). On 27 December he writes from Paris to John Butler Yeats, "I have been here for a month working at *The Player Queen* for Mrs. Campbell" (p. 513). Back in Dublin he writes again to his father on 17 January 1909, "I dictate the prose structure of the new play every morning" (p. 524). On 8 March he tells Lady Gregory, "I did a good morning's work on *Player Queen*" (p. 525). On 29 April he tells his father that the appointment of Norreys Connell as manager of the Abbey will free him for work on *The Player Queen* until November or December (p. 528). A letter written to Sturge Moore on 1 May (*Correspondence*, p. 15) speaks of a two-act version of the play that has been sent to Mrs. Campbell and that has already been superseded by revised versions (Draft 15 is a two-act version of the play in its early form). [But see my note, p. 467 Gen. Ed.] On 10 October Yeats speaks of a new start (*Letters*, p. 535), then on 29 November comes to the high-comedy report of his reading a three-act version to Mrs. Campbell (*Letters*, p. 539). (The first three-act version is Draft 16.) We hear no more about the play until 7 August [1910], when Yeats quotes a passage from Act I, Scene ii, which appears in the verse version of Draft 16 (*Letters*, pp. 533–34). I think Yeats continued putting the play into verse (see Draft 17) throughout 1910 but then laid it aside. On 5 March 1912 he says as much in a letter to his father (*Letters*, p. 568).

The next period of concentrated work on the play came late in 1915 when Yeats made a new beginning. He then wrote Drafts 20 and 21. He was thinking of changing even his title, to *The Woman Born To Be Queen,* and he described the play as "a wild comedy, almost a farce, with a tragic background—a study of a fantastic woman" (12 September [1915], *Letters,* p. 588). This describes Draft 21 well enough. On 11 May 1916 he speaks of working on *The Player Queen,* "which always needs new touches in its one bad place—first half of second act" (*Letters,* p. 614). This seems to point to the many versions of this scene which constitute Drafts 23 through 28. Finally, two references in May 1917 indicate that the play was finished, or nearly so: Yeats dated the "Prologue" to *Per Amica Silentia Lunae* 11 May 1917 (*Per Amica,* p. vi) and wrote in the "Anima Hominis" section, Part 6, of the trouble he had with the play; "I only escaped at last when I had mocked in a comedy my own thought" (*Per Amica,* p. 27). On 12 May he wrote to his father, "I have just made a revision of my *Player Queen,* a prose comedy. . . . It is very wild, and I think, amusing" (*Letters,* p. 625).

We hear no more of the play until Yeats writes on 21 January 1919 of the Stage Society's plans for producing it (*Letters,* p. 654). It was first produced at the King's Hall, Covent Garden, on 25 and 27 May. I do not know exactly what version was produced but suspect it was a version very much like Draft 29, perhaps that version as corrected by Draft 30. No prompt book has come to light, though one may very well exist somewhere. I believe this was the version produced because duplicate copies of it exist, one in the family collection (National Library of Ireland) and one in the papers of Mrs. Patrick Campbell (Princeton University Library) and because the reviews do not mention Septimus's declaration of the end of the Christian Era, which would have been likely to attract attention in 1919. This does not appear in any of the drafts but does appear in the 1922 printings. Yeats later revised three scenes as noted above, perhaps for the revival of the play by the Cambridge Festival Theatre in 1927 (see Draft 31), and included these revisions in the final text of the play which is found in *Collected Plays* (1934).

More than 1,100 folios of prepublication manuscripts and typescripts of *The Player Queen* have survived, and it is certain from various bits of evidence, including cross references that cannot be tracked down, that not all the drafts Yeats made have survived. I have arranged these folios into thirty-one drafts, as nearly as possible in their progressive order. This is not always easy to determine with drafts of only parts of the play, and most of the drafts are partial. I am certain that the drafts of the whole play—6, 15, 16, and 29—are in their progressive order, and my discussion of all the drafts naturally groups itself around these complete drafts. The play reached one conclusion in Drafts 16 and 17, another in the 1922 printings. By the end of Draft 17, Yeats had written a full-length play, largely in verse, which is serious in tone, though it has a comic ending—a "drama," as Chekhov used the term. In the 1922 printings we find the wild comedy we know, though Yeats was still to change a few incidents. I discuss the play's development through Draft 17 in Part 1, its later development in Part 2.

I have enjoyed putting this heap of disordered papers into order, and my enjoyment of that process no doubt partly explains why I undertook this study. I was convinced at the outset, however, that *The Player Queen* was one of the best of Yeats's longer plays—I concurred with the expressed judgments of such earlier students of the play as Norman Jeffares and F. A. C. Wilson. For me the play was also particularly interesting because it was under way during the years when Yeats was forming what he called his "system": Mask and Face, the Self and the Anti-self, Unity of Being, a cyclical theory of history, and so on. All of these concepts found their way into the developing play at some point or other.

Yeats began, as he always did when planning a play, with what he called "scenarios." These are usually bald prose summaries of the plot, though if an idea for an appropriate lyric occurred to him, he would dub it in. Nine separate scenarios have survived, and the manuscript drafts of the play are full of scenarios to which Yeats resorted whenever composition in dialogue became difficult. These scenarios are all without dates, but some of them were clearly written during the long process of drafting the play; they do not all represent advance planning. In none of them is there any hint of the present Scene i. In all of them a group of strolling actors is to play "The Miracle of the Deluge"; in all of them there is a rebellion against the Queen; in all of them the actress who is to play Noah's wife changes places with the Queen and does a better job as queen than the real Queen can do. Often her role-playing leads to her own death, either by suicide or execution. In short, the radical idea that an actress can do a better job of queening than a queen can, that the mask has greater effect than the face, is present from the beginning.

As a guide through the many drafts of the play which follow, two tables are presented: First, a list of those elements from the drafts which are found in the finished play; then, a list of various false leads or clues which Yeats explored but eventually rejected. Both lists include the numbers of the drafts in which the various incidents occur, and both are progressively arranged.

TABLE I

Elements Retained in the Finished Play

1. *Queen to end her retreat.* Drafts 1, 3, 5, 6, 9, 12, 13, 15, 16, 20, 29
2. *The revolt.* 1 through 16, 18, 22, 23, 29

3. *Hidden Player Queen.* 1–3, 6, 9, 11–13, 15, 16, 19–21, 23, 24, 27, 29, 30 (She is hidden in a vat through 16, under the throne beginning with 19.)

4. *The Noah play.* Drafts 1 (unnamed "mystery"), 2, 4–7, 9, 12, 15, 16, 18, 23–25, 27, 29

5. *Nona in love with Septimus.* Drafts 2, 4, 5, 11, 12, 19, 20, 21, 23, 29, 30

6. *Prime Minister tells Queen why she must play her role.* Drafts 2, 3, 6, 8, 10, 12, 13, 15, 16, 21, 23–25, 27, 29

7. *Player Queen sings from her hiding place.* Drafts 3, 6, 8, 12, 15–17, 19, 21, 23, 27, 29, 30 ("The Mask" through 16, from then on "Song from 'The Player Queen'")

8. *Quarrel between Decima and Nona.* Drafts 3, 6, 9, 12, 15, 16, 19, 20, 21, 23, 24, 27, 29

9. *Queen's longing for, and fear of, martyrdom.* Drafts 3, 8, 13, 15, 16, 27, 29

10. *Prime Minister's wish to be King.* Drafts 4, 6, 8, 12, 15, 16, 29

11. *The Old Beggar.* Drafts 4, 5, 7, 8, 11, 12, 14, 16–19, 21, 22, 29

12. *Leader of Rebellion.* Drafts 4–8, 16 (From 16 on, reduced to First Citizen)

13. *Decima locks gate.* Drafts 6, 12, 15–17, 19, 21, 28–30

14. *Decima changes dresses with Queen.* Drafts 6, 12, 15–17, 19, 21, 29

15. *Lobster and wine.* Drafts 7, 8, 16, 24, 29, 30

16. *Scissors with which Decima attempts suicide.* Drafts 9, 12, 15–17, 19, 21, 29

17. *Townsmen attack Septimus.* Reported drafts 11, 12, 19; staged drafts 13, 18, 21, 22, 29

18. *Decima attempts suicide.* Drafts 12, 15–17, 19, 21, 29

19. *Opening scene in the town.* Drafts 13, 16, 21, 22, 29

20. *Septimus believes he has been attacked because he is a poet.* Drafts 18, 19, 21, 22, 29

21. *The two Old Men.* Drafts 18, 21, 22, 29 (Masked in 22 and 29)

22. *Unicorn allusions.* Drafts 19, 21–26, 28–30

23. *Decima cites Septimus's poems.* Drafts 19–21, 23, 27, 29

24. *The dancing contest.* Drafts 19, 21, 29–31

25. *Prime Minister's rage at opening of Scene ii.* Drafts 20, 21, 23–25 (with Queen); 24, 27, 29 (with Players)

26. *Septimus drunk.* Drafts 21, 22, 29, 30

27. *Decima's confrontation with the Old Beggar.* Drafts 21, 29

28. *Popular poets introduced in Scene i.* Drafts 22, 29

These events appear in the following order in the finished play:

Scene i. 19, 21, 26, 28, 2, 12, 22, 17, 11

Scene ii. 25, 1, 3, 4, 9, 6, 15, 7, 8, 5, 23, 16, 24, 20, 13, 27, 18, 14, 10

Commentary

The revolt against the Queen, who at the Prime Minister's urging is to leave her religious seclusion and show herself to her people, is present in the first surviving draft, as are the staging of a play as part of the festival planned to divert the people from their grievances and the disappearance of the Player Queen. In Draft 2 Yeats adds Nona's love of Septimus and has the Prime Minister discuss with the Queen how necessary it is that she fill the role to which she was born. Draft 3 introduces the Player Queen singing from her hiding place, her quarrel with Nona, and along with these the real Queen's longing for, yet fear of, martyrdom. Draft 4 adds two new characters, the Old Beggar, called Rat-hole through many versions, and Barach, the leader of the rebellion. Both roles are reduced in the finished play; indeed, the element of a leader of the rebellion has almost disappeared in the First Citizen's role. Here also the Prime Minister's wish to be King in name as well as fact appears for the first time. In Draft 6, the earliest draft of the entire play, the incidents of Decima's locking the gate on Nona and Septimus and her change of dress with the Queen are introduced. Decima's hunger for the lobster and wine turns up in Draft 7; the scissors that will serve Decima for her attempted suicide are introduced on stage in Draft 9, though the scene where she first uses them is not roughed in until Draft 12. The townsmen's attack on Septimus is reported in Draft 11 and staged in Draft 13 where Yeats first works out the scene that opens the play in the town. No new incidents were invented in Drafts 14 through 17, where Yeats completed the play in its original form.

Here the switch to wild comedy begins. In Draft 18 Yeats invents both the two Old Men who frame Scene i, and Septimus's belief that he has been attacked because he is a poet. This mistaken notion is perhaps no more than implied in the finished play. Allusions to the unicorn begin in Draft 19, where Yeats also invented two of his most effective comic devices: Decima's citation of Septimus's poems as proof of his love, and her staging of a dancing contest by members of the troupe to help her choose a new lover. Yeats opened Scene ii in Draft 20 with the Prime Minister in a rage, a device intended to give the scene dramatic tension. In Draft 21 Septimus is brought on drunk, and Decima and the Old Beggar confront each other in Scene ii. The "bad, popular poets" were added to Scene i in Draft 22.

At the end of Table 1 these events are arranged in the order in which they occur in the finished play; they have been drastically rearranged from the order in which they were invented.

All this is complex enough, but it seems simple when compared with the complication of incidents and ideas which Yeats explored and rejected during the many years he was at work. We have already seen that at first he conceived of his play as a drama, possibly a tragedy. It is also quite clear that for a long time Yeats wanted to write a full-length play rather than a play that would have to share the bill with some other. He had never really achieved this except rather dubiously in *The Unicorn from the Stars*—dubiously because that play had been written, with Lady Gregory's extensive help, to prevent George Moore from using essential features of the plot. And indeed Yeats never was to achieve a full-length play. This desire to develop *The Player Queen* according to a three-act or even a four-act formula led Yeats to plan and develop many incidents that were tangential to his central theme, as Table 2, listing the rejected material, will show.

TABLE 2

Rejected Elements in Order of Their Invention

1. *Tax on sins* (sometimes on lying only). Drafts 1–10, 12, 15, 17, 22
2. *Bringing in tax money in bags.* Drafts 1, 4, 5, 10, 12, 15, 16
3. *Vat for wine or cider.* Drafts 1–3, 5, 6, 8–16
4. *Septimus's old play, which Player Queen has found.* Drafts 1, 2, 4, 7, 8, 11, 12, 14, 16 (beginning with 7 this play concerns a Queen of Babylon)
5. *Love affair between Nona and Prime Minister.* Drafts 1, 2, 4, 5, 7, 8
6. *A clown introduced.* Drafts 1–3
7. *Audience for Noah play summoned or gathered.* Drafts 1, 4–7, 12, 15, 16
8. *Maskers other than Player Queen introduced:*
   Septimus: 2, 12
   Peter: 12
   Prime Minister: 2, 12
9. *Queen enters accompanied by nuns.* Drafts 2, 3, 23–25
10. *Troupe of players searches for Player Queen.* Drafts 2, 3, 8
11. *Player Queen cites her lineage from eagles.* Drafts 2, 6, 8, 15, 16
12. *Exchange between Decima and Septimus before Noah play begins.* Drafts 3, 12, 15, 16
13. *Irish allusion introduced.* Drafts 3 and 6 (To Maeve)
14. *A character named Peter introduced.* Drafts 6 (unnamed), 11, 12, 15 (unnamed), 16
15. *Decima returns to Septimus and to the role of Noah's wife.* Drafts 6–8, 15, 16
16. *Noah play staged.* Drafts 6, 7, 15, 16
17. *The "deeds" of the Player Queen's reign:*
    Confrontation with Prime Minister. Drafts 6, 13, 15–17

Player Queen remains in castle while gold is hidden. Drafts 6, 13, 15–17
Confrontation with rebels. Drafts 6–8, 15, 16
Player Queen and soldiers. Drafts 7, 8, 10, 13–17
Nona captured. Drafts 7 and 8
Confrontation with Septimus. Drafts 7, 8, 15, 16
18. *Queen tries to save Player Queen.* Drafts 6–8, 15, 16
19. *Prime Minister pretends not to know who is Queen.* Drafts 6–8, 15, 16
20. *Decima eating lobster at end of play.* Drafts 7, 8, 16, 21, 29
21. *Nona and Peter ending.* Drafts 15 and 16
22. *Royal portraits introduced.* Drafts 23, 24, 27, 29

Commentary

Rather than follow this table laboriously from first to last, I shall cluster events that seem to belong together. Some of the least promising material came first: In the earliest drafts Yeats has the Nona figure involved in a love affair with the Prime Minister. They are either lovers or betrothed lovers. Nona really wants to marry Septimus and settle down to raise a family. Sometimes the Prime Minister is jealous of Septimus, sometimes sympathetic to Nona, though always certain she hasn't much chance with Septimus. The bare bones, at least, of this configuration lasted a very long time, for Yeats used it as part of various happy endings to his play, wherein clearly he wanted each Jill to have her Jack, as at the end of a Shakespearean comedy. He has Nona carried off (or at least threatened with being carried off) to some remote place by the Prime Minister, thus opening the way to a reunion between Septimus and Decima. In versions with this ending Decima returns to Septimus, quite content to lay aside the mask of Queen.

Yeats spent even more time exploring duplication of his central theme, the relation of pose to reality, of mask to face. In one version (Draft 12) Septimus has imposed his mask of romantic bard on everyone, but especially on Nona and Decima, whereas actually he is common and hard as nails. Then through several versions Yeats developed a character, usually called Peter, as a counterpart to Septimus. Septimus is a romantic lover; Peter takes love lightly. Septimus has nothing but trouble with Decima; Peter is universally successful with the ladies because he is always pleasant, equable, and understanding. But Peter, too, is in one version (Draft 12) a masker; he pretends to be bold and unafraid, when actually he is a coward. Peter was also used at times to help end the play, to solve the problem of what to do with Nona. In Draft 15 (in what I think is a nice touch), Nona and Peter come in at the end costumed as doves. Nona carefully points out that the dove is Aphrodite's bird. While Decima and Septimus have involved themselves with matters of state, she and Peter have better used their time—they have plighted their troth. Nona then joins the hands of Septimus and Decima, and they all live happily ever after. In the finished play there is a bubble, so to speak, that marks the spot where Peter's body descended for the last time. The player dressed as a swan is called Peter, and Decima cuts through his breast feathers so that his arms will be free to play the lute. Though we can only speculate, Peter was probably removed from the play because he was redundant. Nona and Decima represent the Martha-Mary contrast, and it is not necessary to duplicate it. Also the romantic happy ending was eventually superseded by an ironical-farcical ending with grim overtones. The Old Beggar is to be hanged in the morning, no one cares what happens to Nona and Septimus, and Decima is unsure of her fate. In such an ending it would not do to provide Jacks for every Jill.

The question of how far to carry the play within the play continued to trouble Yeats—how much of "The Tragical History of Noah's Deluge" should he show us? In the end he doesn't show us any of it at all; even its rehearsal does not get started. But in many versions a prop Noah's Ark with a gangplank is made part of the stage setting; Decima gets into the mask and costume of Noah's wife, which she later gives the Queen in exchange for royal robes; Septimus, dressed either as Neptune or an angel, speaks a prologue; and the play is actually going on when it is interrupted by the news that a mob is coming. A play needs an audience, so one is gathered by various devices. Its members comment on the effect of playing many roles on the basic or essential character of the actor, an idea with which Yeats began in his earliest scenario and which makes the point that the Decima figure is always acting; she treats people off stage according to the part she happens to be playing on stage—with unhappy results when she is playing Jezebel. I cannot see that staging the Noah play advanced Yeats's purpose in any way and can only conclude that since *Hamlet,* the play within the play has had a morbid fascination for playwrights. The accoutrements of the Noah play—costumes and masks—add to the fantastic atmosphere, and Yeats keeps these.

But clearly the aspect of the play on which Yeats worked hardest was showing Decima in her role of Player Queen, inventing "deeds," so to speak, for her reign. One favorite way of doing this was to have Decima discover quite early an old play by Septimus, eventually called "The Queen of Babylon." The queen in this play gets to her throne after overcoming impossible obstacles (there are many overtones from Cinderella); once there she resists a rebellion, emerging as a successful leader of her troops. Decima is so enamored of this plot and role that she puts them into action; she uses Septimus's play as a scenario for her acts and declaims speeches from it on appropriate contrived occasions. All this is made explicit—she tells Septimus that she is embodying his dreams, actually performing a part which he had only imagined. Also, Yeats has Septimus comment, when witnessing a particularly juicy bit of action or dialogue, that the Player Queen's deeds and words are not her own, that all are borrowed from one of his old plays.

Another way of building up the Player Queen role was to involve her in various confrontations that enable her to assume the role of queen. In Draft 17 Yeats worked out two lengthy exchanges with the Old Beggar, whose braying marks a change of ruler: one just after the Player Queen has taken on her role, the second near the end of the play. She assumes that his crowing or braying foretells her death, whereas he knows that she is not really the Queen and says that her death would bring his powers of prophecy into question. The Player Queen's talks with the Prime Minister were once extensive. He comes in just after she has donned the Queen's dress and recognizes her as a player, but agrees to use her talents so the real Queen can escape. This is possible because only he has seen the Queen. As the soldiers enter, he kisses her hand to seal the bargain. To test her powers, she orders the soldiers to bring the gold from the treasury and scatter it through the streets. The Prime Minister objects; the gold is the source of their power. The soldiers are ready to obey the Player Queen, and in some versions even threaten the Prime Minister with violence until the Player Queen tells them to obey his orders. The Player Queen and the Prime Minister then work out a strategem whereby the Player Queen will remain alone in the castle while the Prime Minister and the soldiers hide the gold, then return and fall upon the rebels, who are attempting to take over the castle, from the rear.

There are in the drafts variants on the Player Queen's effort to get Septimus definitely to reject Nona. One persistent variant has Nona captured by the Player Queen's soldiers and brought to the castle that is under seige by the rebel forces. Septimus pretends to joint the rebels, and in order to gain access to the castle serves as herald to carry their demands to the Player Queen. When they are together, Decima has a set of arm and leg irons brought in, has her soldiers produce Nona, and insists that Septimus put the irons on her. He refuses to perform so cruel an act, and Decima takes his refusal as evidence of his love for Nona. In other versions Septimus tells the Player Queen that he will return after putting Nona in a safe place. The Player Queen sends various persons out to look for him.

Yeats spent a great deal of effort in developing the Player Queen's conception of the true nature of royalty. In draft after draft she addresses the rebels after opening the gates to admit them, telling them that she is an eagle and the descendant of generations of eagles, that they are afraid even to look into the eagle eyes of royalty. She covers her eyes with her hands or a veil so they will not fear her. (This is one of the images developed in "Upon a House Shaken by the Land

Agitation," written in August 1909.) Another way in which Decima asserts her kinship with her imagined royal predecessors lingered until the very latest drafts. The setting of Scene ii is made to include mosaic pictures of the royal line. Decima, sometimes in costume for the role of Noah's wife, appeals to them, claims kinship with them, even says that one of them fondled her as a child. She imagines that they disclaim kinship because of her appearance, and their disclaimer confirms her decision not to play the part of Noah's wife.

Another congeries of rejected conceptions centers upon Yeats's development of the real Queen's role and character. In the earlier drafts she has invented a new tax, usually a tax on her subjects' sins but sometimes a tax on their lies. This produces huge amounts of money for the Queen, and many drafts have the play begin with the Prime Minister on stage watching over the stowing away of the tax money. But the tax on sins has brought the people to the point of rebellion; sin costs so much that they have no money for bread. The Queen, who thinks her proper role is to save her people from their sins, defends the tax and even threatens to add new penalties that will enforce salvation. For instance, her people will all be required to say a rosary every night. While the Queen and the Prime Minister are discussing this proposal and the reasons for the dissatisfaction of the people, they hear a voice singing from the air. It is the Player Queen, who has hidden in a vat high up on the wall that is to be filled with wine or cider and piped to a fountain (a fountain flowing with wine or cider is to have a prominent part in the festivities of the day). The Queen often interprets this voice as a warning to return to her prayers, but she concurs with the Prime Minister's assertion that reasons of state require a royal progress. At the end of many versions of the play the Queen is on stage alongside the Player Queen; she has come forward when Septimus requests a witness that the Player Queen is not the Queen. The real Queen is dressed as Noah's wife and testifies that the Player Queen has taken her place in order to save her. She thinks that the Player Queen is an angel sent from Heaven to save the real Queen from the mob, and when no one is willing to strike the Player Queen, she undertakes to do it, insisting that striking the imagined angel-visitant with a spear will produce a miracle. She is prevented at the last minute by the arrival of Septimus, the Prime Minister, and his soldiers. The Prime Minister pretends to be unable to tell which of the rival queens is genuine. He asks the mob to kneel to the real queen. All except one man, who has been insisting all along that the Player Queen's lips have given kisses and drunk wine, kneel before the Player Queen, who doffs her mask, saying she is tired of queen parts, and resigns the royal power to the real Queen. The Queen will not resume it; the events of the play have convinced her that she is all nun and cannot assume the necessary mask of royalty. Amid cheers and huzzahs the

Prime Minister accepts the kingship; and as the curtain comes down, "The Tragical History of Noah's Deluge" is about to begin with the Player Queen in the part of Noah's wife.

At a late stage in the play's development Yeats tried various beginnings of Scene ii in which the Prime Minister is angry with the Queen rather than with the players, as in the finished play. The Queen has not kept the appointment to show herself to her people. She has sent one of her waiting women, who requests that the Queen be allowed to wear her usual dress, to go barefoot to town over the cobblestones, to say a rosary. The waiting woman reports that the Queen is guilty of a sin of neglect; in some versions the Queen has neglected to dust the side against the wall of an image of Our Lady. On moving it she has found the accumulated dust of years, and even a spider web. In other versions the Queen keeps in her room an image of the Christ child in a cradle. Every night she and her attendants put a hot water bottle at the image's feet—on the previous night they forgot the hot water bottle. The Queen and her attendants come in with a banner bearing the image of a unicorn, explaining the unicorn's association with the Christian story.

A few "odds and ends" should be noted. In a number of versions all members of the company are, like the Player Queen, tired of "The Tragical History of Noah's Deluge"; they have been playing nothing else for five years. In some versions the players comment on the attitudes of the theatrical audience. There is a discussion of the audience's liking realism; people like the play because they like to see themselves on the stage. Members of the audience for the play within a play complain that players are not what they were, that in the old days players could imitate the fighting of cats and overwhelm their audience with laughter by having their pants fall down. In many versions, including the three published in 1922, Decima's eating the lobster at the end of the play is used to provide the curtain line. The Player Queen tosses a lobster claw to the Prime Minister and says to him "Crack that claw."

To end this account of the development of the text, I would like to note that certain allusions do not occur in any manuscripts of the play but are found only in the printed texts. These must be very late, for Yeats has in the existing manuscripts found the language of most of the finished play. They all occur in Scene ii and serve to tie the thought of the play to what Yeats called "the system," that is, to his personal myth, outlined in *Per Amica Silentia Lunae, Autobiographies,* and *A Vision.* Septimus announces "the end of the Christian Era" and "the coming of a New Dispensation." The unicorn should be the new Adam, but, being chaste, he hesitates. Even cold water makes him drunk. Septimus speculates on various ways to arouse his sexuality. They will go to Africa, sing him marriage songs, and play him Ionian music, trying thereby to circumvent the chastity of the Delphic Oracle. But Septimus concludes that they will fail: the Christian Era has ended, but because of the machinations of Delphi the unicorn will not become the new Adam. In short, one of the central themes of the finished play, the need for some god to inaugurate a new era and specifically for a god suited to an era in which

TABLE 3

Scenes of Earlier Play Covered by Scenarios and Drafts of Part 1

Chapter	Act I, Scene i	Act I, Scene ii	Act II	Act III, Scene i	Act III, Scene ii
		Scenario			
2			2		
		3	3		3
		4			
					5
					6
		7	7		
		8	8		
		9	9		
		Draft			
3		1			
		2			2
		3			
		4	4		
		5	5		
4		6	6		6
5			7		7
6		8			8
		9			
		10			
7			11		
		12	12		
8	13	13	13		
		14			14
9		15	15		15
10	16	16	16	16	16
11			17	17?	17

Unity of Being is the ideal, comes into the play very late. We will speculate later, when it does appear, on Yeats's meaning.

I have divided my discussion of the drafts, which follows, into two parts. By 1910 Yeats had completed a prose version of the play in three acts and five scenes. He then turned some, perhaps nearly all of it, into verse. These versions constitute Drafts 1 through 17 and are treated in Part 1. Then in 1915 Yeats made a radical new beginning, which led to the play in two scenes which we now have. These drafts, 18 through 31, are discussed in Part 2. The lines of Draft 16 have been numbered (starting with "1" again for each scene) and all the preceding drafts keyed to it when possible; this has not been possible when the drafts are in verse, since Draft 16 is in prose. In reproducing the early drafts, I have placed the appropriate number after a line when it reaches the form or approximately the form it has in Draft 16. (The numbered lines of Act I, Scene ii of Draft 16 are on pp. 195–205; of Act II on pp. 217–30, and of Act III, Scene ii on pp. 235–45.) In reproducing drafts of Part 2, I have keyed them to the line numbers assigned to the finished play in the *Variorum Edition*. My hope is that these devices will help the reader follow Yeats's progress.

Tables 3 and 4 are schematic presentations of Parts 1 and 2 respectively showing what parts of the play are covered by each manuscript or typescript, giving the

TABLE 4

Scenes of Later Play Covered by Drafts of Part 2

Chapter	Scene i	Scene ii
12	18	
		19
		20
	21	21
13	22	
		23
		24
		25
		26
		27
		28
14	29	29
15		30
17		31

numbers of my chapters in which they are discussed. Table 5 is a list of the changing names of the characters in the play, arranged as nearly as possible in progressive order.

TABLE 5

Changing Names of Characters in Progressive Order

Final Names	*Earlier Names*
Decima	Player Queen, and occasionally others not positively deciphered
Septimus	Poet, Yellow Martin
Nona	Girl, Winny or Winnie, Friend, The Friend
Prime Minister	Bishop, Chancellor, Lord Chamberlain, Minister
Old Beggar	Rat-hole, Old Man

PART 1

CHAPTER TWO

The Scenarios

As NOTED, when planning a play, Yeats began with what he called "scenarios." These were at the outset bald prose summaries of a dramatic action, but as Yeats continued work on them he soon began to develop his characters and write dialogue. His earliest drafts of a play were usually mixtures of scenario and dialogue; often he would begin with scenario, then switch to dialogue. When composition grew difficult, he would switch back to scenario, and so on. Nine scenarios for *The Player Queen* have survived, and in the drafts themselves Yeats frequently shifts to scenario. Not all of these separate scenarios were, I think, written before Yeats began to work on the drafts, for several of them recapitulate exactly events found in the drafts. None of the surviving drafts are much like the first two scenarios, and I think these were written before Yeats began his drafts.

Scenarios 1 and 2

Scenario 1 takes place before a cathedral door, where a group of strolling players is discovered. They are to perform a miracle play, which Yeats does not name, in the cathedral the next day. The principal actress, Libal or Liban, has disappeared. There are riots in the town, and she has gone to watch. Her absence allows the members of her company to discuss her. She has been a very difficult colleague, largely because she can never quit acting. She carries into life the characteristics of the part she is playing on stage, and when she is playing Jezebel, this practice has unpleasant results. But all her fellow actors agree that she is a genius. Yeats is here studying the effect of role-playing on character, the effect of the mask on the face beneath it. He explores this subject for a very long time in the drafts, and it is still present, though there is no specific discussion of it, in the finished play. He also kept to the end the company of strolling players, the performance of a Biblical play, and the disappearance of the principal actress.

In Scenario 2 Yeats names the play to be performed, a Noah play, and states the radical idea of *The Player Queen*—a good actress will make a better queen than one born to the purple without, so to speak, a true vocation; thus, the mask can have more power than the face it conceals. To demonstrate this, Yeats has the Player Queen change places with the real Queen (a device he retained throughout). In the finished play he does not demonstrate Decima's superiority at playing the role of Queen, he merely states it: Suddenly she is Queen, and very good at the job. But through many drafts, the events showing Decima in the role of Queen are rather tediously invented and elaborated. Much was kept from this scenario, much abandoned. Yeats kept the Player Queen's dislike for the part of Noah's wife, combined with her longing for queen roles. He abandoned the Player Queen's leading her troops to temporary victory after she has exchanged roles with the true Queen and the hint of a tragic ending. At the end of the scenario the Player Queen is arrested by the rebels.

Scenario 3

Clearly this scenario was written while the drafts were under way, for it contains plot elements that we will encounter again and again through Draft 17—that is, through the completion of the early two-act (Draft 15) and three-act (Draft 16) versions of the play.

[SCENARIO 3]

Courtyard. A battlemented wall at the back with gate. Cross with stone platform to one side. Gate [with] castle door at the other. Large painted vat at the back. Queen comes down from door of castle, stands looking at vat. Prime Minister follows her. Queen says she is certain she heard something moving in the vat, and even a sound like singing. He says that is merely because she imagines spirits everywhere. That comes of praying too much. She says it is the grey dawn hour that makes her afraid. A voice heard calling "Where is Noah's wife?" She clings to the Prime Minister, terribly alarmed. She always knew there were old ancient spirits. Friend comes in. Explains who she is looking for, but no, they have not seen Player Queen who is to play that day before the people. She tells what a difficulty they are in. They have searched the countryside; she cannot be found. She must be hiding somewhere near the castle. She goes out at one side. The Prime Minister is impatient. They must be down [in] the town where crowds gather. She makes a last appeal to let her stay. She knows that what the people want is prayer. He says that he will never appeal to her again if she does not listen to him now. She reminds [him] of what he has told her, it will be destruction of all. She may even say would he not give back the taxes and what would they care then. But he says no, it is because of their pomp and glory and state for the people obey them. What have they to do with a praying Queen. She must keep her state and show herself to him [them?]. She must be the people's soul made greater, as they understand greatness. She answers rather pettishly that she is doing all he wants. They are about to go out the big door at the back. She looks back longingly. In a little while those players will be dancing their good pious story and doing some real good, not like her. They go out. The Player Queen puts her hand [head?] up out of the vat, singing. A sort of song of apple juice and intoxication founded on the Song of Solomon. The Friend comes in. Delight at finding her. It is almost time to begin. Where has she been? Why has she hidden herself. Player Queen tells her that she has made up her mind never again to dance Noah's wife or any other part that does not make her feel very passionate, very noble, very intense. She runs over the names of various parts, mystery, epic, romance, etc., no, he will never do that, because people don't want those parts. They must please the people. She replies no, they must please her. She is quite certain she can make him do what she likes. He loves her. And he can't get anybody else to dance for him, so he must agree. The other then confesses that she has agreed to dance Noah's wife. The Player Queen has been sitting on the side of the vat. Jumps down, goes to the Friend and shakes her. The other replies yes, but she didn't want to do it; it was only because she couldn't bear to see him unhappy. She gets into this spirit for a moment and reproaches the Player Queen for treating him so. The Poet comes in. There is a gong against the wall at the back. The Player Queen is going over to the gong. He says "O, so I see you've got sense, you are going to call the people." Asks the other what she is crying about. Before she has time to answer tells her to spread out the cloth for the dance, or make whatever preparations it is. The servants come down from the castle. The Dance of Noah's wife. The Poet and the Friend are dressed as the raven and the dove.

Poet makes showman speeches to the crowd. While preparations are being made has lectured the two women on the importance of doing what pays and keeping up appearances. Tells Friend to dry her tears. Mustn't show she has been quarreling with Player Queen. Dance suddenly interrupted by arrival of men at courtway calling out the people have risen against the queen. Some of the people are for flight, some are to go down and help the crowd. The men who arrive distribute badges of revolution.

All go out except players. Poet and Friend are gathering up costumes, etc. Player Queen has locked door of courtyard. She says she won't let them out till he has answered her a question. He cries but it is death if the people find them there. He tells her to give him the key. She says if he comes a step nearer she will throw it over the wall. She then tells him that he must put the other woman out of the company. She pleads with him. She can do all he wants. She can make him famous over the world. He then confesses that he loves the other. The Friend admits it tearfully, but says she had always refused him; she always knew that no one was worthy of him but the Player Queen. The Player Queen in outburst of jealousy says that then they will stay there till the people come. The Poet pleads for his life. Is quite willing to give up the other. The Friend thinks it quite natural. The Player Queen opens the door and bids them go. The Friend lingers behind. What is Player Queen going to do? She is going to die. She hears a distant shouting and goes out. She puts the badge of revolution on a pole, singing. While she does so the real Queen enters. The real Queen is going to take refuge in a house. The Player Queen stops her. Finds out she is the Queen. Tells her there is no use hiding there. The real Queen says but the people are following her. Scene in which Player Queen takes the real Queen's place, putting on her robe, possibly not at present putting on the crown, leaving it at the cross. Queen has been tempted by crown of martyrdom, but is afraid, etc. Thinks it might be presumptuous. Queen goes out. Singing. Or else Queen may escape by different door going round castle. Perhaps merely go to hide in the garden. Prime Minister and lawyers enter.

Player Queen at once plays the Queen. Reproves them. One of the young men say but your Majesty, we have driven off the people, we are your own followers. She asks forgiveness. She has seen so little of her people, nourishing her strength in prayer. That has left her the stronger for the moment of need, a new sword. The Prime Minister stands aside. She speaks to each individually of the young men and to the older men, the moment the danger has come. The young men answer confidently, the older men more doubtfully. She then says that before they go down to the town there is something to be done. The gold must be brought out of the house. The Prime Minister comes forward. Ah Queen, I understand now the game you are playing. It is well. He tells them all to go into the house and bring out the gold. Yes, that must be put in a place of safety. When they are alone he says I know you are no queen. Do not be afraid; I do not know where you have come from or who has sent you, but you will do for this day's work. Listen. We will drive off this attack that is coming. All outside that door is undermined. The people will gather there to break in the door. (Note. The bridge of the moat undermined) Or I will open the door to give them confidence. I have but to take this torch. (Someone had brought a torch from inside the house. He has sent this person away at once.) He points to a stone. "I lift this stone." (He moves the stone.) "Throw in the torch and all the bridge leaps up into flame. But there will be other attacks. Yes, the gold must be in safety." Player Queen: "Give me the torch." "No, no, why should I give you the torch, you are not the Queen." Player Queen: "You said I would serve your purpose this day." Prime Minister: "No no, this is a man's work. You will grow excited, you will not know when to put it in, or you will be afraid." The others have come in. Player Queen: "Dare you disobey me? I demand the torch." She says to the other, "With this torch the mine under the bridge can be fired. This man has long enough kept me from authority. I alone will have the power of life and death." He gives the torch, saying yes, you will do the day's work. Holding the torch in her hand she goes up to the raised place by the cross. Then to the young men who have brought in the gold: "Go down to the town, go scatt[er] the gold through the streets." Prime Minister: "This is madness. What have we become unpopular for, how will we pay our men?" She: "Scatter it, scatter it! You said to the Queen this morning here in this very place that she had but to smile and show herself. I will have victory today by being myself. I will show myself and if they wish then to overthrow us, so be it." He still protests. Refuses to give up the gold. She then says let those who will go with him, go for the gold. The older men go with him, the younger remain with her. (In order to give her sufficient momentum for later parts probably her songs when she is in the cider vat should be love songs. In her conversation with the Friend she might speak first of her love and then of her refusal to play the part of Noah's wife. Perhaps she may even desire a great part in which she can express her love. She can describe herself or be described as one of those people who torture those they love.)

As soon as she is alone she tells them to bring out the crown. She takes the crown in her hand, putting the torch into a torch rest against the wall. She tells the history of the crown, or rather draws it from them by questions. She asks them of some tragic history of the past. Madness or death follow. She asks if it would not be a fine thing for one weary of life or forsaken in love to find that crown. She then puts it upon her head. Shots and cries are heard outside.

One of the young men says to another "Go, call the Queen's servants from the house. Then we can hold the battlements." Another: "Half a dozen can unloose that great stone over the door." Another: "We will put the crossbow men in the tower." Another: "I will go rouse the house." Goes into castle. A man appears upon the wall. He calls out that if the Queen will give up the

Prime Minister they have no quarrel with her. She refuses. The young men approve. She will give up no faithful servant, etc. The man on the wall announces then she must die. The Queen takes up a bow as if to shoot at him. He has no herald's rights, he is a ragamuffin. The Queen: "Ah, I had forgotten for a moment I am a queen." Puts down bow. A young man who is looking through one of the loopholes of the court says they have brought in a fallen tree to break in the door. Young man enters from castle. He says the castle is deserted. Player Queen: "Yes, they have all fled or they have joined the enemy." The young men have all gathered round the man who had been in the castle. She goes to the door. She turns to the others. "Your force can do nothing against them. This is my battle alone." She throws open the door. The crowd come in. "It is the Queen, the Queen herself!" They fall back, leaving a space round her. The people crowd round between her and the young men. The Queen speaks scornfully. They fear the crown upon her head, the mere show of herself. They are about to attack the young men. She commands the crowd to leave them alone. Their quarrel is with her. All that has been done she has ordered, the taxes, everything, she has done. They cry out at her and shake their fists at her. She speaks of her ancestors who ruled over them, or she puts the case of sovereignty more philosophically, the long preparation of the subtlety that they may rule. The young men entreat her to be silent, but she replies she witnesses for her ancestors. Suddenly a figure forces her way through the crowd, the real Queen. She asks if they do not know her, but then remembers no, they do not know her. She asks if she may speak. The Player Queen says it is of her she must ask leave. (Before the entrance of the real Queen the crowd must cry out that the Player Queen must die. It is upon this that the real Queen enters.) The real Queen begins incoherently. She has repented, she was going to do a great wrong, she was going to let another take her place. If she had done that, her soul would be lost. Player Queen says what had that to do with them. Let her to her confessor. She is now in the presence of the people and their rules. The real Queen says, "It is her that I have come back to save. She is not the Queen, she is a very noble person, she has taken my place to die instead of me." The Player Queen laughs. She says that she knows this woman, it was a player that was to have played before her servants that day. She knows her well. A wild, turbulent imagination, thirsty even for death if it give excitement. The real Queen falls upon her knees and then implores them to give her the crown of martyrdom. The other says, "Listen to her, she is jealous even of my death." A man forces his way through the crowd. He is the Poet. He says this woman is speaking the truth. I know that woman there. The Player

Queen mocks at him; he is in league with the other. Talks again of the artistic temperament. The crowd are bewildered. "Why should these people lie?" The others answer "But why should she go to her death?" There is general confusion. The Player Queen says they cannot understand the vanity of artists, and whatever you say to them, that they will believe. She will make this man boast before them all that she was of his troupe and loved him. The Poet cries out that it is true, it was she who played Noah's wife, it was she who loved him. The man who played herald on the wall says that the Poet and the Queen are mummers now as always, playing some game before the crowd. Some cry out to kill all three that they may be sure to have the right one. Player Queen says no, until she dies she is still their Queen. Take these people away. They cry that's right, they have no quarrel with anyone but her, their Queen. She asks by what death she is to die. A man comes forward, says he is the executioner. It is by poison. He hands her the cup. She says no, not that cup; bring me the jewelled cup from the castle. They go for it. (Leave out cup.) She sings a death song over herself. Shouting heard outside. Shouts of a rescue. She sings her refusal to wait and drinks off the cup. She is thirsty for death. The Prime Minister comes in. The soldiers with him cry they have made him King. He mounts up to the steps of the cross. He bids his soldiers shut the gate. He will know who is to suffer for all this. Or else he may pardon all on condition of accepting his rule. One of the young men finds that the Player Queen is not dead. She revives enough to tell that she was but playing her part. She dies. Various ends possible. Young men may refuse allegiance to new king, cross their swords over the Player Queen, swear some allegiance to the memory of her shadow rule. In this case Prime Minister should not come on scene, only messenger announcing him. Or else Poet might come forward and say she could have played a great part after all and made all our fortunes. Or else the Prime Minister might come in just as she is about to drink, and abolish both Queens.

Much of the foregoing will become perhaps too familiar as we work through the first seventeen drafts of the play, though a word should be said in advance about differences between Scenario 3 and the drafts: There is no indication of possible act and scene divisions here and little awareness of how the various parts of the scenario will work up during composition. Parts of it were expanded, parts condensed, such as the plan for the first meeting of the Player Queen and the Prime Minister. Scenarios 5 and 6, and perhaps 2 and 5, plot a tragic ending for the Player Queen. However, such an ending is found *only* in the scenarios; it occurs in none of the surviving drafts, and I rather doubt if it ever did occur. I think the idea that choosing a mask might have tragic consequences simply did not work out dramatically—serious consequences, yes, but not tragic. At the end of Scenario 3 Yeats seems to be playing up the death scene. The Socratic poison cup as a means of execution, the insistence that the cup be jeweled, the revival from unconsciousness for a few last words—all remind us of the extravagance of Jacobean drama.

Scenarios 4 and 5

Scenario 4 provides a variant of the scene in which the Prime Minister insists that the Queen must fill her traditional role for the good of the state. The principal variant is the setting, which is a gloomy wood that frightens the Queen, especially when Nona comes there looking for Noah's wife. Scenario 5 is a plan for the one-time final scene of the play, the confrontation of the Player Queen with the mob, she bent on death while the real Queen and Septimus try to save her. This fragment breaks off before the end is resolved.

Scenario 6

This scenario covers only the end of the play and goes back to the tragic resolution, for it ends with the Player Queen throwing herself over the battlements in a Tosca-like finale.

[SCENARIO 6]

Player Queen July 20

Note. The Executioner to be crowd leader and Herald. Could he make point of the fact that his vanity is touched by executing a Queen? He leads therefore the party to believe in Player Queen as rightful Queen. Executioner lifts sword or otherwise prepares. Poet struggles to save her. People hold him back. He makes a wild appeal. Player Queen for a moment seems shaken, then remembering the Friend has a flash of jealousy or magnanimity. Kneels down. The Prime Minister enters. Tells his people to close all gates. Asks where is the Queen. Suddenly hesitates. Is getting old. Does not know which is Queen. Executioner insists that it is the one he was going to execute. Turns towards her to ask her pardon. All kneel to her and ask her pardon. (Or Prime Minister can bid them ask their pardon from the true Queen.) Player Queen then explains. Brings the real Queen to the Prime Minister. Some lines pointing the moral. Act your part. It is not enough to be, but [stake] your life upon your acting. Turns to the Poet. Says to him, "Tomorrow I shall play . . ." He replies, "Yes, tomorrow, Queen of Sheba." She goes out singing.

When Poet struggles to save her he doesn't emphasize love. She as bef[ore] accepts her death. Prime Minister comes in. As before pretends not to know which is the real Queen. Bids them to ask pardon of the real Queen. Led by the Executioner they select the Player Queen. She walks down amongst them singing two or three lines or speaking or else saying it is not she should pardon, that the play is finished. She begins to mount stone stairs up to battlement. She explains, speaks to real Queen much as before. Friend comes forward and gives back to her her lover. She, mounting higher on the stairs, refuses to accept. Even may plead she knows that she is not fit for life. She may speak even of the enchanted crown. [MS addition.] Pity. Doom. The wild artist's imagination. Suddenly she disappears from the battlement. She has thrown herself from the top.

Surely this is unsatisfactory. The whole logic of the version points to a happy ending, and when Yeats wrote drafts based on Scenario 6, he found this to be so. Except for the "tacked-on" tragic conclusion, we have here the essentials of the final scene in Drafts 15 and 16. In these the Player Queen returns to Septimus and to her place in the troupe, quite content to play Noah's wife.

Scenarios 7 and 8

Scenario 7 works out a concept for the Septimus character that is radically different from any found in the drafts. Here he is completely shallow and commonplace, though so good-looking that both the Player Queen and Nona are in love with him. Here too, the Nona character is quite subservient to the Player Queen, and content to be so. The scenario covers only the scene between these two women. In Scenario 8 Septimus is rehearsing the Player Queen in the role of Noah's wife. At the point where Noah is to beat his wife, the Player Queen comes out of her part and refuses to continue. She demands a role such as the Queen of Sheba, and she reacts violently against Septimus's defense of the common people's liking for realism. Nona, who has gone out or been sent out during the quarrel, returns with news of the uprising against the Queen. The scenario continues with the change of role and costume between the real Queen and the Player Queen, the flight of the real Queen, and the entry of the Prime Minister. The staging of the rehearsal is the unique aspect of this plan.

Scenario 9

This late scenario, which includes the first extant prose version of "The Mask," completed in August 1910, contains the principal events of Act I, Scene ii and Act II as these were worked out in many drafts. Clearly it was written when the process of composition was far advanced.

[SCENARIO 9]

Player Queen

(The Queen in the foregoing scene argues against the Prime Minister who wants her to show herself in state, that being true to oneself and sincerity, that is everything. The people will respect her for that.) Player Queen puts up her head out of vat. She sings a song of which the following is the substance. My beloved sang to me why do you wear that golden mask and eyes of emerald. I would know what you are, I would see your face. Put away that burning mask, I cannot see it without trouble. As I sang to my beloved, if I put away my mask your heart would no longer beat, beat violently. One has calm when one knows what people are.

Ah, you would not sigh for me any longer; I wish for the praise of your sighs. That is why I will always wear my burning golden mask, with the eyes of emerald. Then my beloved sang to me, I do not even know if you are a friend or an enemy.

The Friend comes in, calling out "Noah's wife, Noah's wife!" and seeing the Player Queen says, "Ah, that's where you are! We have been searching for you all night, but I have found you just in the nick of time. As soon as the clock strikes we are to begin the dance of Noah's wife."

The Friend enters. "Ah, there you are. We have been looking for you all night, what have you been doing?" Player Queen: "Lying here in the cider vat, putting my head up every now and then to watch the beautiful young men go past who serve the Queen." (A line or two describing their beauty.) The Friend: "There is no use your sending me to Yellow Martin with that story. I have seen the Queen's people, all grandfathers. While you torture him so." Player Queen repeats a couple of lines of her song and sinks down again into the vat. The Friend: "O, do get out of that quickly. I have brought you a dress for the dance. It will begin the moment the clock strikes." The other, putting up her head. "It will not. I will never again dance that part." (A grotesque description of the [dress] and dance.) "I told Yellow Martin yesterday . . ." (When the Friend blames Player Queen for torturing Martin, she says "You do not love [him?] me." And Player Queen replies, "If I did not love him better than my own soul, would I do him so much evil?" She then sinks down into the vat with her song.) ". . . that he must let me play the Queen of Sheba or Juliet or Herodias" (or a series of names, some Irish). "There is not one of them I could not make up a fine dance for, he doing the words. When I dance and act I wish to make my soul greater, I wish to be something I have only dreamt of, I wish to hit the moon with my head, I wish to become a flame that men can warm themselves by and light themselves by." The Friend: "He will never let you play any of those parts, because nobody wants them. Don't you understand that? It is somebody like themselves that they all want to see." The Player Queen: "He will because there is nobody else to dance for him. Because he loves me, because I torture him, because I am myself, because I am beautiful and because I will never get out of this vat until he promises." The Friend: "There's something I have to tell you. You will be very angry, but I couldn't help it. You are so unkind to him." Player Queen: "What this? What are you going to say? Out with it." "I know I can't dance like you, but I promised . . ." Player Queen: "You promised?" She has got half out of vat, is sitting on it. Friend: "That I will dance Noah's wife instead of you." Player Queen jumps down from vat and begins shaking Friend. The Friend: "I didn't want to promise, no I didn't, but he was so unhappy, and he is so good, and you treat him so." The other keeps calling her names while she shakes her. The clock begins to strike. Yellow Martin comes in with the rest of the costumes. "What are you two quarreling for? Calm yourselves. The people must never see us quarreling. We must only be the people of the dances." The Player Queen is hurriedly dressing herself as Noah's wife. (Or the Poet having scolded them for quarreling may begin to blow a trumpet.) People come in. One says, "I saw them last year. It was the Jonah and the Whale. The man was Jonah. The two women made the four feet of the Whale. It had its mouth open and danced too." Another: "They say she is going to be married to Jonah. I wouldn't like to be married to a man that is all those people." Another: "I'd never be sure it was my own man was in it." (Poet can make showman speeches to the crowd. They have danced before Great Turk or the Great Mogul, or some mythological people. They were presented with twenty unicorns by the Great Mogul, but they all died when they came on the holy soil of Ireland which St. Patrick had blessed.) A few fantastic prose lines. (Crowd may speak one or two sentences, such as he was Jonah last year. That's so, that's so. Or else they may re-echo bits of the Poet's patter. Dance as before. Suddenly interrupted by the arrival of a child calling out, "Run away, run away, everybody run away! The people are coming to attack you. They are coming to attack the Queen." Poet: "Quick quick, gather up the things. We are in the Queen's house; we are all in danger." Some of the crowd, "To the wood! Yes, to the wood." Others: "No, let us stand and fight." Another: "What could we do against the people." Another: "What did the Queen ever do for us that we should fight for her?" Another: "Yes, let us to the wood." They all go out. Player Queen locks the door after them and takes the key in her hand. She says she will not let them pass out until Yellow Martin has promised her something. Yellow Martin says there is no time to be lost. She says that is true. They are the Queen's people, they have taken her pay. And when the people come she will mount up to the battlement and cry out for the Queen. He asks what new frenzy is this? He takes a step towards her. She says if you come nearer I will throw this key over the wall. He says what is it you want. She says that he must put the other woman out of the company. He says what, are you jealous of her? She says yes. Then say if she is first with him and he is first with her? She can make him famous through the world, he [can] make her famous. But last night she came between them. The other woman says, "O, I knew what evil would come of it. I should never have given that promise." Yellow Martin says, "It is well for you and us all three that she gave it. If we do not give the people what will please them, we will starve and die." Player Queen: "I have locked that door. The people are coming up the hill from the town half mad with anger. What reason therefore is there in what you say. How can that move me?" The Friend: "I take back my promise. No, I will not dance. O, Yellow Martin, promise what she wants." (In earlier scene between Queen and Prime Minister he must make more of the extreme anger of the people.) She will do all [he] says. The Player Queen: "Yes, I will go up onto that battlement. I will defy them if they come." Yellow Martin calls Friend to him. "Come here, so and so. Whether it be life or death I say no more. But whether it be life or death here or hereafter, it is to this woman who is mild and gentle and kind I will give my love." The Friend: "O no, Martin, What am I beside her?" Yellow Martin: "Do as you please. I am done with you. You are terrible. You are like a fire." The Player Queen throwing down the key. "Go." She sings a verse of her song. "But I will wear my mask, my burning mask, though he said to me how do I know if you are friend or enemy." The Poet has opened the door. The friend comes back to the threshold. "But what will you do." "Die." The Poet calls her and leads her out.

Nearly all of this is used in some place in the drafts that follow—it is particularly close to Draft 6—and the unicorn who so dominates the finished play has arrived, albeit somewhat incidentally.

Two general points about all of these scenarios before going on to the drafts: First, I believe they were all written before 1910, while Draft 16 was being composed, for none of them anticipates in any way the development of the play which took place after Yeats rejected Drafts 16 and 17. Secondly, there is no anticipation of the character Peter in any of them. Peter, who takes love lightly and is therefore Septimus's alter ego, first appears unnamed in Draft 6; he is named in Draft 11, reaches his point of fullest development in Draft 12, has not quite disappeared from Draft 15, and is very much still present in Draft 16, though his importance has been reduced. These scenarios were probably written during the years 1908–1910, when Yeats was devoting much of his time to the play.

CHAPTER THREE

Drafts 1 through 5

YEATS BEGAN WORK with the scene at the Queen's castle, which became (in Draft 16) Act I, Scene ii. Through many drafts the scene went about as follows: A Bishop/Chancellor/Prime Minister is on stage when the curtain goes up. He is supervising the stowing away of money brought in by a new tax—usually a tax on sins of the flesh but sometimes a tax on the intellectual sin of lying. The day is to be one of celebration during which a hitherto cloistered Queen will show herself to her people and celebrate her coronation or birthday. A fountain flowing with cider or wine and a play based on the Noah story are to be part of the celebration, but the Queen's subjects so resent the new tax that a rebellion threatens. There is also a rebellion in the company of strolling players that has been hired to give the play; the leading lady has hidden herself because she hates the part of Noah's wife and longs for queen roles.

The four earliest drafts are so difficult to read that I do not feel able to reproduce them in any coherent way. I have therefore provided a running summary supplemented by quotations.

Draft 1

Draft 1 begins with some pages of scenario, then shifted to dialogue based on the scenario. The Prime Minister (here *Bishop* or *Chancellor*) is overseeing the soldiers who are locking up the tax money. He must deal with an incipient rebellion over a tax on sins. Though the soldiers of the Queen may grumble, he says, they are essentially loyal men who must show happy faces during the day's celebrations. But they fear the temptations to sin that these celebrations will put in their way—the free drinks may lead to drunkenness, the sight of the women players to lust. They leave, and the Prime Minister has an exchange with a Clown, one of the company of players, who is asleep until the Prime Minister cuffs him awake and sends him out to summon an audience for the play. Once alone the Prime Minister–Bishop doffs his mitre and summons the Nona figure— here merely *Girl*—with whom he is having an affair. She wants to break this relationship and gives many reasons for doing so: the moral example of the Queen, the fact that the Prime Minister's social station is so far above hers that she cannot do anything for him, her desire for a normal domestic life. The Prime Minister jealously interprets her many excuses to mean she is in love with someone else. Septimus, here and through many drafts *Yellow Martin,* comes in with the news that his principal player has hidden herself and that they cannot give the play without her. Here the draft breaks off.

The important point to be noted is that Yeats involved the Nona figure and the Prime Minister in a love affair. This strategem lingered for some time, as we shall see, dwindling at length to a device for disposing of Nona at the end of the play. The Prime Minister has her carried off to his remote estate, thus easing the return of Septimus to the Player Queen by getting rid of the object of her jealousy. In urging his suit to Nona, the Prime Minister makes use of many arguments that will later be transferred to the light-lover Peter (when Peter has been invented)— arguments on the folly of serious or domestic love.

Draft 2

This draft is the first matter found in a large manuscript book of 115 folios with which Yeats must have lived for a long period. It contains the drafts that I have numbered 2, 3, 4, 7, and 11, and has been used from both front and back. (Yeats started from the back of the book when he wrote Draft 11.) Yeats has labeled the book "A2." We will begin at the front.

Draft 2 opens with Nona and the Prime Minister (*Girl* and *Chancellor*) on stage. She has found the script for Noah's wife, where the Player Queen has thrown it down on "the dung pit by the kitchen door . . . between the broken eggshells and an old shoe." The two are, as in Draft 1, having an affair that Nona is trying to break off because she cannot bring anything to their love. The Prime Minister's pride is hurt, though he admits he is too old for romantic love, and he threatens revenge on her "new lover" "because the rights of ministers of state must be respected by all." Septimus (*Yellow Martin*) enters with news that the Player Queen is missing, hence the play cannot be given. She has found an old play by Septimus—"a boyish thing, about a wild, impossible romantic queen, one of those old-fashioned things in sounding verse, no nature [in] it, all convention and high sentiment." She insists on playing this or nothing. The Prime Minister says to find her and let her play what she likes, but Septimus says he must assert his authority and make the Player Queen, to whom he is betrothed, do what he tells her, though he is afraid she may have drowned herself.

Another version, labeled "A.fragment A," takes a slightly different position. Here the Prime Minister has met the Nona figure only the day before. There is no hint of a love affair between them, but Nona has made the Prime Minister her confidant. The recent meeting and the confidential feeling already established are both devices for managing the exposition that now unfolds. The Prime Minister knows of Nona's love for Septimus and advises her against romantic love. The world belongs largely to the Devil, and life is "something to [be] played with strategy, disguises, and ambuscades." As before, Septimus comes in looking for the Player Queen. She has refused the part of Noah's wife and insists on staging an old play by *Yellow Martin*, "a wild impossible play, of a kind long gone out of fashion, all song, verse—no nature in it. A queen defies a rebel people, heroic words, you know the kind of thing, and all written in the style of Seneca, mere oratory from first to last." This leads to a discussion of romanticism versus realism on the stage, and of the people's preference for realism. Again the Prime Minister insists that the Player Queen must be found and a play given; again Septimus insists on the necessity of maintaining his authority over the Player Queen, whom he describes as "all moods, a storm, a perpetual fire." He continues: "If I waivered for a moment, she would lose in me the shaft she clings to, she would torture herself and me to death. I am the floodgate of her flood, the rudder of her ship, the shaft of her spear, the lanthorn to her candle." Septimus leaves, and the Prime Minister comments on the love of the Player Queen and Septimus. Nona has learned the part of Noah's wife, but the Prime Minister advises her not to play it. He woos her with an account of his own bad luck in love, and she is so sympathetic that he follows her as she leaves. The Player Queen, hidden in the vat that is to flow with cider/wine that night, sticks her head up to sing her song, and the Queen, dressed in robes of state, enters in time to hear it. The Prime Minister returns, and he and the Queen discuss the song; the Prime Minister offers to climb up and search the vat. (Yeats kept this piece of business through many of the drafts.) They are interrupted by a troupe of players searching for the Player Queen.

The draft breaks off momentarily, and Yeats writes a whole series of notes to himself that show his great uncertainty about how the play should develop.

Should the Queen have composed Mask of Noah's Wife? to edify her people? This would explain rage of people against players and lighten up plot. It could have been played all over the country by her orders. Or she might have found the play in the convent library and ordered its performance everywhere. Hence exasperation of the people. Both solutions take away from Poet's obstinacy, for Chancellor cannot offer alternative of the play she wants. Motive must be his refusal to show alarm. He should point out that he wears calm [?], straight, and dignified clothes. In which case all through play he should walk with deliberate steps.

If Queen writes or chooses by her confessor, or has written "Mask of Noah's Wife" some one should make a point of its having no characters, or only nameless ones. All through the play there is some confusion between these alternatives: sin/virtue, reality/masquerade.

Young men when Chancellor says they can suffer no ill from the play, seeing what it is, might say it is its dullness that is dangerous, driving them to drink.

These notes are followed by another version of the Queen's entrance. She has just met the troupe looking for the Player Queen and has been disturbed by their wild behavior and the gaiety of their costumes. She had expected players in her play (Yeats momentarily adopts the Queen-as-author idea) to be "dressed more dimly, nothing to rouse their vanity or others' jealousy." But she herself is dressed for a royal progress at the Prime Minister's request, so she does not blame the players. He insists that only the sight of the Queen in her hereditary role will prevent rebellion. She must wear the mask. She counters by saying she wants to be respected for what she is, not for her skill in playing a part. Yeats then writes a series of critical notes, and the draft breaks off.

Draft 3

This draft begins immediately with another version of the Queen's entry in her robes of state. She expresses in extravagant language her objections to role-playing. So dressed she is "a sail spread to the Devil's wind, a pomp, a show, a gilded shadow, an echo, a lighted cloud, a gilded bait for the soul's death, a painted mask." The Prime Minister insists that the state needs her in the role that tradition has assigned her; only thus masked can she give her people élan and a sense of tradition. When she threatens to return to her prayers, the Prime Minister threatens to resign, for he can do no more and fears revolt. When he tells her of the revolt that threatens, the Queen first speaks of the crown of martyrdom that may be hers. This contrast of the crown symbolizing regal power and the crown of martyrdom is still found in the finished play.

"Another version" follows,—an early complete draft of what became Act I, Scene ii in Draft 16. It begins with the exchange between the Prime Minister and the Queen, in language sharpened and improved. (There is an allusion to Maeve, one of the few Irish allusions in the whole mass of drafts.) The possible martyr-dom of the Queen is developed more fully than in the previous draft, but in spite of her fears the Queen and Prime Minister leave for the royal progress into town. The whole troupe of players comes in looking for the Player Queen, who puts her head up out of the vat and sings an early version of "The Mask." They urge her to return to the troupe, but she refuses to play the part of Noah's wife. She must play a queen. When Nona reveals that she has agreed to take the role of Noah's wife, she and the Player Queen fight until Septimus comes in to part them. The end of the draft is much like the end of Act I, Scene ii in Draft 16, even in its language. The other members of the troupe are also tired of the Noah play, but they and the Player Queen agree to give it once more, and the play within the play is about to begin. Septimus is blowing his trumpet to summon an audience as the draft ends.

Draft 4

Draft 4 is very short. It starts with a scenario headed, "Changes to be made in Act I." The principal change is the development of a character named Barach. (Yeats had previously used this name three times: in *The Wandering of Oisin* (III, line 90) and *The Countess Cathleen* beginning with the 1895 version (line 485), and as the name of the Fool in the 1903 and 1904 versions of *On Baile's Strand*.) Barach is the leader of the rebellious soldiers who is sentenced to be flogged. Another new character is Rat-hole, an old man possessed by the spirit of the Old King. Both will flourish in the succeeding drafts. Barach becomes a towns-man, not a soldier, and he leads the rebellion against the Queen. In the finished play he has dwindled to the *First Citizen*. Rat-hole is the protoype of the Old Beggar who rolls on his back and brays like a donkey whenever the crown changes. Through many drafts he will crow like a cock. Here in Draft 4 the Prime Minister assigns him the task of summoning the audience to the Noah play, a task previously given the Clown, who has now disappeared. The Prime Minister is still interested in Nona's love for Septimus and shows his own interest in her by saying that if he were king he would have her carried off. Several versions of the play will end with the rape of Nona.

Yeats concludes these notes with a sketch of an "alternative scene" involving further use of the play Septimus wrote in his youth. Nona is to read parts of this play to the Prime Minister, and hearing them rouses his ambition: He contem-plates the player's masks, and says, "Could I find one of these that suited me, I'd be the king myself." This looks very far ahead; at the end of the finished play the Prime Minister is King. There are other notes which Yeats never worked on in the surviving drafts—the Nona figure is to read out from Septimus's play some passages about the upbringing of a queen. Then at the end when he is King, the Prime Minister is to speak these "as his own history . . . his pose." Though Yeats has Nona read parts of this imagined play in Draft 8, none of the parts read deals with the upbringing of a queen.

Draft 5

This draft is the first to which it is possible to assign at least an approximate date. At the end of the draft Yeats has written a tentative table of contents for the *Collected Edition* published by Bullen, September–December 1908. I quote the plan below:

Vol. 1. Poems (Unwin)
Vol. 2. Poems (Bullen)
Vol. 3. Ideas of Good and Evil
Vol. 4. Celtic Twilight, Kathleen and Hour Glass
Vol. 5. Hanrahan and Secret Rose.
Vol. 6. Discoveries etc.
Vol. 7. King's Threshold etc.
     Deirdre.
     Baile's Strand.
     Golden Helmet.

This plan is quite unlike the contents of the *Collected Edition* as actually published (for instance, all the poems appeared in Volume I), so it must have been made before the final order of that edition was established. This suggests a date at least six months before the publication of Volumes I and II in September. A terminal date for the plan of spring 1908 should not be too far off.

    This draft is also the first example in *The Player Queen* manuscripts of a practice that with Yeats was almost customary—using a single manuscript book for drafts that are not successive but considerably separated from each other in the sequence of composition. In establishing a progressive order among the drafts of many works by Yeats, one must rely on internal evidence rather than on a physical fact such as occurrence in a single manuscript book. In the present instance Act III of the "B" version of *The Player Queen,* which I have called Draft 8, is found in what appears to be the front of the manuscript book that contains Draft 5. The manuscript book in question has no printed label, hence no obvious front or back. Yeats wrote Draft 5 in it, using part of the last sheet of the draft for the table of contents quoted above. Then, when composing Act III of Draft 8, he began from the other end of the book, and wrote on one of the covers "Player Queen B. Act III." The label makes that cover appear to be the front of the book. The internal evidence here simply does not admit of any other explanation. Draft 5 is obviously earlier, probably much earlier than Draft 8. To Yeats blank paper was always an invitation to fill it up.

Whatever the difficulties of establishing the place of Draft 5 among the other drafts, and of dating it, there is no doubt about what Draft 5 is: a working out in dialogue of the scenario from the A2 manuscript book (cf. p. 36) here called Draft 4 and discussed above. This was headed "Changes to be made in Act I." The draft follows that scenario closely. It begins with the Prime Minister (*Chancellor*) gloating over the wealth that the new tax on sins is bringing in. He then deals firmly with a threatened rebellion among his troops, led by a soldier who is first called simply "Soldier," then later in the draft "Barach," as in Draft 4. Yeats kept that name for the leader of the rebel forces for a very long time, though later he made him a civilian and kept the Queen's soldiery loyal. Barach is rebellious because the Queen's new tax on sins is more than flesh can bear; he insists that the Prime Minister hang him, give him his rights, as he puts it. Instead he is sentenced to thirty lashes. The soldiers don't know the Queen by sight. She has spent her life in a mountain convent; even the Prime Minister has seen her only through the grating of a door. Now that all will be changed, for the Queen is about to make a royal progress into town. Meanwhile other soldiers are bringing in barrels of wine to fill the vat over a fountain that is to flow wine as part of the celebration. The soldiers are afraid that drinking the wine will lead to sin, and sin they cannot "afford." The Prime Minister orders them to rejoice: "Hold up your heads, thrust out your chests, let the Queen see you in your holiday manners." The soldiers leave to guard the way to town after stating their loyalty.

Nona (*Girl*) enters with Rat-hole (also introduced in Draft 4), who has all his life been haunted. The ghost of the Old King has recently joined the spirits who possess him. Rat-hole explains his name: "That's it, Rat-hole, because of the way they go in and out." The Prime Minister insists he is a fraud but sends him to summon the people to the play. He then turns to Nona, telling her to warn Septimus (*Yellow Martin*) that the play must begin on time and inquiring whether she still loves Septimus as much as ever. She says she does because he needs her, and that "one must take care of someone." The Prime Minister replies, "If I were king I'd carry you away to some distant castle." This prepares for the rape of Nona at the end of several versions of the play. The draft breaks off, and Yeats writes this note on the opposite page: "Chancellor should have a refrain 'If I were king.' He would hang if he were king, etc. He can use it to the Queen. He wants a feather [the swan feather those loyal to the Queen wear in some drafts?] to be obeyed. He, mere Chancellor, cannot hang." This is followed by the plan for *The Collected Works* discussed above.

CHAPTER FOUR

Draft 6

THIS IS THE LONGEST, most fully worked of the early drafts.
I believe it was written, at least in part, before Draft 7, which follows Draft 4 in
the A2 manuscript book. Before it was done, most of the action and some of the
language of the three-act version of the play (Draft 16) had been worked out, so
Draft 6 has been keyed to the line numbers of Draft 16. Draft 6 is typical of the
early drafts of the play. Though it is more legible than some of them, I have been
unable to decipher many passages. It shifts often from scenario to dialogue and
back again, it is careless about entrances, exits, and speech-tags. Yeats frequently
writes alternate versions, sometimes on the opposite page, sometimes one following another. But by the time the draft was finished, Yeats had invented the end
of the play he was to keep through Draft 16. Draft 6 begins with a scenario.
When Yeats begins his dialogue here he writes blank verse but soon shifts to prose.
Nona is called *Friend* or *The Friend;* Septimus, *Poet.* The numbered lines refer to
Draft 16 (cf. pp. 16 and 196).

[Draft 6]

Queen certain she heard something sing in the vat—always afraid of that.
Prime Minister says it is nonsense. Now they must hurry to town. Enter Girl
calling for Noah's wife. Have they seen her? No. Goes out at back. P.
Queen puts up head, singing out of the cider vat, etc. She will not answer
unless called Queen of Sheba. She has come to say that it will break his heart
if she does not play Noah's wife. How can she treat him so badly. Player
Queen still sings, mocking. Poet enters, anxious. Will she do it? She has
begun blowing on the trumpet. He. "It is all well, she is calling the people."
He and Friend put down boat. The dance as before. Servants crowd out of
castle. Sudden alarm. Fly, etc. No arms. Some to face crowd, some to flee.
Poet and Player Queen alone. She closes gate. He entreats. It is death.
[Several lines undeciphered] If he loves her truly he will give her great parts.

[This is followed by a short essay called "Meditation," which Ellmann prints on
pages 191–92 of *Yeats: The Man and the Masks.*]

Opening of scene. PM is having kegs of gold brought in, or pitchers. He is talking about the new tax. Folly, but [it] has brought in the money. How can people enlarge their minds without sin? We grow intelligent by justifying our passions to our thought. All this time he directs the kegs. [Sentence undeciphered] Scene about vat and spirit might come here. Servants shrinking back. Prime Minister will climb up himself. Suddenly sees Queen. (No, not so good)

Act I, Scene ii

[*Queen*]. Hush, I am almost certain that I heard
     A voice, a humming sound, somebody singing
     But very low.
P.M.   But where?
Queen.   In that big vat.
P.M.   A dream, your Majesty. I set that up
     To hold the cider that by leaden pipes
     Shall run out of the fountain over there
     When we are merry, but it's empty now.
Queen. And now?
P.M.   I'll climb, though Time stiffens me.
Queen. You'd find nothing—it may well have been
     Some ancient spirit, singing the years away.
P.M.   You feared, because you fast and pray so much.
     Describe it anyhow.
A Voice.   Come Noah's wife.
Queen. (clinging to him)
     Listen listen—a most ancient spirit.
A Voice. Where are you, Noah's wife?   53
Queen.   Ah, did you hear?
Voice. O where is Noah's wife?
Queen.   O God have mercy.
P.M. O [word undeciphered] it that you said?
Friend. O sir, it is [a] dancer who is to dance the part of Noah's
  wife before the Queen's servants. She cannot be found
  anywhere. We have searched all the country. She must be
  hidden somewhere here. Did you see her anywhere, lady? And
  today of all days to vanish away, and we to play by the Queen's
  order. (PM should ask if she knows Queen's face. She has

never seen her face. She goes out calling "Noah's wife,
Noah's wife.")

P.M. That woman did not know you. Not one of all your subjects
outside this castle knows you any better. But from this day it
will [be] different. Ah, your Majesty, it is a queen's smile,
her bow that makes our pomp.

Queen. Ah, if I only knew what was right. You are wrong, sir,
to encourage the people to think of outward, needless things.
You are making me do wrong.

P.M. Whether I am right or wrong as you count them, Madame,
I do not know; I am no confessor. But there is much discontent
among the people.

Queen. And I can lay it, it seems, by showing them this poor face.
What is there in this face? There are many better faces.

P.M. The state is in debt. Your father's wars [line undeciphered].
The harvest has been bad. [sentence undeciphered] There
is something besides your rosary, your cell, and your cross.
There is the gold paid to us for the tax. If you do not use
the influence that has come to you from your father, if you do
not smile on them and wear the crown before [their] eyes,
we shall be all killed and the castle sacked. They have
already begun to riot.

Queen. It is their proud hearts that need charity. I will consult
the archbishop at once. We will issue new prayers. Send
someone for the archbishop; that is the first thing we have to
do. I will have all my [?] subjects say a rosary every night for
a month, and the courts must order every man taken rioting
or inciting to rebellion to have [four words undeciphered]
for a month.

P.M. Will your Majesty permit an old man to speak plainly?
It is the Queen's duty to make the people greater by what she
seems. She is the image of what they would be, a symbol, an
image. It is her business [?] to do it, [if] need be for a show,
for a jewel, for an obsequy [?], for a piece of damask.
She can grant to others the government as you have granted
it to me. She may sorrow over her sins, but she must always
seem to be all power and haughtiness. Your state is a mask
which you must wear always on your face.

Queen (*sitting on doorstep*). I would sooner have them respect me for what I am. I knew you were making me do wrong, I knew it in my heart. But now, now you say it out.

[FROM THE OPPOSITE PAGE]

[*P.M.*] I knew what would come of these taxes, and if on the head of all that you insist on new prayers . . .

Queen. But the taxes are just. No one taxed for doing any necessary [?] thing or any right thing . . .

P.M. Ah, that is just it. They are taxed for every sin they commit. Every man that gets drunk, or climbs in at a lady's window, or gambles, or quarrels.

Queen. They are all sinful people, angry because I tax them.

P.M. And if you do not play a Queen's part, all is over with the state.

[RETURN TO RIGHT-HAND PAGE]

Your Majesty may have it as you will. I will send the guards away, but I lay down my office.

Queen (*getting up*). O well, you may have it [as] you please. I will go. Come. But when I look at this spot, when I think of those good players. Now they are doing good to the people with all those pious stories. Ah, they have a good and a pleasing life and a life [word undeciphered] to good.

(*Player Queen puts her head up out of barrel.*)

He.   /164 "I would know what you are in yourself"
          My beloved /165 said to me.
          "Put off that mask of burning gold
          With /166 emerald [eyes]
          That I may know what you are."

[*She.*] "I will not /167 put away my mask.
          It is the mask of burning gold /168
          With emerald eyes that makes
          Your heart beat so /169 quickly
          I would now [?] be praised by your beating heart."

Friend (*at back. Comes in with Player*). I told you all [?] but now there was something you must do for me. You must go

down to the town and come back and tell me what is
happening. Your part in the mystery play is towards the end.
You will have time.

Player. But will the soldiers do me a hurt? They say there
is trouble.

Friend. If you get among the soldiers, put this in your cap. All of
the Queen's party are to wear swan feathers. One of the
Queen's soldiers gave me that.

Player. Did you kiss him for it?

Friend. Don't you ask stupid questions. Go now, and there is the
kiss I promised you.

Player. Good, and everybody does what you want.

Friend. Ah, Noah's wife, ah, I have found you.

Player Queen. Then my beloved said to me "I [do] not
even know if you are a friend or an enemy."   220

Friend. O, there you are. We have been searching for you all
night. What have you been doing?

Player Queen. Lying here in the cider vat, putting my head up
and down during [the] night, watching the beautiful
young men that serve the queen—so tall, so ruddy from   206
their hunting, so bright of eye. All night they have
been playing on lutes and singing songs.

Friend. It is no use you sending me to tell Yellow Martin that
story. He has seen the Queen's people—
all old men with speckled shins from sitting over the fire.   211
Why do you torture him so? If you loved him you could not   214
do [it]. Could I torture him, and I do not love him?

[NOTE FROM OPPOSITE PAGE]

Friend should remonstrate with PQ on her treatment of Poet—
something as follows: Why do you treat him so ill? We
women have so little—all we can do is for them[?]. We have
the greatest power in the world for but a little while. Make a
child or a man perfectly happy even though it is only while
we hold them in our arms. P. Queen. I did not know whether
I would make him happy. I only knew that I would have him
think of nobody but me. Your way loses a man. Friend. Well,
what matter? One man is like another.

[RETURN TO RIGHT-HAND PAGE]

P. Queen (*singing*).

        Why do you wear your burning mask

        Why do you wear your emerald eyes, etc.

        (*Sinks down again in vat but goes on singing.*)

Friend. O do come down out of the vat. I have brought your
dress for the dance. It is to begin in a few minutes. We have
not a moment to spare. Why aren't you like me. I am
friendly with everybody and everybody likes me.

P.Q. (*putting up head again*). I will not.

I have made up my mind that I will never dance that part again.
I will not play the part of a stupid old woman with nothing
worth saying to say for herself. I will not be beaten by Noah
because I will not go into the Ark.

Friend. But Noah does not really hit—you are not beaten.

P. Queen. I must [?] have a great part—a part with fine   232
words and a fine dress. I must say all the things I have   233
dreamed of. I must look beautiful and wear shiny things
or I will not dance. I must grow greater and make those
who look at me grow greater or I will not dance. Bad or
good it does not matter, but I must be like a fire, a light.
I must burn or shine. I must be Herodias, or Maeve, or
the Queen of Sheba . . .

Friend. No, no, no, no. That is no use. He will never let you   242
play any of those parts because the people don't like them any
more. They want somebody like themselves. What do they
care about great people? Now Yellow Martin says that there is
nobody so interesting to them, so obedient, so like themselves
than Noah's wife. She did not like the Ark, he says, but when
Noah took a stick. And it's all in the Bible too.

P. Queen. I will make Yellow Martin.

Friend. You will not. He will never let you play any of those
parts, because we should all starve, because nobody wants
them. Don't you understand that?

Player Queen. He will because he loves me, and because I am
beautiful, and because there is nobody else to dance for him
if I don't, and because I will never get out of this vat until I
have his promise.

Friend. There is something, but I am afraid to say it. I told him
that I will dance in your place. You will be very angry.
(*Player Queen has been sitting on side of vat, but now she
gets down.*)
[*Player Queen.*] You—you did that?
Friend. You make him so unhappy.
Player Queen (*shakes her*). You dared to do that?
Friend. I did not want to but . . . And what does it matter what
part one plays? We should take what comes. [rest of speech
undeciphered]
(*Enter Poet as Raven.*)
[*Poet.*] What are you two quarreling about? Hush, I say. The
people must never see us quarreling. We are their dreams
and we must do what the dream bids us. (*Sees P. Queen
putting on dress.*) You are only just found in time.
[stage direction undeciphered] Quick, put on the dove's robe.
I am already the raven. (*He blows trumpet. The people
gather.*)

[Act II]

First Man. That is the raven. I saw them once in the dance of
Noah's wife before the cathedral at ———. [Yeats's blank]
Second. The last time I saw them it was Jonah and the Whale.
He had a great [three words undeciphered].
Poet (*singing*).

Listen to the holy tale of the Flood and the Ark
Hear the wise words of the raven and the dove.
The Great Turk and the Kubla Khan have heard.
Twenty unicorns they gave us with silver hooves.
But they die when their feet touch Ireland
Because of St. Patrick's curse on all unchaste things.

[FROM OPPOSITE PAGE]

What are you quarreling about? Get on your dress. Ah, I see
that you have put those thoughts out of your head. How
could you play the Queen of Sheba, or Herodias, or
Maeve? What do you know of queens? [four words
undeciphered] You play these old women very nicely. But a
great part? You could not move or speak like a queen. You
would be like a cracked bell, all rhetoric and words. One must

have the passion of a queen to play one, one must be a queen,
one must have the instinct for the pride[?].

[RETURN TO RIGHT-HAND PAGE]

Hear the raven's song and the song of the dove.
Hear this song of the wife of Noah:
"What is the talk of the Flood? There is no flood. I
Say it is all a tale of my husband's to
Take me away from my friends. We gossip too much he says."
Dove: Your husband is cutting a stick
A blackthorn stick in the hedge.
Noah's Wife.
What do I care for my husband?
Let him cut what he will from the hedge.
I have my delph on the dresser,
I have my fire and my kettle
I will do what I please in the house.
Let him go elsewhere with his lies.
I will wait till the flood goes down.
Raven and Dove.
The water is beginning to rise.
The valleys are hidden away.
Noah's Wife.
I will wait till the sea goes down.
[undeciphered line]
I will sit over the fire
I will talk with my friends.
This is all a tale of my husband's
To get me away from my friends.
[same line undeciphered]
Raven and Dove.
Your husband is cutting a stick
A blackthorn stick in the hedge
A heavy blackthorn stick.
Noah's Wife (moving her hands as if cutting a stick in hedge).
Let him cut what he will in the hedge,
I will do what I choose in the house,
I will sit with my friends and talk.

I will not go into the boat,
He has made up a lie of the Flood
To get me away from my friends.
Let him cut what he will in the hedge.

Raven and Dove.

The water has begun to rise
The valleys are hidden away.

Noah's Wife.

I will shut the door with my hands
And keep the water out—
What do I care for his lies?
He is afraid when we sit alone
That we laugh at his ways.
Let him go boating himself. I will
Shut the door with my hands.

Raven and Dove as before.

A thick stick.

Noah's Wife.

O do not strike me Noah.
Put that stick away and I will
Do all that you say.

(*A man comes running in.*)

Player Queen (*to Messenger*). What do you want, you
messenger? Here are none that are not of the Queen's party.

Messenger. Death to all that oppose the people.

(*Players are gathering up costumes except Player Queen, who
has locked door of courtyard after the last who have gone out.*)

Poet. Quick, quick, gather up the brocade the Queen gave us—
leave the rest. We can save nothing but the brocade. (*They go
toward door, find it locked.*) My God, the door is locked.
Who has locked us in? We are lost. Who has done that?

Player Queen (*holds up key*). I have locked the door. Neither   194
you nor I nor that woman will go through that door until you
have promised me something. You must send that woman
away.

Poet. Give me that key.   197

Player Queen. Come a step, and I throw it over the wall and the
cage door is shut. Send the woman away. She has come between
me [and] you.

[ALTERNATE DRAFT FROM LEFT-HAND PAGE]

Poet. My God, put down that banner.

P. Queen. We are of the Queen's party. We are the Queen's
players.

Poet. Will you bring us all to our deaths?

Player Queen. Send that woman away. She has come between
me and you.

Friend. O, she is right. I should never have promised. I will not
play Noah's wife—never, never again.

Poet. Be silent. Listen to me. Whatever I do you will drive
me to ruin. If I promised to let you play . . .

P. Queen. It is too late; for that I will have this woman driven
away.

[RETURN TO RIGHT-HAND PAGE]

Poet. You ask [the] impossible. Would you have us all starve?
Who wants queens to be looking at? (*She goes in front,
displays the key.*) You asked to play great queens, who[m] you
have never seen. You know nothing. You who could not act
the Wife of Lot—no, not even a pillar of salt if you were let
go your own way.

P. Queen. The voices are coming to take you away by death, and
yet you threaten me with starvation. Send that woman away.
O Martin, I am your love, your sweetheart—you are my
friend out of the world. Can't you give me what I ask? Swear
that you will send her away.

Poet. This I will say more—I should be worthy of your love or
any woman's love. I will not swear.

Friend. O, this is terrible. Do what she bids you.

Poet. And this further I say, whether it is life or death or what[?]
not. This woman is more worthy of love than you are, and
whether in this world or in the next I give her my love.

Player Queen. Then it is over. What more have I to do with life?
(*Opens door.*) Go, go.

Poet. Come, she has found her wits again. (*Goes out.*)

The Friend (*about to follow*). O, what will you do? How could
I help it? I did not try to get his love, O no, I did not.

Player Queen (*between her and the door*). I can keep you, I can
keep you. Get him [in] the next world if you like, but let him
. . . (*Friend begins to cry.*) No, you are not worth it. I will
have no sharers[?] even in this. But tell him that this day
I shall [be] Sheba, Herodias, Maeve—all. He shall know what
I can do. Noah's wife, pillar of salt. Go. (*She begins [to] sing
about the mask again.*)

> My beloved said "Why do you [wear] that burning mask
>   with emerald eyes?"
> But I said to my beloved "O better, better than the
>   love that is care and envy and considering[?]
> O, I shall die with my burning mask."
>   (*Real Queen comes in.*)

[*Queen.*] Shut the gate, shut the gate.

Player Queen. It is no use. The people will beat it open. No use
going in there either—all the Queen's servants have fled.
There is nobody there who can save you.

[ALTERNATE SPEECH FROM LEFT-HAND PAGE]

It is no use hiding there. The house is empty. All the servants
of the Queen have fled.

[RETURN TO RIGHT-HAND PAGE]

Queen. O, you are one of the people. You hate me.

P. Queen. I have the swan feather in my hat. It is white for the
virtue that you would have in all our hearts.

Queen. O, where can I hide? They are coming to kill me. They
are close behind, they are running.

P. Queen. It is no use going to hide in the garden; they will
search till they find you. No more that way, they would search.
Here, put this cloak upon you and this hat—they belong to
a woman I am tired of. Queen, no one will know you now.

Queen. Ah, you are a good subject. God will reward you. At first
I thought I should stand still and let myself be killed. I have
often coveted the crown of martyrdom. But then they looked
so angry it was terrible, and besides, it would have been
presumptuous. Ah, you are very noble. How can I reward

you? And you a wandering woman to whom one kingdom
is like another.

P. Queen. Now go, hide among the orchard trees. I take your
part and your place. They will understand nothing but this
crown, and the glitter of it will keep them from you. (*Queen
goes out. P. Queen holds crown above her head and sings to it.*)

> A moment, an hour I am part of the world
> And when I am dead shall be mourned as a queen
> When I am dead there is one that shall weep
> That shall weep me as a queen.
> Here on this stage I shall play out my part
> All that she is, and one when he hears of it
> Shall weep for a queen.

(*Enter soldiers and P. Minister.*)

P. Queen (*on stage*). Lift up your spears, my heart is ready for
them. Why do you hold back? But did you think that a queen
would fear to die? My father looks out of these eyes.
(*Stepping down.*) Blue eyes that have [looked] calmly upon
the spears of your enemies, dark eyes that have seen danger
[five words undeciphered]. I welcome it, this death, crown
of my days.

A Soldier. Queen, we are of your own party. We have beaten
back your enemies; we have come to put you in safety.

Note. Real Queen must have gone out of door again on hearing the soldiers
coming.

P. Queen. Then I am indeed Queen this hour, if never more. You
will obey?

A Soldier. In all things all that [wear] swan feathers obey you.
Your father was not so brave as you are. You are indeed
a Queen.

P. Queen. There inside that door the gold is stored. Go, bring
it hither.

Soldiers. We obey you. (*Soldiers go into castle.*)

Prime M. Why, that is a good thought, whether Queen or no.
Yes, that must be put in safety, we can't risk that in fight.
Lady, I do not know who you are or where you came from—
I have no time for questions—but you will serve my turn

better than the other. Listen to me. I know you are not a
queen, but that matters nothing. None but a few servants
who have fled like their mistress know the true Queen's face.
You reign and I will rule.
(*Enter soldiers. As they come in he kisses her hand.*)
Player Queen. Soldiers, now take that gold and scatter it
through the streets of the town.
P.M. Impossible, impossible. We must have troops [two words
undeciphered]. What, scatter the gold, scatter it through
the streets?
Soldiers. He is right. No, no, we cannot scatter the gold. [seven
words undeciphered] Not the gold, etc. We have not been
paid.
Queen. Then take it, Minister, go with it where you will, but you
are no subject of mine. Whoever stays [with] me stays with
this empty house. I will know this day if I am Queen indeed.
P.M. Quick, there is no time to lose. On, on. I know a place in
the wood where it will be safe. What, scatter the gold? Your
Majesty, give up this thought and come.
Queen. Farewell. Over these three I am queen. (*All go but 3.*)
A [*Soldier.*] Your Majesty, I will stay. ~~You have your
father's spirit.~~ I fought beside him.
[*Soldiers.*] And I, and I.
Another. You have his nose.
Another. And his eyes.
Another. And his voice. I will shut the doors. We will defend
you to the end.
Another. I [will] call your servants from the Castle. We can hold
this place all day.
Another. Half-a-dozen can keep the battlements.
Player Queen. You fought with the King, my father?
Soldier. In many battles. Ah, you have more than his courage.
We were in many dangers.
Player Queen. And his father, and his father. They wore this
crown. It has been in many battles.
Soldier. Yes, now the Danes and now the Normans, always in
danger. Did not Columkille say it would never be at peace?
Player. It has brought many into danger, but never in such danger
as now. 'Twere a good crown for one weary of life.

Soldier. O your father, if I may be so bold, loved his ale and
his cider.

Player [*Queen*] (*shouting getting nearer*). For one crossed in
love—a fine gift for one that had quarreled with a friend to
put up into the [two words undeciphered].

[Act III, Scene ii]

Executioner (*on wall*). I am deputed to declare the people's will.
I am bid say we intend no evil to her Majesty if she will obey
our just demands. (*Soldier draws his bow; she motions it
down.*) Your Majesty has bad advisers—we know who—
and we demand that you dismiss the Minister. (*Shouts outside
of door* [word undeciphered].)

Queen. And if I refuse?

Executioner. Then the people condemn you and him to death.

Queen. I will give up no faithful servant, nor hold any further
converse[?] with rebels. Lay down your arms and then I will
listen. Now hunt this man with arrows if he linger.

Soldier (*at loophole*). They have taken down a great tree; they
are going to break in the door.

Soldier (*coming from house*). There is nobody in the castle; they
have all fled.

Soldiers (*gather round him*). All fled?

P. Queen. You can do nothing against them, this is my battle
alone. I will have all the peril of this crown, and I will have
none suffer for me. (*She throws door open.*)

Voices. The Queen, the Queen herself. It is she [who] has
opened the door. (*They fall back, leaving a space around her.
Some are for attacking the old men who leave the tower.*)

Player Queen. You fear the mere image of sovereignty [?], and
turn on them. It is with me your quarrel is. I accept all. The
taxes, all is my work.

Crowd. Death to the Queen—yes, death.

Player Queen. Who is there among you that dare strike? Your
father's lives, the lives of their fathers before them were
but twigs
woven in the nest that gave the ~~eagle~~ birth. Who
among you all dare face the eagle? Eagle begat eagle up
through all the centuries, and in my eyes all the
eagles look at you. Now strike if you will; look I

will hide their lightning. (*Covers her eyes with her hands.*)   84

Executioner. I do not fear her.

Real Queen (*coming forward from among the crowd*). Let me
  speak, let me speak.

Player Queen. It is of me, the Queen, you should ask
  permission.

Real Queen. Strike at me if you will. She is noble, she has taken
  my place. She is very loyal. I fled, but my conscience stirred.
  I am here to tell the truth. I was going to do a great wrong.
  I was afraid.

Player Queen. Some trouble crazes her. If your soul is troubled,
  lady, get a confessor. Do not speak of it in the market-place.

Real [*Queen.*] I tell you all I am the Queen—I myself am the
  Queen.

Leader of Crowd. Where is your crown, lady?

Queen. Is there no one here who knows me, no one who will
  say what I am?

Player Queen. I remember you now. You were to have played
  before me this day. I have heard of her. All her life she has
  longed to play some great part, at whatever cost. It has crazed
  her at last, and so she goes about dreaming that she is a queen.
  Ah, could you but understand the wild blood of these artists.
  They thirst for all the greatness of the world and dream in
  their folly they could be it.

Man in Crowd. Which is speaking the truth?

Another (*threatening* [?] *with spear*). I say it is the Queen
  that has the crown.

Another. But why should this one try to save her?

Player Queen. She is wearing the dress of Noah's wife in the
  mystery.

A Man. I know that. I saw it at Xmas.

Player Queen. This has been long enough. How am I to die? No,
  not all your spears. I would not thus [be] torn beyond measure.
  I would [go] there on to that stage and die in some seemly way.

A Man in Crowd. I will strangle you with this bowstring.

(Or else the leader of crowd may drive back others. He has
been chosen to kill her.)

Queen. Will no one bear witness for me? Is there no one here

who remembers? And stop this woman who is going to her
death like a wild horse.

Poet. I will bear witness; that is not the queen.

Queen. Yes, yes, she changed with me. She gave me this dress,
I gave her my crown.

Player Queen. What? Here is a new folly. Let this man come
here before me. Put him where he can hear me and see me,
that he may know what is born of eagles faces death. He
will tell of it after, for he too is a player. He and she, they
have planned this mummery. They are so vain, these artists
—O, I know them well. They are so vain. Why I will
make this man say that I was troubled, and that he [and]
I loved, and that he cast me off and so I now seek death, or
but to show myself fearless of it, looking at [it] as eagles at
the sun but to win his praise. I will make him say all that;
I will.

Poet. But it is true; yes, it is all true. (*They laugh.*)

Player Queen. [a long undeciphered speech]

The Friend. It was all my fault. She wanted a fine part, she
thought she could make him give it. He had no one else
to play her parts, and then I promised.

Player Queen (*more laughter*). Why, can you see this was all
arranged before hand. It is a play, a stage play to amuse
you—that is all.

[FROM OPPOSITE PAGE]

Leader of Crowd to be more important. He might begin
"You wish to die." She might say "I have [undeciphered
word] said it—I am weary of life." Men. "It is because of
her sins against the people that she wishes to die."
(*A murmur.*)

[BACK TO RIGHT-HAND PAGE]

Crowd Leader. I say there is a mystery here. I will have no
mumming players here.

Another. I say this woman is not the Queen. It's all mumming.
We're being cheated somehow.

Another. Kill the lot of them.

Another. No, no, we're just men. We will do no wrong. It
was the Queen only that was to be killed. I'll sit here.
We'll have them speak one by one.

All. That's right, that's right.

Man. How will the crown speak?

P. Queen (moving onto stage). I have come here to seek my
death. I am waiting for it. What more is there to be said?

Man. Now you—mummer, Queen, whatever you [are]—you
there in the cloak.

Queen. I see it all now, it is not what I thought. I prayed,
I prayed [for] a great death, and now Heaven has rewarded
me. This woman is not a real woman. She is an angel who
has been sent down from Heaven to take my place. That is
why she is so fearless. Your swords cannot do her any
harm, your bowstring cannot harm her. She is of that
imperishable substance of the Heavens, she . . .

Poet. Spare her. She is my sweetheart. Can you not see she is
but playing? She has reddened her face with raddle—that
is why she has such courage. If you could only see, perhaps
she is very pale.

Queen. Strike at her. All, all your spears, all together. They
will break with . . . You will be struck by lightning. It
—O miracle to tell. I have prayed. It is a miracle.

A Man. If it is a miracle that would be [a] fine thing. But we
must not strike an angel.

[*All.*] No, no, we must not strike an angel. That is certain.

A Man. I am master here. I say that the will of the people
shall be done. She is Queen. She has the crown on her head.
She shall be strangled. These shall be beaten and turned
out of doors.

Another Version

Player Queen. Who is there among you that dare strike?
Your father's lives, and the
lives of your fathers before them were but the twigs   79
woven into the nest that gave the eagle birth. Who   80
among you dare face the eagle? Eagle begat eagle   81
through all the centuries, and all the eagles look out

of these eyes. But strike if you will. Look, I
cover their lightning.
(*They raise their spears. Man forces his way through crowd.*)

Player. Stop. This is no queen. This is not the queen I say. I
will speak. Listen all of you. This is a player of my company.
She quarreled with us but now, and she is seeking for her
death in some wild fit.

[Player] Queen. My people, this is some poor man who would
save me with this incredible tale. You speak in vain, poor
man.

Player. She and I quarreled. She asked a part I would not give
her—a queen's part. We quarreled and I renounced her,
and now . . .

[Player] Queen. This is too much, sir, that even to save me
you should say that I [the] Queen was your lover.
[undeciphered passage] Drive him away, I say. My fathers
are waiting for me; all the skies are full.

Player. No, no, I insist [?]. Take off your hands. She
thought I loved another. She was jealous.

[Player] Queen. You think life precious, not being bred in
eagle ways, to think that I would take it at such a price. And
were it all true what you say, I think the player you
pretend [to] take me for might well refuse. Another
woman has her place.

Player. There never was another—O Mary, that was all
untrue. Will you not believe me and live?

Player Queen. I know him now. He was to have played before
me this day, and now he tries his fables with you. (*They
begin to push him back.*)

Player. Is there none here who will bear me out?

Another Version

[Player] Queen. You are a player. You were to have played
before my people this day and after in the market place,
and now you would save me with this incredible tale.

Player. We quarreled.

P. Queen. I have seen many of your kind and know your
heart. You have longed, for one, to fill some great
place in men's eyes, and to save a queen and claim a

queen all in one mouthful, to bring an eagle to your nest. It
was not love that brought you here. I know that empty heart.
Now go back again. You but keep [me] from my fathers.
All the skies are full of them awaiting me.

Man. Here, put him out of this. He stops the people's way.

All. Out with you.

P. Queen. No stop a moment. I will have no slander striking
suddenly when I am gone, no shaking of the head, no
saying she bribed a player to bargain for her with a foolish
story. I wish to confound him with my own words. These
players are so vain that in a moment I will make him say
I was his sweetheart.

Player. But it is true. (*Laughter.*)

P. Queen. And that he cast me off. (*Laughter.*)

Player. O my God, cannot I make you believe? This woman
was my sweetheart. I love her, I came to save her. She is half-
crazed, she is going to her death. It is all madness [?].

Player Queen. Let him go on. He'll say that I but act before
[you], accepting even death that I may confound his doubts
and break his heart, and then the tale will grow common—I
know his sort—and he will say that it [was] all because
[of] some other woman that came between.

Poet. No, no. It was not true. That was but . . . You fancied
that.

(*They seize Poet, who struggles.*)

P. Queen. Do not hurt [him]. He has not wronged the people.
What death am I to die? [beginning of speech undeciphered]

Real Queen. I, and by listening to him. This girl is not the
Queen—she has taken another's place. I have prayed. I
have been struck with remorse. I was afraid, but now
I am brave again. I myself am the Queen.

P. Queen. One of their company called to play a new part,
seeming earnest. She is dressed to play Noah's wife in the
mystery. I spoke with her this morning.

Queen. She bade me put this dress upon me, and she herself
put on the crown.

Player Queen. My girl, I know your heart. You told it all
to me this day.

Queen. Yes, yes, I was afraid, and you put on the crown.

Player Queen. You all your life longed for some great moment. You told me that. You that could understand what damask is have ever but homespun. You have prayed to God for his great gift, the moment. All these players—they have wild hearts. Is it that you fear that you should so long listen? Look, I am covering up the light of these eyes. Strike, I pray you, for I have found the world faithless.

A Man in the Crowd. Look at that face. No, that is not the Queen. She never [made] those laws. Those [lips] have drunk wine, those lips have given kisses.

Crowd. There is a light in her face. They are right. She never taxed our sins.

A Man. She is wearing the crown; she is Queen.

Crowd. She is wearing the crown; she is Queen.

Leader of Crowd. But all of you make a space. This is the court of the people. We must do all in order. I am the judge, I am executioner, I am witness for the people. I am counselor. All will be done in order. (*To the Queen.*) Now speak.

Queen. Yes, a light, a light, a bright light. O understand; can you not see? She is not a player. He was not speaking the truth, that man. She is an angel. It was because I prayed. They have sent an angel down to take my place.

Leader of Crowd. You are crazy, woman. I say it is time we made an end [to] this.

Men. Yes, yes, she has been condemned to death.

Queen. Yes, strike at her, strike at her. You will not be able to harm her. She is of the imperishable substance of the stars. (*Poet struggles with the men.*)

Leader of Crowd. She has been sentenced to death.

Queen. Strike, strike, and reveal the miracle. Lightning will come from Heaven, strike. [seven words undeciphered]

Enter P.M. Throw up your spears. Shut to the gate.

Cries. The soldiers. We are all taken.

P.M. My men are all around the castle. Ah, we are in time I see. The Queen yet lives. Set those men free. But my eyesight is somewhat bad of late. Which of them is Queen? Ask your pardon of the Queen.

[NOTE FROM OPPOSITE PAGE]

When the true Queen comes to bear witness, the Player Queen should get excited. "No, no, I will not have life. Go, go!" and then recover herself and point to dress of Noah's wife.

[RETURN TO RIGHT-HAND PAGE]

Another Version

P. Queen. I have no more to say, I am weary of this fantastic world. Strike now. Do you fear? I will cover the lightning of the eagle. (*She covers her eyes with her arms.*)

D—— Man. Back, all of you, I say. It is [I] that was chosen to put the Queen to death.

Man in Crowd. Look at that face. She is not the Queen. Those lips have drunk wine, those lips have given kisses. She never put the taxes on our sins.

D—— Man. I said she has got the crown on. I am a plain man, that is enough.

Another. No, I say. [undeciphered name] is a fool. If we all strike her nobody will be able to say who did, and nobody will be punished for it.

All. Yes, nobody will be blamed for it. (*Murmurs.*)

R. Queen. Yes strike. I understand it now. She is not a player. She is an angel. [undeciphered sentence]

A Man. Silence woman. Give me a stick someone. I have nothing to strike with. Ah, the [undeciphered word] of this will do. (*Some begin to test beam.*)

Another. She has gone crazy.

R. Queen. I prayed, and so they sent her down. Let my arms free that I may strike and show the miracle to all. She is of the substance of the Heavens. Your stick will break, your swords will blunt.

P.M. Close the gates. You are surrounded, none of you can escape. Set that man free. Throw down your weapons. Where is the Queen, am I in time to save her? My eyes are old, I cannot see rightly. It is hard to know. (*Loudly.*)

Kneel all, and ask your pardon of the Queen. (*They kneel to P. Queen.*) Ah, I see you have good sight. You are not old as I am. You know the Queen.

Player Queen. You have but arisen against the shadow of a
queen, and so have but done wrong in shadow. I therefore
pardon all. And now I put the play away and take up   279
life again that I had thought myself well done with.   280
I am no queen; those spoke the truth. (*To the real*   281
Queen.) Your Majesty, forgive. (*She offers crown.*)

Real Queen. No. But now when I fled, you taking my place, I
went to the convent to look down upon these walls, and
but then my sin overwhelmed me at the door[?], and I shall
leave[?] this world forever. I was never meant for Queen,
but all a nun.

P.M. You are still the Queen, and a fair one, worthy of men's
devotion.

P. Queen. No, you that have the power are the king, and so
should have the name. Let me be still enough a queen to
give the crown where I will.

P.M. You are the golden mask, the queen by that much right.

P. Queen. Ah, for an hour or a day, but then I'd turn, and
turn to some other mask.

P.M. Then at your hands I take this crown, hands that have
a right to give. I have learned my task from you and will
know how to wear my mask.

R. Queen. So be it. The crown goes to him, the powerful.

P.M. Ah, now your pardon, rebels. Listen. From this day
out we will no more tax your sins, (*cheers*) but from this
out we'll tax your industry, your patience, and your foresight
—all your virtues. Come to the Council. There I will give
out the laws. (*Goes out amid cheers.*)

Friend (*comes from behind the door*). And the giving is
the game. I give to you this man for your sole sweetheart,
and may I be cursed with chastity if ever I so much as smile
at him.

P. Queen. You here?

Friend. I too came back to look for you, but, seeing so many
sticks and scythes, hid behind the stage.

Poet (*taking her hand*). And from this day you will play what
  you please to. Maeve, Queen of Sheba . . .
P. Queen. O no, I am tired of queens. I shall be Noah's wife.

Commentary

After a scenario that begins with the bringing in of the tax money, the Queen
enters. She is dressed for a royal progress into her rebellious town but is doubtful whether she should go or return to her prayers. She defends her course
of action in taxing her subjects for their sins and shows the ascetic's contempt
for normal life. She is very unwilling to play the Queen—that is, to assume
the role fate has allotted her—but agrees to do so at the Prime Minister's
urging. They leave for the town, though the exit is not marked in the manuscript, and the Player Queen sticks her head up out of the vat where she has
been hidden and sings "The Mask." This is almost word for word the version
found in Draft 16, though there the lines are arranged as prose, here as poetry.
(Yeats wrote a nearly final version of "The Mask" into his *Journal* in August
1910.) [Cf. *Memoirs,* pp. 258–59. Gen. Ed.] Nona (*Friend*) comes in with
another member of the troupe whom she sends to town to find out what is
going on. (This becomes part of Peter's role once Yeats invents Peter.) The
Player exits, though the exit is not indicated, and we hear no more of him. After
he leaves, Nona discovers the Player Queen, who has hidden because she dislikes the part of Noah's wife. When the Player Queen learns that Nona has
agreed to take the part, she quarrels with her briefly. Their quarrel is interrupted by Septimus (*Poet*) who shuts them up and starts the Noah play. All
of the foregoing material was to be greatly enlarged before it became Act I,
Scene ii in Draft 16. Here there is no break in the action, and Yeats goes on
directly to what will become Act II. This will begin with comments from the
audience of the Noah play on the character of actors, here done very briefly.

The play within the play, contrariwise, has in this draft the fullest development Yeats was ever to give it. It is in verse, rather rough verse, and includes
in Septimus's preliminary patter an allusion to unicorns who, unlike the unicorn
of tradition, are "unchaste"; there is evidence in the successive drafts of *The
Player Queen* that Yeats became better acquainted with traditional unicorn symbolism while he was writing the play.

Twenty unicorns they gave us with silver hooves . . .

> But they die when their feet touch Ireland
> Because of St. Patrick's curse on all unchaste things.

The finished play is dominated by the image of the unicorn, and the question of its chastity dominates Septimus's thinking. The play goes on till it is interrupted by a messenger who brings news of a rebellion against the Queen. Most of the players flee, though their exit is not indicated, leaving Nona, Decima, and Septimus on stage. Decima locks the courtyard door and demands that Septimus dismiss Nona from the company. Septimus is steadfast; he criticizes Decima's acting amusingly—she could not play Lot's Wife even after she had been changed to a pillar of salt—and he declares his love for Nona. The Player Queen opens the door, Septimus leaves, and, after a few final words from the Player Queen, Nona leaves too. The Queen enters, fleeing from the mob, and the Player Queen immediately offers to change places with her. They exchange clothes, the Queen leaves, and the Player Queen begins singing to the crown when the Prime Minister enters with a group of loyal soldiers. The Player Queen, who thinks they are the mob, addresses them in extravagant language, taken no doubt from Septimus's old play mentioned in Drafts 2 and 4. Much more will be made of this in Draft 8. The Player Queen begins at once to assert her royal power; she orders the soldiers to bring out the hidden treasure. While they are gone, the Prime Minister tells her he knows she is not the Queen but she may serve his purpose better than the true Queen. To seal what he hopes is a bargain, he kisses her hand as the soldiers return with the gold. The Player Queen orders the soldiers to scatter the gold through the streets of the town; the Prime Minister intervenes, saying the gold must be put in a safe place. All save three of the soldiers leave with him to hide the gold, and the loyal three comment on the Player Queen's likeness to her father and on their present dangerous situation. Thus in Draft 16, Act II will end.

An executioner, standing on a ladder, sticks his head above the wall and demands the dismissal of the Prime Minister. (Later this part was assigned to the Prime Minister's coachman, then some of it to Septimus before it disappeared altogether.) If the Player Queen refuses, then she and the Prime Minister are condemned to death. The few remaining soldiers plan resistance, but the Player Queen throws the door open and confronts the mob. During this confrontation she uses the image of the generations of eagles to stand for the long line of aristocrats from which she comes. This entered Yeats's poetry in August 1909 when he wrote "Upon a House shaken by the Land Agitation" and was used again in "To a Wealthy Man," finished 24 December 1912. The image will recur in draft after draft of *The Player Queen*. The real Queen comes forward to identify the Player Queen and save her life, and there is general confusion. The Player Queen continues to goad the mob until Septimus joins his arguments with those of the Queen. He tells them who the Player Queen is, and Nona backs him up. The Crowd Leader sets up a kind of court to try to unsnarl the tangle and forces them to speak one at a time. The Queen now thinks the Player Queen is an angel whom Heaven has sent to take her place, and she expects a miracle to occur. The Crowd Leader decides to execute the Player Queen, to give the others a beating, and to turn them out.

Here the alternate versions begin: There are three of these, and only in the third does the play reach a conclusion. In the first alternate Septimus comes forward and tries to save the Player Queen, but she is too jealous of Nona to accept his help. During their brief dialogue she repeats the eagle image. In the second alternate version, first Septimus comes forward to save the Player Queen, who, knowing the truth, anticipates what he will say to the crowd by telling the truth in a way that will not be believed. Then the real Queen comes forward to back Septimus up. Following an exchange between the real Queen and the Player Queen a man in the crowd says of the Player Queen, "Those lips have drunk wine, those lips have given kisses." This becomes a kind of refrain in later drafts. Again the Crowd Leader sets up a kind of court, and again the true Queen insists that the Player Queen is an angel sent to save her, and she expects a miracle. At this point the Prime Minister enters, stops the mock trial, and asks which is Queen, the Player or the real Queen? The third and final version begins and proceeds to the end of the play, as this was to stand through Draft 16. The real Queen adds to the confusion, if that is possible, when she offers to strike the Player Queen in order to reveal the miracle. Again the Prime Minister enters to the rescue. He orders the crowd to choose between the queens, and all bow to the Player Queen. She, however, comes out of role immediately and asks the Queen's pardon. The Queen refuses to take back the crown because the events of the play have convinced her she is "all a nun," and Decima offers the crown to the Prime Minister. He accepts it, and the former Queen agrees to this. He goes out with the crowd. Nona straightens out matters between Septimus and Decima; Septimus takes Decima's hand and offers her any queen role she wants. She refuses them all and ends the play with a line that stood through many drafts: "I shall be Noah's wife."

CHAPTER FIVE

Draft 7

WE RETURN NOW to the A2 manuscript book, where Draft 7 follows the scenario I have called Draft 4. As has been shown, Yeats worked up this scenario in Drafts 5 and 6. In Draft 7 he concentrates on two parts of the play, the opening of Act II down to the beginning of the Noah play and Act III. In the draft of Act II he is developing the character Rat-hole; in Act III he is working out a confrontation of Septimus and Nona with Decima, who is now playing the part of queen. The manuscript is very difficult, and much of it I have been unable to read. Below is a running summary of the drafts of Act II and of several drafts of Act III, followed by a transcript of a more carefully worked-out version of Act III.

At the opening of the draft an audience summoned by Rat-hole, as in Drafts 4 and 5, has gathered to watch the Noah play. As Rat-hole goes among them, begging, the members of the audience discuss the political situation. The Queen's new tax is now a tax on lies. The discussion moves on to the nature of actors, especially the effect of role-playing on the basic character of the actor. The audience is afraid of Rat-hole and discusses his possession by the ghost of the Old King. Septimus in the role of the Deluge begins the prologue of the Noah play but is interrupted by Rat-hole, who has a seizure and speaks in the voice of the Old King. He demands to see his daughter, the Queen, to warn her of the rebellion and to advise her. His advice, rather cryptic, is "I must tell her to dream right. She must dream herself a Queen. . . . He who is ready to die for his dream, he shall be King." This plan for the opening of Act II is pretty much that found in Draft 16, though there it has been refined.

Yeats leaves Act II and goes on to the planning of Act III. He is working on various schemes that will bring about a confrontation of Decima in her new role with Septimus and Nona. Nona is called *Girl*, and Septimus *Yellow Martin* or frequently simply *He*. In the first version Septimus and Nona have been captured by the soldiers of the Player Queen and are brought before her. Septimus, jealous, suggests that she has won the soldiers by giving herself to them. The Player Queen replies that she is bringing into being certain of Septimus's dreams—that is, the sayings and deeds of the queen-role he has created in his old play. Nona defies the Player Queen, and Septimus asks her if she knows of the mob outside the castle who seek her death. There is a jumble of partial drafts, which move in various directions without making any real progress, ending in a scenario of Act III. This Yeats works up at length in the manuscript that follows. Nona but not Septimus has been captured by the Player Queen's soldiers. Septimus takes the role of Herald for the rebels in order to reach the Player Queen, who has Nona brought in and stages a love test by ordering Septimus to put Nona in chains. He refuses to perform so cruel an act.

Act III

Young and old soldiers and [Player] Queen.

Young Man. We are already surrounded. They are making a
   ram from a great tree to break in the door. But we may
   prevail against them. We have the barrels if powder with
   the fuses ready on the tower over the gate to throw upon
   their heads.
Another. Here are the weapons that you bid us bring you that
   you may ask the saints to bless them before the fight.
[*Player Queen.*] I will ask the saints to bless them, but it is a
   hard thing to keep one's heart high always, a death and
   dark coming. But we have trumpets and haughty words.
   After all, does one not forget all once the curtain has
   gone up?
First Young Man. Queen, I thank you.
Another. I have seen one no word and no trumpet could have
   put courage into. Last night we took the prisoner you
   sent us for last night. We got through the enemy unnoticed.
   They are a vast mob without order. And found her hidden
   in a tree at the edge of the wood. We bound her fingers [?]
   and carried her hither. We got here only just in time, for
   they were closing in about the house. Once here we took
   the gag from her, but locked her in a cell under the tower.
   And through the door the sentry can hear her calling out
   strange wild things against your majesty, that you're no
   queen at all and so [on.] It's certain that she is mad. (*Cries
   outside. Young Man descends from above.*)

Young Man. They are hanging that old beggar man Rat-hole
    almost at the very gate, and I have been watching them
    this hour past. His eyes were ever closed and he was abusing
    them with the voice of the Old [King], calling them rogues
    and thieves, and asking for his daughter. And then they
    seized him and began dragging him to the tree. And at
    that [he] awoke, and began crying and beseeching and
    saying that he knew nothing of what he had said. But
    while he was kneeling and beseeching his voice changed
    and his eyes closed and the Old King's voice came again,
    and then again he woke and cried out and again slept and
    called them rogues, but now they have got him to the tree
    and the rope at his neck. The last time the voice, spirit, or
    whatever called [?] denouncing and mocking them up to the
    [word undeciphered], and then left his yells and struggles.
[*Player*] *Queen.* Have you seen men die before?
Young [*Man*]. Many, yes, in battle form in far times, and
    I have seen a man fall dead, or more often than that been
    near men that died of their wounds or of sickness got in
    camp.
[*Player*] *Queen.* Have you seen women die?
Young Man. I have seen no woman die.
[*Player*] *Queen.* Queer, is it hard to die, or when it comes is
    one glad to be done with it all, or does the world seem
    better at the last and worse to leave, as some good houses
    seem when the horses are round and one's foot in the
    stirrup?
Young [*Man.*] I have only seen men die suddenly, or wasted
    with sickness, and those [who] were wasted thought little
    enough of it.
[*Player Queen*]. Would you be glad to be out of this, young man?
    (*Disturbance at door under arch.*)
Young Man. There has been thrust through the door a
    message from the rebels.
[*Player*] *Queen.* They ask that I abrogate the taxes and hand
    the Chamberlain over into their hands for punishment. I
    will answer as befits my throne.
Another. Here is the Herald who came with it asking to be

34

admitted. None but he is near the gate; there is no treachery
planned.

[*Player*] *Queen.* Admit him; he shall have my answer. There
also speaks another voice than mine, a shadow, a thin night
life, a long-gathering power, a mystery out of the
measureless years. (*Herald enters.*) Leave me all, I will
speak alone with this man. He and I have much to say
with one another. But first bring me heavy chains and
lay them here upon the ground; then bring my prisoner
when I call. This man, these chains, that raving woman
and I have knotted up together from the beginning of the
world. (*Motions them away.*) What can they know of
lives like mine, what when I know now the chain is
tightened and the day of untangling come?

Herald. For whose pleasure will you fasten me with chains;
for which of these young men? (*She takes it* [*in*] *her hand.*)

[*Player*] *Queen.* Has not this iron serpent caught us and
entangled us?

Herald. What entanglement but that that your own frenzy or
wickedness have made, setting yourself up for queen among
these men.

She. Your dream has made me queen. O yes, we are bound fast
enough, and I am on [my] way to death to cast the chain
off there. But do not fear; I will not have you chained
more than you are already.

He. Lay down that iron thing and put this cloak about you
and let us be gone. And the crowds without will ask no
questions, seeing that they think me one of them.

She. I will not go.

He. Ah, so it is as I thought. One of these young gay-dressed
men has hit your fancy. I grow too old for your light mind,
or there's a sameness in the one man over too long. O, I
might have known.

She. No, it is you who keep me here.

He. How I?

She. It is your dream that roots me to the ground. I found it
in the depths of your mind, and when you took your heart
from me I gave myself to that and to that alone.

He. You think nothing of wisdom, of my firmness or my prudence. O, you are a woman all out. You fasten upon my folly.

She. No, no, I have found your secret, that which came to you of old, at the foundation of the world. You could not believe because it was yours, because you had made it. Had it been mine I too would have cast it away. Who believes in anything but in the dreams of others? That which we make in continual hesitancy, in trembling, and in fear.

He. I would that I knew that you were not playing with me, that you have not some young man in your thoughts. You say [you] have it not, and yet you will not come away.

She. Martin, Martin, I was never so much yours, for now that I have lost your love I have your dream. I sing to it, it murmurs to me, I rock it [in] my arms like a child, and I am going with it to my death, and my death shall be but the dream.

He. What test but that I have come here to save you?

He. I would I could understand you.

She. Love me truly and you will understand, or like [?] not understands best.

He. I have never cared for any but you. You have imagined me false in that [two words undeciphered]. You have been jealous of a shadow.

She. I will test you.

He. I am not given to using big words, or swearing upon the book. It is enough that I say I have not been false to you.

She. Be truthful to your words, for now I can test you.

She. You would do as much for a dog. When we love do we not despise all but love? The one we love is the whole love, other women nothing.

He. Yes, she that we love is all.

She. Then the test is certain (*She strikes bell.*) I shall sift your soul. I will draw my fingers through it; I shall know what is there; I shall pass it through a sieve. (*Girl is brought in. They go out.*)

He. My God. So she is in your hands? I thought her safe.

She. Put the chains upon that girl with your own hands, and
   when [?] that's done I'll send to the dungeon and know she
   has gone from your life and mine.

Girl. O save me, Martin. She will kill.

He. So that's what you hid in your thoughts.

She. Put the chains upon her quickly. Those clasps are for
   the wrists, and those others, they go about the ankles.
   I am not in Babylon here, and now can escape alive.

Girl. O my God, my God.

She. Time's passing, and Babylon and the dream are near.

He. I will do no such cruelty.

She. Then you do not love, for those that love think scorn
   of all, or shrink from all but those they love. What's
   she to you if you love me? But it is not so, and I am
   nothing and she is all.

Girl. O, you wicked woman; now I know what you are like.

She. O Martin, I have gone over and over it in my mind, and
   could not know whether you loved or not, and now she comes
   between us again.

He. I have loved and been true, but love that I know of is
   of Heaven.

She. It is not love if there is no night [?] in it.

He. I'll have no more to do with you; this day has been
   enough.

She. Go with your love, go free, I will not harm you. And
   had you clasped those chains upon her, I'd have taken
   them off and been as happy as a bird.

He. Tell me some new wildness. I am [?] [word undeciphered]
   but your thoughts.

Girl. Fool, you think he is my sweetheart, and he has never
   spoken love to me. But now I'll win him from you.

She. Win, but you need [?] have pleasure in. I am going to
   my death, and when I am a ghost I'll haunt the bedside
   where you lie, and when you spread your arms to call him
   to you at the day's end, I'll put my face to yours and
   make you shriek.

Girl. O, let us go quickly.

He. No, I must stay, and cry out who this woman is and save

her from her own madness. They are already at the doors
and calling for her death.

She. Who will believe you? You have but your words; I
have my willing death to give them faith in mine.

He. What are you doing?

She. I have drawn the bolt. (*He steps forward to prevent her.*)
It is too late. (*The people crowd in.*) Here am I, your
queen. I will give my answer to this message to your faces.

Voices (*above*). They are in the yard; we are surprised.

She. Be still. I have done this that none may die for me, and
none abate my fame.

Men. What is your answer? Do you surrender that evil adviser?

She. There. (*Brings the document.*)

Another Man. That is not the Queen. Those eyes have given   66
kisses; those lips have drunk wine.

Man. Silence that fool there. You know the penalty.

She. Yes, it is here. I die.

Voices (*above*). She is your Queen. How dare you threaten   70
her? Rogues, murderers. (*They fill the stairs and are
kept back by armed men.*)

She. I am your Queen, and therefore I die, and dying laugh at
you and so condemn, for such as I have learned from the
cradle when to die seems [?] even to storm the gate of
death.

Man. I have no fear of you. There is an angry writing on
this back that puts out fear, a sort of spell against it,
a crooked figured thing from no wizard hands.

[DRAFT ENDS. The next draft follows, after some notes.]

Middling Act III

When Martin fails and calls for a witness, P. Queen can taunt
him with flight of his witness when real Queen comes forward.
She thinks it is an angel, come she knows not why. She warns
them not to harm her. She can say if she was there that she
might die with her, for she has done much evil. For she wronged
one she knew, and [is] filled with a death-seeking fury.

Player Queen points to dress of Noah's wife and bids them take her away. Do they not see she thinks for death? She's at its door, and argues. Efforts to get witness there. [word undeciphered] man is about to strike her. Queen dares them to touch her. Some cry out yes, she would make another [?] ghost. Young men cry out of the divine vengeance for those that kill kings. It will fall on him or on his children.

Man. Then you shall do it. (*All take up the cry:* "Yes, that is it. No vengeance shall fall on them or theirs." *Young men are dragged down amid the cries of the people. Set to do it or they die themselves.*)

All cry: We will die, we will die. It is worth dying for one like her. If they do they shall [be] met by horsemen and chariots beyond death.

Queen comes forward as before and offers to strike her, for she understands it now. She is angelical.

Queen. If her face grows pale before me, it will be but she'd take upon self the humility of death. A moment before she shows herself again in all her indestructible [?] life. Now you will see the miracle she promised.

[NOTE FROM OPPOSITE PAGE]

Player Queen may be veiled through this. She might take veil from Noah's wife and cover her face with it. She could borrow it with some fanciful mockery. Speaks about giving it back full of roses and apples. But then, no, for what were roses and apples to so good a nun. But she will work some miracle with it. It might be a golden veil. She might speak of the queens of Babylon that gilded their faces.

[CONTINUATION]

Enter Chancellor. He bids them choose Queen as before. He accepts crown as before. In his speech he asks what is to be done with Player Queen. Asks Martin what it should be. He will ennoble her and marry her to him. Martin says that impossible; she has cast him off. Chancellor says fear nothing

more. I have carried off that Girl, she'll love you no longer.
Poet in great excitement rushes to tell her. Can no one find her?
He is ecstatic. He goes out stair crying out "He has carried her
off."

She asks Queen to take her also to convent. Martin appeals to
her. She bids him seek his friend. Chancellor's men have
carried her off. She "So then he was not false, and the day's
work is over." (*Exit.*) Chancellor goes on to propose reward.
Proposes nobility. Martin objects: how could nobility tumble
for a living? Chancellor says she must decide. Where is she?
She comes out eating from her fingers. (*Leaning over balcony.*)
[two words undeciphered]

She. Did you think I wanted to be a countess or a queen
   in earnest. Not I—laid by, I am tired of it. Go
   take your places. Let the play [begin].
Martin. But now you can have what you will—be any queen
   you like.
She. O, I will be Noah's wife.

Commentary

In Draft 7 Yeats is principally concerned with working out a confrontation of
the three principals (Decima, Septimus, and Nona) to precede an already established finale of the play. Before this confrontation occurs, Yeats shows us
the Player Queen in role, queening it to the top of her bent in exchanges with
the loyal soldiers who think she is Queen, and he disposes of Rat-hole by having
the rebels hang him. He will keep this opening of Act III, Scene ii through
Draft 16. Septimus is acting as Herald or messenger for the rebel forces in
order to gain access to the Player Queen. The Player Queen has a set of body
chains brought in, and arranges to have Nona produced when she calls. When
Septimus enters and sees the chains, he thinks they are intended for him. He is
jealous of the soldiers, but the Player Queen says she is only acting out his
dream—that is, his artist's conception of a queen. Several references to Babylon
indicate that Septimus's youthful play will shortly become "The Queen of Babylon." Septimus works into his reply to Decima an idea from Yeats's early poem
"The Cap and Bells" (1894): The Player Queen thinks nothing of his wisdom,
firmness, or prudence; she fastens upon his folly. Though Septimus swears he

loves the Player Queen, she denies this and has Nona brought in. Septimus is to put her in chains to prove his love. He refuses to do anything so cruel, and the Player Queen opens the door to the mob. Yeats now begins to develop the Barach character, the leader of the crowd, though here is merely "Man." Yeats makes various plans for continuing the scene which seem to refer back to Draft 6. He carries over from it the Prime Minister's arrival at the crucial moment, his request that the mob pick out the real Queen, and his acceptance of the crown. Then Yeats begins to plan his conclusion. Shall the Player Queen be ennobled and married to Septimus? He has the Prime Minister carry off Nona to make their reunion possible. The Player Queen, hungry because she has had no breakfast, rushes into the castle for food. At the end she is eating as the Noah play is about to begin with Decima in the role of Noah's wife. Yeats knows a good thing when he finds it: Decima is still eating in the final scene of the revised version of the play published in 1934 (Cf. *Variorum Plays,* p. 758).

CHAPTER SIX

Drafts 8 through 10

AT SOME TIME while composing *The Player Queen* Yeats came to think of Drafts 1 through as 7 as his "A" version. Draft 6 is not so labeled, but the other drafts are. With Draft 8 he goes on to a version he called "B," not all of which has survived. What has survived is found in two manuscripts, one labeled "B. Act I continued," the other "Player Queen B. Act III." Yeats must have written in another manuscript, which he did not save, the beginning of the "B" version, because the surviving part of Act I has its first folio numbered "22." Nothing from Act II has survived except a note written into the manuscript of Act III. From Act III we have a complete version of III, ii, as that is found in Draft 16, and already the scene is nearly finished. The "B" version is in a direct line of descent, so to speak, from the "A" version: in it Yeats returns to ideas he had tentatively explored in Drafts 2 and 3 but never developed, ideas such as the finding of Septimus's old play. He also develops further scenes worked out in Drafts 5 and 6, such as the discovery of the hidden Player Queen. The fragment of Act I is notably less finished than the draft of Act III; such different degrees of finish are a characteristic feature of Yeats's prepublication drafts.

In many of the drafts of *The Player Queen* Yeats seems to be intent on working out some single feature on which he concentrates; in Draft 8 it is Septimus's youthful play, which the Player Queen has found and wants to produce in place of the Noah play and of which she makes a kind of scenario for her actions and words after she has changed places with the real Queen. This imaginary "work" by Septimus was referred to in Drafts 2 and 4; here it is given substance as a play on a Queen of Babylon. Parts of it are actually read out by Nona to the Prime Minister in Act I. The "play" is retained in Drafts 14 and 16, though there it is less important than it is here in Draft 8. The character names used are Yellow Martin, Chancellor, and Girl.

B. Act I continued.

Chancellor. My God, what has happened?
Girl. Has she hidden herself again? I thought it would come
   to that.

Martin. Last night, sir, we quarreled. She said that she would
play no more dull women with nothing to commend them
except that they were like people one knew and pitied.

Girl. Ever since she read that play she has been beside
herself—striking attitudes and reciting speeches.

Martin. That she would wear no more dull dresses, and that
above all things and before all she would never be Noah's
wife again.

Girl. She wants to display herself, and she always hated the
part of Noah's wife because Noah has to beat her to make
her go into the Ark.

Chancellor. Did she know it was the play the Queen had ordered?

Yellow Martin. Yes sir, but she had found an old play of mine
written long ago to be played before Kubla Khan when we
were on our travels—a wild thing full of oratory and poetry,
the kind of thing the pagans wrote long ago. I asked her
what did she know of queens, where could she learn the right
manner, the right walk, the right speech, the right look for
a queen. But no, nothing would move [her]. She would
play my Queen of Babylon; that and nothing else.

Girl. They say she recites in her sleep. When she is awake
she lives in the world like a tiger in a wood.
    (*Chancellor motions her to be silent.*)

Yellow Martin. I was angry and said play she must, and play
what I told her. I have to break her will, sir, or she and I
will be both miserable. I told her that the Queen's
commands must be obeyed.

Chancellor. Well, and what then?

[*Yellow Martin.*] She has vanished, she has hidden herself,
and, O, sir, I am in the deepest anxiety. She is a very wild
strange woman, and the river . . .

Girl ([*to*] *Chancellor*). O, if she would only drown herself
Martin would be so much happier.

Chancellor. Hush. Impossible. Women do not drown
themselves for things like that. She must be in the house,
the garden, or in the wood. Where have you searched?

Yellow Martin. I have searched nowhere.

Chancellor. My God, nowhere? You have searched nowhere
and people coming for the play within the hour, and if there

is no play it will be said through the whole kingdom that
the mutinous soldiers have stopped it. It may be very
serious for the state.

Yellow Martin. It will be death [for] me as well as her if
she has drowned, and yet I have not searched.

Chancellor. What do you mean by telling me that she is lost
and that you will not search; are you well moon-struck?

Yellow Martin. Sir, I have explained that there is between
her and me a struggle, a trial which of the two is master,
and if I show anxiety . . .

Chancellor. And is the policy of the state to give way to a
girl's quarrel with her sweetheart?

Yellow Martin. If we have patience, there will come dinner
time and that will make her hungry. If that does not bring
her from her hole, supper is certain to. Whenever she does
anything that excites her, my lord, it gives her a great
appetite.

Chancellor. But that will be twelve o'clock at night, and
every moment of delay is dangerous. The Queen must
be received with all the usual ceremonies.

Yellow Martin. I ask your pardon, sir, if we have harmed the
state, but it may be you have been so happy in your love
that have [been] loved by some woman of her own will
from the first, a kind woman like Mary there, but we that
love passionate, proud women must keep the mask upon
us though our heart is breaking, for if it slip off maybe
the happiness of a whole life is gone.

Chancellor. I will not hear another word, and I tell you if
she is not found I will put you and all your company in
the stocks, except the lady here.

Martin. Very well, sir, I will tell my company to search by
your orders, but I, sir, will go read a book in the garden,
hoping that she will see me there and understand that I do
not care. (*He goes out.*)

Chancellor. O what a day, what a day; and the Queen late too.

Girl. O here it is, I have found it.

Chancellor (*who is walking up and down*). Found what, girl
—and hurry of all importance.

Girl. The play about the Queen of Babylon Martin wrote long

ago. It's lying here on the ground. But listen. No, It's
gone now. (*Song in the air.*) Did you hear that? A song.

Chancellor. No no, I heard nothing.

Girl. But it was quite distinct; it was her voice. She was singing
that song about Jack and Jill that she always sings when
she has had a triumph over Martin. She is hidden here.

Chancellor. Impossible. There is no place for anyone to hide.

Girl. No, there is no place, for there is no one in the
galleries. It sounded as if it was up in the air. It must be
her spirit. I always knew she'd drown herself in the end, to
get the better of Martin.

Chancellor. Spirits don't sing by daylight.

Girl. They follow old Rat-hole everywhere, and it would be
just like her to go singing in the air after her death.

Chancellor. Somebody was passing by on the road, if there
was anybody at all. What can have kept the Queen; it is
past noon by the shadows on the roof. (*He sits down on
step of stage.*) Give me that book. "The Queen of Babylon,
or Who Should Have the Throne." (*Sits down on stage.*)
Well, well, what's in this play that has upset our plans and
brought the state in danger?

Girl. It's called "The Queen of Babylon, or The Choosing
of a Queen," and tells how the King of Babylon had seven
beautiful daughters, and they, being jealous of the youngest
because the oracle foretold she would be queen, drove her
out upon the road and left her to wander here and there
as a ragged beggar. But you're not listening.

Chancellor (*getting up*). Go on, go on. O, when will the
Queen come.

Girl. But for all they could do she becomes Queen as the
oracle foretold, and there is one great scene in the fourth
act where she outfaces the mob who'd stormed the palace.
There are very fine speeches in it, but Martin says there
[is] no one now could play it or would like it if it could
be played, because now it's real people, [who] would seem
to gather up all the life of the land, who spring into the
unknown like a dive into the sea—no mere maker of laws
nor leader in battle—but the flavour of life, thirst for
what exists, sheer life, the flame that comes from us that

are its fuel, people like themselves, pettish, troublesome,
ordinary people like Noah's wife, they want to see. There is
a passage somewhere that seems to give the meaning. It's
what the priest of the oracle says when she is dead, for
they kill her in the end. It's at her funeral and they have
laid her in a great tomb of bronze.

Chancellor (*at gate*). There's shouting in the town; there
is some mischief there. O when will the Queen come?

Girl. O, here is the passage: "Not leaders alone, but that
which we would be—no means, but end. One better to
follow through bitterness and defeat than to be beside
another in victory. The flame and we the fuel. To look at
her was to make ready for battle, to stand . . ."

[The draft is interrupted at this point and continues with a
new scene on the next page with a different pagination.
(This page is numbered 31, the next 28.) On the verso of
this page is the following, taken, I think, from Yeats's
plans for the Babylon play: "We are not with her as friend
with friend, for we followed her with tumult, often
forsaking and forsook. Was she not with us the one with
the multitude, as lover with beloved?" Underneath this is
the following couplet:

> When all our state is into ruin gone
> I cannot fix my thoughts on Babylon.

Opposite page 31 this note: "Should this be a song, part of
the funeral ode, and sung by the Girl?"]

Chancellor. It was I that planned this; that's what I am paid
for and my back is broad. And now let's hurry there.

Queen. But stop, my lord. I cannot abrogate the taxes, the
only just tax government ever levied, for no good body is
taxed at all, but only the passionate and wild.

Chancellor. I do not question what you do. The Old King
said to me, "You and I are sinful men; she is a saint so let
her have her head." But if the soldiers will not have it
and refuse to obey us . . .

Queen. I cannot put aside the law, for I have sworn before I
die to make the country innocent.

Chancellor. Yet often, your Majesty, we have to choose for a
time the worser course.

[ALTERNATE VERSION FROM THE LEFT-HAND PAGE]

[*Queen.*] My confessor says that it were better that the whole
world perish than one sin be committed.

[DRAFT CONTINUES? GEN. ED.]

Chancellor. I cannot reason with your majesty. I am only
learned in the world's affairs.
Queen. I've thought it all out, and I know that God's law is
absolute and should be like an iron plough in the world.
Chancellor. I am well on in middle life, and I have seen no
straight furrow worth the dying for.
Queen. And they so wicked that they'd take my life.
Chancellor. If your mind is set no matter what outcry may
be in the market-place to undo the taxes, then I can but
say return to your convent.
Queen. You think that I fear martyrdom?
Chancellor. I think you are your father's daughter, and can face
all that time brings you to, but I know that today is not
the day of trial.
Queen. O yes, you doubt me, and no wonder in that for often
and often I have doubted myself, and wondered if I could
do from mere conscience what you and many thousands
do from pride and anger. You think that prayers make
timidness.
Chancellor. I have no such thought.
Queen. You think that the mere naked soul cannot do that
which is done every day by souls in all the armour of the
world, with the pride, the wisdom, and all the blind [word
undeciphered] over it.
Chancellor. Your Majesty wrongs my most loyal mind.
The Queen. No, no, such thoughts are natural. A thousand
times I have said I just [do] all these others do that can
outface the convent by mere believing they are brave,
though their heart trembles. These women know how I
have struggled, but today I'll bring it to the test and show

that I have conquered. Sister Margaret, Sister Mary, have
we not spoken of these things?

Chancellor. Yet running this great risk would endanger the
peace of the state and your own life but to prove that your
prayers have been heard.

Queen. He is thinking that it's mere pride, that I've no right
to seek the heavy cross. But if it comes unsought then all
is well.

[NOTE FROM OPPOSITE PAGE]

Important: At end of play Chancellor says that his work is to
make what Player Queen has done for a moment seem
lifelong, or else to go from change to change, from mask
to mask. They will war on Kubla Khan and sack the garden
in the eastern world.

[DRAFT CONTINUES]

Chancellor. I think but of the state and your own life.

Queen. O no, the state will be the better, for I will speak of
these taxes, and that I'll make them heavier until there's
nothing in the land but what is good and holy.

Chancellor. Do you command it that we go and stand among
the angry soldiers with no gift or favour?

Queen. I command it.

Chancellor. Then I obey. Wildness is breaking out over the
world, and I can see no end to it all. Shall it be before the
night has fallen, angry [?] with some savage crowd, or
telling beads? (*They go out, the Queen first, the Chancellor
following with bowed head. Players come in from garden.
Player sings song about* "emerald eyes and mask of gold.")

[*Players.*] Where is she? Let us search behind the fountain.

2nd. There is no one here.

3rd. She is not in the wood or the garden.

Girl (*comes in from garden*). Look, I have brought the dress,
the dress for Noah's wife.

A Player. Yes, if we can find her we must begin at once. Let
me go up and search the galleries.

Player (*lingering behind other players who have gone up singing into the galleries*). Do not dare it. (*Girl has been measuring dress against herself.*) A woman like that is terrible when she has a lover between her teeth.

Girl. We will find her. She will take the part herself.

Player. I will bet you this old mask of mine that she will play the Queen of Babylon before night falls.

1 Player (*above*). Take off your mask of gold with the eyes of emerald that I may see what your face is.

Player Queen (*rises up in vat and sings*). I will not take off my mask of gold with emerald eyes, for it is that which makes you tremble and desire.

Player. Take it off that I may know if you are a friend or an enemy.

[NOTE FROM OPPOSITE PAGE]

Important. Have I made the Queen too active? Am I right even about the tax on sin? Should the soldiers be merely crying out for war for war's sake. They can get drunk and be sinners.

Very important. Should Queen be merely passive and pious? Should she merely love peace and refuse some war? The Chancellor should take responsibility for refusal. That it is his should be kept back until scene between them. *He should, whether tax on sins is kept or not, be accused of hiding her in convent. Or could the Girl show* [?] *surprise at act? This would give them character.* [Yeats's emphasis. Then from the side of the page] When Chancellor takes money at end of Act II he says that holiness must buy its welcome, for it has an ugly face. It is the bold child that the mother loves.

[Act III is found in another manuscript. With it are two drawings of a possible stage setting. At the end of the MS Yeats has drawn a rough sketch, then, opposite the first leaf of the MS, a more finished drawing, but without labels or description. This shows at rear door and windows with balcony above. All openings have pointed Gothic arches. To L steps leading to a raised platform (throne?) The effect is vaguely medieval.]

Player Queen B. Act III

Note. Act III should play 30 minutes as it is here.

Queen. Young and old soldiers. P. Queen on step or steps of stage.

P. Queen. Heap them all up there, and when I am alone I will bless them. An old form of words that saves [?] from death in battle. Are they all there?

Young Soldier. All, your Majesty.

Player Queen. I never could be in comfort near to so many knives. Have [you] no tale to tell to make time pass? (*Yawns and stretches herself.*) I grow sleepy and lose the right look of a queen waiting for battle, murder, and sudden death. Does no one know the story of the goose girl that became a queen?

Another Soldier. Last night we took one of [the] two prisoners you sent us for.

P. Queen. Ah.

2 Young Soldier. We found her hidden in a tree.

P. Queen. It was the woman then.

Young Soldier. We took her at the wood's edge, but could not find the other evil-doer, the man you spoke of.

P. Queen. Let him go where he pleases.

Young Soldier. We carried her in here before the rogues out there had drawn their lines about the castle.

2 Young Soldier. Has she so much offended, Queen?

P. Queen. O that I could tell you, for I die when I have to keep a secret, but tell I cannot. Did she cry out and struggle to get away? She is both mad and bad.

2 Young Soldier. There was no need to bind her though we had brought these chains. It's certain she is mad, for she cried out wild things against you—that you are no queen, and so forth, but finding that we did not listen became dumb enough and quiet enough.

P. Queen. Quiet enough. That's where her wickedness comes in. O, a million thanks. But I'll not see her yet awhile, not till I am more awful in my majesty. (*Cries outside.*)

3 Soldier (*coming from gate*). They are about to hang that old beggar man, Rat-hole. I have been watching them this

half hour past. He stood there with his eyes closed and
called them rogues and rebels.

P. Queen. And so they seized him and said that he must hang.
I envy him his simple majesty, to be either king or beggar
—no mixture.

3 Young Soldier. When they laid their hands on him to drag
him to the tree he was all beggar, for that woke him and set
him pleading [for] his life, crying, and down upon his knees,
but when they let him go his eyes closed.

P. Queen. And was he King again, being asleep?

3 Young Soldier. His back grew straight, up went his head,
and he began to rail again, to call out for his daughter, or
rather the Old King or the lunacy that is in him spoke up
and called them lousy ruffians, and mocked at them for
thinking they could do hurt to an impalpable spirit.

[FROM OPPOSITE PAGE]

Important, Act II. In scene with real Queen some allusion
should be made to the fact that none know what she is like.
This can be said when her escape is arranged. The veil should
come in. Queen should ask for it to cover her face, nun-like.
It should be gold and belong to the Queen's robe. It could
lead up to the conversation on her being unknown. She could
ask for it, not as at first scene to hide her, but out of modesty.
She is all but a nun.

[DRAFT CONTINUES]

P. Queen. I would that my mother had brought me to haunted
rooms and to old gentle places when I was young. I dare
say now from that on he's gone bravely and been all king.

Young Soldier. No, no, for they dragged him towards the tree,
and he wept through full fifty yards, and said that spirit
was no friend of his and a most wicked thing. Puzzled
again, they would have let him go, but no sooner were
their hands off than the big voice, hoarse as if with
shouting in battle, called them hangmen, nothing but
hangmen, bid them to think twice [?] and be damned for
it, threw such scorn upon them for thinking that they could
twist his cloudy neck. Then Barach got him by the legs and

pulled him to the tree, and now they are all in a hanging
mood and would not pardon him if he were their own
father. There is his last yell now.

P. Queen. So he was all beggar with [the] noose about him, and
now he's dead he'll but consort with beggars. Have you
seen men die before?

Young Soldier. Three or four times in battle, and more times
than that of the camp sickness.

Player Queen. Have you seen women die?

Young Soldier. I have seen no woman die.   34

Player Queen. Is it hard when it comes, or is one glad to be
done with life; does the world seem better in the end and
hard to leave, like some good house when the coach is
round and one's foot upon its step?   37

Young Soldier. I have but seen men die suddenly, or else wasted
with sickness, and those that were wasted thought little of
going and those that went suddenly, nothing.

Player Queen. But to be in good health and to see death and
not to grow pale, that's better than the players do upon
the stage. (*Sudden knocking at door and soldier crosses
to door.*)

A Soldier. This has been thrust through the door—a message
from the rebels.

P. Queen (taking it). Is the man within who brought it?

Soldier. Yes, with a flag of truce.

P. Queen. They ask to have the taxes annulled and that the
Chancellor be given them to punish. I will answer as befits
my throne.

Soldier. The man that brought it asks to be admitted. He is
alone and unarmed.

P. Queen. Admit him. I'll find fitting words to speak—
something—what I cannot tell. But when there's need
there comes into my thoughts a shadow, a thin mighty
life, a long-gathering power, a mystery out of the
measureless years.

A Soldier. She means what comes out of the weight of the
crown. Look how she straightens herself up. (*Martin
enters.*)

Player Queen. Leave me all; I will speak alone with this
man. He and I have much to say to one another. But you

there, stay awhile and lay these heavy chains there close
at hand, and bring that prisoner you took by night [?] when
I strike upon this shield. Keep within reach. This man,
these chains, that raving woman and I have been knotted
up together from the beginning of the world. (*All go.*)
What could they know, even though I know all the secret
what do I know now that the chain is tightened and
the day of disentangling come?

Martin. Is it for me you have that chain, or would you bind
me for some young man's spirit?

Player Queen. Why should I bind you? Are you not already,
both you and I, locked, bound, and tangled with a chain?

Martin. What tanglement but that which your own frenzy and
wickedness have made, setting yourself up for queen
among these men?

Player Queen. I cannot tell who made it, but today it shall be
unmade, for I have dreamed myself and that is a most
mortal thing.

Martin. Quick, throw this cloak about you and come with me;
I told them that I had a sister here.

Player Queen. I will not go.

Martin. Ah, so [you] think that you can fight the people,
and do not care how many get their death.

Player Queen. Only one shall die today, and she being born
of kings—that [have] ever been at war, and hanging [?]
up in chambers where murderer's histories are stitched
in silk—will find a fitting end.

Martin. I see it, I see it all. Some young man with the yellow
down upon his chin has so befooled you that you'll stay
on here though Heaven rained brimstone. O, I might have
known it. I am too old, too quiet, or it may be there's a
sameness in one man. Some man dressed out so neatly and
[in] such colours and with manners so well matching that
the whole man seems to have been bought over the counter.

Player Queen. I have too weighty a business on me for one
like that.

Yellow Martin. No wonder they take woman's fancy—what
else do they think of? They do not make philosophies,
poems, great events.

Player Queen. O, Martin, Martin, your thoughts awry upon
the wind. It is you that keep me here; you that will not
let me seek my safety.

Yellow Martin (standing still). How, I?

Player Queen. It is your dream that roots me to the ground.
It lay once in the pit of your mind, and when you took
your heart from me I gave myself up to it, for I had that
alone.

Yellow Martin. What, is it that old queen of Babylon? O, this
is monstrous. You think nothing of my wisdom, of my
firmness, of my prudence. O, you are a woman all out. You
fasten upon my folly.

Player Queen. No, no, but I have found your secret, the
thing that was born with you, that you had to discover.
How can we believe what we discover? Did we not find
it in hesitation and fear and trembling? How could you
believe in that dream? Had it been mine, I would have
cast it away like an old rag. Who believes in any but
another's dream? I would set yours up before all eyes.

Martin. I would that I knew that you are not playing with me,
that you have not some young man in your thought. You
say you have not, and yet you will not come away.

P. Queen. Martin, Martin, I was never so much yours, for
now that I have lost your love I have your dream. I sing
to it, it murmurs to me, I rock it in my arms like a child, and
I am going with it to my death.

Martin. I would I could understand you.

Player Queen. Love me truly and you will understand, or like
not understanding best.

Martin. I have never cared for any but you. It was your teeming
brain made you think me false.

[NOTE FROM OPPOSITE PAGE]

Act I. Note. Might not Martin have written the Babylon
play when first in love with P. Queen?

[DRAFT CONTINUES]

Player Queen. Beware what you say.

Martin. You have been jealous of a shadow.

Player Queen. I shall soon know if you are lying.

Martin. I am not given to using big words or swearing upon a
  book. It is enough that I say I have not been false to you.

Player Queen. It were well indeed to be careful of your words
  now and not to make them too big, for now I can test you.

Martin. What test but that I have come here to save you?

P. Queen. You would do as much for a dog. Answer me this.
  When we love do we not despise all but love, is not the
  one we love all?

Martin. Yes, surely, she that we love is all.

Player Queen. And other women nothing?

Martin. Yes, nothing.

Player Queen. Nothing. Then the test is sure. (*She strikes
  shield with butt of a spear.*) O, I shall sift your soul. I
  shall draw my fingers through it; I shall know what is there.
  I shall shake it through a sieve and see what the wind
  leaves. (*Girl is brought in. She motions soldier away.
  He goes into house.*)

Martin. My God, she here? I thought I had left her in safety.

Player Queen. Put the chain upon that girl, then take her
  through that door. There is [a] winding stair goes down,
  far down. Leave her there and lock the door upon her with
  this key. Then she will be gone from your life and mine.

Girl. O, you wicked woman.

Martin. So this is your test.

Player Queen. Is she not nothing—did you not say it? Put
  the chain upon her quickly. Those rings are for the ankles,
  these others for the wrists. Quick, quick, I am not in
  Babylon now. We can escape and live. In Babylon there's
  only death.

Girl. O my God, my God.

Player Queen. It is my life I ask of you; if she stays in the light,
  I go to darkness.

Martin. She has done no wrong.

Player Queen. Time passes, and Babylon and the dream are
  near. She's but nothing.

Martin. I will do no such cruelty.

Player Queen. O yes you would. If she bid you, you'd put

those chains on me because you love her, and she is all
and it is I am nothing.

Martin. The love I know has come from Heaven and makes
me gentle.

Player Queen. O no, it's not of Heaven. It is an angry, bitter,
torturing thing, that's hungry in our lips and violent in
our hands; or that's the love one dies for, and what is all
the rest?

Girl. You see the sort she [is], how little fit for one like you,
and it's for her you've slighted me a thousand times. She
hates me because she knows that you and I are like to one
another, souls made for one another.

Martin. I never saw her as she is till now, and I ask pardon
for having wronged in you the better woman.

Girl. Now you have lost him. You first tried him with mad
jealousy, and all the while he thought of you alone, but
now you have shown what you are.

Yellow Martin. I'll have no more to do with her.

Girl (*to Player Queen*). I'll be his sweetheart now.

Player Queen. I would not have hurt her Martin. All I
wanted was to be sure you did not love her. Once you
put her down there I'd have fetched her up, for then I'd
know that she was nothing, and why would one punish
nothing?

Martin. And the day after some new wildness would have come
into your thoughts.

Player Queen. I'll keep them wild forever now, and from this
nightfall I'll begin to punish her, and I'll not leave it
while she lives. Go, go, go free; be lovers. Go to your
marriage, but you'll find little pleasure there, because I'll be
a ghost and haunt. In the depth of the night let her but
spread her arms and call you to her, and I'll see it and put
my face to hers until she screams.

Girl (*to Martin*). Protect me from her; I am afraid. (*She
clings to him.*)

Player Queen. And when you die that shall be no escape, for
I'll so die that I shall be with queens and have great armies
to do my bidding.

Girl. Let us go quickly.

Martin. No, for I must stay, and before the fight begins or after tell who this woman is and save her life in her own despite, for they are already at the door calling for her death.

Player Queen (*going to gate*). Who will believe? Speak what you will, you will but have your word and I my willing death to give them faith in mine.

Martin. What are you doing?

Player Queen. I have drawn the bolt. (*He steps forward to prevent her.*) It is too late. (*Rebels crowd in.*) I am your Queen, and I will answer as befits me the message that you have sent.

(*Soldiers come to balcony above. Rebels take up the arms.*)

Soldier. We are surprised. They are upon us.

Another Soldier. Where are the arms?

Another. Below in the archway.

Another. We cannot get down; they have the stairs.

Player Queen. Be still all; you can do nothing. It was I who did it, for I will have none die for me.

Barach. What is your answer? Do you surrender the evil adviser and take off the taxes?

Player Queen. This. (*She tells message.*)

Voice in Crowd. That is not the Queen. Those lips   66
have given kisses; those lips have drunk wine.

Barach. Silence the fool. You know the penalty.

Soldier (*above*). She is your Queen. How dare you threaten   70
her. Rogues, murderers.   71

Player Queen. It is my will, and maybe I shall die laughing.   72

Barach. I am not afraid of you.

Soldier (*above*). You wicked scoundrel.

Barach. There is a sort of angry writing on my back, a sort of crooked lettering with magic in it that puts fear away. The wizard that made it had nine tails.

P. Queen. It was I who made the tax. I accept it all;
put me to death if you dare. (*Murmurs in crowd.*)   77
For all your boasting you are afraid. Who is there
amongst you that will strike? Your father's lives
and the lives of their fathers before them were but twigs

woven into the nest that gave the eagle birth. Who   80
amongst you dares to face this eagle? Eagle begat eagle up
through all the centuries, and the eyes of all the   82
eagles look at you. But strike if you will. I   83
veil their lightning. (*She covers her eyes with her
hands.*)

Barach. I fear nothing today. Did I not hang your   85
father in that beggar's body, for I knew the voice.

Yellow Martin. Stop—this is no Queen.   88

Drunken Man in Crowd. That is right, that is right.   89
Those lips have given kisses, those lips have drunk wine.

[*Yellow Martin.*] This is no queen, I say. Yes, I will speak.   91
Take your hands off me. What I say is true;   92
she is a player in my troupe.   93

Barach. She has the crown on her head; she says she is the   94
Queen. No man shall turn us from what we've a mind to.
(*Voices* "Take him away, etc.")

Yellow Martin. Am I not one of you? Did I not carry your
message but now when you all feared to? Have I not a right
to be heard? (*Voices* "Yes, yes, he has a right to be heard,
etc.")

Barach. Speak, but let it be short.

Yellow Martin. Give me time; it is a strange tale.

Player Queen. It is no use, good honest man. Even if they
would listen to your incredible tale, I would refuse to   102
accept my life in exchange for becoming less than   103
I am.   104

Yellow Martin. I tell you that she is seeking for her   105
death, and that her high words are meant to pull it   106
on her.   107

Player Queen. People, he but speaks the truth. I
seek my death, because I think it well instead of a   109
few more years of lessened royalty to choose a death   110
that shall be a life forever, and as it were mock at   111
you with sweet laughter.   112

Yellow Martin. Why those big words are not her own; they
are words out of a play. O, if you only knew what this
woman was like, you would understand and listen to my
tale, though it seem incredible.

Player Queen. No, for I would first show them what you
    are like and what you are called [?]. This man is a player
    from a troupe who were to play at my bidding this day,   119
    and now, being loyal, he seeks to save me by a tale of   120
    wild make-believe, such as his craft makes natural   121
    to him.   122

[FROM THE OPPOSITE PAGE]

Note. Act III follows straight on Act II. Only Yellow Martin
to come on stage opening of Act II. Act one to close with
blessing of arms or with putting them under arch on some
excuse or other. She might use excuse of blessing and then
use phrase about being afraid of knives. Her blessing might
take the form of charming words—a sort of hush [?] song—
the arms to lie quiet whoever had to die. Girl could then
fetch Chancellor. She could then tell at end that he was
going to take her away by force.

[DRAFT CONTINUES]

Yellow. I tell you that those robes and crown are not hers,
    though where she came by them I do not know.   124
Player Queen. Poor man, do you think you will make them   125
    believe that anyone could speak with so much calm as I   126
    am speaking with, with such quiet breath, death being   127
    so near, and have no royalty in her? Who could face the   128
    levelled spears but for a borrowed crown and robe?   129
Voices. That's true, that's true, put him out.
Drunken Man. She was never in a convent. Those lips have   132
    given kisses, those lips have drunk wine.
Player Queen. Those up yonder, who would give their lives   134
    for me, would not say that I am less than Queen.
Barach. Out with you.   137
    We'll be played with no longer. (*They begin to jostle*   138
    and pull Yellow Martin.)
Player Queen. Do not hurt him. Leave me still the power to   139
    pardon—that can do no harm. It is I that have been
    wronged. (*To Martin.*) Come nearer, Answer me. Have   141
    we not more than once when I had summoned you before

me, spoken of the nature of artists,

    how they long to have such parts as may make them   144

    seem great in men's eyes, or in some lover's eyes;   145

    to save a queen and claim a queen all   146

    in one mouthful, that is the part he longs to play.

Yellow Martin. It was you that said these things, and   148

    that is why you now would play the part of Queen.   149

Barach. Take him away; we've heard enough.

Player Queen. Let him go. I will question him. Why do you

    not obey me? Am I Queen until I die? (*Murmurs in crowd*

    "Yes, she is Queen until she dies.")

    I will have no slander living after me, no shaking   154

    of the head. You say I was of your company?

Yellow Martin. Give me but time and I will find a witness,   156

    twenty witnesses.   157

Player Queen. When I was of your company, was I not your 158

    sweetheart?   159

Yellow Martin. Yes, you were my sweetheart.   160

Player Queen. Now you see his vanity—the artist's

    vanity. Should I question him further he would say   162

    he cast me off caring [?] her for a fool.

Yellow Martin. No, no, never. That's where the wildness   164

    is.   165

Player Queen. Ah, now he grows more wary.

Yellow Martin. No, no, there never was another, but I

    cannot make her understand, or you understand, or anyone. 169

    I cannot put out the wildness that is burning her. I   170

    cannot save her life.   171

Player Queen. Go to your own sweetheart and tell that   172

    you are so full of falsehood you have hardly escaped   173

    with your life. For me the wide Heavens are waiting.   174

Yellow Martin (*being dragged away*). Is there no one that   175

    will bear witness? There was one, but she is gone. (*Noise*

    in crowd.)

Queen. I will.   178

Barach. Is this your witness?   179

Yellow Martin. No, I do not know her.   180

Barach. Then cast him out. (*Martin pushed out.*) And

    now I'll find out what new trickery is this.   184

    Who are you?   185

Queen. I, not she, am Queen, and yet she is more than I.
   (*Murmurs among crowd* "She says she is Queen."
   Laughter above among the young soldiers—"She Queen.")

A Soldier. That tale can help nothing.

Player Queen. He says he does not know her to make her
   testimony seem the stronger, but so hastily did they make
   their plot that she still wears the dress she wore as
   Noah's wife.

Queen. I put it on to escape. She gave it me; she sought to   194
   save me. But my conscience troubled. I wandered here and
   there. I was afraid, but I came back and I have told the
   truth. She came in answer to my prayer to save me.   198
   She wore this dress. I was afraid of martyrdom and so
   she saved me. She put this veil about me. I think she
   is miraculous.

Drunken Man. She is the Queen. She made the taxes. Her
   lips have never given kisses or drunk wine.

Barach. Silence you fool.

Player Queen. You would pull me [from] the rest I am   204
   seeking to a world I am weary of. But come nearer;   205
   give me the veil that I may wrap myself in it and   206
   look [no] longer on the world.   207

Queen. You will see. She will work some miracle;   208
   do something to lift our hearts to Heaven.   209

P. Queen. No, it is [they] that shall work the miracle, for
   when they strike with their spears I shall become one of
   the great queens of all ages.

A Voice. Kill both of them and then we shall be certain.   210

Barach. But this one first.   211

Queen. She came to save me. You cannot harm me.   212

Drunken Man. Strike at the other. Her lips have given
   kisses, her lips have drunk wine.

Soldier (*above*). When has he prospered that killed queens?   214

Barach. All of you take up your spears and strike all together.   215
   Then no one can be blamed more than another.   216

Soldier. So you would make the ruin greater?

Another Soldier. How can you cheat the thunder?   218

One of the Crowd. I'll not strike   219
   I am always afraid when it thunders.   220

Another. Nor I. She'd be a fearful ghost. 221

Another. Strike at her Barach. It's the work you chose. 222

Drunken Man. There was a ghost that rode a grey horse 223
and broke the rooftree with a blow of his hoof. 224

Barach. Lower your spears then. None of us will take the 225
blame, but she shall not live for all that. 226

Drunken Man. It was in my great grandfather's time. 227

[*Barach.*] Bring down those men to me. I'll find 228
executioners and show them not to rail at us. 229

Queen. Bring a million and they'll not harm that 230
golden pillar. Who knows what she is? May be she has 231
but to lift her hands and the air be full of spirits. 232

Drunken Man. He had drunk wine. And he had golden 233
armour. O, he was a fearful ghost. 234
(*Young soldiers are brought in.*)

Barach. Find one among you that will put her to death, 235
and go free, but if you do not find one then you 236
all shall die. No thunder and lightning will fall 237
on us for killing you. 238

Soldiers. We will die then; she is our Queen. 239

All. Yes, we will die. 240

Queen. No, no, give me the spear. I will strike 241
at [her]. 242

Soldier. Would you strike your Queen, poor woman? 243

Queen. If she were but a queen I would not strike, 244
but she is angelical, come to show me how I should 245
have met martyrdom. 246

Barach. She is crazy, she thinks to reveal a miracle. 247
She will do as well as another. Take the spear, but 248
strike hard. 249

Queen (*taking spear*). Now shall [you] see that golden 250
pillar change into light, or vanish like a flash of 251
fire. 252

Barach. Poise it on your hand, grasped in the middle.

Queen. Or else you will see it blunted, and there will
come a sound as if I had struck bronze.
But look [at] her, [she] is trembling: that is 256
not because she is a woman, afraid of death at 257
the last for all her courage. You cannot understand

as I do the mysteries of Heaven. To test me the better
she is putting on the
humility of death and fear. 260
(*A sudden movement in the crowd. A cry* "The soldiers,
the soldiers. Escape. We cannot do so.")

Queen (*holding spear, who has seen nothing*).
Now, now will I reveal the miracle. One cannot say 261
what will happen. Perhaps Heaven will open and 262
she be carried away in a moment. 263

Martin (*seizing spear*). So I was but just in 264
time. 265

Chancellor. What, two queens, and one against another? 266
Let no one stir. My soldiers are all about you. Lay 267
down your weapons. But which of them is Queen? My 268
sight has grown dim of late. I cannot see rightly.
Kneel all and ask your pardon of the Queen.

(*All kneel to Player Queen asking pardon except Drunken
Man.*)

Drunken Man. Her lips have given kisses, her lips have
drunk wine.

Queen. No, not to me. I am done with being Queen.

Chancellor. Ah, you have all good sight; your eyes are 274
better than mine. 275

Player Queen (*coming down from steps*). Ah, you have but
risen against the shadow of a queen in rising against me, 277
and so have done but shadow wrong. I therefore pardon 278
all. And now I put the play aside and take up 279
life again that I had thought myself well done with. 280
I am no queen. These spoke truth. (*To real Queen.*)
Will your Majesty forgive the mask that I have worn?

Queen. When I ran away and you took my place I was alone
with my own soul. My sin rose up against me, my
cowardice. I vowed to myself that I would leave the world
and the throne, and stay till I die in my convent cell. I
will find out my own soul and cling to that. I can see that life
is but deceiving and being deceived, that who masters it
speak even to themselves in masks. If you will bear the
hard burden, stay on being Queen.

Chancellor. You are still Queen and a 289
most fitting one, worthy of men's devotion.

Player Queen. You who have the power of a king should have   291
the name. Am I still enough of Queen to give the crown?   292

Chancellor. O mask of gold, is not all gold royal?   293

Player Queen. For an hour or a day, but then I change
the mask.   295

Chancellor. So be it, then. I take it at your hands that   296
have most right to give. I have my task from you and   297
am ready for the doing of it. (*He takes crown.*)

Player Queen. Hey-day. So Jill must be herself again although   299
her Jack's away. (*Goes to one side.*) Go to, you fat toad;   300
go to your mudhole.

Girl. I only can set this right.

P. Queen. What have you [to] say to me, viper?

Girl. I will not have Martin, though you bade me come here
out of their hearing. He there, his Majesty, he promised
if ever he became a King to carry me away by force,
against my will to some lonely castle, and now he'll do it.

[FROM OPPOSITE PAGE]

King offers to make M. count. Player Queen refuses to have
him. King impatient. He must find some reward for her, and
fitting what she has been. Martin steps towards her; she walks
away. Girl speaks to her. King will carry her off. Points out
how he looks at her. P. Queen says so the day's work is done.
But what an appetite she has. (*Goes into house.*) Girl tells
Martin that it is all right. King considers title. Martin refuses.
King says P. Queen must decide. Martin hates all show. He
has to tumble and juggle. P. Queen above at window eating
lobster. Won't have title. Might drive her to who knows what?
One part always. King admits she will never do for a countess.
P. Queen asks all to listen to play.

[DRAFT CONTINUES]

P. Queen. But will he do it?

Girl. He swore it to me. Look how he is watching me. I am
going walking alone tonight on the edge of the wood.
That's what he's whispering now.

Player Queen (*stretching her arms and yawning*). So the day   317

is done and all's well. What an appetite I have.   318
   (*She runs into house.*)

Girl (*to King and Martin*). She has forgiven him.   319

King. Then I will make this player count.   320

Martin. Sir, that is impossible. It would ruin   321
   me. I play all sorts of parts. In bad times I   322
   am a juggler, an acrobat. How could a peer of the   323
   realm tumble upon a board? I'd starve.   324

King. She must decide, not you, sir; she, not you.

Player Queen (*above with a lobster which* [*she*] *is eating
   out of her fingers*). What's that I hear? I will not be a   327
   countess. I've been more than that today. This lobster's   328
   good. (*To Girl.*) There, catch. I never was so hungry in
   my life. A
   countess? I that made a King?   332

King (*to Martin*). She's right. It would never do.   333

Player Queen. Have a claw Martin. (*Martin makes   334
   a gesture to stop her.*) O well, if you're on   335
   your dignity. Friends and patrons, we seek once more   336
   your good opinion, if we have deserved [?] something
   for past services. I'll take my shoe to this. (*Begins
   cracking lobster claw with blows of the heel
   of her shoe.*) Take
   all your places and we'll begin the play we had   339
   promised.

King. So be it, let the play begin. If there're   341
   any here who [word undeciphered] should not like the
   play, I'll have them hanged.

Martin. No, you can [play] what you please from this day.
   Herodias, Sheba, any you've a mind for.

Player Queen. O no, no, no. Take your trumpet, mount   346
   up there and blow, for from here out I shall be Noah's
   wife. (*She blows a kiss to him.*)

Commentary

The surviving part of Act I goes back for its principal themes to Drafts 2
and 3. In Draft 2 the Player Queen has found Septimus's old play and insists

on reviving it; she will play that or nothing. Though the Prime Minister doesn't care what play is given, Septimus refuses to let her play it, since he feels he must assert his authority. In Draft 3 the whole troupe of players looks for and finds the hidden Player Queen. Yeats develops these situations in Draft 8.

We cannot tell how the scene began, for clearly the usual opening dialogue between the Prime Minister and the Queen was not used; when this fragment of Act I opens, the Prime Minister is still waiting for the Queen to appear. The opening must have involved Rat-hole, because Nona alludes to him in passing. The draft opens with Septimus, Nona, and the Prime Minister (*Yellow Martin, Girl, Chancellor*) discussing the disappearance of the Player Queen. She and Septimus have quarreled over parts. She hates Noah's wife and wants to play the Queen of Babylon, but Septimus has insisted she play the part he has assigned her. He feels that for both their sakes he must assert his authority. To help establish his image of authority he refuses to help in the search for the Player Queen. As he explains, ". . . we that love passionate, proud women must keep the mask upon us though our heart is breaking." He agrees to tell his company to search for her and leaves. Nona finds Septimus's old play about the Queen of Babylon, and, just as she finds it, she hears the hidden Decima singing. The Prime Minister does not hear her. Nona returns to the play, outlines its action, and explains Septimus's views on why audiences no longer like romantic drama. She is reading out a section of the play when the draft breaks off. When Yeats resumes, the Queen has arrived and she and the Prime Minister are alone on the stage. They are discussing the rebellion. She feels she cannot meet the rebels' demands, for her tax on their sins is a just tax. The Queen uses a notable image in defending her actions: God's law "should be like an iron plow in the world"; the Prime Minister extends it when he answers, "I have seen no straight furrow worth dying for." She has nothing, then, to offer the rebels, yet fears death at their hands. She refers to this death as martyrdom, thereby enrolling herself in the company of saints. She discusses her spiritual and moral state, and at the end she goes out with the Prime Minister to face the rebels. Yeats dubs in the Player Queen's song, on which he had worked in Drafts 3 and 6, by writing, "Player sings song about 'emerald eyes and mask of gold,'" and the whole troupe of players comes in searching for the Player Queen. Nona is with them, carrying the dress of Noah's wife, which she holds in front of her to see if it fits. The Player who is with her warns her not to take the part for fear of Decima. This warning will shortly be assigned to Peter in Drafts 11 and 12, refitting the costume of Noah's wife lingers as a piece of stage business in the finished play. The troupe discovers the Player Queen, and the draft breaks off with an important note about the Queen's character, which shows that Yeats feared he had made her too strong in the draft just finished: "Should Queen be merely passive and pious?" She had certainly not been passive in this draft.

There is no "B" version of Act II, though the continuation of the note just quoted shows that it was to end much as it had in Draft 6, where the Prime Minister leaves with most of the loyal soldiers to put the gold collected from the tax on sins in a safe place. He is made to say "that holiness must buy its welcome, for it has an ugly face. It is the bold child that the mother loves." Yeats may never have written a "B" version of Act II. In Draft 6 he had made good progress with his second act, and he will return to parts of it in Drafts 11, 12, and 13.

Act III in Draft 8 is a further working up and refinement of Draft 7. Nearly all of its events occur there, though little of its language. Many of the events are developed further here—for example, at the opening, both the capture of Nona and the hanging of Rat-hole. This same process of expansion can be observed throughout: Nona is strengthened, she now takes pride in winning Septimus; the phrase describing the Player Queen ("Those lips have given kisses, those lips have drunk wine") becomes a kind of refrain; Barach is more fully developed as the leader of the rebellion; the Queen's conviction that Decima is an angel sent to help her, whose true nature will be revealed by a show of violence leads her to take the role of executioner that she may produce the miracle; the rape of Nona to get her off the scene is more fully worked out; and at the end of the draft Decima is eating lobster, an ending of the play which Yeats kept through the versions published in 1922.

There are echoes or anticipations of other works: twice during the scene Decima stretches and yawns. This became Yeats's favorite device to mark either the desire for love or its fulfillment. He used it in "On Women," finished 25 May 1914, and he continued to use it up through *A Full Moon in March*. I think its occurrence in this draft of *The Player Queen* is the earliest of all. [Cf. David Clark, "Stretching and Yawning with Yeats and Pound," *Malahat Review* 29 (January 1974): 104–17. I had read and forgotten this passage of Bradford's typescript when I wrote that " 'Stretch' and 'yawn' are first used together in 'On Woman,' composed 21 or 25 May 1914" (p. 106). The Player Queen's first stretching and yawning in Draft 8 (p. 87 of this book) has no obvious erotic significance, though, as in *A Full Moon in March,* the man of greatest importance in her life (Septimus) enters soon afterward, as if heralded by the stretching and yawning. The second instance in Draft 8 (p. 101), retained in Draft 16 (p. 244), comes immediately after she discovers that Nona is no longer an obstacle to her love for Septimus and she looks forward to a happy reunion with him. Since these drafts antedate Yeats's 29 November 1909 reading of the play to Mrs. Campbell, doubt is thrown on my conclusion in the article that Yeats got his erotic association for these words from Pound's *The Spirit of Romance* (London, 1910). Gen. Ed.]

The mention of a winding stair on page 92, though only a descriptive detail, is rather startling when we think of all that the emblem of the winding stair was to become in Yeats's iconography, though probably we should not make too much of the various twists and whirls that occur in Yeats's early work.

The refinement of the language of Draft 7 that took place in Draft 8 is apparent throughout. Here are two passages that illustrate it. The first reflects the thought of "The Cap and Bells":

He. You think nothing of wisdom, of my firmness or my
prudence. O, you are a woman all out. You fasten upon my
folly.

Yellow Martin. O, this is monstrous. You think nothing of my
wisdom, of my firmness, of my prudence. O, you are a
woman all out. You fasten upon my folly.

The second describes the charm that protects Barach:

Man. I have no fear of you. There is an angry writing on
this back that puts out fear, a sort of spell against it, a
crooked figured thing from no wizard hands.

Barach. There is a sort of angry writing on my back, a sort
of crooked lettering with magic in it that puts fear away.
The wizard that made it had nine tails.

Finally, the Queen's speech on the mask deserves particular attention, since she has been shown throughout as a downright person who cannot wear a mask:

I can see that life is but deceiving and being deceived,
that who masters it speak even to themselves in masks.

Draft 9

This draft begins with a plan for the scene where Nona (*Friend* or *The Friend* for the first time) discovers the Player Queen hidden in the vat. Nona is carrying a pair of scissors with which she is altering the dress of Noah's wife to fit herself, as she had thought of doing in Draft 8. (This property, the weapon Decima uses when she threatens suicide, is still found in the finished play; getting it onto the stage in a natural manner gave Yeats a good deal of trouble.) Septimus has gone to town and does not know that the Player Queen is missing, a first faint dawning, perhaps, of Yeats's eventual decision to begin the play in town. When Nona says that she intends to take the part of Noah's wife, she and the Player Queen fight. Nona is conceived of as a fickle but generous woman who has had many lovers. Yeats spends a good deal of time planning her quarrel with Decima, then begins to write dialogue in prose. After about a page of this, he begins over again in blank verse. I quote the verse:

PQ. [undeciphered name repeated three times]
Friend.   So that's the place
    Where you've been lying hidden all the night,
    While we have searched in every hole and corner
    And dragged the pond. (*A sob.*) I hope there is a spider
    Crawling about your eyes and that your back
    Aches, and that you have not slept a wink.
    Such wickedness—to hide yourself up there
    When we had thought . . .
PQ.   But where is Druidan?
Friend. So that is why you come out of your hole.
    You'd thought to find if you could blanch his face
    And put a shake into his voice. Then you'd look up
    And skip about the room in two-step
    To see how you had shaken him.
PQ.   Where is he?
Friend. He does not know that you are lost. He went
    Into the town at midnight to buy masks
    And has not yet returned.
Player Queen.   Not yet returned!
    There's nothing that I hate but a bad part,
    And why do you so hate me?
Friend.   Tell me first
    Why is it you make Druidan so wretched?
    You know he wants you, as he never wanted
    Woman before, and yet you are as full of tricks,
    As full of tricks . . . (*Sobs.*) and isn't he worth two of you?

Player Queen. If he but let me have the parts I want
  I'll have no tricks—I'll not be Noah's wife
  And wear a seventy year old mask and stoop
  And after that be beaten with a stick
  Because I'll not believe in the old flood
  And will not go into the Ark.
Friend.   But Laudine [?]
  You are not really beaten—they're only thin laths,
  Those double laths that strike upon each other
  And make a noise.
P. Queen.   But I must have a part
  That's all embroidered in gold and silver,
  And haughty words and a high lifted head.
  I'd like to be a peacock or a sunset
  But lacking that I will be half content
  If I am nothing but a queen from this.
Friend. And you will stop up there until he promises,
  Although we may play nothing at this court
  But Bible plays, to let you play again
  The chronicle of Queen [undeciphered name]
  [undeciphered half line]
  Virtue [?] is lost—all is the same to you
  If but you have embroidery enough
  What do [you] care if we are clapped in prison.
  "I'll stop up here," that's what you think now,
  "Until I have my way."
Player Queen (nods). But such it has for way. [doubtful reading]
Friend (*she takes up dress*).
  Look, look, you have forgotten this.
  You should have padded the old tub with it
  Or better still have torn it to tatters.
P. Queen.   Who is there
  Would dare to play a part that I've been cast for?
Friend. It was too thin at the waist to fit me
  But take it now—look, how I've [word undeciphered] it
  And to height [?]
P. Queen.   How dare you come between?
  You've had a score of lovers in a twelvemonth
  And not satisfied.

Friend.   I've never tortured them
     Or bitten [?] them as they had been a [undeciphered word]
P. Queen. Yes, you are always kind. (*She has got down
               and snatches dress.*)
                              Your kindness
     Tastes as though it had been beer uncorked
     Upon a Saturday and left undrunk
     Till Monday morning on a tavern table
     Between a stale crust and an orange peel.

[VARIOUS ALTERNATE VERSIONS FOLLOW]

                    Not yet returned,
     Not yet returned? Why do [you] hate me so?
     You have loved many—I do not blame you for it,
     One must do something with one's life, or else
     Be like a book that has no writing in it.
     And it may be that you are tired of the sweet
     And long to have men harsher as your wine.
     But why when there is all the world to take [?]
     Do [you] hate me

[ALTERNATE VERSION FOLLOWING "ONE'S LIFE"]

                    And may be
     That is as good a thing as any other.
     But if you have grown weary of the sweet
     And long to have men harsh as is your wine
     When there is all the world to choose a husband [?] from
     Should you hate me?

Yeats diagrams a stage plan and continues with three successive openings of this scene, all in prose. In the first, the Queen, because of her strong sense of duty, arrives at dawn dressed for the festival. She is met by a sleepy young man, a follower of the Prime Minister, whose yawns make the Queen think she is boring him. He explains that he has been up all night bringing in the treasure, and that the Prime Minister is still sleeping. He tells the Queen of the rebellion. Having someone other than the Prime Minister meet the Queen was tried only here and soon abandoned. In the second opening, after making another stage plan, Yeats has the Queen, when she enters, hear the hidden Player Queen singing from the vat, a piece of business already used in Draft 6. The Prime Minister meets her and explains the political situation, which only her appearance among her people can resolve. The third drops the young man who is in the first but keeps the duty-ridden Queen, to whom, again, the Prime Minister explains the situation. The draft ends with a scenario containing further plans for the same scene with elements from all three of the drafts. These drafts, then, explore possible beginnings intended to precede and modify Draft 6, where at the outset the Queen hears the Player Queen singing.

Draft 10

This draft contains two more openings of Act I, Scene 2. I feel very uncertain where they belong in the order of drafts of this scene and particularly uncertain whether they should follow or precede Draft 6. Since they are not of particular interest, perhaps their place in the sequence of drafts is not important. On the first sheet Yeats has drawn a scene plan. Under it is this rubric: "Door into tower to R and L / Raised platform with curtained door at back TR / and courtyard door to LC". In the first version the Prime Minister is discovered onstage overseeing the stowing away of the tax money, the earnings of the new tax on sins. The Queen arrives and hears the Player Queen singing from the vat; she thinks it is a spirit voice. This version breaks off and Yeats tries again, using new characters, two old men, to help with the exposition. They hear a voice singing from the air and interpret it as a warning that Heaven disapproves of the new tax:

Old Man. It is great riches for the state, but this tax on
   people's sins, it is against God. Did not God say that sin
   is unprofitable, and here is profit. Why it's sheer blasphemy.

The Queen enters and hears the voice, which she interprets as that of a spirit warning her that she is doing wrong in leaving her cell. The Prime Minister speaks of the discontent caused by the new taxes, which the Queen defends; he goes on to state the need to reassert the traditional images of royalty: the royal presence, the royal manner. The Queen must embody her people's dreams of a heightened existence. To the Queen these are appearances only, but she finally agrees to go with the Prime Minister. They are interrupted by Nona, who is looking for the Player Queen. The Queen says, rather acidly: "She would better serve your purpose, for it is a player that you want. Why do you not bid me paint my face and learn a part by rote?" Here the draft breaks off.

CHAPTER SEVEN

Drafts 11 and 12

DRAFT 11 was written into the back of the A2 manuscript book. At some point Yeats simply turned the book over and began writing from the back in. Here the play takes a new turn as Yeats begins to develop a character called Peter, Septimus's opposite, who takes love lightly. I am not sure where this and the following draft belong in the succession of drafts; the matter explored is too different from earlier drafts to make exact determination possible. The drafts do make use of certain situations already developed, the just-found early play by Septimus on the Queen of Babylon, the revolt, the hiding of the Player Queen. I sense a shift of tone in this draft, a move toward the comic mode. Septimus is still *Yellow Martin;* Nona is *Martha* or *Winnie.*

Player Queen

Yellow Martin. Look at my clothes.

Peter. And at mine.

Yellow. I shall never get over this.

Peter. The briars have striped me like the ticking of a bed.

Yellow Martin. They pelted me with stones.

Peter. Such a time as I have had.

Yellow Martin. All the town after me.

Peter. That damnable woman.

Yellow Martin. Why don't you listen? Stop moping there.

Peter. I wonder who will mend this.

Yellow Martin. But I tell you this is no light matter; I tell
    you it may be my death with my heart in the state it is.
    And if you do not listen to me, if you will not listen to
    me . . .

Peter. Well, I am listening, but I should think considering
    the hardships I have been through—but do as you like.

Martin. I went down to the town as John of the Books bid
    me, and stood on a high stone and called out that I was a

poet, and that I had come from the east of the world and
that I knew all tales, until I had drawn a crowd, and then
as John of the Books had bid me I began to praise the
Queen, and when I began that they began to grumble
and mutter and then to interrupt me, but I went on but
they grew worse and worse.

Peter. So they would, so they would.

Martin. And yet I said nothing that I have not said about
queens and great persons from one end of the country
to the other, whether among the Gael or the Gaul.
"Sacred saint" I called her, "Crown of lilies" I called her,
"Image of the Heavens" I called her, "A woman without
mortal blemish" I called her, "Queen of love" I called her,
but before I had got out a dozen sentences they tumbled
me over into the mud and hauled [me] through the
streets and pelted me with stones. No, I shall never get
over it. The excitement will kill me; with a heart like mine
one does not get over a thing like that.

Peter. And did you tell them that you had never set eyes
upon her, or so much as knew if she were straight or
crooked?

Martin. I was hoarse, but they would [not] listen. They had set
their hearts on my murder by that time, and murder me
they would [have] if I [had] not met with a troop of
the Queen's soldiers.

Peter. It is all plain. She is coming here today; she is to
show herself to her people for the first time since her
father's death, since she came to the throne. It is the
day of her public coronation, and John of the Books sent
you down there to find out what they thought of her.
(*Speaking in a low voice and looking about him.*) It is
quite plain she is a devil, that she has done some wicked
thing, and that all the people hate her.

Yellow Martin. O miserable life of poet and player, without
a home, going here and there, and never knowing on what
misfortune one will light—from door to door, table to
table, giving a play here, a mystery there, a miracle play
somewhere else, now pelted, now praised.

Peter. Strolling players we are, strolling players we shall die.

And we must take the world as we find, but maybe if you
have had your lamentation out you will hear my troubles.

[ALTERNATE VERSION]

And of all things in the world I most despise a player, but
what of that. I take [the] world as it is. I have never yet
found a man who would give forty shillings a week for
ploughing. But if you have finished your troubles perhaps
you will hear mine.

Martin. Well?

Peter. Look at this.

Martin. Why did you not tell me that before?

Peter. But I did.

Yellow Martin. I am not deaf.

Peter. Your soul, troubled by the cruelty of your dear friend
 the public, forbid you to listen.

Martin. Well, what has happened? Have you too been
 attacked?

Peter. Much worse than that has happened. Your sweetheart,
 Martha, cannot be found.

Yellow Martin. I shall never get over this, and Noah's
 wife to be played at the Queen's homecoming this very
 day and the stage set for it.

Peter. This morning she swore that she would never play
 Noah's wife again, or any part in which she did not wear
 a fine dress, and look young, and talk with beautiful words,
 and do heroic things, and from that moment she cannot
 be found.

Yellow Martin. O my God. I shall die before the sun goes
 down. And such a trick to play on us.

Peter. I have been searching the whole wood through. I have
 been torn by briars and stung by nettles this hour past.

Yellow Martin. What sort of life will I have when I am
 married to her? She does not know what obedience is.
 She is obliged by every law of religion to obey the man
 she is to marry, but she is as hard to control as a weasel in
 the hedge or a hare on the mountain.

Peter. Would you take away her charms?

Martin. Charms, did you say charms? Charms to be the ruin
of them all, to bring her to death's door, and she knowing
right well that everything affects my heart. I have done
with her this time. O, if I only knew where she is that I
may tell her I am done with her. But where can she be?
My God, who knows what may have happened to her.
She is capable of throwing herself into the river to spite
me.

Peter. There is not a hole or corner that we have not searched.

Martin. She is dead—I am sure of it. And she so beautiful, so
graceful. Her long [hair] floating in the weeds. To think
of it. This morning when I kissed her it was the last I
shall ever give. I shall die with her Peter. What was that?
Did you hear?

Peter. No, I heard nothing.

Martin. I heard her voice. I am sure of it. And if it were only
a whisper and there were a hundred feet of wall between
I would hear it. She is alive.

Peter. You have fancied it Martin. There was no voice.

Martin. Yes, yes, she is hidden up on the battlements. O, I
shall die of this—what a relief. Martha, Martha. (*He goes
out. Winny, who has been thrusting her head through side
door, calls out* "Peter, Peter.")

Winny. Look what I have got here. No wonder he imagines
things, hears voices in the air.

Peter. Why what is it?

Winny. The play that upset Martha, the thing she wants to act.

Peter (*taking MS*). It's something Martin wrote years ago.
The ink is faded. Yes, "The Queen of Babylon." He
told me about it once.

Martha. She says that she will never play another part until
Martin puts this on the stage.

Peter. She is a fool to think the people would like anything
like this. Why this is really good. Words it would be
a pleasure to speak. There is a queen and the people rebel,
and at once she's all queens that ever were. Divine right
and all that sort [of] fare—heroic nonsense.

Martha. It does not seem to me a bit like life.

Peter. But that's just what I like. It is what we would be in
our dreams, and always when we do any fine thing we
dream. We play at it like children, and the dream takes
hold, and when we wake we are either lost and hated, or
loved and throned [?], and we wonder because men think
that it [is] we that do it all and not the dream. We hate or
love—are no different from the rest.

Martha. Well, if you want to put that sort of thing on the
stage, you would have to face empty houses, that I know.
It is bad enough to be strolling players, but we'd soon be
strolling beggars.

Peter. O yes, yes, it [would] be sheer starvation. The public's
the vainest of all hobgoblins, for it loves nothing but its
own face in the mirror. They cannot have art, because they
do not know that we must always love what we are not: the
coward loves courage, the sluggish, energy, the sad, delight,
the foolish, wisdom. But they, they [are] all cattle, no all
pigs loving the straw they lie on better than the clouds of
dawn. No, this is not for them, this is a drama for kings.
Listen now how proudly she speaks.

Martha. O what a tear; let me put a stitch in it.

[CONTINUES IN SCENARIO]

Peter begins to recite grandiloquent blank verse passages
from the play—either those or like those the Player Queen
afterwards speaks to the crowd, and as he does so Winny walks
up and down with her needle and thread mending his shirt.
He won't attend to her. At last she turns away and is going
out. The passages may praise noble, aristocratic life. When
Winny finally seizes hold of him for leave to mend the tear,
he may shake it off with "It has been as bad many times"—
some phrases which will bring out the contrast between
himself and what he reads, and after that should come a
very lofty passage.

[DRAFT CONTINUES]

Peter. Where are you going?
Winny. I won't tell you.

Peter. If I allow you to mend my sleeve will you not tell me?

Winny. But you must come here where nobody can hear us.
I do not know who may be hidden behind the walls.

Peter. So you did hear a voice. Well, there is my sleeve.

Winny (sewing). I am going to learn the part, (*looking about timidly*) the part of Noah's wife.

Peter. If you do, Martha, if she is alive, will put you out of the company.

Winny. But Yellow Martin is so unhappy. The people he loves so will come, and there will be no play for them and there will be no money.

Peter. I see what is in your mind—the old thought. You think you are tired of me, and that you are going . . .

Winny. Do not speak so loud.

Peter (in a whisper). . . . to throw yourself at his head.

Winny. O Peter, I never thought of such a thing. You know I love nobody but you.

Peter. You want him because he is slow, thinks he was a weak heart, longs for a quiet life, because he will be always tied to a post like a goat at the roadside, because he is as peaceful as if he were bedridden, because he has all the marks of a good husband.

[FROM THE OPPOSITE PAGE, MARKED *A]

At opening of play soldier might produce a proclamation from rebels announcing that all who take part in festival of the Queen shall be punished. Chancellor could then send on message to Yellow Martin with order he was not to be told about proclamation. A soldier might make himself the voice of the rebels; he might be taken away to be punished. This would make opening of play more serious and make heroism more believable. Would destroy the charm? This man might become leader of rebellion. Rebellion to be of soldiers only.

[DRAFT CONTINUES]

Winny. O . . .

Peter. Do not interrupt. You will want someone whose

drink you can warm, whose clothes you can mend, whose chair you can put to the fire, but it is no use. Even if you were to marry him in church like a citizen, you would beckon to me at the church door.

Winny. You are [the] most conceited coxcomb I ever came across.

Peter (*points to another tear which Winny begins to mend*). But you cannot do it, you will never give me up. Try, I give you leave to try. You will never give me up because you know I would console myself in twelve hours.

Winny. In twelve hours. (*Beginning to cry.*) You would take up with somebody else in twelve hours! That settles it; all is over. I will have no more to do with you.

Peter. It is we faithless ones that are loved the best, win the most beautiful. We are never gloomy, never jealous.

Winny. I will take her place. I will make him happy.

Peter. Then take [word undeciphered] some little part. It is going to be performed before nightfall, and Noah's wife will never be played again. Columkille has foretold it. She is our queen. She makes us do what she pleases.

Winny. Goodby Peter, goodby forever. Columkille has foretold falsely. I will find someone who is sincere, who does not talk nonsense.

Old Man. Then you must find him on the showery [?] top of Ararat. When the flood came the people of the world became fish: cod, herring [word undeciphered] trout, flat fish, stock fish, and leviathan that rules all. And the flood has never gone down, and today there will be a Spring tide, and leviathan will float on the top.

Winny. It is a poor man who has been wandering about the castle since they sent out word of the play.

Old Man. But on the top of Ararat, the ghosts. They have no shape. O, how they shimmer. Leviathan himself swims on the top, and a pretty ghost from Ararat swims on the top. What has she to do with the flood of time?

[BREAKS OFF]

Commentary

The character Peter is entirely new. It seems best to reserve a full discussion of Peter until we consider Draft 12, where he reaches his point of fullest development. Earlier, in Draft 6, Nona comes on stage just before she finds the Player Queen with a man called simply "Player" whom she sends to town to find out what is going on there (see p. 46). This scene will be assigned to Peter in Draft 12. And Yeats has not yet found any neat way of disposing of Nona at the end of the play. Her rape by the Prime Minister seems to violate the principle in romantic comedy that each eligible girl must be found an appropriate mate. Peter will be such a mate for Nona in later drafts. The attack on Septimus, here merely reported, anticipates the beginning of the finished play where the attack is staged. Giving to Septimus a weak heart and fussbudget notions is new and not too happy. Peter's scene declaiming grandiloquent speeches from Septimus's old play while Nona mends the tears in his clothes is a nicely incongruous bringing together of idea contrasted to reality, and it shows Nona's domestic nature. The doctrine of the mask is amusingly stated in this speech of Peter's:

> The public's the vainest of all hobgoblins, for it loves
> nothing but its own face in the mirror. They cannot have
> art, for they do not know that we must always love what
> we are not: the coward loves courage, the sluggish, energy,
> the sad, delight, the foolish, wisdom.

Peter's comments on Nona's desire to win Septimus are more fully developed in Draft 12. At the very end of Draft 11 the Old Man represents a new conception of Rat-hole as a visionary for whom the Biblical flood has actually taken place.

Draft 12

This is for me one of the most interesting early drafts of *The Player Queen*, and for several reasons: To begin with, it is not in Yeats's hand; he dictated it to an amanuensis whom Mrs. Yeats could not identify. It is not the writing of Lady Gregory, Miss Horniman, or Ezra Pound, all of whom served Yeats as amanuenses at various times. Mrs. Yeats suggested Iseult Gonne, but it seems to me Iseult was too young for that role when the draft was written, for I do not think it can be later than November 1909, when Yeats read a three-act version of the play to Mrs. Patrick Campbell. A comparison of the relevant passages in this draft and the only three-act version that has survived (Draft 16) shows that the three-act version is later. The writing of the manuscript of Draft 12 is uniform, bold, and, happy event, completely legible. The writing seems to me that of a mature person who was thoroughly used to Yeats's style; one rarely notices a missed turn of phrase. The manuscript contains no corrections in Yeats's hand, though such are usually found in manuscripts he dictated.

We have observed that in his successive drafts Yeats seems often to be concentrating on some one aspect of his play. Here that aspect is clearly the role of Peter, whose prototype appeared briefly as a nameless "Player" in Drafts 6 and 8, who was developed and named in Draft 11, who reaches his point of fullest development here in Draft 12, who drifts back into a nameless Young Man in Draft 15, and who appears for the last time with name in Draft 16. In the finished play there is still a remnant of Peter, so to speak. The player dressed as a swan is called Peter by the Player Queen at line 333 of Scene II. In all versions where he appears, the character of Peter is the same: he is a light lover who is pursuing or has captured Nona, a rational lover intended as a contrast to Septimus, the romantic lover. In short, a womanizer is opposed to the nineteenth-century conception of *amour courtois*.

Yeats must have had this draft particularly in mind when he wrote his 1922 note to the play. There he says:

> I wasted the best working months of several years in an
> attempt to write a poetical play where every character became
> an example of the finding or not finding of what I have
> called the Antithetical Self; and because passion and not
> thought makes tragedy, what I made had neither simplicity
> nor life. [*Variorum Plays,* p. 761]

Though there are suggestions in earlier drafts that characters other than the Player Queen are exploring their masks, only here do they do so intensely.

[Draft 12]

[LOOSE SHEET INSERTED, WRITTEN IN THE SAME HAND]

Yellow Martin begins discussion by saying "We have found her only just in time, what a miserable night she must have had there." She replies that she has been very happy watching beautiful young men who have come there to wait upon the

Queen. The Player says " 'tis no use telling Yellow M. that,
for he knows quite well there was nobody in the castle but old
men and women, their shins speckled with sitting over the
fire." He asks her why she is always trying to make YM.
unhappy. The Player Queen sings:—"My beloved said to me
I do not know if you are a friend or an enemy" and sinks down
into vat. Yellow M. says Player only vexes her and sends him
away to fetch Winnie and tell her the mysteries are beginning.
The Player goes out. Yellow M. climbs up beside the vat and
begins timidly to remonstrate with Player Queen whose voice
at first comes from the bottom of the vat. He tells her he has
the dress for her to wear as Noah's wife. She says she will
not play a stupid woman no better than herself. She will
never again be beaten by Noah because she will not go into
the Ark. Yellow M. says "But you are not really beaten. Noah
does not really hurt you. I am always very careful not to hurt
you." The Player Queen says she must have a great part with
fine words and fine dress. She must have shiny things to wear.
Her role must be Herodias, or Queen of Sheba, a light or a
fire, or, best of all, play that wonderful part YM told her of
the other day.

[NOTE FROM INSIDE COVER]

Note:—Winnie when she sets Peter to sew the dress could
do so that she may go hide herself to learn the part. ?Should
she tell Peter what she's doing or not? Probably yes.

[TWO NOTES OPPOSITE PAGE 1]

Query—Should not Peter pose in some obvious, perhaps
extravagant way before Winnie; wearing the mask in some
pronounced way? He might, for instance, speak of the troubles
of the town with great courage, perhaps braggadocio, and
when Yellow M. comes in begin to question him with a
nervousness strongly in contrast with his late manner. Perhaps
confess to his fear only after looking to see if Winnie is out
of earshot.
Note 2.—Winnie might tell Player to make the dress merely
that she might go away to sleep in the garden, she being lazy.

He having been charming to her might burst out against her
in fantastic fury the moment she had gone out. One would
then get a scene between YM and Player in which each would
tell the other of his wrongs without listening to him. Ended
by some vehement expostulation from Martin and by Player
saying:—"Well, you do look pretty knocked about. What is
it?" (Showing he had heard nothing) The Player's mask
would therefore be perpetual good nature.

Characters

Yellow Martin. Over sincere. In love with Player Queen, but
incapable of giving way to her caprices, incapable of wearing
a mask. [*Septimus*]

Peter. A light lover. Gives way to every caprice, always wears
a mask.

John Battleaxe. Genial philosopher. [*Prime Minister*]

Player Queen. Values nothing in life but the mask. [*Decima*]

Winnie. Stage rival of Player Queen. [*Nona*]

Winnie upon stage sewing. Peter enters. Goes over to Winnie.
Shows the mud on his clothes and where they are torn.
He says:—

[*Peter.*] O, I am not asking you to mend them. I am sufficient
   of a hand with the needle. You can pity me without fear.
Winnie. But have you found her? Yellow Martin has put me to
   sew this for her to wear in the miracle play, and I must go
   on sewing it. But there will be no play now. He'd never
   let me take the **part.**
Peter. O, you'd play it very well.
Winnie. He'd never dare give it to me, she'd be so angry.
   She'd never let me have any part worth playing, that I
   know. Do you think she has gone and drowned herself?
Peter. Drown herself my dear! Maybe she is somewhere
   listening to us now, waiting to see the audience gather, and
   no play for them to see, and Yellow Martin beside himself.
Winnie. It was a terrible quarrel this time. I never saw her
   so angry. She was as pale as pale. She said she would never

play these dull parts again, and if Yellow Martin wouldn't
promise to give her a part that would show her off properly,
he would never see her again. I don't know what would have
happened, but at that moment John Battleaxe came up and
sent Yellow Martin down to the town to praise the Queen
there.

Peter. Here he is coming now.

Winnie. Peter, you were always so kind——(*She holds out dress
to him.*)

Peter. You want me to sew it for you?

Winnie. Yellow Martin bid me do it, and now he will stand
over me and watch till it is done, and I don't want to make
a dress for her. (*Holding back dress.*) But you must say
you took it in spite of me.

Peter. But I wanted to do something for her pleasure.

Winnie. No no, but that I was tired and that you saw it. You
mustn't say that you've done anything for her. But Peter,
if the threads don't hold, if there's a crack in the seams,
and, I dare say, you were not too good with your needle,
what do I care? Put as big stitches as you like; what does
she deserve but big stitches?

Peter. Where are you going; you have to give me a kiss.

Winnie. No no, you said she might be somewhere quite near.
I must search the gardens, the yards, the battlements.

(*Yellow Martin comes in, covered with mud and his clothes torn.*)

Yellow Martin. What a trade is ours. I am sent down to the
town to praise a queen I never saw before. I praise her as
I have praised queens through half the world, the same
words. And what do they do but begin cursing her and
calling out something about a tax. She's some sort of a devil
it seems. I go on praising her, for John Battleaxe paid me
for an hour, and then they leave off abusing her and begin
abusing me. And then they begin throwing stones at me,
and mud. I hardly got away with my life. I wish I had turned
tinker or seine maker. This woman must be a devil.
Lord, how they hate her!

The Player (*who sits stitching, sings*). Good days and bad days
and all days pass over.

Yellow Martin. Where's Bridget? It's time to get ready for the

play. But 'twill be a poor audience I'm thinking. Where is
Bridget? Tell her I want her. No, I will put on St. Michael's
clothes and be ready for the prologue, and get off these
muddy rags. Tell her to wait me here.

Peter. She cannot be found anywhere.

Y.M. Not found! Not found! O my God, what has happened
to her? She has hidden herself, drowned herself maybe.

Peter. She will come back when she is hungry.

Y.M. You don't know what she is capable of. She is capable
of killing herself that she might look up through the roots of
the grass and see my misery.

Peter (*sings*).

> Woman's delight is the death of her best-beloved
> Who dies in tears and in sighs.

Y.M. Here am I all out of my mind, and you sing your verses
at me. Is there nothing in life that you do not take as a
game?

Peter. Because I take all things lightly, I am master of all.
(*Stands up, puts his arm on poet's shoulder affectionately.*)
If you would only listen to me. Here am I with all my
trifling, with my empty head, and I have won and tired of
half a dozen women while you were losing one. Love is an
art—a science if you will. You treat it as if it were the
inspiration of Heaven. Why do you not give way to her a
little, pretending to think her right when you know she
is wrong?

Y.M. But she wants to play a part that she can't play, and
that nobody wants if she could play it. Such a wild part.
I must not let her hurt herself. Love is a part of wisdom.
I have to bring her mine, my wisdom. How else can we be
the two halves to make one perfect whole?

Peter. No no, love is not a part of wisdom, but of gaiety and
folly. My dear Martin, it is we light lovers who understand
love. We make of ourselves what a woman wishes.

Y.M. But I wish her to be all the perfection I can imagine,
and would be no less myself.

Peter. Seem a little, play a little. If you are jealous try to
seem trustful and happy. If you are full of gloom because
she was cross with you, seem lighter than a swallow. If you

think her foolish pretend that she is wisdom itself.

Y.M. But I love, and she would not think me worthy of her love if I did not show myself strong enough to be her master.

Peter. But only we who love lightly, keeping always our gaiety, are masters. Love masters you and so you are despised.

Y.M. But I love her; what else can I do?

Peter. Ah, that is just the trouble (*He sings.*)

 Never jealous, never sad
 We that love lightly
 Are loved by the fairest
 And loved the most truly.

Y.M. There's somebody coming.

Peter. John Battleaxe. He went off to get gold for the treasury. This is a rich house. We should get rich pay here.

(*John Battleaxe comes in with men who carry bags of gold.*)

John Battleaxe. Come, you two there, help and put this money into the cellar; quick, put it out of sight. What a treasure. I never thought to see the like. Quick! Quick! This yard must be empty when the Queen comes. (*He stops the young actor. The others go into the house.*) No, you mustn't go with them; I wouldn't have you looking at so much gold. There is too much life in your eye. Who knows what dreams it will put into your head? Why, when I look at it I want to be king. It would set you dreaming of some fair lady all silk and satin. There, go to the gate and close it when the Queen has come.

Peter. Is the Queen coming, sir? I have never seen the Queen.

J.B. Why, how could you? She's been shut up in her cell at the convent of ——— [WBY's blank]. But now that her father is dead she has to come out and show herself like another. Get you gone now and make yourself ready for the mysteries. What are you waiting for? This Queen is no young man's dream. A saint, boy, a saint. That is why she has so much gold. It's the reward of Heaven. What are you waiting for?

Peter. Something very strange, sir. I think that I heard a voice singing up in the air.

J.B. What do you mean? What voice?

Peter. I cannot tell; it was very faint. I should have said it
   was the voice of someone that I know.

J.B. You're dreaming. Away with you. Ghosts do not sing in
   daylight. Here is the Queen. (*Peter goes out, but not into
   house. He goes out where Winnie has gone.*)

J.B. Your Majesty is welcome to this house, now for the first
   time since your father's death.

Queen (*to her ladies*). Leave us. (*They go out through the
   gate.*)

J.B. My soldiers wait a little way along the road to guard your
   majesty upon a further way. We are alone. No one can
   overhear us. I have much to urge upon you. The times
   are desperate.

Queen. Hush!   30

Minister. This new tax has roused the people to fury. If we
   would make them loyal . . .

Queen. Hush!   32

Minister. We must shake that crown of yours before their
   eyes.

Queen. Hush, hush I tell you.

Minister. Make their eyes drunken. There's nothing like a
   drunken eye for loyalty.

Queen. Hush, hush! Listen. Yes, there again. I am certain
   that I heard it. Somebody sang very low.

Minister. But where?

Queen. In the big vat.   40

Minister. A dream, your Majesty. Who'd climb up there?
   That is the wine vat. There is a channel from it to the
   fountain in front of the castle, and tomorrow at the rejoicings
   we shall fill the vat with wine, that the fountain may
   spout wine.

Queen. But I am certain.   43

J. B. I'll climb and look, though Time has made me   44
   stiff.   45

Queen. You would find nothing. I think it is some ancient   46
   spirit. There should be many in a yard like this.: Perhaps
   it has been sent to warn me that I should have stayed at my
   prayers.

J.B. You fast and pray too much; it makes one timid.   50

A Voice (*without*). Where are you, Noah's wife?   53

Queen. That is a different voice. It is calling a   54
   most ancient spirit.   55

Voice (*nearer.*) Where are you, Noah's wife?   56

Queen. Oh God, have mercy.

[OPPOSITE THE ABOVE IS THIS NOTE]

I don't think I can use this incident as it is forestalled
by the earlier part of the exposition.

[DRAFT CONTINUES]

(*Winnie passes in the background calling,* "Where are you,
   Noah's wife?")

[OPPOSITE]

Winnie passes along the battlements behind.

[DRAFT CONTINUES]

Queen. Some strange thing is going to happen. I should never
   have left the convent. This yard is a terrible place. I never
   saw a spirit before. It is true, do you think? My nurse used
   to tell me that things change their shape in this yard.

J.B. 'Tis but a stage player. One of those who will play the
   mystery play called "The Deluge." She is looking for some
   other player.

Queen. A stage player in a   76
   fountain flowing with wine? No good will come of it.   77
   It was for this, it was for all this sin that I was
   brought out of my cell. Had my father but lived, I
   should have lived there preparing my soul for Heaven
   till I died.

J.B. The need is desperate. I could not help myself. I have
   ordered great rejoicings.

Queen. Stage player in a fountain flowing with wine. The
   times must indeed be desperate to justify all that.

J.B. Only these rejoicings and your majesty's most gracious
   presence can save us. The crown itself is threatened.
Queen. What wickedness!
J.B. The people are about to break out in riot or in worse.
   It is all because of this new tax.
Queen. The tax is just. I only thought of it after much
   prayer. It is the most just tax sovereign ever laid upon a
   people. No man's house or labour is taxed. No good man
   is taxed at all. But men are taxed for the sins they commit.
   The cup of ale that stirs the blood too much; a whole
   guinea for a lawless kiss, and only copper and small
   silver money for sinful but more natural indulgences, and
   no tax gatherers, but only good priests and monks to make
   out a list of sins and collect the taxes.
J.B. Your people say that sin costs so much they have
   no money for bread. And so great is the discontent
   that many of the soldiers have gone over to the people.
   But if your majesty will smile in the marketplace,
   I think that all may be well. They loved your father;
   make them love you too, and they will let you do what you   112
   please. A piece of cloth, a bit of damask, a smiling
   face, a habit of bowing right up from the ankles and
   not from the waist only, some words of love to those
   you have never seen and may never see again, a little   116
   wearing of the mask, that is all I will have of you. If   117
   you would win obedience, you must seem all the   118
   greatness your people dream of, all that they would
   be if they could, the might of soul their shivering hearts
   deny to them, the wealth their indolence has denied to them.
   All this you must somehow express by the way you stand,
   by the way you smile, by a certain intonation in your voice.
   It is all quite easy; perhaps an hereditary knack. Your
   majesty understands me.
Queen (*who has been squatting crouched up on the doorstep*).
   Sir, I will go to my prayers again, for I would sooner be
   respected for what I am than cajole them with pomp and
   show. It is a lifelong labour to find out what one is. But
   when one has found it there is nothing left but to confess

one's sins. You have made me do many and many a worldly
thing that I hate. But this I will not do. No, you cannot
persuade me to it. I will go pray.

J.B. Then, your majesty, I lay down my office. I was your
father's servant and he left me to be your servant. But
when I can no longer guard your crown, it is time that I
leave the task to another.

Queen (*who has got up*). What am I to do? I wish I had
never been born to live this empty and showy life.

J.B. I see that your majesty will come with me, that you
will show yourself in the market-place, that you will show
your confidence by going amongst your people as if you did
not fear them. I only pray that it may not be already too late.

Queen. Some player with a painted face were better for your
work, some mere painted mask.

J.B. To be great we must seem so. Seeming that goes on for
a lifetime is not different from reality. (*They go out.
Player Queen puts out her head out of the vat. She sings a
song founded upon the following thoughts.*)

[NOTES FROM THE OPPOSITE PAGE]

Query. This scene wants simplification. Should not the
Queen's pose be simply to show herself brave when she is
not, graciousness being merely an expression of this courage?
This would give her a positive emotion throughout, fear, and
the Prime Minister a more decided thing to seeing an
emotional point of view and one that would lead up to the
Player Queen's speeches later on. All fine manners would
be expounded by the Prime Minister as the expression of
courage. He could not do these things himself. He has not been
born to them, which would give a contrast between his
diffidence and the diffidence of the poet. No one would
listen to the poet, he thinks, if he were to attempt certain
themes and so on. It would, however, make the Prime Minister
the reasoner of the play. His character would have to be
wisdom; his entrance would have to be led up to to make the
audience expect wisdom. Query, would it make him too
important? Who else can be the reasoner? Query, the Player—
is he enough in the plot?

[DRAFT CONTINUES]

[*Player Queen.*]
   / 164 I would know who you are
   My beloved / 165 said to me
   Put off that mask of burning gold
   That mask with emerald eyes
   That I may know who you are
   I will not / 167 put away my mask.
   It is the mask of burning gold
   It is the mask with emerald eyes
   That makes your heart beat so / 169 quickly,
   I would be praised by the beating of your / 170 heart.
   But my beloved answered me
   I do not know / 171 if you are a friend or if you are
        an enemy.
(*Enter at back Player and Winnie.*)

Player. We are quite alone here. You said that when I had   172
   finished the coat Noah's wife is to wear you would   173
   give me a kiss.

Winnie. No, I did not. And besides then I was asleep.

Player. But a sleeping kiss is only half a kiss, being all upon
   one side. And there is the coat; don't prick yourself with
   the scissors. They are folded up in it.

Winnie (*she keeps him off with the scissors*). I will give you
   the kiss if you will go down to the town and see what is
   happening. They have begun shouting again, louder than
   ever.

Player. As you will. I shall be back in time to play Raven, for
   I don't come in till the end.

Winnie (*still keeping scissors out in front of her*). I will
   give you three kisses, but not here but outside, outside
   where no one can see us. I have something to say, something
   very important. But Peter, will she ever be found do you
   think? Has she thrown herself into some pond?

Peter. She might maybe go to the brink of the pond, or maybe
   go to the muzzle of a gun and make all the faces of despair
   that she knew of. That's what she'd do and that's all she'd
   do. (*Enter Y.M. just as they are going out.*)

Y.M. Winnie, Winnie, have you found her?

Winnie (to Player). I'll tell you what it is later on.
   (*He goes out.*)
Player Queen (seeing Yellow Martin). Martin, I've had such an
   uncomfortable night of it.

[NOTE FROM OPPOSITE PAGE]

Alternative scene. Player enters sewing coat. Player Queen
sees him and cries "Peter, Peter!" Peter then says, "Look at
that and that. Scratches I got in the briars." Player Queen says,
"Come nearer. I don't want to be overheard. I've something to
ask you. Ah, what is it Peter in you that makes one long to
confide in you? I have been hiding here all night. 'Tis a hard
bed to sleep in. Is Martin near? I don't want him to see
me." Peter answers, "He cannot be far off; he is searching the
whole place like a wild creature. I swear by this." Player
Queen (*playing with Peter's hair*). "How can a woman be
happy who is not loved, and he does not love me, Peter. Oh, I
wish someone would carry me away out of this! I am for the
first man that carries me away. He never does anything I ask,
and makes me act such odious things, and is so gloomy. You
would let me play anything I liked, I know you would."
Peter says, "That is because he loves you too well to be
masked with his love. His love is greater than him, and that
fills him with sorrow. And does not the proverb say that it
is the sweetest fruit on which the worm feeds?" Player
Queen says (*drawing him closer to her*), "Peter, I am
longing to be loved, and by someone who would be merry,
always merry, and let me do what I please." Peter says,
"Then choose a light lover, lady." (*Sings.*)

   True love makes one a slave
   Less than a man;
   The light lover is always love's master
   So much the more is he man.

No. 2 Player. "Who refused to flirt on the pounds [?] don't
prey on wolves." They are the same sort. He and she take life
as a game; the others take it as a trade. Besides, if she made
Yellow M. jealous there would be a duel. Y.M. might kill
him, and if he killed Y.M. she herself would kill him. "Ah,

(*There is a step.*) Let me go. What a devil you are, Bridget.
You wanted to make him jealous." (*Enter Yellow Martin.*)
Y.M. "Now we will begin the mystery."

[PLAYER QUEEN CONTINUED, AFTER "NIGHT OF IT"]

These boards are hard.
Y.M. Oh, my poor child!
Player Queen. But Martin, there have been such beautiful
   young men playing musical instruments in the yard. They
   are the young men who are going to wait upon the Queen.
Y.M. There is not one word of truth in what you are saying.
   They are all old men and old women here, I have seen
   them all. They have speckled shins with bending over the
   fire. (*She sinks down into vat singing* "A friend or enemy.")
   O, do come down, do come down, dear. Here is your dress
   for Noah's wife. Why do you not answer me? There will be
   a great crowd here in a minute or two. The stage is ready,
   John Battleaxe has engaged us to play to the people. Won't
   you answer? If you'll play for me I'll promise you something.

[NOTE ON OPPOSITE PAGE]

Query? Note. Use vat to utmost as dramatic incident. How
can it be used? He can look down into it; they can sit on the
two ends of it. She can put her head up and down, etc.

[DRAFT CONTINUES]

(*She puts her head up again.*)
Player Queen. You promise?
Y.M. Yes, I've thought it all out when I heard you couldn't
   be found.
Player Queen. You won't ask me to do it again? (*She jumps
   down.*) O, I am stiff. (*Stretching herself.*) But nothing
   matters now that you are going to let me do what I want.
Y.M. O no, I didn't say that.
Player Q. But you said you'd promise.
Y.M. I'll promise not to let Noah beat you because you won't
   go into the Ark. I know he doesn't hurt you, but you don't

like being beaten before the audience. He can shove you instead.

Player Q. O Martin, let me once, only this once, play that part you told me of, the play you wrote when you were a young man, or write me one of those parts you told me about that you still sometimes think of. Those great queens, Herodias, Queen of Sheba, and that Queen of Babylon. Why must I go on playing in an ugly dress as an ugly old woman, and speaking words no better than I use myself when I'm ordering the dinner?

Y.M. My dear, that would be quite impossible. Nobody cares for such things. Maybe it was different long ago. None of them have ever seen, or met anyone who has ever seen, a great king or queen speaking splendid words and dressed in cloth of gold. They could never realize it.

Player Q. But you and I will make them. Dear, listen to me. (*They begin to walk up and down, she with her arm round his neck.*) I have learned a great deal, learned from you, learned from Peter too. I know what men of genius say when they talk to one another, all that mysterious philosophy.

Y.M. No no, I have to think of everyone's good, what you can do and what I can do.

Player Q. I remember your own words, what you said the other day. I know that you were timid about your own thoughts, and nothing seems true that we find out for ourselves. Only the most delicate mind can discover the truth, and that mind is always hesitating. The truth comes to us like the morning lost in clouds, hesitating; that we are only confident about the ideas of others. But there must be people like me to take up your thoughts, to believe in them because they are not our own, to put them on our faces like a mask.

Y.M. It is easy to see you want something from me when you remember my words so well.

Player Q. Let me become all your dreams. I will make them walk about the world in solid bone and flesh. People looking at them will become all fire themselves. They will change; there will be a last judgment in their souls, a burning and dissolving. Perhaps the whole age may change, perhaps the

whole age may learn. It is only by continual struggle, by
continual violence we force the gates of Heaven. That
no one is worthy of art, worthy of love who's not always
like those great kings and queens in soul and body, like a
runner, like a racer.

Y.M. (*who has stood still watching her enthusiasm*). My dear
child we should all starve.

Player Q. Starve because we bring them instead of poor
miserable words as common as the mud of the roads, words
like [word undeciphered] birds, and instead of thoughts
about going here and there, of buying and selling, thoughts
about dull business, the meditations, the chaos that our
souls are immortal.

Y.M. No no, I am older than you and I know what the people
want. They want Noah's wife and characters of that kind.
Aren't they just like her themselves? She won't go into
the Ark. Is she not just like themselves, tame and quiet
and peaceable, and her thoughts on household things. I mean
after she's been beaten. What are you doing?

Player Queen. I am going into the vat once more.

Yellow M. Then we are all ruined. In a little while the
audience will gather. There will be no play. Perhaps they
will attack the play, and John Battleaxe will be angry.

Player Q. Do not be afraid. I shall make everybody happy. In
a little while they will bring the cakes and wine. They
will pour them into the vat. They will not see me. I shall
turn into wine and flow through the pipes and everybody
will get drunk.

Yellow M. But it is ruin. I can never show my face again
anywhere. Do you not understand? This is a great festival,
the coronation almost, and if I do what you want me we
are ruined all the same. We shall become like Tom the
Fiddler; he would sing no song that did not please him.

Player Queen. Yes, like Tom the Fiddler; that's what I want.

Yellow M. And there he goes in rags, and the women take
the clean clothes off the hedges when they see him passing
by. But no no, I'll never give in to you, I will break up the
company. We shall all take to other trades. I shall eat
fire at a fair. What a life! And Peter, oh, he'll take purses

on the highway, I know he will. And what'll become of
you? And as to Winnie, think of her Bridget. What good
can she come to?

Winnie (*who has just come in with Peter*). I understand you,
Yellow Martin. What Peter can't get from the rich
merchants by violence I am to get out of them by love.
But no, I have no fancy for that life.

Y.M. She is ruining us all.

Winnie. No, I prefer to choose my men for myself. I don't
want men who go all out of shape from sitting all day on
a stool. That being so I prefer my present way of life. Give
me that dress.

Y.M. What are you going to do?

Winnie. Play Noah's wife myself if she won't. I've learned
every word of it.

Player Queen. You! You dare to do that?

Winnie. Well, you see the fate he has prepared for me if I
don't. O Peter, help me.

Player Q. Give me that dress! Go to your rich merchants if
you like. What else are you fit for? I am going to play
this part.

Yellow M. So you've changed your tune now?

Player Q. I will have no one come between you and me.

Winnie. You wouldn't play it to please Martin, and now you
play it to keep me from getting a chance.

Player Q. Go away, I shall find my own way of making
Martin do as I want. Quickly; go behind the curtain. Call
the others out of the castle. All get into your costumes.

Winnie. She's going to strike me!

Yellow M (*who has gone to the door*). Quick, quick. Get
into your costumes. What are you dancing for? The crowd is
beginning to come.

Player Q. (*beginning to dance*). I strike you! Am I not beaten.
I am the most patient beast in the world. (*She dances on the
robes of Noah's wife.*)

Yellow M. Here is somebody. Quick, what are you doing there?
(*An Old Man puts his head round the corner of the door
and says.*)

[*Old Man.*] May I come in? I saw the deluge; I saw the
flood rise.

Peter. It's old mad John that wanders the country.

Mad John. No priest, no brother. Then I may come in. Dancing, dancing. That's right. That's right. They all danced before the deluge. No no, it was the waves that danced. They all rose; they all danced. Up, up, up they came. (*He keeps time with his arms while she dances.*)

Yellow M. Go, go, get into your dress. (*She goes up steps posturing, finishes dance on platform, and goes behind curtain.*) [This is marked with a ?] There, there, get into your costume. You go, Winnie, too; get into yours. But first send the other players to us. Ah, here they come, ravens, doves, Noah's sons. Get dressed, get dressed. I will blow the trumpet.

[THIS PAGE HAS BEEN CROSSED LIKE AN OLD LETTER. HERE IS WHAT I CAN DECIPHER.]

Possibly Player Queen should first declare herself Noah's wife with mock praises of the character and do her dance on the platform so as to get a better exit. She might say, "Ha, I am Noah's wife today, patient and beaten. Tomorrow I shall cut off heads (*with threatening gesture to Winnie*). I shall be Queen of Babylon." Her dance could then start with a movement of triumph, or with a movement as if she were crowning herself. During her dance when she thinks of herself as queen she might, if not dancing on platform, motion Winnie back from her. Winnie would shrink away. In this case Player Queen will announce beforehand that when queen she would banish Winnie.

[DRAFT CONTINUES]

Player Queen (*puts her head out through the curtain*). But next time, Martin, you will let me play Herodias, or the Queen of Sheba, or a queen of Babylon.

Y.M. Keep your head in. None of you must be seen till you are in costume. (*Blows trumpet.*) You a queen! What do you know of queens?

Player Queen. There are a hundred queens inside my ribs.

Yellow Martin (*blows trumpet*). Put in your head. You've eaten off pewter and brown earthenware.

321

Player Queen. That is why I long for Babylon and Nineveh,   324
    a hundred horsemen and golden armour, a great silver   325
    chariot on men's heads upon great silver spears.

Yellow M. (*blowing trumpet*). You a queen, whose father
    spent his life hedging and ditching?

Player Queen. That is why I hunger for cloth of gold and
    a multitude to see my straight back and my high head.

Martin (*blowing trumpet*). There is too much of that high head.   327
    Here is the audience coming. Keep it out of that.
    O, that I had the courage to break it once in a while.
    (*Player Queen keeps her laughing face thrust through
    the curtain. The audience begins to arrive.*)

Act II

(*Scene as before. Few old peasants and countrymen.*)

Winnie. Is it worth beginning with an audience like this,
    and Bridget in such a mood? Who knows what she may
    say or do?

Yellow M. What a day of ill luck. But I never broke faith yet.
    Ah, here is somebody else. (*A gaunt old man comes in
    saying* "Is there any priest here or any monk?" *He is met
    with a general cry from the country people* "Not one!
    Not one!")

Winnie (*who has gone to the gate*). There is not a soul on
    the road. We have no larger audience than we see here.

Madman. We are few, but we are holy. The wickedness of
    the world has left us. Let the flood pass over all the rest.

A Peasant. Begin the play, sir; you'll have no more than us
    here. I wouldn't have come myself if my sins hadn't left
    me these ten years.

Another Peasant. I've brought a present for the players. Look
    into my basket, sir. Butter and eggs and a fat chicken. I
    never saw a play in my life. I would not have come
    but for that. How can we live without sinning?

One of Queen's Servants. Do not be afraid, neighbour; you
    needn't be looking at those windows. There's not a man
    left in the house now we are out of it. Still less a priest
    or a monk. Don't leave us without the play, sir. I saw one
    once; it was all about Abraham.

Madman. First everything has to be swept away. Abraham
comes after. But there is more in this flood than one
can see at a glance. Listen to me, neighbours. It's not
now altogether a natural flood. It's natural and it's more than
that. (*He goes about among the crowd trying to get
somebody to listen to him. They break away when he tries
to speak to them.*)

Woman. Go away, Michael. There's a penny for you.

Michael. There's mysteries in this flood. There's secrets
in this flood.

An Old Man. Look, he's putting on his dress as an angel.
Those are the wings he has in his hand. He goes up on
that platform there and then the play begins. The Flood
comes out of that door over there. The Flood's got a
trident and a long beard.

Mad Michael. Before the flood men were spirits, nothing but
spirits. But afterwards they had bodies. The flood of space
and the flood of time they call it. Those that were drowned
did not die. No, no. They were the people that became like
the beasts, a multitude of things. They changed, they change,
they change always. But those in the Ark now, they do
not change, oh no.

Another Man. And who's going to play Noah? (*During this
scene players with various properties in their hands cross
from the castle to behind the curtain.*) I never like to know
who plays this part or that part. I like to think there is the
angel himself, and Noah himself. I am just like Mad Michael
when the play begins.

Another Man. I saw this play once, and I was angry with Noah's
wife when Noah began to beat her as I am with my own.

A Child. What are the players like, grandmother, when
they're not acting?

An Old Woman. Why just like you and me; what else would
they be like?

Old Man. I would not like to say that, ma'am. They don't
think the same thoughts as we think. How could they and
they letting on to be such good people and such grand people.
(*A man with a trident and a bundle containing a beard
crosses.*)

Mad Michael. The flood is rising, it is rising; a terrible
flood. 'Twill change the world.

Another Man. It must be queer to be so many different people.

Mad M. This flood now, the flood of space they call it, and
time and the body. A bad flood and a wicked flood it is.

The Man (*who has just spoken*). There's something for you,
Michael; go away. Yes, it must be a queer thing. One
would not know the name one had been christened by at
the end of it.

Mad M. The Angel, the Angel is going to speak. He will
tell us are we to be changed, are we to be drowned. That's
it, that's it, changed or drowned. O, there are secrets,
secrets, People of the Ark, now they are not drowned.
But all the rest, all changed, all turned into fish.

Y.M. (*who is dressed as Angel*). Listen neighbours, all of you,
to the tale of the great flood. God was angry because the
souls of men . . .

Peter (*who comes running into yard*). Stop! Stop the play.
The people are mad; they have broken out against the
Queen. They have pelted me with stones because they said
I was of her party. They began to pelt me the moment I
gave them her invitation.

Y.M. Silence, all of you.

Peter. I had to run for my life.

Y.M. Get your breath.

Peter. It is no use hiding in the house. I heard them say
"burn down the Queen's house, throw everything that
belongs to her into the flames." To the woods! Become
hares and rabbits. The leaves are too damp to burn.
(*Peasants, etc. troop out.*)

Mad M. (*going out*). I shall be the flood! I shall be the flood
myself.

Another. Have they murdered the Queen do you think?

Mad M. I will rise up, up.

Another. Come, come, old man. That crowd from the town will
like you no better for being too holy.

Another. Quick, quick! I see them at the bottom of the hill.
(*They go out.*)

Poet (to the players). Come back, come back! What, would
  you leave all this behind? The mob would tear it to pieces
  or burn it out of mere lightness of heart. Quick, quick!

Peter. And murder us out of that same lightness of heart if
  we stop.

Y.M. Put that on your shoulder, and that on yours. Let the raven
  lie there. I made him out of an old black coat of mine.
  But hoist up onto your backs the heads of the doves.
  Begone now and put them out of sight somewhere. (*All the
  players except Winnie, Y.M., and Bridget go out.*)

Y.M. (to Winnie). Put down those scissors; take up that trident
  and wig. I will bring the angel's wings and God almighty's
  beard. My God! Who has locked us in?

Player Q. I have locked the door. Neither you nor   194
  I nor that woman there will go through the door till I
  please.   196

Yellow M. Give me the key.   197

Player Q. Come a step nearer and I will throw it   198
  over the wall.   199

Y.M. For God's sake, let us open the door.

Player Q. Not yet.

Poet. The people are mad with excitement. They will
  beat us and illtreat us.

Player Q. I will make them kill us if you do not promise
  what I am going to ask.

Y.M. I will if you ask nothing beyond my power. What
  you asked me today I could not give you.

Player Q. O, 'tis not that old thing that I should ask you now.

Yellow M. What new craze has come into your head?   208

Player Q. That you put this woman away.

Yellow M. She has done no wrong.   211

Player Q. She has come between you and me.   212

Y.M. Once rid of her you would do what you   213
  pleased with me. I will sit here and take my chance
  with the crowd. They will beat me, but you would ruin me.

Player Q. Then I will stand up there on that platform, and I
  will cry aloud the praise of the Queen until they kill
  us all.

I will say of her all that I have ever imagined of the 217
queens of Nineveh and Babylon. 218
Y.M. I too have a voice. I will tell them that we are people
like themselves, living by our trade as best we can.
I will tell them why you praise the Queen to their face. I
will tell them that you are crazy, and that you have planned
it all for vengeance upon another player.

[FROM THE OPPOSITE PAGE]

How is one to make the animosity of the mob plain to the
audience? Should they have already killed or ill-treated those
connected with the coronation festivals, over and above what
they have done to Yellow Martin? Is some incident visible
to the audience necessary?

[DRAFT CONTINUES]

Winnie. Promise whatever she asks; nobody will understand 221
you. How could they when we do not understand her
ourselves? She will make them think what she pleases.
Promise to send me away. (*She whispers into Y.M.'s ear.*)
Player Q. Ah, what are you whispering? To promise and 224
then to say you did it under compulsion so need not 225
keep. Promise that way if you like, Yellow Martin.
But I will have her bound by such an oath that if she
breaks it she will feel the Devil pulling her to bed
by the toes.
Winnie. O my God, O my God! Who would have thought 229
she was so wicked? Yes, yes, I will go away and never 230
come back, and dance for my living and turn juggler
and eat swords.
Y.M. Hush, hush, you little fool. I will not part with you 232
so easily. She will open the door before they come. (*He
puts his arm upon shoulder of Winnie to comfort her.*)
Player Q. Ah, now I understand. I have been blind. 235
You love her. You are making love to her under
my eyes.

[FROM OPPOSITE PAGE]

Perhaps at the very opening of the play Y.M. might come in hunted by a hooting crowd whose faces one might see for a moment through the little windows in the wall. But this would need some reconstruction. Or they might follow Queen and hoot her till they were driven away by John Battleaxe's soldiers.

[DRAFT CONTINUES]

Winnie. O never, never! He never did such a thing.

Player Q. Is that also told under compulsion?

Yellow M. You are trifling away the time with this wildness. Here are a hundred pounds worth of dresses, of costumes given to us by the Queen. You will have them all burned or torn to pieces.

Player Q. If I loved another's sweetheart, I would take him boldly. I would not lie about it.

Y.M. When have you seen me change about like a weathercock? When have I been false to you? Open that door.

Player Q. She's been trying to get you for months. Why else would she take my place, and a part like that too. If she didn't love you, why would she take it?

Winnie. But I swear . . .

Player Q. No need to whisper to him now that you don't need it. He knows.

Y.M. I will say no more. Keep the key. I will sit down here. Let them burn the clothes. Let them beat us if they like. What does it matter? There's no help for it.

Player Q. No, you can go. I care for nothing now. There is the key. But Martin, I never would have thought you would do this. I loved you so. "I will never change," you said.

Y.M. (*taking key and opening doo*r). There's no time for words, and I'm in little mood for it. You've gone too far this time. I will put this woman in safety. I will not have her suffer because of your folly. See to yourself. No, go your own way. The wood is wide. Or stay here if you have a mind to. (*Winnie and Y.M. go out.*)

Player Q. He is gone, he is gone! And 'tis all my own fault, and now I will never see him again. (*She takes up the scissors and holds it up as if she were going to kill herself. She may possibly sing a dirge over herself. The Queen comes in and shrinks back from the uplifted scissors.*)

The Queen. O, do not kill me. I will give you money—anything you ask.

Player Q. It was not you I thought to strike, but another.   270

[FROM OPPOSITE PAGE]

Note—Make Yellow M. angry earlier? Should there be a side gate for the wood, or two side gates, one going to the town, one going to the wood, or should one even reverse the whole scene, making it like the scene in a Greek play with the palace in the background? Note. Possibly the Queen in her entrance in Act I should come in trembling, having been hooted by the people.

[DRAFT CONTINUES]

The Queen. Then it was to protect me. But what could one do? I will call my servants.

Player Q. They have all run away.   273

Queen. Then let us shut to this big door. The mob was close   274
behind me. I could see their spears.

Player Q. No, no, they would break it down. No use going that way either. You are the Queen.

The Queen. Yes, yes, they are going to kill me.

Player Q. No use hiding in there. No wood will cover you, no cave will hide you. They will search till they are certain thay have got you.

The Queen. O my God!

Player Q. But I will save you. Listen. I have often thought to myself, ah, if I could be but a queen, even for an hour, I would be happy. Put on this old cloak and give me yours and that crown.

The Queen. But they will kill you.

Player Q. I will tell you a secret. It was for myself I was   297
getting ready that knife.

The Queen. O, how wicked. The church says we must not do   298
    that. Was it love?   299

[END OF DRAFT]

Commentary

Draft 12 is in many ways a new beginning: the character names are partly new, the multiple approach to the problem of the relation of mask to face is an extension of the idea that an actress makes a better queen than a born queen, and many of the plot formulas to which we have become accustomed are altered. Again I sense a slow shift of tone toward the comic mode, for example in the opening exchange between Peter and Yellow Martin.

The loose sheets of scenario inserted in the manuscript seem to have been written before the draft, for their matter is included in it. This is the plan to have Septimus (*Yellow Martin*) and Peter find the Player Queen and to give to Septimus the arguments urging the Player Queen to return to the role of Noah's wife. The notes opposite page 1 of Draft 12 (cf. p. 120) are not worked into the draft that follows. They have to do with Peter's mask: should he pretend to be brave, though actually he is a coward, or, another possibility, should he pretend to perpetual good nature whereas actually he is irascible? Yeats does nothing with either idea.

Act I opens with Nona (*Winnie*) on stage, working on the costume of Noah's wife. Peter enters with clothes torn and mud-stained in an unsuccessful search for the hidden Player Queen—an incident used previously in Draft 11. Nona is thinking of taking the part of Noah's wife, but says that Septimus would never let her. Peter encourages her to take it, and they discuss the latest quarrel between Septimus and the Player Queen. They see Septimus approaching, and Nona asks Peter to finish the Noah's wife costume—she doesn't want to make a dress for the Player Queen. Septimus comes in with his clothes torn and mud-stained like Peter's; we learn that he has been attacked by the angry townsmen while praising the Queen. Yeats is slowly moving toward an opening scene in the town which he will put into Draft 16 and which is still found in the finished play. We soon find that the similarity of appearance of Septimus and Peter, their torn and muddy clothes, is appearance only; they are completely unlike. Septimus learns of the disappearance of the Player Queen, but we are spared talk about his weak heart. That theme from Draft 11 has been dropped. Peter makes his first statements about the nature of love as he conceives it, a passing fancy that should be taken lightly: "Because I take all things lightly, I am master of all," and, later, "Love is not a part of wisdom, but of gaiety and folly."

The Prime Minister (*John Battleaxe*) enters with the gold produced by the new taxes and announces that the Queen will arrive shortly. Her father's recent death has forced her out of seclusion. Peter, taking the place of the soldiers in earlier drafts, hears the voice of the hidden Player Queen who is singing from the vat. The Queen enters. The Prime Minister urges upon her the necessity of playing the role her birth has allotted her for the good of the state. Nona comes in looking for the Player Queen; her exchange with the Queen and Prime Minister has nearly reached the form it has in Draft 16. After Nona goes out, the Prime Minister reemphasizes his argument that the Queen must play her part, ending with a statement that is pure Yeats: "To be great we must seem so. Seeming that goes on for a lifetime is not different from reality." The idea of the mask is in the process of becoming the concept of the Self and the Anti-self. The Queen and the Prime Minister leave for the progress into the town. Yeats dictates a criticism of the scene just finished, exploring the idea that the Queen, too, become a masker. Though fearful, she is to pretend to courage. He wonders whether he might make the Prime Minister the reasoner of the play, or perhaps assign that role to Septimus.

The Player Queen sticks her head up out of the vat and sings "The Mask," already worked on in Drafts 3, 6, and 8. Peter and Nona come in. He has finished the dress for Noah's wife and gives it to Nona with a scissors wrapped up in it—a new device for getting that necessary property on stage. Nona is sending him to town to find out what is going on, a scene kept in Drafts 15 and 16, though the name Peter is not used in 15. Nona kisses him and he goes off to town. Septimus comes in and finds the Player Queen; but before going on to that, a note from the opposite page should be dealt with, a plan for an "alternative scene." Here Yeats has Peter find the Player Queen, who makes love to him most outrageously with the purpose of arousing Septimus's jealousy. Yeats did not work up this happy idea—"happy" because at the very outset it would demonstrate the Player Queen's bitchery. In passing we should admire Yeats's Homeric and operatic strategy of keeping the Player Queen's first entrance late.

During the scene that follows, the Player Queen has everything her own way. Septimus is sorry she has spent so uncomfortable a night. She pays no attention but tries to arouse his jealousy by describing the beautiful young men who wait on the Queen. Septimus knows her description is a total fiction; he has seen the Queen's attendants, all old men whose shins are speckled from sitting near the fire. Yeats uses this detail elsewhere in his work but here so far as I know for the first time. It occurs again at line 12 of *At the Hawk's Well*, composed in the winter and spring of 1915–1916, and in the 1934 *Collected Plays* Yeats put it into one of the songs in *A Pot of Broth* (line 268). [But see line 228 of *On Baile's Strand* in *Variorum Plays*, first appearing in *Poems*, *1899–1905* (London and Dublin, 1906). Gen. Ed.] It is a traditional sign of old age and the sedentary life. Yeats makes full use of the vat in which the Player Queen has hidden, a property of which we are already rather tired but which seemed to fascinate him. Septimus promises her something—he doesn't say what—and she, thinking he means she won't have to play Noah's wife again, jumps down. Septimus's promise refers only to a new piece of stage business: instead of Noah beating his wife he will shove her. They go on to discuss romance versus realism, and the Player Queen's speeches become very Yeatsian, as in "Only the most delicate mind can discover the truth, and that mind is always hesitating," and in the hope she expresses that a new way of art may change the age, a first apocalyptic hint in a play that was to become decidedly apocalyptic. Yeats's idea that art might change an age was as old as the 1890s, when he expressed it in many poems and stories, perhaps most clearly in his poem "The Secret Rose." Septimus insists on realism; given the tastes of the audience any imitation of Tom the Fiddler who "would sing no song that did not please him" would mean starvation for Septimus and his company. Nona overhears Septimus's prediction that Peter will become a highwayman and she a whore, and to save herself and the others from such a future she offers to play the part of Noah's wife. The Player Queen won't allow this and agrees to play, though she shows her contempt for the Noah play by dancing on her costume. Rat-hole in his new identity as Old Mad or Mad John, begun in Draft 11, enters and comments on the dance, and Act I closes with the Player Queen behind the curtain, sticking her head out between its two halves while Septimus threatens to break it with the trumpet he is blowing to summon the audience.

Act II. The audience that comes in response to Septimus's trumpet blasts is a poor one. The Rat-hole character is shortly added to it, and he and the audience discuss the flood, the nature of actors, and so on until Septimus begins his prologue. Peter runs in with news of the revolt against the Queen, and audience and players flee, leaving Septimus, Nona, and the Player Queen. Septimus is trying to save properties, an action derived from Draft 6 but elaborated here and kept in the finished play. The Player Queen locks them in; again, this action is first sketched in Draft 6, is worked up here, and forms part of the finished play. The Player Queen lets them go only when she becomes convinced that Septimus loves Nona. Septimus leaves with no promise of return to rescue the Player Queen, as in subsequent drafts. Decima threatens to kill herself with Nona's scissors—this is a new development, which will be kept—and the fleeing Queen enters. She thinks the Player Queen is threatening her but is soon reassured. The Player Queen is planning to change roles and clothes with the Queen when the draft breaks off.

In addition to all the new and changed business that Yeats invents in this draft, he is beginning to think seriously, in places almost philosophically, about his characters. This is new. Up to now Yeats has been almost exclusively concerned with working out his dramatic fable; his practice through many drafts has seemed to indicate that for him as for Aristotle plot was the soul of a dramatic work. Here he is rounding out his agents, so to speak, making us aware of different aspects of their characters. The characterization in *The Player Queen* is unusually brilliant, a point to which I shall return in my final consideration of the play.

CHAPTER EIGHT

Drafts 13 and 14

DRAFTS 13 and 14 were written in the same tablet, on the cover of which Yeats has written "Player Queen IV." This must mean that he conceived of it as the fourth version of the play, because the draft is not a sketch for a new fourth act. Though none of the surviving manuscripts is numbered, this is the fourth version of the play if we consider the "A" versions the first, the "B" versions the second, and the Peter versions the third. For once, the two drafts in the book are closely related, Draft 14 being made up of bits that fit into and expand Draft 13. Draft 14 can be dated approximately, for it contains notes for Yeats's preface to Synge's *Deirdre of the Sorrows:* Yeats dated the finished preface April 1910, so the draft must have been written before then. Both drafts are partial only, concerned with new conceptions of parts of an already existing play, or with the extension of old conceptions.

Yeats's most notable change results from his decision to have the play begin in town. He was moving in this direction in Drafts 11 and 12 in which Septimus comes in from the town with his clothes torn and mud-stained. There the Prime Minister has sent him to the town to praise the Queen, and her disaffected people have attacked him. Yeats now composes a scene set in town in which Septimus has an encounter with the mob. Here is the new beginning:

[At the head of the MS, a sketch of the scene. It seems to show the bases of three large columns spaced across the stage.]

A group of morris dancers, etc. in the shadow. They point out to one another the Queen's palace. They have never seen a queen. No one has seen her. Why are there no crowds? O, the crowds are in the market-place. Let them go there. No, they will get a better view where they are.

Act I. Scene 1.

[FOUR PAGES OF A CANCELED BEGINNING.
THEN SKETCH OF A STREET.]

A Street.

Townsman. The Queen is certain to pass this way.

2 Townsman. No, they say she will take the other way, the shorter way.

1 Townsman. We shall know soon enough by the shouting.

[A BREAK IN THE MS, THEN A NEW BEGINNING]

Countryman. We shall see her if we stand here.

2 Countryman. We shall see fine clothes. We shall see cloth of gold.

1 Countryman. We shall not then. My sister's child is horseman in the castle, and she says that the Queen of Surrico will wear nothing but the nun's dress she wore these ten years.

2 Countryman. I'd not believe that. Her father wore cloth of gold. I tell you it is law that a queen wear cloth of gold; the Chamberlain will see to that.

1 Countryman. "The Chamberlain will never get her to do it," says my sister's child, "clever man though he thinks himself."

2 Countryman. I'd not have come if I'd known that. But I'll not believe it. The Chamberlain will just spread out the dress, and he'll say, "Wear that. Your father when he was dying said you were to wear that," or some other thing he'll make up on the moment.

3 Townsman (*coming in hurriedly*). What are you doing here?

1 Countryman. Is it not this way the Queen comes when she goes from the castle to the market-place?

3 Townsman. Cannot you read that notice?

1 [*Countryman.*] No sir, we've had no schooling. We are countrymen.

2 Countryman. Will you not read it to us?

Townsman. "The silence of the people is the lesson of princes. Let the Queen of Surrico pass through your empty streets. Let no voice applaud her; let no head bow before her. By order. Tom of the Moon."

Countryman. And what kind is this Tom of the Moon?

Townsman. One who was chosen last night by the Guilds and given control of the people.

2 Countryman. I'd not like to go against the people, but could they punish us for not cheering?

2 Townsman. Take off your cap. It's Tom of the Moon you are
talking to.

1 Townsman. You're a fool, Mike. Do you want to have me
hanged or shot? This Queen until this day from her girlhood
up has not so much as shown herself to her people.

2 Townsman. But we'll give her a lesson this day.

1 Townsman. Silence!

2 Townsman. Let her be Queen or nun; let her choose.

1 Townsman. Were you or I chosen to speak for the people?
(*A murmur*) Three months ago the Old King died, and
what, I ask you, was the first act of this woman who had
been hidden from girlhood in her cell?

1 Countryman. She put the priests over us sure enough.

2 Countryman. Marriage costs half a year's profit.

1 Countryman. And to die is sheer ruin.

1 Townsman. And now a tenth of all our wealth has been taken
from us to build a shrine of gold and alabaster for St.
Winifred. We may go naked, but the dead saints shall
have good clothes.

2 Townsman. St. Winifred is the worst robber of all.

Countryman. Maybe now a saint's prayers would serve us well,
for we have had the blight up my way these three years.
But I'd not go against the people.

2 Countryman. Nor I either. We live in a lonely spot, sir,
and who knows what man might set our thatch alight?

Townsman. Then we are all true men. (*They shake hands.*)
Let her pass in silence. There is no law to make us shout.
(*They gather in a knot at one side of the stage. Three
priests, dressed rather like Spanish priests, come in,
followed by soldiers with bags on their backs.*)

Soldier. Make way, make way there in the Queen's name.

1 Townsman. What holy relics do you carry to the castle today?

2 Townsman. It's the money for St. Winifred's altar—a tenth
of all we have.

1 Townsman. No, no, they have saints bones; they have robbed
some cemetery of saints.

Soldier. Way, in the Queen's name.

1 Townsman. No, we'll not make way until we [hear] the
blessed names of those you carry on your backs.

2 Townsman. It's the tenth of all we have.

1 Townsman. Blessed relics, blessed relics. The flesh is wild, but there's no dishonest laughter from dry bones, nor have they kissed this long time.

Priest (*he and the soldiers have been whispering together*). Friends, will you not let us pass? We are peaceful men, we but do the Queen's business. And this day of all days.

Townsman. This day of all days, I tell you, that the flesh we have still upon our bones, this dying lazy lecherous flesh shall work its miracles too.

Priest. Sir, you talk sedition and blasphemy.

Townsman. Read what is written there, and then go tell your Queen what you have read, and tell her that you have besides a message from one you met on the way, from Tom of the Moon.

Priest. Sieze this man.

Townsman. Seize, but you cannot hold. (*The soldiers seize him and drag him off, followed by the people fighting with them; the two priests remain behind.*)

1 Priest. May God grant that they hold him. My nails are tired pulling down these notices. This is the seventeenth.

2 Priest. There'll be no more notices; they've done their work, I think. Did you see the look he gave when they took him?

1 Priest. He had an angry look.

2 Priest. Worse than that. I am getting an old man now, and I've seen many quarrels between men and men, and the crowd's with them that are set over them. All's but grumbling for a long time and then something happens, and the knives are out.

1 Priest. O, this will pass over—a little stone throwing maybe.

3 Priest (*running in*). O, poor Father Peter.

2 Priest. What has happened?

1 Priest. Come away. He struck Father Peter with a knife, and Father Peter fell, and then before we could seize [him] he got into the crowd. But come, or they will kill us.

1 Priest. I saw it in his eyes. (*They go out as crowd enters.*)

Barach. Why did you let the money go? With that we could have bought over the soldiers.

Countryman. This is a hanging business.

Barach. Yes, it's hanging, or it's our rights back again and
   our money in our pockets. There's no turning now. That's
   a little thing to send the spirit out of you.

2 Countryman. You think we are fools because we're from the
   country and have no schooling.

Barach. You've some villainous lie in your throat.

2 Countryman. You worked this quarrel up on purpose.

1 Countryman. Do not go against the people, Tom.

Barach. I killed [him], if he is dead, to defend my own life.
   Would you live and see more, and I chosen for the work?

Townsman. Yes, you were chosen. You are a true man.

Barach. Is this mountainy man to tell lies, lies against me?

Townsman. No, no, we know you; you [are] a true man. But
   maybe we had best go hide before they send enough men
   to take us.

Barach. Then go back under the priests' rule. Let St. Winifred
   have her altar, one tenth of all your money.

Townsman. What would you have us do?

Barach. To the market-place; get all the guilds together [?]
   and there I'll tell you what to do. But this day there shall
   be an end made, and a change in the state. [From the
   opposite page] Did not Moses kill an Egyptian? I am
   your Moses; I will bring you back out of the house of
   bondage. (He should be made firm and heroic. Now they
   can trust him. He should proclaim the murder.)

Townsman. That's right—to the market-place.

(*Enter Yellow Martin with masks.*)

Yellow Martin. Come to plays, gentlemen. Come and honour
   the Queen and see great art. The story of Noah and [the]
   Flood to be performed this day in the Queen's honour in
   the great yard of the castle. Here now is old Noah's mask; he
   has lived a thousand years; and here is his wife and she
   had seven hundred; and here is the angel's mask, and he
   is eternal. They have been to the mask maker to be repainted.
   Now it stands to reason that they've wisdom, they have
   been so long in the world.

Barach. There must be no play this day in the Queen's honour,
   but get you to the market-place, and when this day's work
   is over . . .

Yellow Martin. What, to the market-place? Sir, queens are

more to my fancy. They have something over [?] dignity
when they know their trade.

Barach. There is a dead man between us and the Queen.

Yellow Martin. What have I to do with your disputes? Here
is my world. I am getting angry. I must speak to you in
earnest, I see, as becomes the united ages of those I carry—
seven thousand patient years. He that plays for kings or
queens or nobles has the chance of a wise man for patron, but
he that plays for the people has the certainty of a fool.

Barach. Do you call us fools?

Townsman. Come away; there has been enough trouble for one
day.

Barach. I'll have no man call the people fools. (*They seize
him.*)

Yellow Martin. I that have played before the Great Turk and
the Doge of Venice, and such words were never spoken
to me. But I can see it all.

Barach. I tell you, sir . . .

Yellow Martin. I can see it all. Some rascal, some dunce
that copies Seneca, has put you up to this—only worthy
to play in the market-place.

Townsman. Do not answer him. There has been enough
trouble this day.

Barach. He has called us fools. Well, let him. Neither him
nor any other shall call us fools when this day's work is
over. (*They go out.*)

Yellow Martin. Some lover of bombast has done this. O
gold-haired Apollo, when with fiery wheels I can hear
him. No, and Noah and Abraham for me.

[End of Scene 1]

On the opposite page under the heading "Rewrite on this
plan" Yeats wrote an outline of Scene 1 which introduces
more resistance by the Countrymen to the claims of Tom
of the Moon. Otherwise the outline is very like the scene just
written. No rewriting of Scene 1 according to this plan
has survived. Yeats then went on to write still another
opening of Scene 2 which drops the bringing in of the tax
money and has the Queen on stage when the curtain rises.

Act I. Scene 2

Queen standing by great window. She is in robes of state.
The Chamberlain comes in. He is silent. Bowing, he then
speaks.

Chancellor. Your Majesty. (*The Queen does not answer.*)
    Your Majesty, I have been told that you would speak to me
    before setting out.

Queen. Hush.   30

Chancellor. The soldiers are waiting to conduct your majesty.

The Queen. Hush.   32

Chancellor. I have still hopes that your father's memory, the
    crown and dress of state, all that they have been accustomed
    to bow before, the familiar symbols . . .

Queen. Hush, listen. Yes, there again. Someone is singing   36
    very low.   37

Chancellor. I think I hear it now, though I have not the   38
    hearing I once had. But who is it and where is it?   39

Queen. In the big vat there.   40

Chancellor. That vat is for the festival tonight. It is empty, but
    it is to be filled with wine.

Queen. There, again. I am certain.   43

Chancellor. I will climb and look, though Time has   44
    stiffened me.   45

Queen. No, you would find nothing. Have you ever heard,
    Chancellor, that ghosts walk in an old house like this?

Chancellor. I believe in no ghosts but those that [are]
    between men's ribs, pushing aside their own natural souls.

Queen. Yes, I have heard of those ghosts. When my father
    died there was an omen. One of the servants made a
    strange noise like a cock. I myself once heard a cock
    crowing out there—crowing in the foam of the sea.

A Voice. Where are you, Noah's wife?   53

Queen. Ah, that is a different voice. It is calling   54
    some ancient ghost.   55

Voice. Where are you, Noah's wife?   56

Queen (*clings to Chancellor*). Ah there, there again.   57

Voice. Where are you, Noah's wife?   58

Queen. O God have mercy. (*The Friend comes in. The*   59
    Queen has shrunk into the shadow.)

Chancellor. That name sounded strange; who are you calling?   60

Friend. Somebody stranger than the name, now   61

    one thing, now another, a joy and a torment. Where   62

    can she be? She is to play [in] an hour or so, and she cannot   63

    be found.   64

Chancellor. You are the troupe who came yesterday.

Friend. She cannot be found. We have searched everywhere,

    and she is such a good player. We are nothing without her,   69

    and Yellow Martin will be certain she has thrown

    herself into the sea.

Chancellor. Your manager?   71

Friend. Yes sir. He will be out of his mind with   72

    grief, for they are to be married. O, he has such a   73

    time with her, but I see you cannot tell me anything.   74

    Where are you, Noah's wife, where are you? (*Goes out.*)

Chancellor. The ghosts have gone, your Majesty. Many

    prayers have made you timid, and this shadowy place.

    Let us go out into the town among your people. Do not

    let us delay. But I had forgotten, your Majesty had

    sent for me.

Queen. May I take off this robe of state, this gold, this

    crown, these griffins and roses? I have renounced the world.

    Let me wear today as on other days the simple dress I

    wear in my cell.

Chancellor. You are a Queen.

Queen. But I have vowed to resemble St. Winifred in my life,

    and she was simple and humble.

Chancellor. She begged her way through the world and wore

    rags.

Queen. Ah, maybe if I did likewise I should be happier.

Chancellor. I see that we have not banished the ghosts. We

    are indeed, your Majesty, nothing without them. But the

    all important thing is that the right ghost is in our ribs,

    and you, your Majesty, need a queen in your ribs and not a

    saint. You have put crosses of gold and altarpieces full

    of precious stones into every church because you thought

    more of Heaven, but you should think rather of your

    kingdom, upon possessing the earth, and that being so

    must [wear] this gold, these griffins, these roses. You smile

on those that you have never seen and will never see again
as if you loved them. A little bowing from the knees down
and they will forgive you a thousand errors. You must
seem greater and kinder and wiser than woman ever was.

Queen. Cannot one save one's soul and be a Queen?

Chancellor. There is great discontent. I do not think even
the soldiers are to be trusted. The whole town is on the
edge of riot. Show yourself in a nun's habit, and they will
see in it a confirmation of their fears. They [will] look
for nothing but more taxes, for they will say if she does
not love the world, how can she love us?

Queen. Chancellor, I do not know what to say. A holy book has
said that it were better that the whole world should perish
than one sin should be committed. (*Going to window.*)
O blessed ones, you are in the still sky; it [is] with you only
that there is peace.

Chancellor. If your Majesty seeks martyrdom, I have no more
to say.

Queen. No, no, not that. I am not worthy. No, no, that
were presumption.

Chancellor. If today you play the saint, you die, and that
you say is presumption; but if you play the Queen you
will live and rule your kingdom.

Queen. I will go then, for it is a sin either way, but
if you were in my place could you play a part?

Chancellor. I need your help because no ghost has ever put
his toes into my shoes.

The draft breaks off, and on the opposite page Yeats writes a
note that seems to refer to Act III, Scene 1 as he was to develop
it in Draft 16. It is the only anticipation of that scene that I
have found: "Must be some earlier part. Allude to players
having forgot all their clothes." In III, 1, of Draft 16 the
company of players is waiting for the Player Queen to let down
their everyday clothes from a window of the castle. They had
forgotten them when they fled from the mob. The manuscript
continues with an expanded scene for the end of Act II as
that was developed in Draft 16. The Player Queen has just

changed roles with the real Queen when the Prime Minister and
soldiers return. This is her first try at queening.

Soldiers (*kneeling*). The Queen, the Queen.
Queen. Go with them someone and bring out all the money
    and heap it there at my feet. Go quickly; by your obedience
    I will judge if I am Queen indeed.
Chancellor. That is a good thought. That gold must be put in
    safety; with that we can make armies. But who are you?

[Then this note which seems to refer to another draft which
Yeats was following. The cue-in words "my Queen" are
not found in any surviving draft.] "After 'my Queen' read
'We have broken the crowd for a moment, but tomorrow
they will gather in greater power.' "

Soldiers. The money is the [word undeciphered].
Queen. Then go and bring it here. We'll out and scatter
    it about the city streets.
Chancellor. My God, what do you say? We need it all.
Queen. Yes, to scatter. I let you kiss my hand but now,
    and did you great honour, and already you disobey.
Chancellor. It is soon to talk of obedience.
Queen. Are you not my Chancellor?
Chancellor. You have some thought of bringing them round,
    you think, because they complain of the tax. How
    little you know them that you . . .
Queen. It may be that I have no thought but to be obeyed.
    What are you waiting for? I have given my orders.
Chancellor. Your orders! Let no man stir.
[*Soldiers.*] But sir . . .
Chancellor. For thirty years you have obeyed me in all.
Soldiers. My lord, she is the Queen.
Chancellor. A pretty Queen. Easy earned and easy spent;
    that is her way.
Queen. If you would speak some slander [?] upon us, I
    shall be forced, much as I honour your grey hair and long
    service, to order out of respect to the high place I hold . . .

Chancellor. You could order these to wait [?]. Good God, I
do believe the knaves would do it. (*Taking her arm.*)
What are you doing this for? You will spoil all, and it was
a good game, worth playing.

Queen. But there's a better. Have you been so long in the
world and not found that women love power?

Chancellor. You are laughing. You'd know how far your
power goes, that is all.

Queen. One has strange dreams in a cell. It is a turbulent
place.

Chancellor. But now that you have seen that they would
drown me like a blind puppy, you are content are you
not?

Queen. What is power if it [is] not that one may give?

Chancellor. So you would still scatter? What have I brought
upon myself. Well, for this day I must take the Queen
luck sends me.

Queen (*to Soldiers*). Let the Chancellor have his will. I
but wished to see if after all these years of piety, which I
must confess have vanished as a dream vanishes, I would
know if I'd obedient servants. Soldiers, you would obey,
would you not, in everything you would question; even
if it seemed against myself—to run myself in danger?

Soldiers. You are Queen.

Queen. Now you too. Will you not promise to do my will
in all, if it be not against the state?

Chancellor. In all, fair lady, that is not against the state.
There, hoist the bags upon your backs. We'll put [them]
in safety before the crowd has had time to gather again.
Quick. Your Majesty should go in the midst of us. Do not
delay; let us set out.

Queen. I stay here.

Chancellor. Alone? That is impossible.

Queen. I will close the great gates. I shall go up on the
battlements. I shall stand there alone. They will gather
round the walls. I will mock at them. You will come behind
their backs and fall upon them. They will cry out. I shall
be like some Queen of Babylon, some terrible queen.

Chancellor. They will burn the gates.

Queen. If they burn the gates, you shall have the longer to
gather a host.

[NOTE ON OPPOSITE PAGE]

Queen must go to her cell to pray.
Chancellor. But you, they may kill you.
Queen. They shall kill no Queen after me.
Chancellor. I'll not permit it.
Queen. But I command. It is not against the state.
Chancellor. Nor will they permit . . .
Soldiers. She must not remain alone. (*Murmurs.* "No, no.")
Queen. Then I will take off this crown and robe, for [I]
am not a Queen.
Chancellor. Well, have it your way, if you're so wild. Well,
so be it. March. We must return to save her Majesty.
Queen (*holding Chancellor back*). Tell me, is there anyone
with long yellow curls wandering around the castle,
outside the gate?
Chancellor. No one, lady.
Queen. He has not come back. He said he would come to look
for me. He has forgotten me.

Draft 14

This draft consists of bits from various parts of the play,
none of which duplicates material in Draft 13. Yeats begins
with a scenario for an opening of Act II as that appears in
Draft 16. It concerns Rat-hole:

> He should struggle to get past to enter castle. They should
> hold him back. Then one should say he knows who it is. They
> must shake him awake. They do this. Then old man asks what
> has he been doing? Who has been in him? A king. He should
> beg them not to let him go from them. He should describe
> what he feels [?]. They should shrink back. He begs them
> to hold him. Beat him if they like. It is terrible not to know
> who one is. They all shrink back till he is left alone.
> Then the trance falls on him and he begins to mutter
> about his daughter—what she should do.

Then, after a few speeches between the Friend and Yellow
Martin, in which she reports the finding of the Player Queen,
Yeats moves on to a new scene, which is unique and which
was not worked into any surviving draft of the whole play.
It appears that Yeats intended it to follow Act III, Scene 1
in Draft 16 (this is very short), but did not use it. Some
soldiers desert the party of the Prime Minister and return to
the castle because they cannot bear to leave the Player Queen.
They gain admittance through an open window with a rope
hanging out of it, presumably the window and rope the
Player Queen uses in III, 1 to let down their clothes to her
fellow players, and by which she had planned to escape
until Septimus rejected her.

PQ is shown before a mirror.
PQ (*recites, book in hand*). "Day darkens round me. The
   shadows grow more and more. Alone I stand upon this
   desolate [word deciphered]." No, no; there is a better
   passage here. "Bury in this heart your swords. I take them
   gladly, being most weary." Now if I could put these
   together . . .
1 Soldier. Your majesty.
PQ. Who is that?
1 Soldier. We ask your pardon.
PQ. My pardon?
1 Soldier. We are deserters.
P. Queen. Deserters? But why do you come to me?
1 Soldier. We could not leave you alone, whatever the
   Chancellor might do.
2 Soldier. We could not leave your father's daughter alone
   in this great house.
1 Soldier. We slipped away. We found an open window.
2 Soldier. That window over there, beyond the pillars.
1 Soldier. There was a rope hanging from it.
P. Queen. O, I forgot the rope.
1 Soldier. And we climbed in.
2 Soldier. Pardon us, your Majesty.
P. Queen. You have disobeyed a commanding officer. It is a
   serious thing.

1 Soldier. How could we leave you alone and in danger? I
   fought under your father. You have his eyes.

2 Soldier. I was with him too. You have the very colour of
   his hair.

3 Soldier. It is your Majesty's walk that is most like.

P. Queen. O, then if you see [?] my father in me, and fought
   under him, it was as though he spoke to you.

1 Soldier. And bid us come.

P. Queen. Well then, I pardon you.

1 Soldier. We thank your Majesty.

P. Queen. No more [?].

1 Soldier. Your Majesty must be hungry. May we go bring you
   food and wine?

Soldier. Ah, they're at the door. I can see the light of their
   torches.

P. Queen. Go, set the food and wine within there. They
   cannot break down the great gates.

2 Soldier. We will stay with you. We will die with you if
   need be.

1 Soldier. Do not fear anything. I know a secret sign—mother
   told me. Always when this throne is going to change there
   is someone who is possessed, who cries out in a trance, who
   makes the sound of a cock.

2 Soldier. Yes, I have heard that too.

3 Soldier. They are talking out there. (*Listening at door.*)
   They are going to get wood to make a fire to burn down
   the door. But let them do what they will, they cannot
   harm you for the cock has not crowed. Whoever is to die
   today it will not be the Queen, for the throne cannot change.

[DRAFT BREAKS OFF]

Commentary

I find it difficult to place Drafts 13 and 14 in the sequence of drafts, and have
placed them here because I wish to get all partial drafts out of the way before
I discuss Drafts 15 and 16, both full drafts of the play in its early form.

Where they correspond, Drafts 13 and 16 are alike in many ways: Both use the name "Surrico" for the mythical kingdom where the play takes place, and only in these drafts does Yeats name it. Both begin the play in the town; both share much of the same language. In short, Draft 13 is moving either toward Draft 16 or away from it. I have concluded it is moving toward 16, largely through a comparison of the openings of I, 2 and the end of II, the only places where the two drafts correspond closely. The language of these scenes seems to me on the whole more finished in 16 than in 13. My conclusion is an opinion, not a conviction. For working against it is the fact that I, 1 in Draft 13 includes Septimus (*Yellow Martin*) whereas I, 1 in Draft 16 does not. Draft 13 also includes a confrontation of Townsmen and Countrymen which is not found in 16, though Yeats gives to the group of entertainers in 16 some of the re- sistance to Tom of the Moon/Barach expressed in 13 by the Countrymen. Both Septimus and the confrontation of Townsmen and Countrymen are found in the finished play, and we will see that Yeats established them there in Drafts 21 and 22. Both of these place Septimus in the town, and 22 works out the confrontation. In short the scene as found here in 13 seems more effective than the scene as found in 16, and, however that may be, it is nearer to Yeats's final plan.

As for the relation of Draft 13 and 14 to Draft 15, I am simply unable to decide which is earlier. The only parallel scene in these drafts is the opening of I, 2, and the internal evidence as to which version is the earlier does not seem to me conclusive. Clearly 13 and 14 are not so closely related to 15 as they are to 16; I can find no certain evidence for saying more than this. I have put Draft 15 where it is largely because I wish to consider the two-act version of the whole play side by side with the three-act version.

At the opening of Draft 13 the countrymen are debating whether the Queen will wear her nun's dress or the cloth of gold that custom stipulates for such occasion when a group of Townsmen enters and tells them that all rejoicings in honor of the Queen have been forbidden. The source of the people's dis- content is no longer a tax on sins but increased costs for the sacraments of the church and special levies for building a new shrine honoring St. Winifred, the Queen's patron. The Countrymen agree to join the Townsmen in disciplining the Queen, and the whole group is gathered to one side of the stage when three priests enter, followed by soldiers with bags of money on their backs. The leader of the Townsmen, Tom of the Moon, insists that the bags contain relics, saints' bones, and will not let them pass. The priests order his arrest and he is dragged off by the soldiers, his followers struggling to free him. Two priests stay behind to discuss the discontent; another returns to report an attack on the soldiers and the freeing of Tom of the Moon, now suddenly metamorphosed into our old friend Barach. A priest has been killed.

The Townsmen and Countrymen are quarreling among themselves, the Townsmen supporting Barach, the Countrymen hesitant, when Septimus enters with several actors' masks in his hands. He has brought them to town to have them repainted. He invites both groups to the Noah play, whereupon Barach tells him that all celebrations have been forbidden. Septimus begins a tirade on the absolute importance of art, which contains antipopulist sentiments. Barach's followers seize Septimus, who insists that they and Barach have been put up to attack him by followers of Seneca, who dislikes his plays. Septimus is released and the crowd leaves. Septimus is addressing Apollo when the draft breaks off.

Yeats then drafts an opening of Act I, Scene 2 which drops the new beginning of Draft 12 and goes back to Draft 6 and its derivatives. The Queen and Prime Minister are on stage, the Queen has heard the hidden Player Queen singing, and Nona comes in calling for Noah's wife. In this part of the scene the language of 13 and 16 are much the same. Nona goes out, and the Prime Minister makes his now familiar plea to the Queen that she play her role for the good of the state; he says that if she does not she may face martyrdom, and so on. One new element is introduced: before the death of the Old King a cock has crowed. This sign that the throne was about to change is used in subsequent drafts, and a sign invented later after many cocks had crowed (the Old Beggar brays like a donkey when the crown changes) is still found in the finished play. The draft is broken off as the Queen and Prime Minister are about to leave for the town.

The manuscript continues with another conclusion for Act II, a version of the scene following the Player Queen's exchange of roles with the Queen. Yeats has already worked extensively on Act II in Drafts 6, 7, 11, and 12. In 6 the audience for the Noah play gathers and the play is under way when a messenger arrives with news of the outbreak against the Queen. The players flee except Septimus, Nona, and Decima, who locks the door on them, begs Septimus to dismiss Nona, lets them go when she supposes Septimus loves Nona, and exchanges roles with the Queen. Then, after the Queen's flight, she confronts the Prime Minister and Soldiers. Yeats worked over the early part of Act II in Draft 7, where he added Rat-hole's seizure by the spirit of the Old King. He tried a slight variation of this in 11 and a more radical variation in 12 which concentrates on the exchange between Nona, Decima, and Septimus after Decima has locked them in. These various drafts of the early parts of Acts II must have satisfied Yeats, for now he picks up the end of the act where he left it in Draft 6.

The Player Queen stages a trial of strength with the Prime Minister and wins. She orders the soldiers to scatter the royal treasure through the streets, and only when she finds they will obey her and not the Prime Minister does she order them to hide the money. She will remain in the castle and engage the crowd so that the Prime Minister and the soldiers can fall on them from the rear. As they go out, the Player Queen asks them to look for Yellow Martin.

Draft 14 is even more fragmented than Draft 13. Yeats began with a scenario on Rat-hole, which has been canceled. The last sentence of this makes Yeats's conception of Rat-hole clear: "The old man describes his state of medium-ship." He then writes an uncanceled scenario describing Rat-hole's seizure by the spirit of the Old King which interrupts the performance of the Noah play. This is a working up of a passage in Draft 7. It is followed by a scrap of dialogue between Nona and Septimus in which Nona announces she has found the hidden Player Queen. This was no doubt added because Septimus, having gone to town to have the masks repainted, does not know that the Player Queen has been hiding. The final item was, I think, intended to follow III, 1 in Draft 16. The Prime Minister and his soldiers have left with the treasure. The Player Queen is alone, looking into a mirror and practicing speeches from Septimus's old play, "book in hand." Three soldiers come in. They have deserted the party of the Prime Minister because they could not bear the thought that the Player Queen was alone in the castle. At the end of the scene they are listening to the besieging rebels and taking comfort from the fact that according to tradition the throne cannot change until a cock has crowed No cock has crowed, so the Player Queen cannot die.

CHAPTER NINE

Draft 15

DRAFT 15 is a short version of the whole play. The manuscripts and typescript of it have no act or scene divisions, but they contain sections corresponding to Act I, Scene 2; Act II; and Act III, Scene 2 in Draft 16. I have indicated where these parts begin. The play starts at the castle of the Queen with the rolling in of the tax money, continues with the exchange between the Prime Minister and Queen before they go off to town, the finding of the Player Queen, and the preparations for giving the Noah play (I, 2). This is followed by the beginning of the Noah play, the news of the rebellion, the quarrel among the three principals, Decima's exchange of roles with the Queen, and the encounter with the Prime Minister and the loyal soldiers (II). Then the Player Queen is shown in her new role, and queens it until she is rescued by the Prime Minister and his forces. She gives up her mask of queen and returns to the troupe, content to play the role of Noah's wife (III, 2). I think it likely that this short form of the play represents its state early in 1909. On 1 May Yeats wrote to Sturge Moore that he was revising the second act. He says in his letter that Mrs. Campbell has a two-act version of the play that is already out of date.

What follows is a transcript of the manuscript version, which was written out carefully in three bound exercise books with numbers on their covers. This is a more accurate version than the typescript dictated from it, though the typescript has been used without comment to supply readings missing or obscure in the manuscript.

[I, 2]

P.M. This is the last of them. What a treasure: gold,
 silver, and copper. What are you stopping for? Why do you
 not roll the keg there into the door? Quick, quick. O never
 had the state such a treasure.
Servant (while the others roll in keg). Sir, if I may speak.
 Just now we thought we heard a voice singing or

speaking in the air. John here says it was announcing the anger of Heaven upon us for having put a hand to this gold, but I thought it more like a love song.

P.M. There is an echo in the yard. It is the echo that you heard. Doubtless someone was singing in the Queen's room. Now get you gone. (*They go.*) Ah, your Majesty. I thank you for having come so promptly and with your crown and dress of state.

Queen. Hush.   30

P.M. There is much discontent, but it is not yet too late. At least I hope . . .

Queen. Hush.   32

P.M. This new tax. And there is not one who has ever seen your face.

Queen. Listen. Yes, I am certain. Someone sang very low.

P.M. But where?

Queen. In that big vat.

P.M. A dream, your Majesty. That is the cider vat. The fountain is to pour cider tonight.

Queen. No, no, I am certain.

[Note.] P.M. should himself think the voice ominous of evil to the state.

P.M. I'll climb and look though Time has made me stiff.   44

Queen. You would find nothing. I think it is some ancient spirit. The courtyard is full of them. It may have been sent to warn me that I am doing wrong in going among the people and leaving my prayers.

P.M. You are afraid because you fast and pray too much. It makes one timid.

A Voice. Come, Noah's wife.

[Note.] P.M. should warn Queen how serious things are. He is, he knows, risking her life on this desperate chance.

Queen. Listen, listen. A most ancient spirit.

Voice. Where are you, Noah's wife?   56

Queen. Ah, there again.

Voice. Where are you, Noah's wife?   58

Queen. O God, have mercy. (*Enter Friend.*)   59

P.M. Who is that you call? The name sounded strange.

Friend. One stranger than her name. Now she is one thing,
   now another. A joy and a torment. But where is she?
   She has to play before the Queen's servants all but
   this moment, and she cannot
   be found.   64
P.M. It is one of those for whom we have set out this
   stage.
Player. And after that we go into the market-place and we
   play there. But we have searched the woods and all the
   countryside and she cannot be found. And she is such
   a good player we are nothing without her, and Yellow
   Martin will be out of his mind with sorrow. Ah, I see
   you cannot tell me. (*Goes off crying* "Where are you,
   Noah's wife.")
Queen. Stage players too, and a fountain flowing with cider.
   I think no good will come of it.
   Is it to preside over a revel that you have bid me meet   78
   you here?   79
P.M. I have asked your Majesty to meet me here in all your
   robes of state that I may show you to your people. Your
   Majesty except in the one matter of the new tax has
   always left me to manage this state, and now I hold this
   necessary. To make the first sight of your face the more
   memorable, I have called these players. While you and I
   are in the town among the people they will show themselves
   here to those of your servants or their children who are too
   old to go to the market-place, [undeciphered passage]
   and tonight while they are playing in the town that vat
   will be filled with cider and the pipes will carry the
   cider to the fountain before the castle gate.
Queen. And it is for this sinful scene that I am brought out of
   my dear cell, the nest where my soul is bred for Heaven?
P.M. There is great discontent, and all I can hope is that
   it is not yet too late for your Majesty's sacred presence, the
   graciousness you have been bred to, to keep the riots down.
   It is this heavy tax. I bade your Majesty to meet me here in
   all your robes of state.
Queen. What riots, discontent? Yet is the tax most just. Indeed
   it only came to me after much fasting and wakefulness
   and prayer. The most just tax sovereign ever lay upon

a people. No man's house or land or labour is taxed; no
good man is taxed at all. But men are taxed for their
sins. A crown for the cup of ale that stirs the blood too much,
a whole sovereign for a lawlass kiss, and only coppers or
small silver coins for sinful but more natural indulgences,
and no tax gatherers, but only good priests to make out the
list of sins and to collect the taxes.

P.M. Not only does the tax seem strange to your people, but
they say sin costs so much they cannot keep money to
buy bread. Many of the soldiers I brought for your
protection have gone over to the people's side. But
if your Majesty will smile on the people, I think all
yet may be well. They loved your father, and
make them love you too and they will let you do what you   112
please. A painted cloth, a piece of damask, an always
smiling face, some words of love to those
you have never seen before and may not see again—a little   116
wearing of the mask—that is all I ask of you. If   117
you would have obedience, you must seem all the   118
greatness your people dream of being and having, the
might of soul their shivering hearts deny to them, the
greatness of wealth they have in their dreams.

Queen (*squatting on doorstep*). Sir, I will go again to my
prayers, for I would sooner they respected me for what
I am than cajole them with pomp and [word undeciphéred]
show. It is a life-long labour to find out what one is, and
when one has found it there is nothing left to do but
confession of sin. Ah, you have often made me do things,
worldly things, that I hate. But you will prevail against
me no more. I will go in and pray.

[Note] P.M. should use following illustration: we can be
sincere ourselves, only when this watery world has been
consumed and all become spirit.

P.M. Then, your Majesty, I lay my office down. I was
your father's servant, and he left me in your care,
but when I can no longer guard your crown it [is] time
that I gave up the task to another.

Queen (*who has got up*). What am I to do? I wish I had
never been born a Queen, born to this empty life.

P.M. I see your Majesty will come. I have but one hope—
    that we are not already too late.

Queen. Some player with a painted face were better for your
    work, or a mere painted mask.

P.M. To be great we must seem so, and seeming that goes on
    for a lifetime is not different from reality.

    (*Exit. P. Queen puts her head up out of vat.*)

[*Player Queen*] (*sings*).

        / 164 I would know what you are in yourself
        My beloved / 165 said to me
        Put off that mask of burning gold with / 166 emerald eyes
        That I may know who you are.
        I will not / 167 put away my mask
        It is the mask of burning gold
        / 168 With emerald eyes that makes your heart beat so
              / 169 quickly
        I would be praised by the beating of your / 170 heart.
        But he answered to me: I do not even
        Know / 171 if you are a friend or an enemy.

Friend. Yes, there is something going on. There has been
    shouting, and I saw crowds about the city gate. You must
    go quickly and come and tell me what it is all about.

Young Man. We are quite alone here. You said when I had   172
    finished the coat that Shem (?Noah's wife) is to wear . . .

Friend (*takes scissors and coat*). Give me the scissors.
    You will be back in time for your part in the play.
    Shem only comes on at the end.

Young Man. But you promised to kiss me if I made the coat,
    and another if I went this message.

Friend. Why of course, there is a kiss then. There, go now,
    you dear thing, and run quickly. But be careful of
    yourself, and if they are fighting do not go near them.
    (*He has gone through centre gate. She kisses her hand.*
    Seeing Player Queen.) We have been in search of you all
    night. What have you
    been doing? Yellow Martin has been so unhappy, and I   202
    have been so anxious.   203

Player Queen. Lying here in the cider vat, putting   204
    up my head every now and then during the night, watching   205
    the beautiful young men that wait upon the Queen. So   206

tall, so ruddy from their hunting, so bright of eye.
All night they have been playing upon
lutes and dancing.   208

Friend. It is no use sending me with that tale to Yellow
Martin. He has seen the Queen's people—
all old men with speckled shins from sitting over   211
the fire. She won't take a young man or a young girl   212
near her, but only old people who are making their souls.   213
Why do you torture Yellow Martin so?   214

Player Queen. Because I love him and want him to be always   215
thinking about me. I am not like you. I am not
content with a kiss, to take a
kiss as a kiss and tell everybody what pleases him.   217

Friend. You are making Yellow Martin so unhappy and so angry.   218

Player Queen (*sings*). My lover said to me I do not   219
even know if you are a friend or an enemy. (*Sinks*   220
down in vat.)

Friend. O do come down out of that vat. I have brought   221
your dress as Noah's wife. We have only a few minutes   222
before we begin.   223

[NOTE FROM OPPOSITE PAGE] Some of this might go in
conversation with Young Man who is going to town.

P.Q. I will not.
I told Yellow Martin that I would never play that part   225
again. I will not play a stupid woman no better than   226
myself, without a thing worth doing or saying. I will   227
never again be beaten by Noah because I will not go into   228
the Ark.   229

Friend. But Noah does not really beat you. You are   230
not hurt.   231

P. Queen. I must have a great part, a part with fine   232
words and a fine dress. I must say and do all the   233
things I have dreamt of. I must be beautiful and have   234
shining things to wear. I must grow greater and make all   235
those that look at me grow greater. Bad or good, it does   236
not matter. But I must be a fire, a light. O, he must   237
make a play about—O, about the Queen of Sheba, or Herodias,   238
or somebody of that kind.

Friend. No, no, no. That is no use. He will never let you   242
    play any of those parts. The people don't like them
    any more. They want somebody like themselves—what do
    they care about those great people. Now Yellow Martin
    says there is nobody so interesting to them, so patient,
    so obedient, so like themselves when they are not angry
    or excited as Noah's wife. That is after she was beaten.
    It is all in the Bible too.

P. Queen. I will make him give me the part I want. I   247
    will never come down out of this vat until I have his   248
    promise.   249

Friend. Then stay there altogether, or until you turn
    into cider, and maybe that will please you if enough
    people get drunk.

Player Queen. He will because he has no-   253
    body else to play for him.   254

Friend. He will not. There is somebody else.   255

Player Queen. You would not dare to do such a thing.   256

Friend (*half crying*). He was so unhappy, I could not   257
    help it. No, no, I could not.
    (*Player Queen who has been sitting on vat jumps down
    and seizes Friend.*)

P. Queen. You, you, you did that—you snail, you jellyfish.

Friend. I did not want to, but he was so unhappy.   261

P. Queen. O, O, you.
    you poultice of rotten apples, you damp cheese.   260

Friend. Don't kill me.   264

P. Queen (*throws her off, gasping*).
    Give me that dress, you empty shirt on a clothesline.   267

Friend. But you said you would not play.

[*P. Queen.*] Give me that dress. I will have no one come
    between me and Martin. I shall find my own way of getting
    what I want.

Friend. There, have it if you will, I never wanted it.

Poet. What are you two quarreling about? We must keep
    behind our masks. Why you might be seen from the
    windows. What right have players to show your quarrels?
    What have you been doing to . . .

Friend. O Martin, I knew no good would come of it, I

should never have promised. She has shaken me so, and
so, and she has called me such names.

Player [*Queen.*] It is time to begin by the dial on the tower.
Blow your trumpet, Martin. I shall play Noah's wife for
you this day, Martin, but I shall find my own way of
making myself a queen. (*She has put on costume and goes
behind stage. She keeps her head out through curtains.*)

Martin. Keep your head in. I want none of you to be seen
when the audience comes in. (*Blows.*) You a queen?
What do you know of queens?

Player Queen. There are a hundred queens inside my ribs.   321

Martin (*blows*). Put in your head. You, that have eaten
off pewter and brown earthenware.

Player Queen. That is why I long for Babylon and Ninevah,   324
a hundred horsemen in golden armour, and great silver   325
chairs carried upon men's heads upon two great silver spears.   326

Martin (*blows*). You a queen, whose father spent his life   327
hedging and ditching?   328

Player Queen. That is why I long for cloth of gold and men
to look at me and see my straight neck and high head.

Martin (*blows*). There is too much of that high head—   331
keep it in. O that I had but the courage to break it
once in a while.

Note. It is here perhaps that she should pull in her head. May
P. Queen say somewhere that she needs all the listening
Heavens for the great spectacle of herself?

[II]

(*Martin blows a long blast. Old men and women and children
come in. Some of them carry chairs which they arrange.
Some stand while the chairs are being put in place. They
talk.*)

Old Man. That's the man who speaks the prologue. I heard
him in the market place once. He pretends to argue
with Noah's wife through the curtain, then after that
the play begins, and you see him again but with a mask
on his face and he up on the stage and a big stick.

Another Man. I never like to know who plays this part or
that. I like to think it's Noah himself is there,

and that it's some friend of ours that is telling us
all about it and when it's the prologue that one hears.

A Child. What are the players like, grandmother, when they
are not acting?

Old Woman. They are just like you and me. What else would
they be?

Old Man. I would not say that now. They don't think the
same thoughts as we think. How could they, and they
letting on to be such grand people or such good people
every day of their lives?

Another. It must be queer to be so many different people.
One would not know what name one had been christened
by at the end, I would think.

Another. Ah, it must be like the creating of the world
over again, and becoming all the birds and the beasts
oneself.

Old Man. Hush, he is going to begin. You always know he
is going to begin when he puts down his trumpet and
settles his shirt round his neck.

Poet. Listen to the tale of the great flood that was in
old times. It rises. It has covered everything, still
and bright but for the dullness of the raindrops. It
covers the woods and the valleys and the towns. The
birds fly over the woods. They are bewildered by their
own images in the water. They cry out and flap wildly.
Noah has made a big wood Ark. Noah's wife keeps indoors.
She will not leave her dishes and her dresser and her
meat-safe, things she keeps over the fire. She does not mind
the flood. She says it will go down again before Spring.
She will not go into Noah's boat.

Noah's Wife (*within*). I will not.

Poet. Listen to her now, but presently her husband will
come and you will see how he will master her, telling
her that she will be drowned if she won't [do] as he
bids her, and all because she wants to go gossiping
here and there among the neighbours, making them admire
her, showing herself off to the wide world. Wives
and husbands, you will learn a good lesson, for he will
lesson her finely.

Noah's Wife. He will not.

Poet. Be quick, I tell you. I see him coming over the
hill, and when you see the bit stick that he has you
will obey him.

Voice. I will not.

Poet. You fool of a woman. Then he will lay the stick
about your shoulders and make you run before him all
[the] way from this to the boat.

Voice. If he dares, if he dares. O, you will see what I
will do.

Young Man (*in gate*). Quickly escape, all of you, to the
woods. They are coming to attack us.

Voices. It is the tax. O my God. It's the rooting out of
their sins.

Poet. Get your breath.

Young Man. I went down to the town to see what the noise
was. There was a great shouting. The people cried out
against the Queen and all that are of the Queen's party.
No, no, do not go into the house. I heard them cry
burn her house down and throw all that belongs to her
into the flames. To the woods. Become hares and
rabbits. The leaves are too damp to burn. (*Servants
troop out.*)

Poet. What, would you leave all behind? No, let the raven
lie there; I made that out of an old black coat of my
own. There, go now with the pigeon heads over your back,
(*Young Man goes out.*) Put them out of sight somewhere.
(*To Friend.*) Put down that scissors, take up the Devil's
hoof. I carry God almighty's beard.
(*Finds door locked.*) Who has locked us in?   191
We are lost.

[NOTE FROM OPPOSITE PAGE]

Poet should speak prologue with some [word undeciphered]
symbolical headdress. Moon or sun [astrological symbols] or
Raven or Neptune.

[DRAFT CONTINUES]

P.Q. I have locked the door. Neither you nor   194

I nor that woman there will ever go through that door until I

please.   196

Poet. Give me that key.   197

Player Queen. Come a step nearer and I throw it   198

    over the wall.   199

Poet. For God sake, let us open the door. The mob are

    coming hither. They are mad with excitement and anger.

P.Q. Then promise what I ask.   203

Poet. I will not give you parts beyond your powers.

Player Q. It is not that now that I am asking.

Poet. Then what new crazy thing are you asking?

Player. That you send this woman away.

Poet. She has done no wrong.   211

Player Queen. She has come between you and me.   212

Poet. Once rid of her you could make me do what you   213

    please. I will sit here and take my

    chance of the crowd.   215

Player Queen. I will stand here and cry aloud the

    praise of the Queen. All that I have ever imagined

    of queens of Ninevah or Babylon I'll say of her.

Poet. I'll too have a voice to tell what a girl speaks to

    them, and for what wild revenge upon another player

    you have planned.

Friend. No, no. Promise, or [her?] anything. Nobody would under-

    stand. Why, when we who have known of her always cannot

    understand her, how could they? Promise to send me away.

[*Alternate version*]

Friend. O, I'll promise. I'll go away. I'll dance for

    my living, and turn juggler, and eat swords.

[DRAFT CONTINUES? GEN. ED.]

Poet. Hush, hush, you little fool. I will not   232

    part with you so easily. She does not mean what she   233

    says. She will open the door before they come.   234

Player Queen. Ah, now I see. I have been blind. You

love her; you have been making love under my very
eyes and have forgotten me.

Friend. O never, never.

Player Queen. And now you lie about it. If I loved   240
another's sweetheart and could take him, I'd [take]
him boldly. I'd carry him off under her eyes as
though my hair and eyes and all my beauty that won
him were an army, but you . . .

Poet. Wildness heaped on wildness. Think what you will.
I'll answer you no more, but give me that key.

Player Queen (*throwing it to him*). There, there. I
care for nothing now. (*The Friend seizes it, opens
door, goes out.*)

Poet. There is no time now for words. I will put this
woman in safety in the wood, and then I'll come for you.

Player Queen. O my beloved one, anybody is the same to
her, but I love only you out of the whole world. O,
he is gone. O false, O falser than imagination can
create [?]. But you will be sorry, you will be sorry.
(*Taking up scissors.*)

> When he finds me lying there
> A knife in my heart
> I shall be so like a queen
> Like a queen indeed
> He will love me then.

[Yeats cancels this song, and writes "She may sing a dirge over
herself."]

(*Enter real Queen.*)

Queen. O, do not kill me. I will give you money, anything
you ask.

Player Queen. It was not you I thought to strike, but another.   270

Queen. Then it was to protect me, but what can one do?
I will call my servants.

P. Queen. They are all fled.

Queen. Then let us shut to these big doors. They are
close behind. O, I could see their spears.

P. Queen. No, no. They would break it down. You are
the Queen.

Queen (*quickly*). Yes, yes. They are going to kill me.

P. Queen. No use hiding in there. They will search   282
till they find a queen. I will save you. Listen.
I have often thought that [?] if I could turn a queen
even for an hour I would be happy. Quick. Put on
this old cloak and hat and give me yours.

Queen. But they will kill you.

P. Queen. Listen, I will tell you a secret. It was for   297
myself I was getting ready that knife.

Queen. O, how wicked. The church says we must never do   298
that. Was it love? (*P. Queen nods.*) I have never
known what that is, but they say it is terrible and
makes people very wicked. O, they will kill you. It
will be the crown of martyrdom. It will take you away
from sin. I have often thought I would like the crown,
but then it seemed presumptuous, and O, I am so afraid.
But if I were a sinner—of course
I know we are all sinners—but I mean really a sinner,   304
a sinner in myself, I would think as you do. It would
wipe everything out, Heaven would be sure. O, I will
go and hide in the wood. No one will know me now. (*Exit.*)

P. Queen. Should you find a man there, Yellow Martin he
is called, hiding in [the] wood, you will tell him what
has happened.

Queen. Your lover? I will tell him. I will say she is
going to Heaven and beseech him to repent.

P. Queen (*putting on royal robes and singing*).

    I will array me for my [death]
    In a splendid way.
    I will put a wreath on my head
    And then I will die,
    And when my lover comes to see me dead
    Then he will weep and love me true
    And love me truly for ever and ever.

(*She has just got into robe and crown when P.M. and
soldiers enter.*)

Player Queen. Lift up your spears. My heart is ready
for them. It is a queen's heart. I have the same

heart the king my father had when he led you in the
battle, and I can accept death as lightly.

A Soldier. We are of your own party, your Majesty, all
Queen's men, and we have driven back your enemies
and come to put you in safety.

P. Queen. Then I am indeed Queen for an hour if never more.
You will obey?

Soldier. As we obeyed your father. You have his spirit.

P. Queen. Then go through that door where the gold is
stored and bring it here. It must not lie useless
there. (*Exit soldiers.*)

P.M. (*coming forward*). I do not know who you are, except
that you are not the Queen, but that is a good thought.
We shall need that gold before this rebellion [is put]
down. Listen to me. I have no time to question you.
I do not care who you are. All I want is a brave mask,
a bunch of feathers on a stick. No one here has seen
the Queen's face but a few servants. You and I will
play out this business and save the state. She has
fled—God knows where. Do not answer, play on, play
on. That is all I ask. The times are desperate. (*As
soldiers come back with gold.*) I thank your Majesty
for these new honours. (*Kissing her hand.*)

P. Queen. Take all that gold and silver and scatter it
through the streets of the town. While I am Queen I'll
give and give, and when I cannot give, I'll die. (*Murmurs
of astonishment.*)

P.M. O no, no. That will never do. No, you are spoiling
all your own good thought. We must put it safe in
the very heart of the wood.

Queen. But now I let you kiss my hand, and now you are
disobedient.

P.M. Play your part out.

Q. Queen. Yes, as I conceive it in the depths of my heart.

P.M. But without the glitter of this we can do nothing.

P. Queen. Am I nothing? If there is any rival to draw
men's thought from the glitter, I would cast about
me from my own soul.

P.M. But they will kill you.

389

P. Queen. That is but another scattering.

P.M. Crazed. It's a pity, it's a pity. Lady, I have to
pay these men, and many more that will obey me if
they know I have the way to pay them.

P. Queen. Do as you please. Go, take it, but go from me.
Whoever is my loyal subject will stay merely because
I bid him.

P.M. Lady, no one will stay with you. [But] with this treasure
we can reestablish all this state again. We'll not scatter, no.
But where it is the power will be. What, scatter it in the
streets? No, I have a better use for this fiery grain. (*P.M.
as he goes out.*) No, no, we'll not scatter. Why the state
is but a gatherer up of things.

P. Queen. And when the body is scattered, who can say
But that the soul is singing on its way.
(*Exit P.M. and soldiers, all but three.*)

1 Old Soldier. I will stay with your Majesty.

2 Old Soldier. And I.

3 Old Soldier. And I. I could not bring myself to desert you. I
fought beside your father, and you are his very image. Your
nose precisely . . .

2 Soldier. I fought beside him too. You have his eyes.

3 Old. I fought beside him too. You have his hair.

P. Queen. Over you three, then, I am Queen. It is enough.

1 Soldier. I will shut the big door.

2 Soldier. I will call your servants out of the castle. With their
help we may keep the place all day. A dozen can keep
the battlements. (*Goes to house.*)

1 Soldier. The door is the danger. We must have enough to
throw the battlements on their heads.

[NOTE FROM OPPOSITE PAGE]

Details about flight of Queen should be put into mouth of actor
who brings message of riot. No sooner did they see Queen and
Minister than they attacked the troops. The Queen has fled and
now the people are struggling [?] with the troops, and the
troops are giving way. Queen could add more detail.

[DRAFT CONTINUES]

Queen. The King, my father, he was in danger often like
this and he wore this crown.

1 Soldier. Many dangers. Now the Danes, now the Munster
men. But he had not your courage, though he was a
great man, and did not Columkille say there would never
be peace for those that wore this crown?

P. Queen. It has brought many into danger, but never into
such danger as this. A good crown for one weary of life.

1 Soldier. O, your father, if I may be so bold to say so,
loved his ale and cider. He would sing over his cider.

P. Queen (*meditating* [?]). A good crown for one crossed in
love. A fine gift for one that had lost a friend. A crown to
set one singing. (*Sings over crown.*)
O grant me, O masters of fate, the moment
That tries the soul. The only gift in life that I covet.
Give me that though I be broken in fragments and
scattered.

[III, 2]

(*P. Minister's coachman climbs up on wall and crouches
upon it. Another man shows his head above wall.*)

Coachman. I have been chosen by the people . . .

Soldier. Why it's the Prime Minister's own coachman.

Coachman. . . . . to tell your Majesty . . .

Other Man. Keep up your head and don't touch your cap.

Coachman. . . . . that you must give up the Prime Minister to
be put to death by the people.

P. Queen. I will give up no faithful servant.

Coachman. Then I am bid say that if you do not your Majesty
must die.

Other Man. Ah, there you've done it.

Another. He's touched his head to the Queen.

Another. Pull him down.

Another. Put a knife into him. (*Coachman and other man
disappear.*)

Soldier (*at loophole*). Big Tiegue the Miller has flung his
knife at Tom Coachman. He but just missed his ear. Ah,

now they've brought up a big tree. They are going to beat
in the door.

Soldier (*coming out of castle*). There is nobody in the castle.
They are all fled. (*Others gather round him.*)

2 Soldier. All fled.

3 Soldier. They'll kill us. I'll be saying a prayer.

Queen. No, no, this is my battle alone. I will have all the
perils of this crown; no one shall share it with me. (*She
opens the door. They shrink back from her, seeing her
before them.*) You fear the mere image of royalty, yet it [is]
with me that your quarrel is. I accept it all. It was I who
made the tax. (*A murmur* "It was she who made the tax.")
What are you afraid of? I am she that you have condemned
to death. (*A murmur.* "Yes, we have condemned her to
death, etc." *She goes up onto stage.*)

Who is there amongst you that dares strike? Your father's lives,   78
and the

lives of their fathers before them were but twigs   79
woven into the nest that gave this eagle birth. Who   80
among you dares to face this eagle? Eagle begat eagle up   81
through all the centuries, and the eyes of all the   82
eagles look at you. But strike if you will. I   83
veil their lightning.   84

A Voice. Let all strike together and then no one will be to
blame after. (*Voice,* "Yes, no one will be to blame after."
They raise their weapons.)

Player (*comes forward*). Stop, stop. This is no queen.
This is not the Queen, I say. Yes, I will speak
I tell you it is true. I tell you she is not the Queen.
She is a player of my troupe. (*Murmurs:* "Not the Queen.   93
A player of his troupe.")

Coachman. Isn't she wearing the crown? (*Chorus:* "She is
wearing the crown.")

P. Queen. It is no use, my poor man. I know who you are.
You are one of the players who played before my people
this day, and now you are trying to save me with this
incredible tale.

Player. She is seeking for her death. Those robes are not
hers, that crown is not hers.

Queen. Poor man. Think you that I could look upon you
   now with so much calm and speak with quiet breath
   had I no royalty within me? Who could outface the
   leveled spears for a borrowed crown and robe?   129

Coachman (*to Player*). Out of that with you, interfering
   with the justice of the people. (*To the crowd.*) What
   shall I do with this man that rebels against the people?

P. Queen. Do not hurt him, let my last breath be a prayer
   for pardon. I understand his kind. I have seen many
   of them. These artists. They are ever longing to fill
   some great place in men's eyes or maybe in some lover's
   eyes. And to save a queen and claim a queen all   146
   in one mouthful, what greater part than that? (*They
   are hustling him away.*)

Player. Let me go, give me time. I will call witnesses.
   I will prove all.

P. Queen. Let him go; I will question him a little.
   Why do you not obey me? Am I not still Queen waiting
   to die? (*They let him go.*)
   I will have no slander living after me. I will have no shaking   154
   of the head. No one will say that I was less than
   Queen. I will refute his story with my own questions.
   I will lay open his hidden motive. I know these players,
   their vanity and folly. I will make him say—I can hardly
   bring myself to speak the words—that I was his sweetheart.

Player. But it is true. She was my sweetheart. (*Laughter.*)

P. Queen. And that we quarreled because I had grown
   jealous. And that now I but play the part of queen
   to make myself seem noble in his eyes, and show him
   that he did me wrong in liking another instead of me.
   These players are so vain.

Player. No, there never was another. But what's the use   168
   I can't make her understand, or you understand. I   169
   cannot save her—I cannot put out the mad fire that
   is burning in her. I cannot save her.

P. Queen. Go to your own sweetheart [and tell her] that   172
   you have escaped and hardly with your life, there being so
   much falsehood in you, and cease to claim a queen for
   whom all the wide Heavens are waiting, one that you are
   not worthy even to look upon.

Player. O my God, is there no one that will witness for
    me? There was one, but she is fled. Who will bear
    witness?

Queen (*coming forward*). I will.

Player. I do not know you.

P. Queen. Another to pull me from the rest that I am
    seeking to a world I weary of. A poor, crazed player,
    dressed as Noah's wife, and seeking a greater part.
    But no, I will not be robbed. Here, here in my heart,
    your spears. Strike, strike. I will speak no more
    in this world.

A Countryman. Look, look at her face. She is not the
    Queen, she never made the law. Those lips have given
    kisses and drunk wine.

Queen. It was I who made the law, I am the Queen. I
    will make all plain. (*Chorus:* "She says she is the
    Queen.") And you that say she has drunk wine and
    given kisses do not know of whom you are speaking.
    You would tremble if you knew.

Coachman. I say that the one who wears the crown is
    Queen.

Queen. The crown is mine.

Countryman. She has the right lips. She made the law.

Coachman. I say this. Kill both, and then we'll know
    that the Queen is dead and cannot come to life again
    to tax us. Put them there side by side and we will
    kill them both together.

Queen (*who has been seized*). I am safe among you. You
    cannot touch me, there would be thunder. Can you not
    see that there is a miracle? (*Chorus:* "A miracle. She
    says a miracle." *They let her go.*) I did not know at first. She
    took my place to die instead of me as I thought. I went away
    and then my conscience brought me back. But the moment
    I saw her I knew that she was an angel, who had, because
    of my prayers, come to take my place. Now strike at her,
    thrust your spears at her. They will fall back as from smitten
    bronze, or they will pass through her as it were mist. She is
    the messenger of God. (*Chorus.*) Look at her face. Can you
    not see she is above fear? There is no human life in that
    mask, all is immortal, [two words undeciphered]. The

grave cannot touch her. [Two words undeciphered] With
this sword I will strike her on the heart, then you will see
the miracle. You will fall upon your knees when the sword
glances from her. She seeks it here, that is why she cries for
you to strike her, but I will have all the glory of making
the miracle [take] place.

P.M. (*throwing up spears*). What, two queens, and one against the other?   266
     Let no one stir, my soldiers are all around you. Lay   267
     down your weapons. But which of these is Queen? My   268
     eyes are old and cannot see rightly. Kneel all, and
     ask your pardon of whoever of them seems most the queen.

Queen. No, none to me. (*All kneel to P. Queen.*)

P.M. Ah, you have all good sight, you are not as old as
     I am. You know the Queen.

P. Queen. You have but risen against the shadow of the queen,
     and so have done but shadow wrong, I therefore par-   278
     don all. And now I put the play away and take up   279
     life again that I had thought myself well done with.   280
     I am no Queen, those spoke the truth. (*To real Queen.*)   281
     Your Majesty, forgive me.

Real Queen. No, no. But when I fled and you took my place
     I was alone with my own soul, and all [?] about [?] me my
     sins rose up against me, and I made a vow that if I lived
     I'd leave the world for some convent cell and there spend
     all my days finding out what my own soul was, what is
     eternal in me. I was [not] meant for Queen, I am all nun.

P.M. (*to P.Q.*) So you are still the Queen, and a fair one,
     and worthy of men's devotion.

P. Qu. You who have the power are the king, and should have
     the name of king. I am still enough a queen to give
     the crown.

P.M. You are the golden mask, and all gold is royal.

Queen. I am royal for an hour or a day, but then I'd change
     the mask.

P.M. So be it then, I take it at your hands that have most right   296
     to give. I have learned my task from you and will know
     what mask to wear.

P. Queen. So be it, so it be not on my head.

P.M. Come with me, rebels turned honest, and here without

on the woodside swear to me, your new King, allegiance.
From this day out you will be no more taxed for your
sins. We will but tax your virtues—your industry, your
patience, and your thrift. (*Exeunt. He goes out bowing to
P. Queen.*)

P. *Queen* (*to Poet*). Go you too your way, go to your
sweetheart and ask her pardon because you have sworn you
did not love her. Go ask her pardon. What do you linger
for? (*Enter Friend and her young man wearing the doves'
heads.*)

Friend. I will not have him, nor any but this young man here.   312
While you've been getting up some riot here, he and I
have been busy to more purpose. For now we give thanks in
the likeness of Aphrodite's own bird, and this shall be my
olive to the Ark. (*Puts hands of Poet and Player Queen
in one.*)

P. *Queen.* I will go through it all again to bring this moment.

Poet. From this day you can play the Queen of Sheba,
Herodias, or who you will.

P. *Queen.* O no, I am tired of queens. I shall be
Noah's wife. (*In Poet's arms.*)

Commentary

I am uncertain just where this version belongs in the progressive order of drafts.
There has been no complete version of the play since Draft 6, and Draft 15 is
clearly later than that. Its relation to the partial drafts that I have placed between
these complete versions is less clear: as a whole, Act I, Scene 2 shows a definite
advance over preceding drafts; Act II is in about the same state as it was in Draft
12; Act III, Scene 2 abandons the rather strained love test involving Septimus,
Nona, and Decima, and this is clearly an advance. I have placed Draft 15 here
because on the whole it shows greater finish than the other drafts, and because
placing it here will permit direct comparison with Draft 16.

Act I, Scene 2. This desperately worked-over scene has most of the incidents
that are by now so familiar: the bringing in of the tax money; the Player Queen's
song from the vat overheard by the servants; the Queen's arrival and her hearing
the voice of the Player Queen, which she takes as a warning that she should not
leave her prayers; the Prime Minister's exhortations that she should fulfill the

role her birth has assigned her, interrupted by Nona's (*The Friend*'s) searching for the Player Queen; the Queen and the Prime Minister's departure for town; the Player Queen's mask song; the scene between Nona and the Young Man she is sending to town (this was part of Peter's role—one of the most noticeable things about this draft is the absence of Peter); the discovery of the Player Queen and her exchange with Nona; the entrance of Septimus (*Poet*); and the preparations for giving the Noah play. Yeats writes 74 lines he will keep in Draft 16. The largest number of lines finished in drafts earlier than this was 28 in Draft 13.

Act II. This version of the act is noticeably shorter than the version in Draft 16, but it contains most of the incidents found there. After a very brief discussion by the audience on the effect of role-playing on actors and the nature of theatrical illusion, the Noah play begins. There is no Rat-hole in this version to interrupt it. The Poet does a full prologue, and the dialogue has started when the Young Man comes back with news of the outbreak against the Queen (again, part of Peter's role in versions containing Peter). The audience and most of the players flee, but Septimus, Nona, Decima, and the Young Man stay behind to rescue the properties. Decima locks the gate after the Young Man leaves and demands that Septimus send Nona away. When she comes to think Nona and Septimus are in love, she lets them go; Septimus says he will return for her. The fleeing Queen arrives; Decima proposes she take the Queen's place; they change clothes; and the Queen leaves. The Prime Minister enters with the loyal soldiers, and he and the Player Queen have a quarrel over what is to be done with the gold. All save three old soldiers go out with the gold; the three soldiers tell about earlier troubles in the kingdom, and Decima sings over the crown.

Act III, Scene 2. The rebels are besieging the castle; the Prime Minister's coachman climbs up on the wall to shout their demands that the Prime Minister be dismissed. He forgets his new role and, coachman-like, touches his cap to the Player Queen. She opens the gate to confront the rebels and gives her speech about being descended from eagles. Septimus comes forward and tells the truth, but the crowd will not believe him. He asks for a witness and the Queen comes forward. She has come to believe that the Player Queen is an angel sent to save her and that a miracle will take place if she is struck. [The Queen calls Decima an angel as, in *The Resurrection*, the Greek will call Jesus a phantom. Cf. *Variorum Plays*, p. 923, Gen. Ed.] Enter the Prime Minister to the rescue just in time; he asks the crowd to bow to the Queen; they all bow to the Player Queen. The Player Queen admits to her play-acting, but the real Queen refuses to take back the crown: "I am all nun"; whereupon the Player Queen offers the crown to the Prime Minister, who agrees to take it. The Player Queen tells Septimus to go to his sweetheart, when Nona and the Young Man enter, costumed as doves. Nona points out that they resemble Aphrodite's own bird and that, appropriately, they have plighted troth. She joins the hands of Septimus and Decima, and Decima is quite content to rejoin the troupe and play Noah's wife. This denouement seems to me the most charming the play has had or will have. Clearly in this scene we are moving toward those outrageously concatenated events that are part of farce, though the mode of language is as yet farcical only in spots.

CHAPTER TEN

Draft 16

ALL THAT YEATS has done so far builds toward this draft of
the play in three acts, by far the longest play he had ever written or was ever to
write. It or something like it must have been in existence by 29 November 1909,
when Yeats reported on his reading of a three-act version of the play to Mrs.
Patrick Campbell (*Letters,* pp. 539–40). The draft includes parallel versions of I,
2, one in prose and one in verse. Here they follow each other, first the prose, which
is the earlier, and then the verse. They are too unlike to be printed opposite each
other effectively. Yeats was still at work on this draft in August 1910 when he
quoted from the verse version of Act I, Scene 2 in a letter to his father. The draft
of the play is preceded by a scrap of another early version of Act I, Scene 1,
only part of which has survived. (Cf. p. 16 for explanation of line numbering.)

[16a]
[Loose papers from the back of the A2 MS book]

*People with Clown, Jack-of-the-green Man, and a creel of
banners. They meet the* [undeciphered] *and the Fell Seller.*

Fell Seller. Where are you going?
Man with creel. To the city gate, sir, to put these flags upon
   it for the Queen's coming, to make it gay.
Clown. And I and Jack the Miller here, leaves about him,
   are to keep the spirit going till she comes.
Fell Seller. It is her monks and her priests that have set you to
   it, but let the black gowns tremble and fly if they've a mind
   to. I am Peter the Fell Seller, and I tell [you] that I and
   the butchers and the sieve makers and the smiths and the
   tinsmiths and the carpenters of this town will have none
   of your flag flying nor your clowning. How much had you to
   pay the priest when your daughter married?
The Man. A year's savings.

Fell Monger. And when your son was christened and your
   wife's churching after?
A Man. I sold a field to pay for it.
Fell Monger. And what are they taking from us to build the
   big church?
A Man. A tenth they ask of all, and they say that [four words
   undeciphered].
Jack-in-the-green. He's in the right, I'll bring her no green.
   Hasn't she set her black cattle to browse on us?
Man with banners. I'll take these home to my wife to make a
   patchwork quilt of. There's not a man in town has ever
   seen her face.   •
(*Enter Priest and two soldiers.*)
Priest. Seize that man. He is the stirrer up of riot.

[NEXT SHEET MISSING]

Fell Monger. You, painted face, go call out the sieve-makers,
   and you the smiths. Bring all to the market-place. And as you
   go, Jack-of-the-green, bid the butchers close their shops
   and bring their knives with them. I'll get the coopers,
   and with thick [?] cudgels, and stop the play in the castle
   yard. We'll show her gloomy faces this day.

[NEXT SHEET MISSING]

Priest. Then are you the Devil's relics.
Barach. I care not, so they work miracles.
Priest. What miracles can your like work?
Barach. Make your Queen as mournful as yourselves.
Priest. The Devil's relics hang in chains. Their master is prince
   of the air. Seize that man, and charge him with high treason.
Barach. You dare not. (*He is seized.*) A rescue, a rescue.

[Draft 16]
Act 1 Scene 1

[*Though the lines of Draft 16 are numbered for comparison
with earlier drafts, Act I, Scene 1, is left unnumbered because
there is no similar draft.*]
A street, windows high up, an image of a saint on the wall. A

*suggestion of a Spanish street in the architecture, but nothing
very definite. It is a street in the country of Surrico, which is
unknown to history though known to legend. A man with a
basket, a clown, a juggler, and a jack-in-the-green man come
in at one side. From the other comes a big man with a red
face, Barach, the ferret seller. He is accompanied by another
man, artisans, and tradesmen. Their clothes vaguely suggest the
middle of the 15th century.*

Barach. Where are you going?
Man with basket. To the castle gate to put this string of
    flags upon it.
Barach. And you?
The Clown. To keep the sport going till the Queen comes, and
    to get pennies.
Barach. And you?
Jack-in-the-green. To keep Tom Clown company.
Barach. Can you read that? (*He points to a notice pasted on
    the wall.*)
Clown. No sir. Will you read it to us?
Barach (*reading*). "Citizens of Surrico, the Queen of Surrico
    who today shows herself at last to her people must be
    received without honour, without cheers, without flags,
    without shows. And player, juggler, fiddler, piper, clown,
    or the like who shall this day practice his art is hereby
    condemned to the stocks. Signed, Barach, the fell maker."
Jack-in-the-green. Sir, we are country people, new come to
    town. Who is this Barach who can order people to the
    stocks?
Barach. I am Barach, and I have been made captain of all the
    guilds.
Townsman. Yes, that he has, that he may show our will to this
    Queen that no sooner did she come to the throne . . .
Barach. Silence!
Another Townsman. This Queen, who till this day from her
    girlhood up has not so much as shown her face amongst
    us . . .
Barach. Silence!
Townsman. . . . but keeps her cell like a nun . . .

Barach. Were you or I chosen to speak for the people? (*A murmur.*) Three months ago the old king died, and this woman who has hidden from girlhood in her cell took his place. What was her first act, I ask you?

Man with basket. To put the priests over us, true enough.

Clown. A marriage costs half a year's money.

Jack-in-the-green. And to die a sheer ruin.

Clown. And now we've to give a tenth of all our goods to make a church and a convent for St. Winifred.

Jack-in-the-green. St. Winifred is the worst of all.

Barach. Put Jack-in-the-green in the stocks.

Jack-in-the-green. I've no mind for the stocks, mister. Away with the green. (*Begins taking them off.*)

Clown. I'll go wash my face.

Man with b[asket.] I'll give these flags to my wife to make patchwork quilts.

Juggler. The Devil takes all juggling from this out. I'll cut purses.

Barach. Then we are all friends, all of the one mind to give this Queen a lesson. (*Voices, "all, all." They shake hands, gathered in a knot on one side of the stage. Three priests, dressed rather like Spanish priests, come in at the other side followed by some soldiers who carry a sort of litter on which are bags containing money.*)

Priest. Make way, make way there in the Queen's name.

Barach (blocking way). What holy relic do you carry today?

Man in crowd. It's money from the hearth tax.

Barach. No no, you have some saint's bones. Death has picked them bare so that no shred of the world sticks to them, nothing of this ever-changing, cloudy flesh.

Priest. Make room. Fall back in the name of St. Winifred.

Man in crowd. It's the hearth tax for St. Winifred's new church and convent.

Barach. No no, it is a holy relic. The flesh is wild, but there is no dishonest laughter in dry bones, nor have they kissed this long time.

Priest. Out of the way.

Barach. Yet it may be that this flesh that's still upon our bones, this lying lazy lecherous flesh, this cloud passing away, shall turn to miracle worker and after that sing laudy.

Priest. Go back in St. Winifred's name.

Barach. Read what is written there, and understand that we
   shall make your Queen as chopfallen as yourselves if you
   have not made her so already. You know me now, Barach the
   fell seller.

Priest. Seize that man.

Barach. Seize, but you dare not hold.

Priest. Seize him and bring him to the castle. (*The soldiers
   try to drag him away; the people follow him offstage.
   Soldiers and people fighting. Two priests remain behind,
   one middle-aged and one young priest.*)

Young Priest. Did you notice how his mind ran upon dry
   nettles.

Priest. Well, what of that, Brother?

Young Priest. That the world is near its end. Evil spirits
   are breaking out of the ground already as if they were
   nettles.

Priest. They say last night that mad Martha . . .

Young Priest. A very holy woman.

Priest. The moon was full, and she could see plainly the
   Devil rooting with his horns in the five acre meadow beyond
   the crossroads, and his wife looking on in the likeness of
   a ferret.

Young Priest. Why was he rooting, Brother, and why was his
   wife in the likeness of a ferret?

Priest. How could she find that out and she in so great a
   fright? (*Third Priest comes running in.*)

Third Priest. They have rescued him, they are bringing him
   back here. The soldiers hardly got the money safe away.

Second Priest. They are coming. (*The Priests run off. At the
   other side Barach and his followers come in.*)

Barach. Why did you let the money go? We could have bought
   the soldiers with it. You there, with the floured face, and you
   juggling Tim, and you John Tapster follow the two that
   pulled my notice down and see to it that you have sticks to
   make their backs as soft as their bellies. I am the law this
   day. Let no man take down my notices.

Clown. We have no mind for the hangman's welkery [sic] that
   creaks at crossroads.

Barach. Do you think, fool, that you'll be safe after this

day's work? I tell you that we must finish it and put fear
into them, or they will find some trick to hang us. No
pulling down flags, nor cleaning faces like yours, nor
scattering greens will serve our purpose now.

Man in crowd. Best hide before they send enough men to
take us.

Juggler. You worked the quarrel up, bring [brought?] our
necks in like danger with your own.

Man in crowd. What if he did, thereby he brought you into our
fellowship. Is not fear the root of affection?

Barach. This is no time to quarrel; will you.go back into the
priests' power? What mercy will they show you; they that
having neither wife nor child nor sweetheart are as tyrannous
as old maids.

Man in crowd. I have to stand up before all the congregation
because of Red Sarah.

Another. What can we do?

Barach. Take the castle; when we have it the soldiers will
declare for us.

Man in crowd. But [the] great gates, shall we beat them down
with our fists?

Barach. The gates are open to admit those that would see the
players that were to play there this day, and there's none
to guard the castle but old men, their shins speckled with
the fire.

Man in crowd. Death to the Queen.

Barach. No, there's something unlucky in queen-killing. We'll
send her priests away; then she shall marry and bear children
to reign after her. What have we to do with saints? We want
a Queen like the Old King her father who was a good
sinful man.

All. That's it, that's it.

Barach. One that will wear fine clothes and have enough sins of
her own to pardon ours. One that won't talk to us of laying
up treasures yonder when we've a mind to put down an
enemy.

Man in crowd. True enough, the men of [blank] undersell
our linen.

All. To the castle, to the castle.

Barach. And let no man shrink, we've but to do and all the
people will be with us. So to the castle, for there is
naught against us but mere breath. (*An old ragged beggar
comes in; they all shrink back from him.*)

Man in crowd. It's the ghost-ridden man.

Clown. That's an unlucky thing to meet at the outsetting of
the day's work.

Barach. Do not come near us.

Rat-hole. Why do you go away from me? Can I help it if they
take hold of me? How can I help it, and I asleep? Do I
call them? What do I know of it?

Barach. Get from the way.

Rat-hole. I am walking along or sitting, maybe, and I begin
to shiver and all in a minute I lose grasp of my thoughts
and my tongue, and it's some old dead man that's speaking.

Barach. There's money for you, but never come near me again.

Another. And there.

Another. And there. (*All fling him money as they go out.*)

[End of Scene 1]

Act I Scene 2

*Courtyard of castle. To the right of stage a raised platform on
which is a representation of the bow and part of the body of
Noah's Ark. Another part of the platform is curtained off, or
there is a curtain door with the words "House of Noah"
written above it. Above this platform and at the back of stage
rise the walls of the castle. At some distance above the ground
there are a row of arches something like an Italian loggia, a
place where people can stand and look down into the courtyard.
Underneath this loggia at the back is a great archway through
which one sees heavy gates, which are now open, giving a
glimpse of a street beyond. At one side close to the archway a
door opens into the castle. At the left side of the stage is a high
wall containing a small door and showing above the trees in
the garden. In the middle of this wall there is a fountain, some
Neptune or the like holding a shell from which at present no
water is flowing. Above the fountain is a vat of a temporary
nature, which is connected with the fountain by pipes. There*

*may be on either side towards front of stage two towers so
placed that the street scene of Scene 1 can be used as a front
scene with these towers as permanent wings unchanged
through play.*

*Soldiers bringing in the litter with bags of money. Directed by
the Chancellor they carry it into the house.*

Chancellor. Set it within there; shut the iron door of 1
 the cellar upon.it. The state has hardly seen so much 2
 money these twenty years. (*Two soldiers who have 3
 lingered behind are gaping up into the air. A song
 is faintly heard.*)

First Soldier. Listen, did you hear that? 4

Second Soldier. Yes, yes, quite clearly, but it's gone again. 5

Chancellor. What are you gaping up into the sky for? 6

First Soldier. Just now we heard a voice high up in the air. 7

Chancellor. Well, what did it say, unless it spoke treason? 8

First Soldier. I heard it cry out vengeance on those that 9
 took that money from the people. I heard that plainly, 10
 Chancellor. 11

Chancellor. I said I would have no treason repeated. 12

Second Soldier. It sounded to me like a love song or some 13
 sort of vanity. 14

First Soldier. A love song, was it; who'd come out of the 15
 grave to sing a love song? 16

Second Soldier. Love song it was. (*The other soldiers 17
 have returned from the house.*)

Chancellor. Well, get you out of this, and remember that 18
 while I am Chancellor here I'll have no tales of pro- 19
 phesying voices whispered in taverns. 20

Second Soldier. I said it was a vanity. 21

Chancellor. You know your duties, to join your fellows, 22
 and to keep watch, you and they, without being too 23
 much noticed. You are to keep the side streets to be 24
 at hand if needed. I and the Queen will walk down the 25
 main way unattended, in seeming confidence. Now go. 26

(*They go out. The Queen has come in unnoticed, the
Chancellor having followed the soldiers under the arch. She*

*comes from the house or from one of the towers in front of
the stage. She stands close to the fountain as if listening.
The Chancellor turns into the courtyard and sees her.*)

Chancellor. Your Majesty, I am most grateful that you	27
should have heard my prayer and come without delay and	28
alone.	29
The Queen. Hush!	30
Chancellor. With crown and dress of state.	31
Queen. Hush!	32
Chancellor (*walking up and down*). There is still a chance,	33
a desperate chance although it be, that with the glitter	34
of the crown, your father's memory to help . . .	35
Queen. Hush, listen! Yes, there again. Someone is singing	36
very low.	37
Chancellor. I think I hear it now, though I have not the	38
hearing I once had. But who is it and where is it?	39
Queen. In the big vat there.	40
Chancellor. That is an empty vat to be filled tonight with	41
wine. The wine flows from it to the fountain.	42
Queen. Yes, I am certain.	43
Chancellor. I will climb and look though Time has made me	44
stiff.	45
Queen. You would find nothing. I think it is some ghost.	46
This ancient courtyard should be full of them. Maybe	47
it was sent to warn me that I was doing wrong in coming	48
with this show upon me and not staying at my prayers.	49
Chancellor. You fast and pray too much, it makes one timid.	50
Someone singing out there in the street. That is	51
all it is.	52
A Voice. Where are you, Noah's wife?	53
Queen. Ah, that is a different voice. It is calling a	54
most ancient ghost.	55
Voice. Where are you, Noah's wife?	56
Queen (*clings to Chancellor*). There, there again.	57
Voice. Where are you, Noah's wife?	58
Queen. O God have mercy. (*The Friend comes in from the*	59
garden. The Queen has shrunk back under the arch.)	
Chancellor. Who are you calling? The name sounded strange.	60

The Friend. Somebody who is stranger than the name, now   61
   one thing, now another, a joy and a torment. Where is   62
   she? She has to play in a minute or two and she cannot   63
   be found.   64

Chancellor. You and she then are of the troupe that came   65
   this morning, for whom we have set up the stage yonder.   66

The Friend. She cannot be found. We have searched [for]   67
   her in every corner, even in the wood beyond the town;   68
   and she is so good a player, we are nothing without her,   69
   and Yellow Martin . . .   70

Chancellor. Your manager?   71

The Friend. Yes sir. He will be out of his mind with   72
   grief, for they are to be married. O, he has such a   73
   time with her. But I see you cannot tell me anything.   74
   Where are you, Noah's wife, where are you? (*She goes*   75
   out.)

Queen (*coming from under archway*). A stage player and a   76
   fountain to flow with wine, no good will come of it.   77
   Is it to preside over a revel that you've bid me to meet   78
   you here?   79

Chancellor. I have asked you to meet me here that I may   80
   show you to your people and so end this long seclusion.   81
   These players are but part of the old customary celebra-   82
   tion, habit that was made before you and I were born.   83
   When royalty shows itself, there must be joy about it.   84

Queen. And it was for this, this worldly, perhaps sinful   85
   scene that I was brought from my dear cell where the   86
   soul is prepared for Heaven.   87

Chancellor. There is great discontent, and I have no hope   88
   but in your majesty's face and gracious words to save   89
   the state from riot, maybe from rebellion. This tax   90
   for St. Winifred's new church and convent, and the ever-   91
   growing power of your priests . . .   92

Queen. Can they not give Heaven its share? Why should the   93
   needs of this life that is full of illusions and false   94
   images seem more important than the needs of the life   95
   beyond where there is reality? Have not I, a queen,   96
   with joy given up all but my bare cell? Is not this   97
   life but infancy and that to come maturity? I would   98

be the mother of my people and make them, as we make 99
children, even with blows, prepare for what is to come. 100
Chancellor. The soldiers alone are to be trusted, and who 101
knows how long we may trust them? Some few have joined 102
rioters. 103
Queen. I will make all this country innocent or die attempt- 104
ing, nor will I turn back because the state may die too. 105
Was it not St. Winifred of Barbary herself who said "Bet- 106
ter all life should perish than one sin be committed"? 107
Chancellor. I have not brought you here to argue with you, 108
I know your thoughts are fixed. If your majesty will 109
but smile in the market-place, if you will but speak a 110
few empty words, all may be well. They loved your father, 111
make them love you too and they will let you do what you 112
please. A painted face, a piece of damask, a smiling 113
face, a bow that is not from the waist only but given 114
with the whole swaying body, some words of love to those 115
you have never seen—and may never see again—a little 116
wearing of the mask, that is all I ask of you. If 117
you would have obedience, you must seem to be all the 118
greatness your people dream of being and have not might 119
of soul to be, all that their shivering heart denies 120
them. 121
Queen (*who has been huddled up on the threshold of the*
house, or upon one of those stones shaped like a sugarloaf
which one sees by gates). St. Winifred of Hungary would 122
never have taken so worldly a likeness. She went in rags 123
and eat her food out of a dish full of ashes. You bid 124
me to sin. How could I show myself to my eternal judge 125
if I pretend to be what I am not? 126
Chancellor. Then I had best go back to my own home, and let 127
the kingdom go to the ruin I cannot prevent now that its 128
Queen seeks martyrdom. 129
Queen. Martyrdom? Ah, now I see your meaning. You think 130
I am committing a great sin and would call me back from 131
it, that I am seeking martyrdom at my own time and will, 132
and not leaving that to God. If that were indeed true, 133
if you had seen into the depths of the soul—for the soul 134
is very strange . . . 135

Chancellor. Your Majesty, I am not skilled in these things.   136
   I was but thinking of the ruin that will overtake this   137
   state. I saw in imagination these towers burning,   138
   everything I had hoped almost against hope to prevent   139
   by appealing to the loyalty of your people . . .   140
Queen. But it is all true. I can see it now. I drifted   141
   into that sin. I did not understand what I was longing   142
   for until this minute. They put St. Winifred of Barbary   143
   [to death]. I had hoped to win her crown, her fame   144
   in Heaven and on earth. I have longed for it and then   145
   I have wondered if I should have the courage. St.   146
   Winifred was not like other women. O, do not let us   147
   delay. You have saved me from a great sin and I am   148
   thankful. (*Going towards the gate but then stopping.*)   149
   But to go, that too is a sin, to show myself in all this   150
   gold; the poor anatomy, the flesh full of original sin   151
   covered with embroidery as though it were some precious   152
   thing. O, how hard life is when one passes the door   153
   of one's cell.   154
Chancellor. Come, your Majesty, I am like a falconer that   155
   bears upon the wrist a hawk that struggles to lose it-   156
   self in the heavens, and all I understand is to keep   157
   the jesses tight; yet it may be, before the day end,   158
   some murderer's hand may cut them.   159
Queen. You think that death may come unsought; a true   160
   martyrdom would bring forgiveness for every sin.   161
Chancellor. We both risk our lives.   162
Queen. I pray to God that I have the courage.   163

(*Queen and Chancellor go out of gate at back. Player
Queen puts her head out of the vat. She sings a
thought* [*song*] *founded upon the following thought.*

   "I would know who you are in yourself, my beloved   164
   said to me. Put off that mask of burning gold with   165
   emerald eyes that I may know what you are. I will not   166
   put away my mask. It is the mask of burning gold,   167
   it is the emerald eyes that make your heart beat so   168
   quickly. I would be praised by the beating of your   169
   heart. But my beloved answered me, I do not even know   170

if you are a friend or an enemy." (*While she is singing*   171
a young man, the player Peter, and the Friend come in
at the back. Seeing them the Player Queen becomes silent.)

Peter. We are quite alone here. You said when I had fin-   172
ished the coat that Noah's wife is to wear you would   173
give me a kiss. There is the coat. Don't prick your-   174
self with the scissors; they are folded up in it. I   175
am going down to the town to see what all the shouting   176
is about. I shall be back in good time. Japhet doesn't   177
come until the end of the play.   178

The Friend. You think the one we are looking for has gone   179
down to the shouting?   180

Peter. No, she never goes far off. She is somewhere about   181
here, keeping her eyes on Yellow Martin, angry as she   182
pretends to be.   183

The Friend. O, she was not pretending this time, and he   184
was not pretending. It was such a quarrel. O, I am   185
getting afraid, afraid that she may have killed herself.   186
I have often heard her say that she will do that some   187
day, and that then Yellow Martin would be sorry.   188

Peter. Kill herself! Why you are as foolish about her   189
as Yellow Martin. Put her out enough and she will play   190
at doing it, and maybe go to the point of looking over   191
the river brink or down the muzzle of a gun and making   192
all the faces of despair that she can think of. You   193
are too kind to her and to everybody.   194

Friend. You were always so wise. There is the kiss I pro-   195
mised you, but don't forget to come back in time. Why,   196
they are shouting again. Be careful of yourself, and   197
if there is any quarreling do not go too near them.   198
(*He goes out through central gate. She turns and*
sees Player Queen.) O, I have found you only just   199
in time, and here is your dress. Come down out of that.   200
We have been searching for you all night. What have you   201
been doing? Yellow Martin has been so unhappy, and I   202
have been so anxious.   203

Player Queen. Lying up here in the empty wine vat putting   204
up my head every now and then during the night, watching   205
the beautiful young men that wait upon the Queen. So   206

tall, so ruddy. All night they have been playing upon   207
lutes and dancing.   208

The Friend. It is no use sending me to Yellow Martin with   209
that story. He has seen the Queen's people. They are   210
all old men with their shins speckled from sitting over   211
the fire. She wouldn't let a young man or a young girl   212
near her, but only old people who are making their souls.   213
Why do you torture Yellow Martin so?   214

Player Queen. Because I love him and want him to be always   215
thinking of me. I am not content like you to take a   216
kiss as a kiss and tell everybody what pleases him.   217

The Friend. You are making Yellow Martin so unhappy.   218

Player Queen (*singing*). "My beloved said to me I do not   219
even know if you are a friend or an enemy." (*She*   220
sinks again into the vat.)

The Friend. O, do come out of that. I have brought you   221
your dress as Noah's wife; we have only a few minutes   222
before we begin.   223

Player Queen (*putting her head up again*). I will not come   224
down. I told Yellow Martin I would never play the part   225
again. I will not play a stupid woman no better than   226
myself, without a thing worth saying or doing. I will   227
never again be beaten by Noah because I will not go into   228
the Ark.   229

The Friend. But Noah does not really beat you; you are   230
not hurt.   231

Player Queen. I must have a great part, a part with fine   232
words and a fine dress. I must say and do all the   233
things I have dreamt of. I must be beautiful and have   234
shiny things to wear. I must grow greater and make all   235
those that look upon me grow greater. Bad or good does   236
not matter, but I must be a fire, a light. O, he must   237
make a play about the Queen of Sheba or Herodias, or   238
somebody of that kind. I have found out that when he is   239
alone he thinks of people like that, and he would like   240
to write of them. I am going to be his secret thought.   241

The Friend. No, no, that is no use. He will never let you   242
play any of those parts. The people want what they are   243
used to. Some of them like pious people and others what's   244

like themselves. Who wants to see and hear those heathen   245
   kings and queens with their big words?   246
Player Queen. I will make him write the part I want. I   247
   will never come down out of this vat till I have his   248
   promise.   249
The Friend. Then stop there till you turn into wine, and   250
   then maybe you'll be pleased if enough people get   251
   drunk.   252
Player Queen. He will do what I want because he has no-   253
   body else to play for him.   254
The Friend. He will not; there is somebody else.   255
Player Queen. You would not dare do such a thing.   256
The Friend (*half crying*). He was so unhappy I could not   257
   help it. I have promised; how could I help it?   258
Player Queen (*who has been sitting on edge of vat jumps*
   down and seizes her, shaking her). You did that,   259
   you poultice of rotten apples, you damp cheese.   260
The Friend. I did not want to, but he was so unhappy.   261
Player Queen. O you snail, you jellyfish, you trough of   262
   pig's feeding.   263
The Friend. Don't kill me.   264
Player Queen. Give me that dress.   265
The Friend. Help, help!   266
Player Queen. Give me that dress, you empty shirt on a   267
   clothesline. (*She throws her off, gasping. Players*   268
   come running in from garden and house.)
The Friend. Don't let her have it. She'll tear it in   269
   pieces.   270
Player Queen. How dare you come between me and Martin?   271
The Friend. I said I'd play the part, and look how she's   272
   shaken me, and she's called me such names.   273
Player. One of you must take it, or we'll all starve.   274
   What's to take us to the next town if we're not paid   275
   here.   276
The Friend. I daren't play it now. She's terrible now   277
   that she has a man between her teeth.   278
Player Queen. Give it to me, I'll play it. So you still   279
   want to go on all fours in the pig's belly, and to be   280
   the front legs or the hind legs of a cow, or to flap   281

your wings like a bird, and maybe to peck like a hen? 282

Player. What does it matter so long as we're paid for it? 283

Player (*who carries a flute*). As for me, I want to walk 284
in purple, but who wants to see me in it? 285

Player Queen. You are like me. 286

Player. I have no man between my teeth, but my pipes wail 287
for Babylon. (*He blows a note or two.*) 288

Player Queen. And you scorn this? (*Holding up dress of* 289
Noah's wife.)

Player. I scorn all but cloth of gold or the blood of the 290
shellfish. 291

Player Queen. Then I promise to you that before the year's 292
out you'll have a fine dress and fine words to speak. 293
Martin shall write for me of a queen of Babylon; she 294
will wander the roads as a beggar, shaking her rags on 295
the wind, put out by jealous sisters. But she shall 296
come to her own again when all the city is raging. She 297
shall be like the harsh sweet juice of the grape burst- 298
ing through the skin of the world, and when she is dead 299
they will say of her "We were a multitude, and yet when 300
we looked at her each one of us seemed to be alone." 301
(*She throws dress down upon the ground and begins dancing*
upon it, dancing her scorn. The others stand around,
laughing and applauding. Enter Martin.)

Player. Here is our queen, sir, but somewhat out of con- 302
ceit with her kingdom. 303

Martin. I did not expect to find her so soon; I thought 304
she would hide till supper-time. 305

Player Queen. O, I shall make you tremble yet, stony- 306
hearted though you seem. 307

Martin. Well I know the value of your threats, so go 308
dress for your part. And the rest of you get into 309
the shapes of Noah's beasts as soon as you can. 310

Player Queen. Threats or none, I may be capable of more 311
than you know, or than I know. I am called the Beggar 312
Maid of Babylon, and I have wandered by Euphrates 313
seven years, but who knows what I am? 314

Martin. How could you play a queen? (*He is taking a long* 315
trumpet out of its case.) Where could you get the look 316

of a queen or the manner of a queen? Hurry, there is   317
no time to be lost. Go behind there and dress. And   318
you there, put down that flute and find your pigskin.   319
I am going to give the signal for the play.   320
Player Queen (her head through curtain of Noah's house).
There are a hundred queens inside my ribs.   321
Martin (blowing). You that have eaten off pewter and red   322
earthenware.   323
Player Queen. That is why I long for Babylon and Nineveh,   324
a hundred horsemen and golden armour, and a great silver   325
chair carried above men's heads on two silver spears.   326
Martin (blowing). You a queen, whose father spent his life   327
hedging and ditching?   328
Player Queen. That is why I hunger for cloth of gold and for   329
multitudes to see my straight back and high head.   330
Martin (blowing). There is too much of that high head.   331
Pull it out of that or I will break it with my trum-   332
pet. (*She keeps her head out, laughing for a moment,*   333
and then draws it in.)

[End of Scene 2]

Act I Scene 2

Palace of Surrico, lit by a great window to R. At back a large
fountain with huge ornamented cistern or vat above. The Queen
is standing close to window, listening. At first her figure alone
is in light. Gradually the Chancellor comes into the light.

Chancellor. Your majesty. (*No answer.*) They say that you
would speak . . .
Queen. Hush. Hush.
Chancellor.   That you would speak . . .
Queen.   Hush.
Chancellor. Would speak with me of some affairs of state.
I have come quickly for the household troops
Are waiting to conduct your majesty.
Queen. Hush.
Chancellor. I have hopes that so familiar things
Your father's crown, the embroidered dress of state,
All that they have been taught to reverence . . .

Queen. Listen. There, there again. Now I am sure of it.
Someone is singing.

Chancellor.   You have but dreamed a voice
For we're alone.

Queen.   And you would dream it too
If you had but the hearing of your youth.

Chancellor. Where could the singer be?

Queen.   In that great vat.

Chancellor. In that great vat that I've had hoisted up
To hold the wine the fountain is to flow with?
You took the bubbling of the wine for singing;
But that's not so, for now I think of it
The vat is empty still.

Queen.   There, there again.

Chancellor. I'll climb and peep though Time has stiffened me.

Queen. No, you'd find nothing in it. Chancellor,
Do you believe that there are ghosts that walk?
And if they walk, why may they not sing too
In an old house like this?

Chancellor.   A ghost, so be it,
And while it's singing in the vat of wine
It cannot hurt. And even when night falls
And it has run between men's ribs and pushed
Their own minds out, I'll take my chance with it.
We statesmen have to fear a deadlier breed
Of ghosts than that.

Queen.   The night my father died
One of the servants, in a trance or sleeping,
Crowed like a cock. And I myself have heard,
Standing at sunrise by the window there,
A cock that crowed amid the foam of the sea.

A Voice. Where are you, Noah's wife?

Queen.   A different voice
And it is calling to some ancient voice.

Chancellor. This one is more substantial.

Voice.   Noah's wife!

Queen. There, there again.

Voice.   Where are you, Noah's wife?

Queen. O God (*She shrinks back into the shadow as the
Friend comes in.*)

Chancellor. Why do you cry so strange a name?

The Friend. I'm calling one that's stranger than the name,
Now one thing, now another—joy and torment.
She knows that we're to play within the hour
And she has vanished.

Chancellor. You're of the troupe of players
That came last night?

The Friend. She is the candle stick
For we are but the tallow. And Yellow Martin
When he went out at dawn had such pale cheeks
I am sure he thought to find her in the sea.

Chancellor. Your manager?

The Friend. Yes sir. He will go crazed
If she has done a mischief to herself
And there is nothing that she would not do
To make him wretched when that mood is on her.

Chancellor. What, kill herself?

The Friend. Yes sir, for she has grown
So bitter and hard-hearted since she loved.

Chancellor. You play a story from the scriptures?

The Friend. Sir
We have played nothing else for these five years.
Where are you, Noah's wife? (*Goes.*)

Chancellor. Five years ago
We made a law, at your most urgent wish,
Forbidding under penalty of prison
All plays that were not warranted for truth
By holy writ, and thereby roused the ghost
That startled you. You say too many prayers,
Your Majesty, and that has made you timid.
But now the ghosts are gone, and the sun out
Upon the sea, and not a cock in the foam
Has crowed since dawn. Let's quickly to the town.
But I'd forgotten. You had sent for me,
There's something you would say.

Queen. May I put off
This robe of state, the griffin and the roses,
All this gold? For I wear under it
The plain old dress that I have always worn.

Chancellor. But you are Queen.

Queen.   So much the greater need
    That I should wear such plain and simple stuff
    As will remind me of my littleness
    Before the eyes of God.
Chancellor.   Your Majesty,
    I would not set my will against your will
    But that the times are desperate. There is none
    That we can trust. The very soldiers murmur,
    The mobs begin to riot. Show yourself
    In a nun's habit with a saint's face
    And there is not a mother's son but thinks
    How can she love us if she hates the world
    That sets our hearts aglow.
Queen.   What must I do?
Chancellor. Go dressed in all the pride of your old fathers'
    And then bow down, and not with knee alone
    But with the body, and so smile
    To knaves that you have never seen before
    They'll think you love them, and dream ever after
    That all the charm of the wild flesh of the world
    Has passed them by in gold embroidered slippers.
Queen. You'd have me like that player that went out.
Chancellor. I would not take the play from holy writ,
    Our need's too great for that.
Queen.   Must I deceive?
Chancellor. Queens that have laughed to set the world at ease
    And kings that cried "I am great Alexander
    Or Caesar come again," but stir our wonder
    That they may stir their own, and grow at length
    Almost alike to that unlikely strength.
    And those that will not make deliberate choice
    Are nothing, or become some passion's voice
    Doing its will, believing what it chooses.
Queen. I have prayed against all passion, as God knows
    And every day with that old saint have said
    'Twere better that all human kind were dead
    Than even one man sin.
Chancellor.   Then my work's done
    Exchange that circlet for a martyr's crown
    And find a holier chancellor at Heaven's gate.

Queen. You're angry now.
Chancellor.   My business was the state
    And not to save the soul that is but breath.
Queen. And I must go alone?
Chancellor.   If set on death.
    Youth that can dream of Heaven may well go die
    But age must love substantial things and I
    Shall get my goods and take myself away.
    The mob will burn this house down before day.
    Yes, I am old, and love my life.
Queen.   But sir . . .
Chancellor (*going*). Youth is a plague.
Queen.   Come back.
Chancellor (*returning*).   Then you will wear . . .
Queen. Whatever pleases you.
Chancellor.   That gold embroidered dress? (*She nods.*)
    You'll bow and smile? Be full of graciousness
    To wicked men and those you have never seen? (*She nods.*)
    You will put on the Queen and off the nun? (*She nods.*)
    Pray God we are not too late.
Queen (*as they go out she says this prayer* [?] *off stage*).
                But no, not one
    Although for this time I have given way
    Shall make me dress my body from today
    In wanton[?] gold, no not a man on earth. (*Voice dies away.*)
P. Queen (*putting head up*).
    "Put off that mask of burning gold
    With emerald eyes."
    "O no my dear you make so bold
    To find if one be wild and wise
    And yet not cold."

    "I would but find what's there to find,
    Love or deceit."
    "It was the mask engaged your mind
    And after set your heart to beat
    Not what's behind."

    "But lest you be my enemy
    I must enquire." (*Puts head down again.*)

Peter. What was it set them quarrelling last night?

The Friend. I cannot tell—I heard his voice and hers
  And when the day broke she could not be found
  And he went out and by the look on his face
  I knew he thought to find her body in the surf.

Peter. And love sent you to keep your eyes on him
  And see if he were pale.

The Friend.   What a wild tongue you have.

Peter. And now being in the vertigo of love
  Would mortify your love by finding her
  And putting her in Martin's arms again.

The Friend. Of all men you're the last that I would meet
  When my heart's full.

Peter.   And you that cry aloud
  How pale he was, she has broke his heart at last,
  Are of all women her he'll think the least.
  For do you think that he would have her kind,
  That she can make him suffer, for he knows
  That her delight is but to give him pain,
  Because to one so passionately made
  Love would be nothing if it lacked
  Thunder.

Friend.   O leave me.

Peter.   But I am wrong
  You do not care if you are thanked or no
  It's not love's vertigo, it's love's deceit
  That drives you. It hates a rival so
  That it would give that rival everything
  That it might home and brag itself the better
  Before a looking glass.

The Friend.   How dare you say so?
  How can I prove that I have no such thought?

Peter. By coming to the town. We'll find her there
  Or if we do not we'll find what's astir
  For they've been shouting in the streets this hour
  And as our parts but come at the play's end,
  We'll not be missed. I have been cast for Japhet.

The Friend. I cannot go with all this trouble here.

Peter. They quarrel every time the moon is full.

The Friend. But last night's quarrel was the worst of all

And when I came upon her by midnight
At the big window there, she talked of death—
I have told no one this—and by sea water;
After that, of moonlight.

Peter.   Did she lean out?

The Friend. Yes.

Peter.   Her thoughts were running upon death.

The Friend. You think she's drowned?

Peter.   I said her thoughts.
    She loved her life so well she longed to crush
    Death even like a grape upon her tongue.

The Friend. If she were living she'd have hid herself
    Where she could keep an eye on him, and here
    In the pale shadows and the stony [?] light
    There's not a corner that a mouse could hide in.

Peter. You're hoping in your heart that she is dead.
    For Martin loves her and she loves the moon [?]
    And you love Martin.

The Friend.   For all the harm she does
    I've never wished that harm should come to her.

Peter. Wish them no worse than that they'll love too much
    For happiness. But if you should love me . . .

The Friend. Love you?

Peter.   We'd both of us be happy.
    Because I am not gloomy or quarrelsome,
    Jealous, or self-deceiving, turning all
    My soul into incredible shapes of frenzy
    But live that every separate sense may keep
    It's own delight.

[CANCELED VERSION]

    For I am neither quarrelsome nor jealous
    Nor full of self-deceit, nor do I turn
    My soul into incredible shapes of frenzy
    Nor lose my own delight by running all
    The senses in each other.

[WBY HAS WRITTEN:] ? what version

The Friend.   You've never been in love.

Peter. And that is why you'll fall in love with me.

The Friend. I fall in love with you?

Peter.   For peace and quiet
    And so to bring youth's heartache to an end.

The Friend. Never.

Peter.   You must, for it's in the book,
    But better start the day than end with it.
    So come and find her in the town. You will not?
    Well, we shall be together at the end of the day.
        (*He goes out.*)

Player Queen. Martha.

The Friend.   I've found you.

Player Queen.   And the day is just begun.
    That is not true, the thing that Peter says.
    I know that you love Martin, for [I] have watched you.

The Friend. It seems as if the whole world knew of it
    But I myself.

Player Queen.   But you'll not take him from me.

The Friend. Have I not searched all day that I might find you?

Player Queen. What was it Peter said?

The Friend.   Seeing that I have searched
    That I might give you to the man you love
    Because I know his heart's so set on you
    That it would cease to beat if you were gone,
    You need not fear.

P. Queen.   When he and I have quarreled
    I dread the very mouse that squeaks under the floor
    Yet cannot keep from quarreling because
    As I would have my soul and his soul one
    There is no differing thought too slight to seem
    As it were a wedge thrust down into the soul.

The Friend. Let that fantastic Peter go his way.

P. Queen. And if I sent you with a message to him
    You'd not make love?

The Friend.   Make love to Yellow Martin?
    And [he] without a thought that's not of you
    Because he thinks you drowned.

P. Queen.   You will tell him
    That I've been hidden in this vat all night

And morning, and would not come out
But that I'm sore [?] with the hard boards [of] it.
Where are you going?

The Friend.   To tell him what you say.

P. Queen. But you must tell him that since dawn came up
I've had my eyes on beautiful young men
That waited here to hold up the Queen's train.
One played the lute, one juggled with a sword
As if the world were but a golden cage
  And they canary birds.

The Friend.   He'd not believe me.
He's seen all those that are about the Queen
And there's not one but has got speckled shins
With drowsing at the fire. If she could help it
She'd never see a head that was not bald.
And were the message true I should not take it.
Why do you torture Yellow Martin so?

P. Queen. Because I'd have him think of me all day
And all the night until the scared moon fled
Before his desperate thoughts, and the male sun
Sprang out of bed.

The Friend.   That will break his heart
Or end his love for you before you're done.

P. Queen (*sinking in vat*).
But lest you are my enemy
I must enquire.
O no my dear let all that be
What matter so there is but fire
In you, in me.

The Friend. O do come down.

P. Queen.   I'll tell you everything
I found a play that Martin wrote in his youth
So proud and drunken that it is as though
He'd plucked the sun where it hung upon a cloud
Like a burst grape and crushed it into lines,
It's all about a Babylonian woman
That went in rags awhile and then was queen
And I'll play nothing else until I've played it.

The Friend. But you will go to prison if you play it

For since the Old King died no play's allowed
That is not taken from the scripture.
Play. Queen.   What matter.
There is a scene so fine at the end of it
That it is worth the price. I have it here—
A high and feathery scene. All Babylon
Has risen in arms to put the queen to death,
And she outfaces them and takes the spears
Into her breast. And there's a good scene too
Where her lover says "You have no heart."
She sings a song about a mask and face
    "O put off that burning mask."
The Friend. I will not listen. If you should play that play
We'd be imprisoned first and starve after
Or else go wandering through the world.
Player Queen. There's a fine part for you—I know mine best,
    [doubtful reading]
I'll help you with it.
The Friend.   It is Noah's wife
That must be played upon the stroke of twelve
It has been cried in every street, and crowds
Are coming up from every side to listen.
Player Queen. What, would you bring to life that wrinkled mask
That Noah beats about the ribs because
She will not go into his Ark, and set her up
For crowds to look upon, that half-drowned rat
Though she escapes the world's first ruin, waiting
But the fire?
The Friend.   But Noah does not really beat you.
P. Queen. Sorrowing for my true life is what I'm playing
And to be kicked around, beaten for an hour [?]
Is all my share of the world. Go,
Till Martin says I may do what I please
While the hour lasts I'll stay in this big vat,
But give me the old dress to make a cushion.
The Friend. I ask most solemnly for the last time
That you come down and get into this dress
And play what you have played a hundred times.

> You have been praised for it—it pleases everyone,
> And Martin's choice.

P. Queen.   He's a most obstinate man.

> But now the winds all blow in Babylon [doubtful reading]
> And he must choose as I do from this out
> For there is not a soul could take my place.

The Friend. There is.

P. Queen.   There is not one in all the company

> Dare take a part that has been given me.

The Friend. There is.

P. Queen.   No, no, he must endure me.

The Friend. He will not, for I'll take the part myself.

P. Queen. You?

Friend.   I have searched for you and so besought

> You cannot think I would rob you of it.
> For my own sake, and now for Martin's sake
> I'll play it.

P. Queen.   Give me that dress.

Friend.   No, no.

Player Queen. I'll have that dress.

The Friend.   No, for you'd tear it up.

Player Queen. You poultice of rotten apples, you damp cheese.

The Friend. Let me go.

Player Queen.   Trough of pig's feeding.

The Friend.   Help!

P. Queen. You empty shirt on a clothes line.

The Friend.   Help! (*Players come in.*)

> Don't let her have that dress, she'll tear it up.

P. Queen. How dare you come between me and my lover?

The Friend (*crying*). I said I'd play the part because she would not.

> She said that she was tired of Noah's wife
> And wanted something with a better dress
> And no old wrinkled mask.

A Player.   She's in the right.

> I too scorn everything but cloth of gold
> And purple as the shell fish.

Another Player.   I am a genius

> And have I been allowed to show it? No.

I have played nothing for twelve months or more
But the hind legs of a cow, the two hind legs.
Another Player. Yes, but they say the prison floor is damp
With toads upon the ground, bats in the roof.
Another Player (an old woman). I too have had a man between my teeth
And been as bitter.
Another Player.   Though I am not in love
My pipes begin to wail for Babylon.
The Friend. But she has broken Yellow Martin's heart.
A Player (an old woman). What is that heartbreak but the fiery nest
(The phoenix nest—life is but born of life)
Where life, the holy phoenix, comes from life?
Now my own mother told me . . .
A Player.   What's the use
Of running through the generations when we need
A heavy curse that could weigh down with chains
Sink in the earth, or scatter in the sea
All art that puts [us] in a sorry shape
Or leaves us nothing finer than our neighbours
Or gives me people [?] low?
Player Queen (is dancing).   That's it, that's it.
Put chains on it, down to the grave with it,
Trample it underfoot, heap scorn on it.
We should be young and beautiful and speak
Fine feathery things.
Another.   Trample it down—leap on it.
All. Leap on it, leap on it.
Martin (coming in). Stop dancing there and get into your dress;
Here are the masks, begone and put them on
We have no time to lose.
Friend.   It was I that found her.
Yellow Martin. Found who?
Player Queen.   You do not know?
Yellow.   I know
That the hour's about to strike, the play begin.
PQ. You do not know that I've been lost since dawn?
Yellow Martin. You'll like that long-nosed mask. How should I know?
I went at dawn and walked upon the shore
And saw the sun rise.

P. Queen. It's not to be endured.

He knew before he went to bed last night

That he had driven me to some desperate purpose.

Yellow Martin. They say there is a cock that crows in the foam.

PQ. Let it crow where it please.

Yellow Martin. That fits you better.

And after that it flies at a man [?]

And crows a second time.

P. Queen. But am not I

Of more account than fifty cocks and hens?

Yellow Martin. But I heard nothing and so went to town

And bought new masks—that bristled chin for Noah.

P. Queen. I might have drowned myself as I had planned

And you'd care nothing for it.

Yellow Martin. Long chin for you.

P. Queen. I thought that you had gone to search the sea

For my dead body. (*Cries.*)

Yellow Martin. Now all go dress.

Do what you please, my dear, you cannot shake me

And though you strike you bruise yourself alone,

Striking with that wild hand a thing of stone.

P. Queen. I'd take that thing of stone and let it drop

Upon the stonier ground; then take it up

And throw it down again until it broke.

Yellow Martin. Ah that's the hour. I knew it was on the stroke.

Act II

Same scene as before. Old servants of the Queen, directed by the Friend, arranging chairs and benches.

The Friend. Put that there. That will be enough, the young people will stand or sit on the ground. (*To Martin.*) A poor audience so far, none but the Queen's servants. We have not often played to cooks and gardeners.

Martin (*who stands listening*). Listen to that, they are cheering for us in the town. We shall have a big house soon. (*He goes to the gate where he stands looking out. The Friend continues to make herself busy with one*

thing or another. She now begins to arrange the stage,
going in and out of Noah's house. There can be a litter
of things, players' masks perhaps, which she puts into
the house. The servants stand in groups talking. With
one of them is a boy of about nine or ten.

Boy. What are the players like? 9

First Servant. Much like the rest of us. 10

Second Servant. No, but slippery as the eels in the ri- 11
ver. 12

Boy. O Grandfather, how can they be like us, and they 13
sounding out all those grand things to one another? 14

First Servant. The boy's in the right. Why shouldn't 15
they be better than us. Don't they say that Noah's 16
flood is as good as a sermon? 17

Second Servant. Well, when I was that little chap's size 18
there's many a time I took the clothes off the hedge 19
because the players were coming. This is the way I 20
take it it is with they and their like. If I am 21
making a wall I take a piece of soft mortar to stick 22
the stones together, and before it hardens you can 23
slap it here and there into any shape takes your fancy, 24
and now if that mortar should never harden, what sort 25
of a wall would it make? That's what a player is, mor- 26
tar that never hardens. Maybe he's a saint one moment, 27
but when he's out on the roads I'd sooner he found bare 28
hedges. 29

Third Servant. But that's all wrong, for when a man has 30
got a soft soul like that and never lets it harden 31
and can take what shape he likes, won't he take the 32
shape that's respectable and most pleasing? Maybe 33
you yourself now would be the better for a new twist. 34

Second Servant. I say the shape a man's born to and will 35
go to judgment in is the best shape he'll get. 36

First Servant. But what shape is he born with? Is he to 37
go to judgment as a young lad like your grandson there, 38
or a hale man like Tom the gardener, or an old man like 39
myself? Maybe now we have no right shape of our own 40
at all. 41

Second Servant. Doesn't everybody know that when you die   42
    and go to Heaven you have a likeness of you of thirty   43
    years and keep that always? I'd sooner have my choice   44
    shape and be judged by that.   45
Fourth Servant. What, Tom, would you paint your face and   46
    you going before your maker? Five and fifty years now I have   47
    been watching the crows pecking, and there was a thing some   48
    wise man said, Aristotle of the Books or another, that   49
    keeps running in my head. "To know your own true shape,"   50
    he said, "that's what a wise man has to do and what he's   51
    here to do, and when he's found it he's free of the court."   52
Fifth Servant (joining the group). It was not Noah and the   53
    flood, nor Michael and the Dragon either that they   54
    showed us in the Old King's day. Do you mind Christmas   55
    and Easter then, and do you mind that day the King   56
    came back from the wars and the play-actors were in the   57
    big hall? O, that now was a play, I tell you.   58
First Servant. Hush, man. Don't speak of that before the   59
    child.   60
Fifth Servant. There was the Old King, and they brought   61
    him a leather jack full of ale.   62
First Servant. Come away, child, and help the lady to put   63
    the form right.   64
Fifth Servant. There was a player, and a great tumbler he   65
    was, and they cut the points of his breeches so that   66
    they fell down. O, he was a great man I tell you,   67
    before Prester John he played.   68
Second Servant. O, I mind that, I mind that. It was a   69
    great trick he had, and the Old King he up with the   70
    leather jack and he flung it and hit him fair and   71
    square where the breeches ought to have been.   72
Fifth Servant. We'll never see players like that again.   73
    He'd been over the whole world. Prester John he played   74
    to.   75
Second Servant. I'd die of laughing when I think of the Old   76
    King. Fair and square he hit him. How he did jump,   77
    and the Old King gave him his hat full of silver.   78
First Servant. There's no fun in the players now. Where's   79

the man that can make cats fighting and dogs fighting   80
    with his mouth?   81
Second Servant. When I think of the Old King and that lea-   82
ther jack! (*Yellow Martin comes back from gate.*)   83
Martin. Take your seats, take your seats. (*To Friend.*)   84
    They are still shouting in the town, but I'll not   85
    wait another moment. Not one of them for all their   86
    ardour has shown himself in the street; there's not a man in sight.   87
The Friend. Well, what does it matter. The Chancellor pays   88
    us whether the yard is full or empty.   89
Martin. O, it won't be big enough to hold all that will   90
    be here before the play is finished, but the shadow   91
    on the dial up there has come to the hour, but if they   92
    have a mind to be late, I have not. They'd honour us—   93
    listen to that—but it must be in their own way it   94
    seems. When we played before the emperor the arts   95
    were not bid to wait, nor did the Doge of Venice keep   96
    us idle at his pleasure. Get into your clothes. Now   97
    I will speak the prologue without more delay. (*Friend   98
    goes behind curtain. He stands on platform and begins a
    prologue. "Nobles and gentlemen listen to me." Rat-hole
    who has come in while he has been talking with his eyes shut
    and walking in his sleep.*)
Rat-hole. I am an old sinful fighting man, but you are   99
    the King.   100
Martin. Who is this man?   101
A Servant. Rat-hole, sir, he is in his sleep.   102
Rat-hole (*moving about, all shrinking back from him as he
    moves*). Must I wander always in Purgatory for my sins,   103
    must I endure pains when I had thought my daughter   104
    had put all to rights? Obey my daughter, I say, then   105
    I shall be forgiven my sins.   106
Martin. Be silent or leave the yard.   107
Rat-hole. Obey my daughter, she will set all to rights.   108
Martin. Are you pretending to have a devil, you old rogue?   109
Servant. He can't help it, sir. It's the Old King gets   110
    into him and puts him to sleep.   111
Martin. It's all acting.   112

Servant. O don't touch him, sir.   113

Martin (*shoving Rat-hole*). Get out of this, this is   114
   our stage. Go to the market-place.   115

Rat-hole. A sinful, merry man I was, but she'll set all   116
   to rights, and then no need to wander.   117

Martin. Well, if it is a devil, little do I care so long   118
   as you wake. (*Begins to shake him.*)   119

Rat-hole. Will you have your King burn forever?   120

Martin (*shaking him*). You'll get no money here, so stop   121
   that, I say. (*Rat-hole wakes.*)   122

Rat-hole. Thank you, thank you. (*Martin lets him go.*)   123
   He's been in me again, the old thief of a king. He'll   124
   bring me to my death. What did he say? O, sir, if   125
   he has said wrong, don't blame me for it, that terrible   126
   long tongue he has.   127

Martin. Sit there now and be quiet, (*Going back to platform.*)   128
   whatever you're at.   129

Rat-hole. I can't help it, sir. It's because of him and   130
   the likes of him I got my name. It was father gave   131
   it, God rest his soul.   132

Martin. Well, if you have a devil keep yourself awake by   133
   sitting straight up.   134

Rat-hole. Rat-hole, sir, that's my name, and I don't wish   135
   harm to anybody. (*To the others.*) Don't be afraid   136
   of me.   137

Martin. Hush!   138

Rat-hole. And he should know better, and he an educa-   139
   ted man and a king too.   140

Martin (*beginning prologue, which will be in rhymed verse*).
   Nobles and gentlemen, now let your troubles cease.   141
   The world is safe awhile. It has yet to be consumed   142
   by fire—that is the consuming of all forms and ima-   143
   ges—but once it was near drowned by water. From   144
   water generation comes, but that's a mystery.   145

[Alternate version following line 441: "For you behold in me
   the patriarch Noah not abashed for all the deluge that soon
   shall cover hill and wood and field. The world, I know,
   shall be consumed by fire, that is the consuming of all form

and images, but those that are born [to] be hanged escape
drowning. Now water is the mother of change, but that's a
mystery."]

Servant. That's great talk. I don't understand a word   146
he's saying.   147

Martin. And now must we all look upon that high story   148
set out for simple minds in simple words, and there-   149
fore I repeat that I am Noah, and that the flood.   150
There soon will be but little land. (*Noah's beasts*   151
come from behind the curtain, singing in procession.
They gather round Noah. They sing to him to be saved
from flood. They are very vain. They praise themselves,
delighting in all sorts of absurd qualities. Noah
tells them that [if] they are drowned it does not matter,
there will be plenty to take their place, but each
beast thinks [of] itself as unique. Then he tells them they
could all be saved but for his wife who will not go
into the Ark. She will not leave her dishes and her
dresser. Noah's wife comes to door and says, "Do not   152
let them mind the flood, it will go down before Spring."   153
Noah answers that she may go gossiping with her
neighbours, making them admire her, showing herself
off to the wide world. "Wives and husbands, you will   154
learn something now, for I will lesson her finally."   155
The argument goes on, getting more and more fierce,
among the lamentations of the animals, until Noah is
about to beat his wife. Peter runs in dusty, and
his coat torn.

Peter. Fly, all of you, the crowd are coming hither with   156
torches to burn down the castle.   157

Yellow Martin. But the soldiers, the Queen's authority?   158

Peter. The Queen has fled.   159

Servants. The Queen has fled, the Queen has fled!   160
There'll be nobody to eat the dinner. We'd best look   161
after our own skins, etc. (*They go out.*)   162

Peter. We had best follow them.   163

Martin. I will not fly. What quarrel have they with art?   164
Art is above their quarrels. Every place we have been   165

there have been these petty quarrels, but all is for-   166
gotten when we come.   167
Peter. I tell you there is no time to lose, they hate us.   168
Look at me. I bid them come to the play and they fell   169
upon me and beat me.   170
Yellow Martin. What furious folly fills their minds? Now   171
if they would but study the great masters of our art ...   172
Peter. We are condemned to the stocks. The whole town is   173
placarded with it.   174
Yellow Martin. It is some rival poet who has done this, one   175
of those followers of Seneca that comes from the univer-   176
sities with his heathen passions. They are eating the   177
world like maggots.   178
Peter. There is no time to lose, we must escape as we are.   179
Yellow Martin. Gather up the properties. Don't throw   180
your masks away. Put down those scissors. Go find   181
God's beard and the Devil's hoof. Where are you going?   182
(*Players have begun to troop out.*)
Rat-hole (*who has fallen asleep again*). Bring them to me,   183
someone bring them to me that I may curse them. Where   184
are they? Why don't you lead me? I am your king. Ah,   185
there they are, there they are. (*Shouting in the distance.*)   186
May they shrivel, may they gutter, may they drop into   187
tallow.   188
Yellow Martin (*who has been taking Noah's boat in pieces*).
They are gone, the cowards. We could have carried the   189
whole Ark away, but I've the beard and the hoof.   190
(*The Player Queen has slipped behind him and the gate
and locked it.*)
Yellow Martin (*finding gate locked*). Who has locked us in?   191
We are lost. I who have played before the emperor will   192
be put in the stocks.   193
Player Queen. I have locked the door. Neither you nor   194
that woman there will go through the door till I   195
please.   196
Yellow Martin. Give me the key.   197
Player Queen. Come a step nearer and I will throw it   198
over the gate.   199

Yellow Martin. For God sake let me open the door. If   200
    they have been stirred up by one of those followers   201
    of Seneca, they may take our lives.   202
Player Queen. Then promise what I have to ask.   203
Yellow Martin. Anything, so long as it is not beyond   204
    my power, or to give you parts you are not fitted   205
    for.   206
Player Queen. It is not that old thing that I am asking.   207
Yellow Martin. What new craze has come into your head?   208
Player Queen. To turn this woman out of the company and   209
    to drive her away.   210
Yellow Martin. She has done no wrong.   211
Player Queen. She has come between you and me.   212
Yellow Martin. Once rid of her you could do what you   213
    please with me. No, I will stay here and take my   214
    chance with the crowd.   215
Player Queen. And I will say aloud, "Pray to this Queen."   216
    I will say of her all that I have ever imagined of the   217
    queens of Babylon and Nineveh.   218
Martin. I too have a voice. I will tell them what a   219
    crazed one speaks, and what revenge upon another player.   220
The Friend. Promise whatever she asks. Nobody will under-   221
    stand you. (*Aside to Martin.*) You can say afterwards   222
    that you promised under compulsion.   223
Player Queen. Ah, what are you whispering? Promise, and   224
    then say you did it under compulsion, and so need not   225
    keep it? Let you promise so if you like, but I will   226
    have her bound by such an oath that she will feel the   227
    Devil pulling her out of bed if she breaks it.   228
The Friend. O my God, O my God! Who would have thought   229
    she was so wicked. Yes, yes, I will go away and never   230
    come back, I will dance for my living and eat swords.   231
Yellow Martin. Hush, hush, you little fool. I will not   232
    part with you so easily. She does not mean what she   233
    says, she will open the door before they come. (*He   234
    puts his arm on the shoulder of the Friend to comfort
    her.*)
Player Queen. Ah, now I understand. I have been blind   235
    indeed. You love her, you are making love to her un-   236

der my eyes. That is why you would have allowed her 237
  to take my part from me. 238
The Friend. O no, no. 239
Player Queen. And now you lie about it. If I loved some- 240
  body else's sweetheart, I'd take him boldly. I'd 241
  carry him off under her eyes as if I had been an army. 242
Yellow Martin. Wildness heaped upon wildness. Say what 243
  you will, I will answer no more. I will take my chance 244
  with the crowd. 245
Player Queen. There, I care for nothing now. There is the 246
  key. (*The Friend seizes it, opens the door and runs out.*) 247
Yellow Martin. I will put this woman in safety. She is 248
  too panic stricken to shift for herself. Then I will 249
  come back for you, though it's little you deserve it. 250
  (*He goes out, Player Queen following him to the gate.*)
Player Queen (*at gate*). Come back to me, come back to 251
  me, I was wrong. No, I will not follow. I will never 252
  see him again. (*She takes up the scissors.*) 253

[THE DRAFT CONTINUES IN SCENARIO.]

Martin and girl go towards gate. Player Queen moves as if 254
following them. She shrieks out abuse at them. She says she 255
will tear the girl's eyes out and pull Martin's plaits off. She 256
cries as she turns back from the gate that she would like to 257
kill her, to kill him, to kill herself. Sees scissors and 258
picks them up. "Here, I'll kill myself, I'll kill 259
myself. You'll find me dead. You will be sorry when 260
you find my dead body." Opens the neck of her dress 261
to kill herself. Says "No, he wouldn't care. I 262
should look so ugly, such a bundle, a bolster. I 263
should only be a figure of fun, a dead Noah's wife." 264
She begins taking off the clothes, cutting at them 265
contemptuously, while the Queen is seen hurrying in 266
from the gate. Queen, "Help, help!" Player says 267
"Who is that," putting up her hand with scissors. 268

[CONTINUES IN DIALOGUE.]

Queen. Do not kill me. I am not in a state to die. 269
Player. It is not you I thought to strike, but another. 270

Queen. Then you yourself are hiding. I will call my   271
    servants.   272

Player. They have all run away.   273

Queen. Then let us shut that big door. The mob is close   274
    behind me. They had spears. I could see their spears.   275
    I could have faced them and died, but not on a day like this,   276
    the first since I came to the throne that has not been lived   277
    in the presence of God, a day of vanities.   278

Player. No use shutting the door. They would but break it   279
    down.   280

Queen. O, they will never rest till they have killed me.   281
    (*She goes toward house.*)

Player. It is no use hiding in there, for they will search   282
    the house. That is why the servants have run away.   283

Queen. What shall I do?   284

Player. I will help you. Put on these things. Nobody   285
    will know you.   286

Queen. But they will find you. They will think you know   287
    something.   288

Player. O, I will know what to do, I will know how to   289
    put them off. A player and a jester goes free every-   290
    where.   291

Queen. But is there not someone else here, someone who   292
    will see me changing?   293

Player. No, there is no one here.   294

Queen. But there was someone, someone that you wanted to   295
    kill.   296

Player. I will tell you a secret. It was myself.   297

Queen. O, how wicked. The church says you must not do   298
    that. Was it love? (*Player Queen nods.*) They say   299
    it is a terrible thing, that it makes people very   300
    wicked. I have often longed for the crown of martyrdom,   301
    and though I was afraid now it would have been different   302
    if I were a sinner, as people are who love. Of course   303
    I know we are all sinners, but I mean really a sinner,   304
    a sinner in myself. The crown would wipe everything   305
    out, Heaven would be surer. But tell me, is it true   306
    what they say, that love is a joy?   307

Player Q. It is not a joy. It is the worst of things.   308

It is torturing and being tortured. It is hatred.   309
It is all a deceit. It would be better out of the world.   310
The more one feels, the less one prospers in it. It   311
is a game where it is the one that puts on copper takes up   312
gold.   313
Queen. There are voices. They must be at the turn of the   314
   street.   315
Player Q. You must slip away into the garden, and after   316
   that escape by lanes and byways.   317
Queen. Give me that veil.   318
Player. You will not need it. They will not recognize   319
   you.   320
Queen. It is not that. They have never seen me,   321
   but I would not like to show my face to so many   322
   men.   323

[CONTINUES IN SCENARIO.]

The Queen goes off. Player Queen takes up clothes,   324
looks at them, suddenly begins putting them on, singing   325
a song founded on "A ship a ship is sailing, sailing   326
on the sea, and it is deeply laden with good things   327
for me. Raisins in the cabin and almonds in the hold.   328
The sails they are of satin, the mast it is of gold."   329
She puts crown on her head, walks up and down in queen-   330
like attitudes. Soldiers come in. Player Queen tries   331
to hide behind curtain. Soldier. "Where is the Queen?   332
We have beaten the rebels back, the mob is scattered,   333
Where is the Queen." Player Q. peeps round fountain.   334
One soldier in front sees her and cries out "Here is   335
her Majesty." They all come before her and cry out,   336
kneeling on one knee, "God save the Queen."   337

[CONTINUES IN DIALOGUE.]

Chancellor (*coming in*). Close the gate, mind the gate.   338
   Those rebels are not defeated yet. They will reform   339
   and attack us again. The town is with them. Go you first [?]   340
   and see if the gold is safe. It was put down there this   341

morning. Bring up the gold. We will put it in safety at 342
any rate. Where that is, government will soon follow. 343
(*They go.*) Now, your Majesty . . . Who is this? 344

Player Q. The soldiers said I was their queen. 345

Chancellor. You are not the Queen. I never set eyes on 346
you before. 347

Player Q. I am wearing a queen's dress and crown. 348

Chancellor. Yes, the Queen's dress. But who are you, 349
why did you do it? Whoever you are had a good thought 350
in personating the Queen. 351

She. The soldiers thought I was the Queen. 352

He. If one could keep them and all the town thinking 353
that, the Queen would be safe. 354

She. I'll do it. I have played all parts. I have always 355
wanted to play a queen. 356

He. You are a player! Ah, it is a pity you haven't the 357
right blood. They will know you are no queen. 358

She. You are as bad as Yellow Martin. I'll show you I 359
can be a queen. 360

He. It is not so easy as you think to get the mastery 361
over men, and shut the mouths of those that are against 362
you. 363

She. Never fear! Ah, this crown has put great courage 364
into me. I feel as if I had worn it all my life. I 365
will master you and all. 366

He. Poor girl! It may be with the loss of your life you 367
will save that of my Queen. 368

She. How is that? 369

He. I have but few men. I can leave but a few to guard 370
this castle. The people may rise again. If they come 371
here and see you in that dress, it is you they will 372
kill in place of the Queen. 373

She (*coming to him*). You think they will kill me, taking 374
me to be a queen? 375

He. They will, certainly. 376

She. If they kill me, I will be laid out and waked. They 377
will say [I died] with courage like a queen. They will 378
lay me out in these robes. If a man should come in, 379
very tall, with yellow hair in plaits, to the wake, 380

give him a good place beside the bier. Let him cry 381
for me. Do not turn him away. Let him cry until his 382
heart breaks. 383

He. Play it out anyhow. The soldiers are coming back. 384
Go on your knees, murmur your prayers. No one will 385
doubt that you are our Queen. 386

She. No, if I am a queen, I will be a real one. I will 387
reign. (*Gives him her hand to kiss as soldiers come* 388
in.) Take that gold and silver and scatter it through 389
the streets of the city. 390

Chancellor. No, that will never do. We must keep that 391
money safe. We must keep it to buy more soldiers. 392

P.Q. I let you kiss my hand, and yet you disobey me. 393

Ch. It is soon for you to begin to talk of disobedience. 394

P.Q. You are my Chancellor. 395

He. There is no time to stop for folly. I know what is 396
best to be done. Soldiers, take up those bags and 397
carry them out of the town. 398

She. No, leave them where they are, I have given my 399
orders. 400

Ch. Your orders! (*Soldiers look doubtful, but do not* 401
touch the bags.) Take up these bags, I say. 402

Player Q. No, but leave them there. 403

Chan. Do as I bid you. You have always taken my orders. 404

A Soldier. But this, sir, is the Queen. 405

Chancellor. A pretty Queen. Queens know better than to 406
squander what cost toil and blood. It is light 407
women who squander, strolling players and the like. 408

A Soldier. That is treason! 409

Another Soldier. He is a rebel! Turn him out! 410

Another Soldier. Hang him! 411

Chancellor. Listen to me. You know me. 412

Soldier. We do know you, but never till this moment . . . 413

Chancellor. As for this woman . . . 414

Soldier. He calls her a woman! Out with him! 415
(*They seize him.*)

Chancellor. Fools, fools! Let me speak. 416

Player Queen. Who are you going to obey, my Chancellor 417
or me? 418

Old Soldier. You to be sure. I fought beside your 419
father. 420

Another. And I! 421

Another. And I! 422

Another. You have his eyes, you have his hair, his 423
very look. 424

Player Queen. Obey me then, and take the gold and scatter 425
it. 426

They. Yes, yes, we will. 427

Chancellor. Stop! Stop! She is no queen. (*They all 428
cry out,* "Gag him. Hang him! Throw him to the 429
hounds!" *They drag him towards the gate.*) 430

Queen. Set him free! Let him go! (*He is slinking a- 431
way dejected. She comes down. The soldiers leave
a way for her. She says, putting her hands on his
shoulders and turning him round:* "Forgive me. These 432
soldiers are so rough. It was for love of me they 433
did it." *He grunts angrily. She says,* "Dear old 434
friend, I don't care whether the gold is scattered or 435
not scattered. I only wanted to try my subjects' 436
loyalty. Have it your own way. Don't be angry with 437
me. Remember how often I have played about your 438
knee.") 439

Chancellor. Bid them to come with me then. 440

Player Queen (*to soldiers*). Go with my faithful servant. 441
He has the profit of the state at heart. I will remain 442
here in the city. It is my place. My father would 443
have done it. (*All but a few go out with the Chancellor.*) 444

The Old Soldiers. Let us stay with you. There will be 445
danger yet. 446

Player Queen. Go, one of you, and look through the gate 447
and see if there is a man, a tall young man with yel- 448
low hair, looking for something. (*Soldier goes and 449
looks out.*) If it should chance at any time through 450
the night you should see such a one, come and give 451
me news. (*Soldier comes back and says there is no 452
one there.*)

[End of Act II]

Act III Scene 1

The same as Scene 1, Act I. Yellow Martin and his players,
who are still in their fantastic clothes, come in.

Yellow Martin. This is the place. We were to meet by this
lamp under the niche with the saint in it. Here is her letter;
it was thrown from a window. She is within there, and it
is here that we will all get our clothes so that we can escape.
But she herself! My God, the mad game that she is
playing out.

Player. There's not a soul here. Can the rebels have taken
her messenger?

Yellow Martin. There she is, there at the window, she herself.
Go, leave me with her for a while. I will bring her back to
us. (*All go out of sight except Yellow Martin. Player Queen*
is standing at a window holding a torch, or else her face [*is*]
lit by the light of the one lamp, or perhaps all the light is
from within the house. The window may be partly stained
glass.) Dear, do not follow this caprice any further, find
some means of escape. The town is in a most murderous
mood. (*The Player Queen stands motionless and silent.*
Yellow Martin continues.) O my dear, is it because I have
refused you what you asked, those wild queens to play? Or is
it that other thing, that cruel thing you asked me, that is
driving you to your death, maybe, for a caprice? (*He*
pauses for answer. She remains silent, and so remains
throughout his speech, though he often waits for her
answer.) O, could you but know how utterly I long to give
you all you ask, but I knew you would despise me if I gave it.
I love you with every kind of love—with a love full of
passion and with a love like that of old men who are
indulgent and kind, being past desire. Yet I know I must
seem the coldness your wild heart has need of, the strength
amid its wandering, the mountain for its cloud. Why will
you not speak to me? All night I have wandered round the
castle because I knew you were within it, wandering
without hope. Twice I saw a woman at a window with a
torch, standing as you do now, and twice as I came near the
torch was put out. Are you so hard and bitter you will not

answer? O, if I could but know what you were.

(*Players return.*)

A Player. We must hurry. It is posted up on all the walls; we are to be seized and put into the stocks.

Yellow Martin. One of those followers of Seneca, I am certain. They hate us; they value nothing but what does not come out of Plutarch. They hate our holy tales; they will have nothing but tortured passionate souls. My God, if it is one of them, they will take our lives!

Player. They are searching for us in the lower streets.

Yellow Martin. No wonder, no wonder, with a real quarrel on their hands, something worth fighting about and killing people for.

A Player. Unhappily I have been so upset by their shouting that I cannot use my wings. (*He is dressed as a bird.*)

Another. I am only the two front legs of the cow, and I have quarrelled with the hind legs, but if it is a follower of Seneca we will combine against him.

Another (*who is a fish*). I thought myself safe enough this not being a Friday, but those new dramatists are all heathens and keep no order in their diet.

Player. Have you the clothes, Martin?

Yellow Martin. Speak to her; maybe she will answer you.

All (*cry*). Our clothes! Our clothes!

Player Queen. I have an enemy who is still amongst you.

Yellow Martin. An enemy?

Player Queen. She that deceived you and me.

Yellow Martin. And do you mean that you will not give us the means of safety while this girl is with us?

Player Queen. She deceived you and me.

Peter. This is monstrous. Because she has an illusion of this sort in her head, we must all to the stocks.

Yellow Martin. You mean that you will not give us the clothes unless we promise to send her away? (*The Friend begins to cry.*)

Player Queen. Decide quickly; the people are mad with excitement. Decide before they search these streets.

Yellow Martin. I promise. She shall be sent out of this company. (*Player Queen begins lowering clothes on rope.*

*All the players except Peter and the Friend seize them
eagerly.*)

Peter. But that cannot be. Where is she to go?

Yellow Martin. There are your clothes; pick them up. How
dare you rebel against my authority? I'll do as I think right.
I will have no disobedience. Do not dare to answer, but have
no fear. I have taken you all over the world and never left
any of you in want. Go to the dark places under the old
church of St. Winifred, change as quickly as you can. I will
follow you. (*They go out, leaving him alone with
Player Queen.*)

Player Queen (*above*). Now I know that you love. All's well
again, and the world made afresh. O Martin, I was bent on
dying. I have fastened the rope to the window bar, and
there are knots on the rope for my feet. I will climb down to
you. There is nothing to come between us now, and I am
certain that you love none but me.

Yellow Martin. You and I are lost to one another.

Player Queen. But she is to be banished, she cannot come
between.

Yellow Martin. But you have banished me.

Player Queen. You?

Yellow Martin. But did you think I would let her go alone out
amongst strangers, wandering in the winds, a beggar, from
door to door? I go too, and if she will let me I will take
care of her all her life through.

Player Queen. He loves her, he loves her!

Yellow Martin. No. But better with a woman that I do not love
than with one I love who is full of torturing, passionate
caprice.

Player Queen. He has never loved me.

Yellow Martin. Never loved! And your face has come between
me and all life.

Peter (*running in*). Master, master, come quickly; they are
close at hand.

Yellow Martin. Yes, between me and all life, torturing and
tortured. Why should love be so bitter a thing?

Player Queen. To those who are without faith.

Peter. Come away, come away. (*He drags him out. Player*

Queen speaks in rhyme, repeating the same words she had
used when she thought to kill herself in Act II. The crowd
drag in Rat-hole.)

Barach. I'll have no man cursing me before the face of the
people.

Another. Better leave him alone; you'll have no luck if you
harm him.

Rat-hole. Let me go, let me go. How can I help it, how can I
stop him, he that speaks out of my mouth. O, he is the
wicked one, a terrible cursing one.

Barach. Hang him I say, that will stop his cursing.

Rat-hole. Am I not a poor man, an oppressed man, a miserable
man like the rest of you?

Barach. Give me that rope there.

Another. No, I say. How could we have luck if we harmed
him?

Barach. How shall we have luck if we let him curse us; doesn't
a curse hang in the air seven years?

Others. That's true, that's true. Best hang him.

Rat-hole. Have mercy!

Another (*throwing Rat-hole down*). Stop your noise. I say if
you hang him, those that are in him, that make him their
house, so to speak, will be houseless. And may[be] it's you
or I they'll lay hold on next, or maybe they will come out of
a bush and you going home of a market day and scare the
horse and break your neck.

Another. That's true. There's a tree on a road over the hill
yonder, and something comes out of it.

Another. Where will your luck be if you offend them?

Rat-hole. Am I not one of you? Amn't I oppressed too. What is
it having to pay for buryings and marryings and christenings
and for putting up big churches, like having them inside you
crying out and making wicked talk?

Another. If we hang him he can't curse, whatever's inside
him, that's certain.

Another. He's beginning to shiver. That's how it takes him.
Then his eyes close and he begins to curse.

Rat-hole. It's coming, it's coming. Will no one shake it out
of me? Will no one shake me awake again? I am going
asleep, I am going asleep. (*He begins to grope about, and*

*they shrink back from him. Then he speaks in a dreamy
voice.*) They are all against my daughter, may they burn
down to a candle end.

Barach. I'll not be cursed; I'll crack a ghost's neck for once.
I'll do it with this rope.

Player Queen (*who has been standing watching*). Subjects and
rebels . . .

Barach. It is the Queen.

Rat-hole. All against my daughter, she too against my daughter.

Player Queen. We meet face to face at last. You rebel against
the right sustenance of the priests and the church, and of
all that I abate nothing. (*Murmurs in crowd.*) But that I
may punish rebellion I shall lay upon you yet heavier
burdens. Between you and me the quarrel is to the death.

Barach. Yes yes, you speak true. It is to the death, the death
of you or us. (*The queen goes from the window, perhaps
passing along the other windows. The crowd shouts* "Death
to the Queen. To the castle gate. Tonight we set a new
goverment in this land. To the gate, break in the gate. But
first let us crack the neck of the ghost.")

Rat-hole. They shall all wither.

Another. Drag him along, we'll hang him before we go to
work.

Barach. All day I have been longing to crack the neck of some
ghost.

Rat-hole (*who is dragged along, laughing loudly*). You will
hang me in the wind, I, that am but breath.

Barach. We'll hang you on the side of the Red Lion.

Rat-hole. I laugh because I am breath. You shall be blown
away because you are against my daughter. Come on and
twist my cloudy neck.

[End of Act III Scene 1]

Act III Scene 2

*The Courtyard of the Castle as before. Player Queen and
Soldiers. Shouts without. Soldier comes from within the Castle.*

Soldier. The battlement that is above the gate has been
loosened. We have but to wait until they are gathered

1
2

underneath, and a few thrusts of the crowbar will fling   3
    it up on their heads. (*More shouting without.*)   4
Player Queen. Ah there, there again.   5
Second Soldier (*coming from gate*). They are dragging an   6
    old beggar to the Red Lion Inn to hang him on the   7
    sign. (*A scream outside.*) That is the last; they   8
    have choked his cries now. It was that old man who   9
    believed, or said he believed, that your father's   10
    ghost was in him. At first he spoke up to them in   11
    the voice he puts on for kings. And then the King   12
    or his courage went out of him and at the last he went   13
    yelling, big Barach pulling him by the heels.   14
Player Queen. So he was all beggar when he came to die.   15
    And yet yonder, it may be, beyond death, are all the   16
    things we thirst for: wild adventures among blue   17
    mountains, a lovely life we but see in brief dreams,   18
    and after we fantastically copy. Now if the thought   19
    had come to him, the right lasting thought, he might   20
    not have been remembered with beggars.   21
Soldier. I know not, your Majesty. In truth I never gave   22
    much thought to it.   23
Player Queen. They only seek my death, and were that   24
    finished you would go safe.   25
Soldier. Do not fear, your Majesty, that I or any here   26
    will shame his father, let the day bring to us what   27
    it please. And yet I think it will carry both you and   28
    us to safety.   29
Player Queen. Have you seen a man die before?   30
Soldier. Three or four times in battle, and more times   31
    of the camp sickness.   32
Player Queen. And women?   33
Soldier. I have seen no woman die.   34
Player Queen. Is it hard when it comes? Does the world   35
    seem better at the end, like an accustomed house when   36
    the coach is round and one's foot is on the step?   37
Soldier. Those that died suddenly died without thinking,   38
    and those that were wasted with sickness, being weak   39
    and weary, cared little enough about it.   40
Player Queen. Yet an old beggar who has gone from door   41

to door, been out in rain and wind, worn ragged and 42
lousy clothes should have been glad to rush out upon 43
the air. And what's all life, poverty, forsaken love 44
like all else, but a tearing into tatters, a jarring 45
and a breaking to make the soul free and make it glad 46
to be gone. (*More shouting outside, this time nearer.*) 47
Soldier. They're getting noisy again out there. (*He* 48
goes to gate.) They have carried up a great tree set 49
upon a cart; they have brought it to ram in the gate. 50
First Soldier. Then we'll to the battlements, your Majesty; 51
crowbars will need all our hands. Your Majesty need 52
not fear; the gates will not fall but to many blows. 53
(*Player Queen sings a verse of her song in Act II, and*
as she does so unbars gate and throws it open. The
crowd stand hesitating, expecting some snare.)
Player Queen. What do you stand back for; do you fear 54
some plot? This yard is empty; I have no weapon in 55
my hand. Here is the life you seek. 56
(*The soldiers show themselves at a window above.*)
Soldiers (*above*). They are in the yard; they've broken 57
in the door. 58
Player Queen. I will have none die for me. I alone thirst 59
for the blue mountains where I shall fight dragons yet. 60
Barach. Seize the galleries. The soldiers are in the gal- 61
leries. 62
Player Queen. There is no need for that; you are a mul- 63
titude and armed. No one here can do anything against 64
you. 65
A Drunken Man in the Crowd. That is not the Queen. Those 66
lips have given kisses and drunk wine. 67
Barach. Silence the fool. (*To Player Queen.*) You must 68
die. (*The crowd shouts* "Death, death to the Queen, etc.") 69
Soldier (*above*). She is your Queen. How dare you threaten 70
her. (*The soldiers above shout* "rogues, murderers, etc.") 71
Player Queen. It is my will, and maybe I shall die laughing. 72
Barach. We are not afraid of you. There is a hunger and 73
thirst in our purses that drives us on. (*Crowd shout* 74
"Down with the priests, down with St. Winifred's church, 75
etc.")

Player Queen. It was I who ordered all, I accept all. 76
Put me to death if you dare. (*Murmurs in the crowd.*) 77
Who is there among you? Your father's lives and the 78
lives of your father's fathers were but twigs 79
woven into the nest that gave this eagle birth. Who 80
amongst you will face this eagle? Eagle begat eagle up 81
through all the centuries, and the eyes of all the 82
eagles look at you. But strike if you will; I 83
veil their lightning. (*She covers her face* 84
with her hands.)

Barach. I fear nothing today. Did I not hang your 85
father in that beggar's body, for now I know the 86
voice. (*He raises his spear to strike her; others* 87
do the same.)

Yellow Martin (*coming forward and throwing himself between*
them.) Stop! This is no queen. 88

Drunken Man in the Crowd. That is right, that is right. 89
Those lips have given kisses and drunk wine. 90

Yellow Martin. This is no queen, I say. Yes, I will 91
speak; take your hands off me. What I say is true. 92
She is a player of my troupe. 93

Barach. She has the crown on her head. She says she is 94
queen. No man shall turn us from what we have in mind 95
to. (*Voices in the crowd* "pull him out of that, etc.") 96

Yellow Martin. Am I not one of you; have I not a right 97
to be heard? She is seeking for her death. I will 98
explain everything. Give me time; it is a strange 99
tale. 100

Player Queen. Honest man, it is no good. Even if they 101
would listen to your incredible tale, I would refuse 102
to accept my life in exchange for becoming less than 103
I am. 104

Yellow Martin. I tell you that she is seeking for her 105
death, and that her high words are meant to pull it 106
on her. 107

Player Queen. My people, he but speaks the truth. I 108
seek my death because I think it well, instead of a 109
few more years of lessened royalty, to choose a death 110
that shall be a life forever and, as it were, mock at 111
you with a sweet laughter. 112

Yellow Martin. Why those very words are not her own, but   113
   from a play I once thought to write. O, if you but   114
   knew what this woman is like, you would understand and   115
   listen to me. My story would not be incredible.   116
Player Queen. They would not listen, for I would show   117
   them what you are like. This man is a player from   118
   a troupe that were to play at my bidding this day, and   119
   now, being loyal, he seeks to save me by a tale of   120
   wild make-believe such as his craft makes natural   121
   to him.   122
Yellow Martin. I tell you that that robe and crown are   123
   not hers, though where she came by them I do not know.   124
Player Queen. Poor man, do you think that you will make   125
   them believe that anyone could speak with so much calm   126
   as I am speaking, with such quiet breath, death being   127
   so near, and have no royalty in her? Who could face   128
   levelled spears for a borrowed crown and robe?   129
Voices in Crowd. That's true, that's true. Pull him out   130
   of that, etc.   131
Drunken Man. She was never in a convent. Those lips have   132
   given kisses and drunk wine.   133
Player Queen. Those up yonder, they would give their lives   134
   for me, but would not seek to save me by a base means   135
   or say that I am less than Queen.   136
Barach (*trying to shove Yellow Martin aside*). Out with you;   137
   we will be played with no longer.   138
Player Queen. Do not hurt him; leave me still the power to   139
   pardon. That can do no harm. It is I that have been wronged.   140
   (*To Yellow Martin.*) Come nearer, answer me. Have we not   141
   more than once, yesterday and today when I have sum-   142
   moned you before me, spoken of the nature of artists?   143
   How they long for such parts as will make them seem   144
   great in men's eyes, or in some lover's eyes. (*To   145
   the Crowd.*) To save a queen and claim a queen all   146
   in one mouthful, that is the part he plays.   147
Yellow Martin. It was you that said these things, and   148
   that is why you now play the part of the Queen.   149
Barach. We've had enough of this.   150
Player Queen. Let him go, I will question him. Am I   151
   not Queen until I die? (*Murmurs in crowd, who*   152

let Martin go, "Yes, she is Queen until she dies.")   153
I will have no slander living after me, no shaking   154
of the head.   155
Yellow Martin. Give me but time and I will find a witness,   156
twenty witnesses.   157
Player Queen. When I was in your company, was I not your   158
sweetheart?   159
Yellow Martin. Yes, you were my sweetheart.   160
Player Queen. Now you have seen his vanity, the artist's   161
vanity. Should I question him further he would say   162
that he cast me off for some other woman's sake.   163
Yellow Martin. No, no, never. That's where the wildness   164
is.   165
Player Queen. Ah, now he grows more wary; you'll see   166
he'll mend his tale.   167
Yellow Martin. There never was another, but I cannot make   168
her understand, or you understand, or anyone. I   169
cannot put out the wildness that is burning her. I   170
cannot save her life.   171
Player Queen. Go to your own sweetheart and tell her that   172
you are so full of falsehood you have hardly escaped   173
with your life. For me the wide Heavens are waiting.   174
Yellow Martin (being dragged away). Is there no one that   175
will bear witness? There was a woman, she was with   176
me but now, but she is gone.   177
Queen (forcing her way through the crowd). I will.   178
Barach. Is that your witness?   179
Yellow Martin. No, I do not know her.   180
Barach. Then cast him out.   181
Yellow Martin (who is being thrust through the gate).
I will get help; I will save her in spite of herself,   182
in spite of you all.   183
Barach. Now I will find out what new trickery is this.   184
Who are you?   185
Queen. The Queen. (*The crowd murmur,* "She says she is   186
Queen." *There is laughter among the soldiers above.*   187
They repeat the phrase of the crowd. A soldier cries
"That tale will help nothing, woman.")   188
Player Queen. He said he did not know her, but yet it   189
is all part of his plot. He said it to make her tes-   190

timony seem the stronger, and yet so hastily did they	191
make up their plot that she still wears the dress of	192
Noah's wife.	193
The Queen. I put it on to escape, she gave it me. She	194
sought to save me, but troubled in conscience I wan-	195
dered hither and thither in the garden there. I was	196
afraid, but now I have come to tell the truth. She	197
came in answer to my prayer, to save me. She wore	198
this dress. I was afraid of martyrdom. I think she	199
is miraculous.	200
Drunken Man. That is the Queen; that's the convent mouse.	201
Her lips have never given kisses or drunk wine.	202
Barach. Silence!	203
Player Queen. You would pull me from the rest that I	204
am seeking to a world I am weary of. But come near,	205
give me the veil that I may wrap myself in it and	206
look no longer on the world. (*She takes from the*	207
Queen the golden coloured veil, spoken of in Act II,	
folds it about her and remains silent and motionless	
to what follows.)	
The Queen. You will see that she will work some miracle,	208
do something to lift our hearts to Heaven.	209
A Voice. Kill both of them, and then we will be certain.	210
Barach. But this one first.	211
The Queen. She came to save me. You cannot harm me;	212
there would be thunder.	213
Soldier (*above*). When has he prospered that killed queens?	214
Barach. All of you take up your spears and strike together,	215
then no one can be blamed more than another.	216
Soldiers. So you would make the coming ruin greater?	217
Another Soldier. How can you cheat the thunder?	218
Man in Crowd (*throwing down his spear*). I'll not strike;	219
I'm always afraid when it thunders.	220
Another. Nor I; she'd make a fearful ghost.	221
Another. Strike at her Barach; it's the work you chose.	222
Drunken Man. There was a ghost that rode a grey horse	223
and broke the rooftree with the blow of a hoof.	224
Barach. Lower your spears then. None of us will take the	225
blame, but she shall not live for all that.	226
Drunken Man. It was in my great-grandfather's time.	227

Barach. Bring down those men. I'll find executioners,   228
    and show them not to rail at us.   229
The Queen. Bring a million, but they'll not harm that   230
    golden pillar. Who knows what she is? Maybe she has   231
    but to lift her hands and the air be full of spears.   232
Drunken Man. He had drunk wine, he had golden armour.   233
    O, he was a fearful ghost.   234
    (*The soldiers are brought down.*)
Barach. Find one among you that will put her to death,   235
    and go free. But if you do not find one then you   236
    shall all die. No thunder and lightning will fall   237
    on us for killing you.   238
Soldier. We will die then.   239
All. Yes, we will die.   240
The Queen. No, no, give me the spear. I will strike   241
    at her.   242
Soldier. Would you strike your Queen, poor woman?   243
The Queen. If she were but a queen I would not strike,   244
    but she is angelical, come to show me how I should   245
    have met martyrdom.   246
Barach. She is crazy, she thinks to reveal a miracle.   247
    She will do as well as another. Take this spear and   248
    strike hard.   249
The Queen (*taking spear*). Now shall you see that golden   250
    pillar change into light or vanish like a flash of   251
    fire.   252
Barach. Poise it on your hand; now grasp it in the middle.   253
The Queen. Or else you will see it unchanged, for there   254
    will come a sound from it as though I had struck bronze.   255
    But look at her, look at her, she is trembling. That   256
    is not because she is a woman and afraid of death at   257
    the last. You cannot understand as I do the mysteries   258
    of Heaven. To teach me the better she has put on the   259
    humility of death and fear.   260

Note. She might possibly uncover her face just as the Queen is
going to strike, and the Queen might see that she is pale. This
might give a final scene. Player Queen, however, not speaking.

    (*A sudden movement in the crowd, a cry of* "the soldiers,
the soldiers.")

The Queen. Now, now I will reveal a miracle. One cannot 261
 say what will happen, perhaps Heaven will open and 262
 she be carried away in a moment. 263

 (*She raises the spear again. The crowd is all in confusion.*
 The soldiers are forcing their way in, but she pays no
 attention to them.)

Yellow Martin (*seizing the spear*). So I was but just in 264
 time. 265
Chancellor. What, two queens, and one against another? 266
 Let no one stir; my soldiers are all about you. Lay 267
 down your weapons. But which of these is Queen? My 268
 sight has grown dim of late; I am sometimes strangely 269
 mistaken. Kneel all of you and ask your pardon of the 270
 Queen. (*All kneel to Player Queen except Drunken Man.*) 271
Drunken Man. Her lips have given kisses and drunk wine. 272
 (*He kneels to real Queen.*)
The Queen. No, not to me. I am done with that. 273
Chancellor. Ah, you have all good sight, your eyes are 274
 better than mine. 275
Player Queen (*coming down from platform*). You but rose 276
 against the shadow of a queen in rising against me, 277
 and so have done but shadow wrong. Therefore I par- 278
 don all. And now I put the play aside and take up 279
 life again that I had thought myself well done with. 280
 I am no queen; those spoke the truth. Your Majesty, 281
 will you forgive the mask that I have worn? 282
The Queen. I know not what is happening, nor what new 283
 change has come, but I know now that life is deceiving 284
 and being deceived, that those who are powerful in it 285
 speak even to themselves from behind masks. If you will 286
 bear the hard burden, stay on being Queen. I will to 287
 my convent cell forever. 288
Chancellor (*to Player Queen*). You are still Queen, and a 289
 most fitting one, and worthy men's devotion. 290
Player Queen. You [who] have the power of king should have 291
 the name. Am I still enough of Queen to give the crown? 292
Chancellor. O mask of gold, is not all gold royal? 293
Player Queen. For an hour, for a day, but then I change 294
 the mask. 295

Chancellor. So be it then. I take it at your hands that   296

 have most right to give. I take my task from you and   297

 shall be obeyed because you gave it to me.   298

Player Queen (going into the crowd, with a complete change of

 manner). Hey-day. So Jill must be herself again although   299

 her Jack's away.   300

Chancellor. Before the moon is up all here must swear al-   301

 legiance, but our first work shall be of bounty. This   302

 day must be a happiness to all. You players make your   303

 peace with her to whom the state owes all. When that   304

 is done the state will show her its gratitude.   305

The Friend (goes up to Player Queen). I only can make this   306

 right.   307

Player Queen. Go to your mudhole, you fat toad.   308

The Friend. Call me what names you like.   309

Player Queen. What have you to say to me, viper? Go   310

 to Yellow Martin; he has chosen you.   311

The Friend. I will not have him, nor any but this young   312

 man here. *(Pointing to Peter.)* While you've been   313

 stirring up some riot here, he and I . . . *(She whispers*   314

 in her ear.)

Player Queen. What! He is your lover?   315

Peter (coming forward). For the last month.   316

Player Queen (stretching her arms and yawning). So the   317

 day is done, and all's well. What an appetite I have.   318

 (She runs into castle.)

The Friend (to Chancellor). She has forgiven him.   319

Chancellor. Then I will make this player Count.   320

Yellow Martin. Sir, that's impossible, it would ruin   321

 me. I play all sorts of parts, and in bad times I   322

 am a juggler and an acrobat. How could a peer of the   323

 realm tumble on a board? I'd starve.   324

Chancellor. It is she who must decide it, sir. It is   325

 not you that I would honour.   326

Player Queen (coming out of the castle with a lobster in

 her hands and eating a piece of the claw out of her

 fingers.) What's that I hear? I will not be a Coun-   327

 tess. I've been more than that this day. This lob-   328

 ster's good *(To the Friend.)* There, catch. I've   329

never been so hungry in my life, not even when we   330
  played to the Doge of Venice and I outdid myself. A   331
  Countess? I that made a King?   332
Chancellor (*to Martin*). She's right. It would never do.   333
Player Queen. Have a claw, Martin. (*Martin makes*   334
  a gesture to stop her.) O well, if you are on   335
  your dignity. Friends and patrons, we seek once more   336
  your good opinion. We have deserved something for past   337
  services. (*She takes off shoe to crack lobster.*) Take,   338
  all, your places. We shall begin the play that we have   339
  promised. I'll have my meal during the prologue.   340
Chancellor. So be it, let the play begin. And if there's   341
  any here that won't applaud, I'll have him hanged.   342
Yellow Martin. No, no, for I must make you a new one. For   343
  from this day you can be what you like—Herodias, Sheba,   344
  or any queen you have a mind to.   345
Player Queen. O no, no, no. Take up your trumpet, mount   346
  the platform there, and blow, I'm tired of queens.   347
  From this day out I will be Noah's wife. (*She blows a*   348
  kiss to him.)

[The End]

Commentary

In what follows, I shall summarize Yeats's earlier progress before going on to consider what he accomplishes in Draft 16 in an attempt to pull together the whole record of his process of creation so far. By now the kite has a long tail, but we shall soon get a new kite.

Act I, Scene 1. There were a few preliminary preparations for this scene in Drafts 4, 5, 13, and 16a, and the idea of having Septimus come in from the town where he has been attacked by the citizens while praising the Queen— this occurs in Drafts 11 and 12—perhaps suggested having the play begin there. In Drafts 4 and 5 Yeats invented the character Rat-hole, the mediumistic old man who has lately become possessed by the ghost of the Old King. Yeats introduces him now at the end of Scene 1 very briefly. In Draft 13 Yeats planned and wrote a scene in town where a group of countrymen have come to watch the Queen's entry. A group of townsmen enters and tells them all rejoicings in honor of the Queen are forbidden. The soldiers and priests who are conveying money to the castle come in and are attacked by the townsmen. During the attack a priest is killed. Septimus enters and invites the townsmen to the Noah play. They say it, too, is forbidden. They seize Septimus but release him just before the draft breaks off. In 16a Yeats assembles various celebrants who hope to add to the fun—a clown, a man with banners, and a jack-in-the-green. They are persuaded to join the rebels. The draft breaks off as the fight between the townsmen and the Queen's party is beginning.

Scene 1 in Draft 16 grows out of these beginnings. As he did in Draft 13, Yeats sets his play in Surrico, known not to history but to legend, and pushes it back in time to the Middle Ages. The opening stage direction in Draft 16 is long and detailed and seems to contradict Yeats's statement in the 1922 note to the play that he planned his action against an imagined background made up of Gordon Craig's screens, as do his several drawings of possible stage settings. Again the celebrants are planning to produce a properly festive atmosphere for the Queen's visit to town, but they are prevented by Barach, leader of the rebellion. The Old King has been dead three months. The tax on sins has been dropped as in 13; here it is the cost of the rites of the Church that has outraged the people, that and a capital levy to build a church to St. Winifred. Priest and soldiers come in carrying money to the castle, and Barach challenges them. He insists the bags contain relics, saints' bones; this enables him to say a few things about the sinful flesh as. opposed to the sinless bones. Barach is arrested and taken away; the priests speak of various omens of evil that have occurred. Barach escapes, and plans to attack the castle. He wants to overthrow the power of the priests but does not plan to kill the Queen. He will force her to marry and live a normal life. At the very end of the scene Rat-hole comes in. We are told of his possession and of the crowd's fear of him.

Act I, Scene 2

The play started here in many drafts, and forms of the scene occur in every preceding draft except 7 and 11. Here is an outline of its complicated genesis:

Draft 1. A new tax on sins is bringing great treasure to the state, but the citizens are on the point of rebellion. The Queen is to leave her retreat; a Noah play is to be given by a troupe of strolling players honoring this occasion. The actress who plays Noah's wife has hidden because she dislikes the part.

Draft 2. All of the above is kept. To it is added the Nona figure's search for the missing Player Queen and a reference to Septimus's old play, the reading of which has made the Player Queen so discontented with the role of Noah's wife.

Nona has learned the part of Noah's wife and wonders if she should play it. The missing Player Queen is heard singing. The Queen enters, dressed for the royal progress. She objects to the role-playing required of her.

Draft 3. The discussion of the Queen's dislike of role-playing is extended. When the Queen persists, the Prime Minister threatens to resign and hints that the Queen faces martyrdom. The Player Queen's song about the mask is introduced. The whole troupe of players looks for the Player Queen and finds her. When Nona admits she has learned the part of Noah's wife, she and the Player Queen fight. Septimus comes in and breaks up their quarrel. Though the rest of the troupe are tired of the Noah play too, at the end end of the draft they are preparing to give it once more. The Player Queen has her head stuck through the curtains of the stage within the stage and is exchanging gibes with Septimus as the scene closes. A contrast is being developed between the Queen's dislike of role-playing and the Player Queen's love of it.

Drafts 4 and 5. Yeats considers having the soldiers, led by Barach, rebel, and he introduces Rat-hole, progenitor of the Old Beggar.

Draft 6. This is the first complete version, made by drawing on all the above. It opens with the exchange between the Prime Minister and Queen, goes on to the mask song, the scene between Nona and the player she sends to town, and the discovery of the Player Queen. The exchange between the Player Queen and Nona is very brief and breaks off when Septimus enters. Fourteen lines are finished.

Draft 8. A discussion of the Player Queen's disappearance comes first, and Septimus takes part in it. His old play has now become a play on the Queen of Babylon which the Player Queen will make a scenario for her words and deeds. The exchange between the Queen and Prime Minister has been removed from the outset of the scene and placed in the center. The whole troupe of players finds the Player Queen. Nona carries the dress of Noah's wife and shows that she is thinking of taking the part by holding it against her to see if it fits.

Draft 9. A verse version. The Player Queen sings from the vat. Nona enters with the dress of Noah's wife which she is altering to fit herself, using a pair of scissors. When the Player Queen hears Nona's plan to take the part, they fight.

Draft 10. Two further versions for the opening of the scene down to the exit of the Queen and Prime Minister. A rearrangement of material already worked out.

Draft 12. A new plan for the opening, introducing the light lover Peter discussing the missing Player Queen. Nona is making the costume for the Player Queen, a task she gives to Peter. Septimus returns from town and learns that the Player Queen is missing. Then the tax money is brought in and the Queen arrives. The mask song follows, and the exchange between Nona and Peter whom she is sending to town. Septimus finds the Player Queen and, after many objections, she agrees to play the part of Noah's wife once more. As the scene ends, the play is about to begin. Thirty lines are finished.

Draft 13. This covers the opening of the scene down through the exit of the Queen and Prime Minister. The Queen adds the detail of the cock that crowed when her father, the Old King, died. Twenty-eight lines are finished.

Draft 14. This contains a scrap of dialogue where Nona reports to Septimus that she has found the Player Queen, which was inserted into 16.

Draft 15. Contains the whole scene, but no Peter. The arrangement of the parts of the scene is pretty much that which Yeats keeps in 16. Seventy-four lines are finished.

Draft 16. There are two versions of this scene, one in prose and one in verse. The verse version, which is in Yeats's hand, has been inserted into the binder, and the prose version, which is in typescript, is found in loose sheets at the end of the play. The prose version is clearly the earlier of the two, so I discuss it first. As the scene opens we are aware of the skillful weaving together of already worked-out elements. For the opening of the scene in which soldiers hear the hidden Player Queen singing, Yeats goes back to very early drafts. The scene between the Queen and the Prime Minister (*Chancellor*) follows Draft 13 closely, even in its language, down to the exit of Nona (*The Friend*). From there on down to the exit of the Queen and Prime Minister, Yeats finds new expression for old ideas to state the Queen's objection to the role she is called on to play. A fascinating detail here is Yeats's anticipation at lines 155–59 (p. 200) of the falcon image in stanza 1 of "The Second Coming" nearly a decade before he wrote that poem. The mask song is old, of course; Yeats doesn't change a word, though it is arranged as prose—perhaps a mistake by his typist. The scene between Peter and Nona was worked out in Drafts 12 and 15 (there *Young Man*), though none of the earlier language is carried over. Nona finds the Player Queen, and the scene after she is found had all been worked out, even to most of its language, down to the entrance of the other players following line 268. When Nona and Decima talk about what the audience wants, Nona says, "Who wants to see and hear those heathen kings and queens with their big words"; this is perhaps Yeats's wry comment on the reception of his heroic plays. From here on, the language of the scene between the players and the Player Queen is largely new, as is much of the matter down to the entrance of Septimus (*Martin*) at line 302. There is an echo of Draft 8 in the Player Queen's words about the Queen of Babylon at lines 300–301. In this version Septimus is made more nonchalant in his attitude toward the Player Queen than he had been in earlier drafts. The close of the scene from line 321 on is taken from Drafts 12 and 15.

The verse version is surprisingly independent, in both its language and action; it hardly seems that Yeats wrote the verse with the prose before him, since so few of its words are carried over. It should also be noted that the incidence of couplets is unusually large for Yeats's dramatic verse. At the beginning, the Queen's mistaking the voice of the hidden Decima for a ghost is built up, and the Queen recalls that one of the servants crowed like a cock when her father died. This looks forward toward the eventual end of the play where the Old Beggar's braying is the sign of a new reign. Then Nona comes in looking for the Player Queen and has her by now familiar exchange with the Prime Minister and Queen—though the scene is longer than usual, expansion being a characteristic feature of this draft. The dialogue between the Queen and Prime Minister that follows is similarly extended: we are told of the ban on all plays except Biblical plays, then the usual exchange occurs on the Queen's duty toward her people, which is to assert custom and ceremony. Yeats quoted a passage from this exchange in a letter to his father written 7 August 1910, the passage on page 208 beginning "Queens that have laughed to set the world at ease." In his letter Yeats added this comment: "My theme is that the world being illusion, one must be deluded in some way if one is to triumph in it" (*Letters,* p. 534). The Queen agrees to make the progress into town, and Decima raises her head from the vat and sings the first twelve lines of "The Mask," which now, except for one word, have the form in which Yeats first printed them in December 1910 in *The Green Helmet.*

The following scene between Peter and Nona is considerably changed. This is to be Peter's last appearance; in subsequent drafts he is gone from the play. Again as in Drafts 11 and 12 he is wooing Nona, commenting in no friendly way on her love for Septimus while he is pressing his own suit. This scene is much longer than the equivalent scene in the prose version, where Peter says nothing of his own interest in Nona. Here and throughout the version in verse I feel the influence of Draft 12, in both incident and tone. Nona now finds the Player Queen, and the usual exchange occurs in a slightly varied form. At the outset the Player Queen accuses Nona of loving Septimus, and Nona does not really deny this, but merely says that Septimus is obsessed by thoughts of the Player Queen. The Player Queen's concept of love is extravagantly romantic. We are again reminded of the identity of Yeats when the Player Queen says that she would have Septimus think of her "all night until the scared moon fled" (p. 213), anticipating the line "As trips the sacred moon" in "He and She" of "Supernatural Songs," which Yeats had so much trouble getting printed correctly. The Player Queen introduces a reference to Septimus's youthful play on the Queen of Babylon, which was not mentioned in the prose form of this scene, and comments on it. It is made to include "The Mask," which must mean that Yeats intends us to think that she has derived her song from the old play. The scene ends with the usual fight; the Player Queen hurls insults at Nona, and the other players come in to break up the quarrel. One player is an extravagant romantic like the Player Queen. Septimus enters from the town and either does not or pretends not to know that the Player Queen has been missing. This scene is greatly enlarged, though Yeats breaks it off at an earlier point in the action than the corresponding scene in the prose. All in all we are left with the impression that the prose and verse drafts of this scene are by no means exact equivalents; their tone especially is different—the prose drier, already perhaps heading toward farce, the poetry recalling Yeats's earlier romantic conceptions of his play.

Act II

This act has been worked on in part or whole in Drafts 4, 5, 6, 7, 11, 12, 13, and 15, though it was not worked over quite so much as the preceding scene:

Drafts 4 and 5. The character Rat-hole was invented in these drafts, and he was associated with the Noah play. He was to go call the audience to see it.

Draft 6. This begins with a brief exchange between the members of the audience on the effect of role-playing, and in it the play within the play is most fully developed. It is broken off when a messenger brings news of the revolt. The players flee, except for Septimus, Nona, and Decima, who locks them in. She finally gives up the key when she becomes convinced Septimus loves Nona. The real Queen enters; she and the Player Queen exchange dresses. The Prime Minister arrives with the loyal soldiers; there is an argument about what to do with the treasure, ending when the Prime Minister and most of the soldiers leave to put it in safety. Two lines are in final form.

Draft 7. Here the interruption of the play by Rat-hole's seizure is introduced, and the Old King speaks through him. The draft breaks off at that point.

Drafts 11 and 12. There is just a scrap of Act II in Draft 11. Rat-hole has now become an Old Man for whom Noah's flood is a reality. Draft 12 assembles most of the incidents previously explored but breaks off midway through the scene between the Queen and the Player Queen. Here Yeats first worked out his conception of roughly the first half of the act. He kept twenty-four lines from this draft.

Draft 13. This concentrates on the parts of Act II not covered in 12. The general development is that found in Draft 6. The Prime Minister and the loyal soldiers come in; the Prime Minister knows the Player Queen is not the Queen; she tests her power with the soldiers and then gives in to the Prime Minister. As he leaves with the treasure, she asks him whether he has seen Septimus.

Draft 15. This brief version is little more than half as long as Act II in Draft 16; it telescopes the incidents in the scene and omits the scene between Rat-hole and Septimus altogether.

Draft 16. Here Yeats pulls together and expands ideas, nearly all of which are to be found in earlier drafts. The comments of the audience that has gathered to see the Noah play are expanded so much that the discussion of the effect of role-playing on actors grows tedious. The extended simile comparing the actor to mortar that has not hardened strikes me as unhappy, but perhaps only because it is the nature of mortar to harden—the physical object used in the comparison cannot act as the comparison requires it to. Failures of this kind are very rare in Yeats's work. The longing for the old slapstick days of fallen pants and imitations of natural sounds is no doubt a covert criticism of the theatrical audience. Yeats used the business about the imitation of fighting cats later in his unpublished dialogue "The Poet and the Actress," though there the violin and not the human voice imitates the cats. Like the other incidents, the interrupting of the Noah play by the possessed Rat-hole has here its longest form, and it becomes very funny when Septimus tells Rat-hole to keep himself "awake by sitting straight up." Septimus's remark that the world has yet to be consumed by fire recalls *The Unicorn from the Stars,* Act II, line 73, and makes it seem likely that Yeats was responsible for the earlier passage. It is Peter once more who brings news of the rebellion and of danger to the players. Septimus's replies to Peter are delightful: "What furious folly fills their minds" (line 171, p. 223) is highly theatrical; the reference to followers of Seneca is amusingly pedantic (line 176). Even much of the language of the exchange between Decima and Septimus and Nona after the gate is locked is carried over from earlier drafts. The Player Queen's exchange of roles with the Queen and the final scene between the Player Queen and the Prime Minister had all been worked out before. Yeats does rewrite them, for there is almost no carry-over of diction.

Act III, Scene 1

Nothing in the earlier drafts anticipates this scene in any way except a note in Draft 13 which reads, "Must be some earlier part. Allude to players having forgot all their clothes." The question whether there were earlier drafts which have not survived cannot be certainly answered, though I think it likely that there were. The draft that we have here does not seem to me to have the characteristics of Yeats's early drafts, such as uncertainty of language and many false starts. However, the fact that only a typescript has survived might conceal such characteristics, though I have no doubt that the typescript was based on a manuscript version.

We can date the composition of this scene rather closely from a passage Yeats wrote in his Journal on 20 September 1909:

Thought for Player Queen Act III

That the heroism of love is to feel, shudder, and yet withstand; to do what one knows is necessary, even to the seeming cold, to seeming an enemy, and all the while to be on fire. Or, [that] it is easy for the light lover to be wise in love. They wear their mask without suffering; they have not to cut themselves in two. This would seem but an empty subtlety to the jealous Player Queen. She would have right to talk so, not hero. (From the MS) [Cf. *Memoirs,* p. 232. Gen. Ed.]

This points to a version of the play that still contains Peter, as this version does, and the thoughts are very like those Septimus (*Yellow Martin*) utters in his first long speech to Decima on page 231.

This speech establishes the highly romantic tone in which much of the scene is written—one might even call it melodramatic. Certainly the verbal texture is wildly extravagant in places, though this is curiously crossed by farce when the players talk as if they had taken on the physical qualities of the birds and animals they are dressed to represent, as when the player dressed as a bird says "unhappily . . . I cannot use my wings." The scene degenerates into out-and-out melodrama when the Player Queen speaks to the rebels and when they proceed to the hanging of Rat-hole. Yeats does not quite stage this hanging, but here for the only time he presents it directly. Always before the loyal soldiers have reported it to the Player Queen as they watch the actions of the mob through a loophole. The unsatisfactory nature of this whole version of the play, a topic to which we will return, is most obvious here.

Act III, Scene 2

There are many antecedents; parts of the whole of it are found in Drafts 2, 6, 7, 8, 14, and 15.

Draft 2. The only anticipation of Draft 16 is the eagle metaphor that the Player Queen uses when she confronts the mob. In Draft 2 this is thought of as part of Septimus's (*Yellow Martin's*) early play; the Player Queen cites it when describing the play to Nona. It concerns the actions of the queen who is Septi-mus's central character: "Here she speaks of her fathers as the true eagles—here she feels their eyes looking to her, and at the end she goes to death so firmly and sure." Yeats does not again specifically assign this to Septimus's play, but Decima is still using that play as a kind of scenario in Draft 16.

Draft 6. Here, by the time he was done, Yeats got the main lines of his scene established and wrote seven lines which he kept. The Player Queen is besieged in the castle; she opens the gates to the mob; Septimus and the Queen come forward to identify her and save her; the Prime Minister enters and rescues the Player Queen, who then makes him King; Nona gives back Septimus, and Decima returns to her place in the troupe as Noah's wife.

Draft 7. Here Yeats first explores an alternate version which he only got rid of in Draft 15. The Player Queen has had Nona (*Girl*) captured. Septimus, acting as herald for the rebels, brings their demands to the Player Queen, who stages a love test. Septimus is to put Nona in chains. When he refuses, the Player Queen opens the gate to the rebels. The draft proceeds as in 6 until the very end, where the Prime Minister has Nona carried off.

Draft 8 keeps the love test and goes along much like 7 down to the point where Decima opens the gate to the rebels. After this point Draft 8 reaches nearly final form, and Yeats finishes or nearly finishes 162 of his 348 lines.

Draft 15. The love test is dropped, and Yeats recasts the scene pretty much along the lines it has taken in 6: the rebels' spokesman addresses the Player Queen, who refuses their demands and opens the gate to confront them; Septimus tries to save the Player Queen, and the real Queen who thinks the Player Queen an angel sent to save her is about to strike her when the Prime Minister arrives. He is crowned, Nona presents the Young Man as her lover, and they all live happily ever after. This version is only about half as long as Draft 16; in 15 Yeats seems to be compressing, in 16 expanding.

Draft 16. Yeats picks up most of the ideas he has been experimenting with in the early drafts, except for the love test that Decima devises for Septimus, and writes a melodramatic version of the end of the play, with a shrill tone and sudden improbable reversals. After a discussion of death brought on by the hanging of Rat-hole, the Player Queen opens the door to the mob. By taunting the members of the mob, she tries to enrage them to the point where they will kill her, though one drunk man in the crowd insists she is not the Queen: his "Those lips have given kisses and drunk wine" becomes a kind of refrain. She succeeds in spite of Septimus's efforts to save her. The Queen comes forward to speak. She has become convinced that the Player Queen is an angel sent to take her place, and she is about to strike her with a spear when the Prime Minister enters with his troops. Asked to identify the real Queen, all save the drunken man bow before the Player Queen. She, however, immediately discards her role, makes the Prime Minister King, discovers that Nona and Peter are lovers, and returns to her role of Noah's wife while stuffing herself with lobster. Her histrionics have made her hungry.

At this point Yeats had worked at *The Player Queen* for more than three years, filling reams of paper with drafts, yet little had come of it. His play is unsatisfactory; indeed, one cannot see how it could have been successfully produced. Act I, Scene 1 is exposition: We hear of a recluse Queen who allows her priests too much power, who is forcing a capital levy on her subjects to build a church to her patron saint. Her subjects have found a leader and are on their way to her castle where they intend to force their Queen to lead a more normal life. Yeats's efforts to give these events the atmosphere of legend do not succeed. The scene fails even as an exposition for it is an exposition of events, not of ideas, and the play was to be a play of ideas, of the relation of art to life, of the function of the mask in developing depth of character, and so on. The exposition of these ideas simply does not get under way: the play begins on the plot level only. Scene 2 is better. The Prime Minister in his first talk with the Queen makes a case for the necessity of the mask, and the Queen, who cannot play the part her birth has assigned her, is successfully contrasted with the Player Queen, who is always playing a part. The central issue of the play is expressed in the mask song, which deals with the need of the mask even by lovers. The contrast of Decima and Nona is also successful, the eternal feminine opposed to the domestic woman, Lilith versus Eve. But even here Yeats seems to be starting more hares than he can pursue. The appeal of realistic art, especially of realistic plays, concerned him greatly during these years, when it was becoming clear that he had established a theater that was especially successful with realism; but does a discussion of this question belong in *The Player Queen?* Septimus arrives finally but much too late, and he does not do much. We do not even know for sure what he has been doing before he arrives. Indeed, the contrast between the man of affairs and the artist (Prime Minister and Septimus) hardly gets started in this version of the play. In the verse draft of this scene things are somewhat better. Peter is good in his dialogue with Nona, and Nona herself begins to take on a more definite outline.

In Act II the opening is simply dull, probably the worst thing one can say of a theatrical enterprise. The discussion of the effect of role-playing and the longing for the good old days are related to the main themes of the play, but they are not urgently stated and are in any event tangential. I cannot see how staging the

Noah play advanced Yeats's dramatic purpose, and it is instructive to note that in the finished play he does not stage it. One must conclude that the Noah play is there to provide a dull part for Decima to dislike. When the rebellion occurs and Septimus assumes that the rebellion is against him and his company, a revolt of life against art, Yeats does express a dramatic idea that will be central to the finished play. Septimus is so fully the artist that he can see violence erupting only between rival schools of art—he has no sense of politics at all. But the theme is introduced far too late in the play. The struggle of Decima and Nona for Septimus is good and will get better. Then comes the switch of parts between Decima and the Queen. This is the crucial event in the play: everything has led up to it in the sense that all the initial events are contrived to make such a switch seem possible, and everything will lead away from it. Yeats's whole enterprise started, indeed, with the radical idea that a good actress could do a better job as queen than a true queen. It is therefore logical to show Decima in role immediately, enforcing her whims on the Prime Minister, though the quarrel over what to do with the money seems pointless.

The low point is reached in Act III, Scene 1. Since no early drafts of this scene have survived, it seems safe to conclude that Yeats had not considered it as carefully as he had his other scenes. The opening with the Player Queen manning the empty castle and letting down the clothes to her fellow actors unhappily combines hyperromanticism with farce; the attack on Rat-hole is much too violent for so fragile a structure as Yeats is building. Scene 2 had been worked over often, and it is better, but surely it is much too busy—masquerade carried to the point of seeking death, angel-visitants, violent reversals. And the pure farce at the end seems merely tacked on to the play it concludes.

Yeats had set out to write a drama of ideas, a play about his developing doctrine of the mask; his dramatic result at this point is anything but that. The ideas have been submerged in complicated intrigue. Part of his trouble comes, I think, from his obvious desire to write a full-length play—he seems to be trying to put in everything he can think of. This often happened with Yeats's works in the early stages, the number of correlatives in the drafts of the opening of "Byzantium" being a case in point. He often began with an idea, an abstraction, and assembled too many and ill-assorted correlatives to express his idea. Then he had to discard the ones that worked badly and point up the ones that worked well. It will be instructive to see him doing this in later drafts of *The Player Queen*.

But I think the main trouble comes from the fact that at this point Yeats's controlling ideas were simply not sufficiently developed to sustain a play. He made an entry on the mask in his Journal in March 1909, which he later included in the "Anima Hominus" section of *Per Amica* and then much later put into "The Death of Synge" (Section VI). I quote it as he originally wrote it to show his thinking about the mask while the sixteen drafts were under way:

> I think all happiness depends on having the energy to assume the mask of some other self; that all joyous or creative life is a rebirth as something not oneself, something created in a moment and perpetually renewed; in playing a game like that of a child where one loses the infinite pain of self-realization, a grotesque or solemn face put on that one may hide from the terrors of judgment, an imaginative Saturnalia that makes one forget reality. Perhaps all the sins and energies of the world are but the world's flight from an infinite blinding beam. [Cf. *Memoirs,* p. 191. Gen. Ed.]

This fits *The Player Queen* well enough, but is there enough to it to make a play? Still ahead for Yeats were the developments that grew out of the idea of the mask, the relation of the self and the anti-self expressed in "Ego Dominus Tuus" and *Per Amica Silentia Lunae,* and the doctrine of Unity of Being expressed in "If I Were Four-and-twenty." As yet, Yeats simply had not developed an intellectual framework finished enough, or strong enough, to sustain a drama of ideas.

CHAPTER ELEVEN

Draft 17

A SORT OF ADDENDUM or pendant remains to be disposed of which I have called Draft 17. In this draft Yeats is composing a continuation of the poetic version of Act I, Scene 2 which he had put into the typescript of Draft 16. Scene 2 was under way in August 1910, when Yeats quoted a passage from it in a letter to his father. Such evidence as there is points to a 1910 date for this continuation: With the manuscript are four pages of revisions for *The Land of Heart's Desire,* some of which were printed in the London 1912 edition of that play, the ribbons used to tie up the faery child's hair, for instance (*Variorum Plays,* lines 322–23). The year 1910 seems a probable enough date for the writing of these revisions. One page of the manuscript contains a note that seems to refer to Miss Horniman's withdrawal of her subsidy of the Abbey Theatre; this event took place in 1910. I have concluded, therefore, that in 1910 Yeats was at work on a verse draft of the play (with a few prose passages left standing) which was independent of but closely related to Draft 16. The surviving passages are all concerned with the events of Acts II and III; there are no versions of the matter found in Act I. Presumably Yeats never made a verse draft of I, 1, the events of which seem ill-suited to poetry, and had completed his verse draft of I, 2 and put it into Draft 16.

We noted that the poetic version of Act I, Scene 2 was not a mere putting into verse of the prose version, that it was sufficiently unlike to have independent status. We noted, too, that very little of the diction of the verse echoes the diction of the prose. These same characteristics are found in Draft 17. The very state of the manuscript amply testifies that Yeats is composing in verse rather than versifying a text already set. There are many cancellations, and many alternate versions of single passages are left standing. Also, the incidents are, in many places—particularly in Act III, Scene 2—different from the incidents of Draft 16. Draft 17 was written on loose sheets of notebook paper which are in complete disorder, and the writing is very difficult to read. After many days of work trying to arrange the sheets in some sort of order, I am still not certain of my arrangements; many passages I have been unable to read. In short, I am not able to recover a coherent version of Draft 17 full enough to print, so I have had to be content to present it in summary and quotation.

The drafts begin where the version in verse of I, 2 leaves off, with Septimus's (*Yellow Martin's*) announcing that the hour for giving the Noah play has struck. This pushes forward the beginning of Act II, which now starts with the scene in which Septimus summons the audience by blowing a blast on his trumpet while the Player Queen sticks her head through the curtain of the Noah set and insists she can play queen's parts. I quote the beginning of Act II, a characteristic sample of this version:

Act II

Servants arranging seats.

Yellow Martin. Though the clock's struck and all the town had word
    That we begin upon the stroke, the hall
    Is empty as at midnight. Give me my trumpet.
    I'll blow a blast to shake the spiders down.
    When the crowds hear that customary sound
    They'll all come trooping. I've no faith [in] clocks
    It was the Chamberlain that gave the order
    As if my trumpet was not good enough.
    I tell you that there is [no] pauper's brat
    Nor beggar on the road but that his heart
    Cries out for trumpets.

P. Queen (*head through curtain*). There are a hundred queens.
    Inside my ribs.

Yellow Martin (blows). Queens in your ribs?
    You have eaten from red earthenware
    And drunk from horn and puncheon, you a queen?

P. Queen. So much the more I long for Babylon
    A hundred horsemen 'rayed in golden arms
    A throne of ivory lifted high in the air
    Upon two silver spears.

Yellow M. (blows).   You a queen
    Whose father rubbed down horses at a tavern,

P. Queen. I long the more for cloth of gold, the more
    For multitudes to look at my straight neck
    The high subduing carriage of my head.

Yellow Martin. High head or no, unless you take it in

I'll break it with this trumpet. (*She stays a*
moment laughing, and puts in her head.)

[THERE IS NO TRANSITION TO THE NEXT PASSAGE.]

Martin.　　　　　　That should have made
　　The children pluck their fathers by the sleeve
　　And pull them to the palace stair and up it.
　　Ah, there they come—we'll have a crowded house.
　　(*He arranges bench.*)
　　I'll put the benches closer—you find out
　　If there are more within. They have their dream
　　Of politics and money, griefs and cares
　　Until our trumpet sounds, and the dream's gone
　　And our reality stares blank upon them.
　　But sometimes, as about a pillowed head
　　At the first waking, the dream clings awhile
　　And therefore we need patience.
The Friend (*at window*).　　　　The crowd has passed
　　They did not even lift an eye upon us,
　　But ran below there with their faces flushed
　　And turned the corner of the hilly street
　　That runs in[to] the market.
Martin.　　　　　　　　It is their loss.
　　Five minutes more and we begin the play.
　　Call out the servants. (*To servant who brings new bench*)
　　　　　　　　We have no need of that,
　　But bid your fellows come and take their seats.
　　Five minutes by the clock and we begin
　　And after that we'll say the house is full.

[CONTINUES AFTER A BREAK]

　　If no one comes we'll say the house is full
　　And after, though the Queen and the town come
　　We'll keep them out. To be so played upon,
　　We that were honoured by the Pope of Rome
　　The Emperor of the East and Prester John.
Boy. What are the players like, I mean when they are not playing.
1 Servant. Much like the rest of us.

Servant. No, but slippery as the eels in the river.

Boy. O grandfather, how can they be like the rest of us
     and they sounding
  Out all those grand things to one another.

1 Servant. The boy's in the right. Why shouldn't they be better than us?
  Don't they say that Noah's flood is as good as a sermon?

2 Servant. Well, when I was a little chap there's many a time
  I took . . .

[Yeats breaks off with comment "and so on in typed versions down to 'Leather-jack!' " This cues into Draft 16 at page 218.]

Peter. Stop, stop the play, for the whole town's in arms.
  One half are fighting with the soldiers
  The other half, with murder in its eyes,
  Run hither.

Martin.   I knew it would come to this.

Peter. The Queen had scarcely shown herself before
  The market filled with cries, and hearing that
  She ran away.

Servant.   They'll burn the castle down.

Another. They'll hang and burn for the mere sport of it.

Yellow Martin. Here, gather up the masks—carry that trident.

[End of page. I am not certain that what follows was intended to continue directly.]

Peter. We're safe enough, it is the Queen they hate.
  I fell into their hands, but when I cursed her—
  I do not know if she be fair or foul
  Or they but thought her breviary
  Is all the life she has—but I cursed well.
  I had by heart a passage from a play
  That curses Jezebel. What did they care
  So that it was but wild and violent?

Yellow Martin. It is not the queen they turn at, but at us,
  Or if at her, it is to strike at us
  Across her body. But an hour ago
  They showed me something written on a paper
  And after seeing that I would defy them still
  Had killed me but they fell to quarreling.

Peter. Why should they kill us, we're no politicians?

Yellow. Take up these things. What, are the servants fled?

    If they but helped we could have saved the Ark.

    I'll answer while we are at work. Those clowns—

    Those groveling [?] players—that delight the common sort

    Have worked up the mob.

Peter.   They pelted me with stones.

Yellow Martin. It has been coming on the world for years.

    Gross laughter, God's most ancient enemy,

    Has risen in arms against our nobleness.

P. Queen. Then let us put our finest dresses on

    And in crimson words, and one a crown on head,

    And all with the most haughty fearless looks we know,

    Meet martyrdom.

Yellow Martin.   Have done with that wild talk

    And help me with this bundle. (*To Peter*) You are to take

    God's beard and Gabriel's breastplate and this trident

    To the great door. We'll follow in a trice.

This is very like Draft 16, though Septimus's comments about the inspirational effect of his trumpet blasts and his insistence on the absolute importance of art to the point where he regards the world of everyday affairs as the dream while art is the reality shows Yeats heightening the already excessive romanticism of his play. Septimus's words that "Those clowns— / Those groveling players— that delight the common sort / Have worked up the mob" supply a still further clue to the date of this draft. In his Journal entry for 6 August 1910, Yeats wrote: "As a simplification of *Player Queen* Yellow Martin should suspect not a follower of Seneca, but some low buffoon."

The scene that follows between Septimus, Nona, and the Player Queen, ending with the departure of Septimus and Nona, has the general form it takes in Draft 16, though again the rhetorical mode is extravagant. Here is the Player Queen on Nona's coming between her and Septimus:

    Love is a hidden war, a bout of fence

    And a long wrestle on a dizzy edge

    And she dared come between, and set her feet

    Beside our feet on that high trampled place.

Then, when Septimus asks what is to happen to Nona if she is thrown out of the company, Decima answers:

She'll peck at the world as though she were a bird
And find what food she needs. But you and I
If we should lose this bitter food of ours
Would famish, for the circle of the earth
Has not another meat that's to our taste.

Presumably at this point Septimus and Nona leave and the draft takes a new turn. Yeats has Rat-hole (here *Old Man*) come forward—he seems not to have left with other members of the audience of the Noah play—and talk to Decima. This scene is still found in the finished play. Only fragments of their exchange remain. Then the fleeing Queen enters and Decima offers to take her place. This follows the plan of the scene in Draft 16 fairly closely, though there are some changes. The Queen tries to bribe Decima, for instance, and when Decima offers her the dress of Noah's wife, the Queen thinks she is offering her "a sober dress to die in" in place of her regal fripperies. When the Queen talks of love she speaks strongly:

Love is a fearful passion I have heard
No single sin, but holloing on a troop,
Anger and lust and shame and sacrilege
For there was Heloise; and someone told me
Lovers go naked into bed.

This seems to be followed by another scene between the Player Queen and the Old Man, whom she has apparently sent into the castle to sleep after their first encounter. The drafts are very difficult here. For the first time Yeats works out the Old Man's prophetic function, though there have been such straws in the wind as the Queen's report in Draft 13 that a cock has crowed at the time of her father's death. Here the Old Man says that he crows three times like St. Peter's cock whenever the throne is about to change hands. Already he is looking for straw, as he is in the finished play where he brays like a donkey whenever the crown changes. The straw seems more appropriate to a donkey than a cock; is Yeats already half-thinking of a change? The Old Man knows that the Player Queen is not the Queen, and in a canceled passage Yeats has him demand Decima's borrowed robes to sleep on:

For you but play at being Queen, and he
That makes me sleep and gets me by [the] throat
Is real. I am therefore in a sort
An honourable vision. So strip off that gold,
It's the straw colour, and I'll sleep on it.

The scene between the Prime Minister (*Chancellor* or *Chamberlain*), his loyal soldiers, and the Player Queen follows. Yeats writes a maze of drafts, 22 manuscript pages, and I have found no thread to help me through it. He follows the general plan of the scene in Draft 16: the soldiers mistake the Player Queen for the Queen, though the Prime Minister knows she is not; the Player Queen tests her power but finally gives in to the Prime Minister over the disposal of the royal treasure; he departs with it. Then Yeats has the Player Queen insist on staying in the castle alone as in Draft 13, which suggests that he was planning a scene along the lines of III, 1 in Draft 16. A small group of soldiers deserts the Prime Minister and returns to the castle to protect the Player Queen, as in Draft 14. There are some nice passages; for instance Yeats writes this couplet for the Player Queen to sing when the Prime Minister tells her that her play-acting may cost her life:

> She thrust her hand into wild Fortune's hair
> And clung an hour and then dropped off and died.

Later, when he is about to leave her, the Prime Minister says:

> Play it out,
> Climb up the sky. When play and passion meet
> Then do the hours go by us on proud feet.

This scene ends as it does in Draft 15 when the Player Queen has one of the soldiers go look for Septimus.

Only two scraps survive which belong, or at least seem to belong, to the equivalent of III, 1 in Draft 16; they come from the passage where Septimus tells the Player Queen he is going with Nona, that this is the result of her cruelty.

The draft of the final act is labeled Act IV, Scene 1, which indicates that Yeats was planning an even longer play than Draft 16. It is quite different from that draft: At the opening the Player Queen is alone on stage, strutting about in her royal clothes. The cock crows, and the Player Queen takes this as somehow aimed at her. She dismisses the crowing:

> Go ride a hen, go ride a hen old bird
> Go and set eggs, for I've my part to learn.

She then declaims speeches intended for the mob that she will encounter, perhaps more lines from Septimus's play on the Queen of Babylon. Here is a characteristic bit:

> As if the blood in my veins
> Were not as old as are the moods of poets
> That are so wild and simple none can say

How they were born or whence, or anything
But that they are our masters still. Who was it
First sang the eagle cock, old bird of the gutter,
Or learned a nightingale, or taught the swan
Its scales, that when it drifts out of the world
It leaves the echoes ringing?

She has still another encounter with the Old Man, whose agony, at the time of
crowing, in a new dispensation is compared to the agony of Christ:

I wandered for three days like a lost dog
And had an itching in my throat and sweats
That might have drowned me.

He knows the Player Queen is not the Queen, and he insists his crowing does
not foretell her death. She insists it does:

Listen, Old Man, my night
Is falling swiftly, and you are the bird
That sings it in. That is my chosen night and that
    the cloud
That's blotting out the day.

She says she has intentionally left the gate open so the mob can get to her.
The Old Man thinks she is trying to undermine his authority as a foreteller of
the death of kings. She hears the people coming and sends the Old Man to safety.
Here is the end of the draft:

P. Queen (*covering her eyes with her hand, weeping*).

I will forgive death
And never rise to haunt you from the grave.
But I'll not look upon the edges of the knives
Nor know the moment, for it is not death
But death's mere moment that is terrible.

(*She crouches down.*)

My mother when I was conceived
Had laid her by the tide
That cast a flake of yellow foam
Upon her quivering side.
How therefore could she help but fill
Her needle's eye with gold?

A Soldier. Your Majesty.

Player Queen. But why do you not strike?
Strike, strike, before my courage runs away.
How therefore could she help but fill
Her needle's eye with gold?

Soldier. Your Majesty. (*She turns and sees them all bowing
or kneeling before her.*)

Player Queen. But who are you?

Soldiers. Your men
Who've driven off the rebels for a while.

Player Queen. Then I am Queen?

Here the draft breaks off at a point which seems to indicate that Yeats is once more about to wrench would-be tragedy into farce. Did he intend to go back to the ending invented for Draft 6 that has been with us so long, the ending where the Player Queen returns to her troupe? We cannot be sure. Yeats has invented for this version the song beginning "My mother dandled me"; a full draft of the song with a variant fifth stanza is included in the manuscript. We do not know the date of composition, but Yeats printed it in *Responsibilities* in May 1914 and used it in the later versions of *The Player Queen.*

PART 2

CHAPTER TWELVE

Drafts 18 through 21

WE HAVE NOW come to the exciting moment in the development of *The Player Queen*, the moment of breakthrough, so to speak, the moment when at last Yeats begins to find the characters, the incidents, and the language he will keep in the finished play. The breakthrough occurs in Drafts 18 through 21, and an inscription on the back of folio 24 of Draft 20 enables us to date it quite precisely: Yeats wrote "Player Queen rejected. Nov 1915 partly verse." This date is confirmed by the fact that in Drafts 19, 20, and 21 Yeats introduced "A Thought from Propertius" into the play: Ellmann has dated this poem November 1915.

Since Yeats had worked on Draft 17 late in 1910, he had revised his early plays, particularly *The Countess Cathleen, The Land of Heart's Desire,* and *The Hour-Glass;* he had written most of the poems in *Responsibilities* and had them published; he had invented a new dramatic form, the play for dancers, and written and produced *At the Hawk's Well,* his first essay in that form; he had begun his *Autobiographies* with "Reveries over Childhood and Youth," which he had just seen through the press, and was continuing his autobiography in the manuscript known as "First Draft." I do not think he had done much work on *The Player Queen* in these years. There are only two references to it in his letters: On 15 March 1912, he wrote his father that he had put the play aside while revising his early plays. Then, at about the time of the breakthrough, on 12 September 1915, he wrote his father from Coole that he hoped by the time he was to return to London in October he would have almost finished the play that he now describes as "a wild comedy, almost a farce, with a tragic background." This must refer to the new version of *The Player Queen* on which he was at work, a version so new, indeed, that Yeats was considering a new title, *A Woman Born To Be Queen.* It is this new beginning that we are about to examine.

I think it no accident that Yeats achieved his breakthrough while "Ego Dominus Tuus" was under way. The final manuscript of this poem is dated 5 December 1915, and Yeats had been working on it for some time before that.

Here Yeats expresses fully the doctrine of the self and anti-self, which had been maturing for many years. Your anti-self is more than a mask which you might don merely for the fun of it—as Decima dons the mask of Queen in the early drafts of the play and then says toward the end that having been Queen for a day she is quite ready to change her mask. Your anti-self is your eternal opposite, your daimon, tutelary spirit, or guardian angel. Decima expresses the concept of the anti-self when she says in Draft 21: "Septimus told me once that nobody finds their genius till they have found some role, some image, some pose that liberates something within them or beyond them that had else been dumb and numb." And this image or anti-self is, as Yeats says three times in *Per Amica Silentia Lunae,* "of all things not impossible the most difficult." Yeats returned to *The Player Queen* in 1915 a greater artist than he had been in 1910, and with a deepened concept of what his play was about.

Draft 18, which is printed below, is a version of what became Scene I in the finished play. The action takes place in the rebellious town, and Yeats has invented two old men who will eventually serve as a frame for the scene. Septimus (here *Wounded Man*) has come to town and become involved in a brawl between the Queen's men and the town's men. He thinks he has been attacked because he is the exponent of an ideal art, an art that enhances life. At the end he goes off to put his troupe of strolling players in a safe place. Yeats writes in prose; indeed no verse draft of any part of Scene I has come to light; I doubt that any was written. All numbered lines in drafts in Part 2 are keyed to the line numbers of the *Variorum Plays,* pp. 715 ff.

[Draft 18]

[Yeats draws a plot of the stage, showing two windows opposite each other with a light behind them. The backdrop for Scene II seems to be in place.]

A street corner. A lane leading off upstage on each side of corner. The lane to left dark, that to right lit by a lamp high up on wall of house at back. Two windows opposite each other in lighted lane. There is a tremendous noise behind the scene and in the dark lane. Two heads come out of the two windows in the lighted part. They are silhouetted against the lighted wall behind. Men come running from the right and down the lighted lane. Presently there is a lull. The fighting is more distant.

Man at Window. They are fighting in Gallons Lane.
Second Man at W. I hear that for myself. They have been

fighting every night this week.

First Man at W (*to passerby*). What are they fighting about?

2 Man at W. The young fool is running to get his head broken. He won't answer. It's a bad time to live in.

First Man at W. And getting worse every day.

2 Man at W (*to passerby*). You down there, what's the news? No use, he won't answer either. Running to get his head broke. Maybe there'll be stones flying.

First Man at W. There they go again. Better pull in our heads. (*Noise gets near again. Nothing can be heard but confused shouts, which drown each other. The clash of steel. A mass of figures run across stage. They are seen for a moment in black outline against the light to right. After them come men with bags. The noise now dies. Heads come out again, at first timidly. They draw back again.*)

First Man at W. It's all safe, There's nobody in our lane. They're all for new stone throwing.

Second Man. But there in the main street?

First Man. They can't throw. They have bags. It is the Queen's men, they that have the bags on their backs.

Second Man at W. Maybe yes or maybe no. It might be the citizens. They say that arms are to be brought in tonight, Auguburn[?]; spearheads, shot, lead shot.

First Man. That's all talk. They have been talking that way this—I tell you they are Queen's men. (*The men with bags pass. An old man with a stick comes from right.*) What's going on, friend, what's the trouble?

Old Man (*turning*). Trouble enough, trouble enough. There's an itching in my throat, a tickling and a scratching and an itching, and when there is that in my throat the world changes.

Second Man at W. What's that you are saying?

Old Man. The bird comes up in my throat. My throat itches all day and night, and then about noon I crow.

First Old Man at W. He's mad, we'll get nothing out of him.

Old man. About noon I crow. Now why should I crow at noon? Noon is not cockcrow. But when I crow the world changes.

Second Man at W. I know him. I know who he is. Did you see his figure as he came out of the light?

First Man at W. A heavy man and he limping.

Old man (*sitting on ground and rocking himself*). Only for kings and queens it comes, but there's nothing in the world so bad for the throat.

Second Old Man. That's him, that's old man Ganaton [?]. The night before the Old King died, and nobody then thinking his death near, he jumped up on a wall and made a noise as though he'd been a bird on a dunghill. It's a queer wise thing madness is.

Old Man. Can you tell me now if that street there will bring old Ganaton [?] to the Queen's Castle? For old Ganaton [?] must sleep before he crows. He must lie as if he were dead, and then the bird's ready when he wakes. God, but it's hard on the throat. Up that street now, is that the way?

First Man at Window. Better put in our heads, better have nothing to do with it. Lord, what a time of mischief we live in. (*Heads go in.*)

Old Man. They are afraid of old Ganaton, afraid of old Ganaton. (*He goes off chuckling. The heads come out again.*)

First Old Man at W. He's gone. A holy man himself would be afraid of a man like that.

(*Two men come down this dark lane talking.*)

2nd Man at W. And there's nothing in the world he will crow for but a crowned head, they say. Hush. There's someone coming.

First Passerby. Is it hurting you much now?

Second Passerby. No, no, but I am weak from the loss of blood.

First Passerby. Put your arm on my shoulder.

Second Passerby. I knew it was madness to attack them like that. We should have waited till the whole town was out.

First Man. That's the way always—nothing planned, all done on the impulse of the moment. They'll be very bitter after this. I saw one of their men fall. Well, here we are at your own door.

Second Man. What I mind most is that I was knocked out before the big fight. When are they to gather?

First Man. Two hours after dawn.

Second Man. They are to finish it this time.

First Man. Yes, it's death. Once it begins it is her life or ours.

1 Man at Window. What was it friend, what was the fight for
tonight?

First Passerby. So that is you, Aghvay [?], sitting up there like
a jackdaw in a cage while we were shedding our blood.

Second Man at Window. We were in our beds when we heard
the noise.

First Passerby. So there's another jackdaw.

First Man at W. What could two old men like us do?

First Passerby. You could carry shot. But the poor will know
how to pick their friends when the great day's through.

Second Man at Window. Yes, yes, we are with the poor. Why
should not we—does [not] all the world know? It was only
yesterday that I gave a shilling, a whole shilling, Allon [?],
to a beggar.

First Man at Window. We were in our beds, we did not know
it was the poor that were fighting. It might have been the
rich fighting among themselves. Don't they often fight among
themselves? We did not even know who was fighting. We
heard a noise and put out our heads.

Second Old Man at W. Allon, you were always a good neighbour,
you will tell us all about it. You will tell who was fighting.

Passerby. The old Chancellor was bringing the tax money, the
money that the Queen has drained out of us for the last
twelvemonth, from our shops and from our farms, from the
tax collector to put it in the Queen's castle for the better
keeping of it. Some of our hotheads made an attack, and the
rest [of] us because we're fools joined in, but they drove us
off. It was a foolish business, for there were not a hundred
of us.

1 Man at Window. Anyone killed?

Passerby. Three of our men and one of theirs. We let the dead
lie. (*He goes out.*)

2 Man at Window. Are there any that we know among the
killed?

First Man at Window. Aghway[?], did you ever see the Queen?

Second Man at Window. No, but I often see the light in her
tower, the tower where she prays. I can see it now, up there on
the hill.

First Man at W. I too have never seen her, but I cannot see the light from my window.

Second Man. When the late King lived the lower windows used to shine very late, especially the windows of the big room where they eat and drank, but now they are seldom lit.

First Old Man. Tomorrow is to be her birth[day]. It is an impious thing to choose her birthday to murder her and maybe to burn her house.

Second. Maybe they will find her at her prayers and be afraid to kill because of the ill luck.

First Old Man. We live in terrible times.

Second Man at W. Do you hear that? It was like a groan.

First Man at W. There it is again.

Second Man at W. Aghway [?], there is a wounded man in the street.

First Man at W. I will get my lanthorn and go down.

Second Man at W. It is dangerous to go out on a night like this.

First Man at W. I would not have him die there. Maybe it is one of us shall be lying there next. These are terrible times.

Second Man. The streets seem quiet enough now. I would not believe there had been all that noise if I had not heard it myself. (*He leans out of window. First Man has come out below.*)

[*First Man.*] Here he is. Come down and bring a bottle of wine. (*Second Old Man comes out while the first is raising up wounded man and holding the lanthorn to his face.*)

Second Man. He's coming to. Drink some of this wine.

Wounded Man. The scoundrels. Where are they gone, where are the scoundrels gone?

First Man. The fight's over. The streets are empty now.

Wounded Man. I told them what I thought of them though. To think of the scoundrels attacking me, and all because of art. Play and players alike is [are?] too good for their understanding.

First Man. I don't understand you. Were you of the Queen's party or of the town? Don't be afraid to speak. We will do you no harm.

Wounded Man. I am not afraid to speak. I know nothing of Queen's men and Town's men. I was at bars, sir, in your

town—which let me tell you, sir, is a . . . But I beg your
pardon. I have drunk your wines and so I must not speak
badly of your town, but if you knew the provocation I have
had . . . I'll thank you for your arm. Ah, now I am better.
(*Gets up.*) . . . you'd understand why I say it is the Devil's privy.

2 *Man at Window.* But where then, sir . . .

Wounded Man. To be set upon by a pack of ignorant curs, who
think they know more of the arts than I do.

2 *Man at Window.* But where then, sir, have you come from, if
you are neither of the town nor one of the Queen's men?

Wounded Man. I am Aglamore [?], the player, a name that
may be known to you.

2 *Man.* No sir, but we are out of the world and the way of its
news this long while. Old age, sir, is a form of ignorance.

Wounded Man. I came yesterday with my players who have
played before half the crowned heads of Europe. We are
to play tomorrow before the Queen and all the court the
famous play of Noah's Flood by the Queen's command.
I am the poet and the chief player and the manager.

First Man. We are to take part in the birthday celebration, it
was to have been a great show, they tell me. But if you are
not one of the Queen's men, or one of the town's men, was it
not, if I may be so bold, a chance blow of [a] stone that
left you the way you are?

Wounded Man. Did I not tell you they were stirred up by some
jealous, envious, rancid poet, or rascally, out-at-elbow actor,
paid I doubt not to attack me, or drunk on [?] bad art and
worse criticism. "Out of my way," says I,—they were packed
in the street like herrings—"I am to play at the Queen's
birthday, and my rehearsals begin at dawn." And then some
rascal said I had no business to play before the Queen, and
others were for turning me back, and then one of them said
a deal I could not understand, but I saw it all plain enough.

First Old Man (chuckling). He thinks it was all some quarrel
about his play-acting.

Second Old Man. That he does.

First Old Man. You're on the wrong track, friend; it's a
little quarrel of our own. You see, there's a Queen that never
shows her face, spends her time praying up there, and the

taxes they go up and up. And some blames the Queen for
that and some the Old Chancellor, but all [say] why
should we pay taxes for a Queen we never see, what is the
good of a Queen like that, they say.

Second Man. And they hit you because you insulted them. Now
do you understand?

Wounded Man. My good man, you live as yet out of the world,
and you are old and age is a form of ignorance, and you do not
know that this moment the entire world is being divided on
certain great artistic questions—restoring classicism, medieval
symbolism, and so on. Then they have not argued tonight,
they have begun to murder.

First M. I tell you the town is preparing to attack the castle, and
if there's murder done it's the poor Queen that will be
murdered.

Wounded Man. The man that struck me was no fool; he
understood how great the issue is. He knew that between
two forms of art lie differences of civilization, the whole
world of the years to come. But you see nothing. If they are
going to attack the castle, it [is] but to destroy us the better.

First Man. It's in his head the wound is.

Wounded Man. And so goodbye to you and my thanks to you,
for I must put my people in safety. They must leave this town
at once. (*He goes.*)

First Man. That's a bad blow on his head.

Second Man. I don't know. Maybe now it's not the blow that
makes him talk like that, for I have heard that the players
and the poets too are not what they used to be. A heady,
headstrong, fantastical lot, that's what they are, I am told.

First Man. Do you mind that birthday of the Old King when
you and I were lads, and the King's players'd come from
foreign parts.

Second Man. Mind it? That I do. He was a man. Do you mind
how he made the quarreling of cats with his mouth, and
you'd have thought the whole yard was full of them, and after
that when I'd thought nothing in the world could have got
another laugh out of us, do you mind what he did then?
(*They dig each other.*)

First Man. That I do. Down fell his britches, and the Old
   King, how he did laugh.
Second Man. Up he took the flagon in his hand, it half full
   of wine, and he flung it.
First Man. He did, and struck the player right on the buttocks.
   And after that what did he do but fill the flagon with money
   and give them to the players, so pleased he was with the way
   he'd hit him.
Second Player. That was a good time to live in, friend. There
   were men in those days, real men I tell you. Where would
   you find a player like that now?

Commentary

This draft would be theatrically effective—the off-stage and on-stage noises
with which it begins in the dark are sure-fire, like the drunk which Yeats was
shortly to add. Rat-hole has become an Old Man who still crows like a cock
(though crowing is "bad for the throat") whenever the throne changes occu-
pants; he is now presented in the mode of farce when he worries about the condition of his throat. He is on his way to the castle, which he knows will be the
scene of his next crowing. Then two men who have been involved in the fight
to which we have listened come in and explain it to the old men and of course
to us: the fight was an attempt to stop the tax money from being taken to the
castle, a carry-over from Draft 16. Then there is more necessary exposition
about the recluse Queen before the old men hear Septimus groaning. The two
play the Good Samaritan, one rather reluctantly, and are amused to discover
that Septimus thinks he has been attacked because of his art. They are unable
to shake this illusion, and Septimus goes off to put the members of his troupe
in safety. As the scene ends, they are talking about the good old days and the
degeneracy of modern actors. The actor who imitated the fighting of cats and
whose britches fell down has been transposed from Act II of Draft 16.

   Draft 19 is a prose version of part of Scene II, from the point where Nona
(still *The Friend*) finds the hidden Player Queen to the end of the play. The
diction of the early parts of the draft is quite different from the diction of
Draft 20 and 21 down to line 557, where Nona snatches the key from Decima.
From this point on, 19 and 21 are similar, though 19 is seen to be a crucial
draft only when one regards its incidents and not its language. Six of its pages

have been lost: the first surviving folio is numbered "7," and the numbering continues uninterrupted to "32." The lost part must have contained the opening scene down to the exit of the Prime Minister (here *Lord Chamberlain*) and the Queen: it would have contained the exchange between the Prime Minister and Queen on her unwillingness to play the role her position has assigned her, the search for the missing Player Queen, and the exchange between Nona and the Prime Minister on the necessity of giving the Noah play as scheduled, though not necessarily in that order. Yeats tried various arrangements of his opening incidents in these drafts. The actual manuscript opens with the Player Queen's song, goes on to her discovery, her liking for queen roles, her disagreement with Nona; it continues with the rehearsal of the play within the play, broken off by news of the rebellion, Decima's demand that Nona be dismissed from the company, her scene with the Old Man, her exchange of identity with the Queen, and her sudden marriage to the Prime Minister. This might stand as an outline of the finished play, and the fact that it could so stand testifies to the extent of Yeats's breakthrough.

[Draft 19]

(*Player Queen creeps from under throne singing* "My mother dandled me, etc." *Friend enters.*)

Friend. Thank God I have found you. (*Player Queen goes on singing song.*) We have searched the whole place, we have been searching for hours. (*Player Queen winds up her song.*) Here is the dress of Noah's wife. Get into it quickly. We are to rehearse at once—dress rehearsal.

Player Queen. No.

The Friend. You won't play? What is to be done?

Player Queen. I am tired of playing old women. I will never play another.

The Friend. But that is the play everybody wants to see, and it has been billed all over town.

Player Queen. Do you think I would have lain in that hole all night till I'm blue with the cold and my foot asleep if I was going to give in now? I will never again play that old woman and be beaten because I won't go into the Ark. I am fit for better than that. I'll tell you what I am fit for—I know it now. I am fit to play a queen. I saw a woman trying to be queen just now and she did not know how to do it, but I know.

That is why I came out, I knew at last what I wanted to do. I have
been laying there all night saying to myself "what is it you
want," then all in a moment I knew. He can put in Cleopatra,
or Herodias, or Solomon and Sheba—I don't care what so long
as I can be a queen. I must be young, I must be splendidly
dressed. Everybody who looks at me must say "that is the very
fountain of life, that is all I have ever dreamed of."

The Friend. Well, if you won't play the part, I will. I have
learned it, and in a very short while I will have changed this
dress till it fits me. (*She shows scissors.*)

Player Queen. Yes, you may play it, but you will be hissed.
Everybody will abuse you and blame you when the play fails. I
heard what you said just now. "We can do without her; she is
[not] the only one who can play the part." O, I heard.

The Friend (*beaten down*). That's quite true, I'll be hissed and
everybody blame me; but I'll play, I'll play. I'll do it for Yellow
Martin's sake; he won't have to break our contract then. O,
why do you treat him so? There's not another woman in the
company that would treat him as you do. [He] is now down
drinking in the town and it is all because of you.

Player Queen. "She does it all to plague Yellow Martin," I
heard that too. Yes, I do it on purpose.

The Friend. On purpose, and he loves you so. I know you have
denied yourself to him this last month. Somebody will
take him from you, and then you will be sorry.

Player Queen. No, never. You are a simple child. I will tell you
what I have learned from life. You will thank me some day
when you have a man of your own. I have had lovers—a score
I think. They tired of me and I of them. And then when I met
Martin I resolved to keep him. First I made him marry me, and
then to make him so mad about me that he would think of me
all day and all night. Do you know that men only love the
unknown, the mysterious, and the unconquered? Perhaps you
too like the rest dream of taking him from me. He has been
to see you to tell you his troubles and to ask your sympathy.
Listen to what he sings of me. (*Sings.*)

"She is worthy to walk with Pallas Athene to the altar,
So comely, so high of head, so stately,

A fit prey is she for a centaur
Drunk with the unmixed wine.''

Do you think if I were ever at his beck and call he would have
sung like that of me? I am loved as a mistress in her first
fortnight, though I am his wife. I never kiss unwooed, and
when he woos he suffers. I am his dreams—what does any
man care for reality—and when I act his dreams shall be
in me. (*Sings.*)

"Had Solomon such joy of Sheba
Under the shade of the palm by the still marble?
O upon me, poor wretch that I am,
Should Sheba have gazed with envy.''

Do you say I do not love?

The Friend. You think that you hold his heart because you
   make him miserable. I know those poems before you say them
   —not their words but their beats, five and four. He made
   those poems between two and three in the morning, and he
   made them upon my back.

Player Queen. Leave!

The Friend. He made one of them Thursday night, and one of
   them Monday.

Player Queen. Yes, yes. He gave me one on Friday morning
   and one on Tuesday morning, that is true.

The Friend. And you hid them there under your dress and you
   thought no one else knew of them, and he told nobody. But
   tap, tap, tap, he made them between my shoulders. You know
   now which of us two has the right way of loving. (*Enter
   Stage Manager.*)

[*Stage Manager.*] Ah, you have been found. Quick, to work. Get
   on that dress. What are you standing there for like a woman in
   a trance? (*Player comes in with animal masks.*)

A Player. Quick with your animal heads. We have but an hour
   before the play starts. We cannot wait for Martin. We have
   only an hour for a rehearsal.

Player [*Queen*]. No, all must listen to me. She there has
   taken my husband. He was with her Monday night and
   Thursday night. She has been planning this for months.

The Friend (*in tears*). He was so miserable. She made him so
    miserable I could not help it.

Player Queen. And now she thinks she has triumphed over me.
    But she has not. I have planned it all. I have done all I
    could to drive him away and to drive him to her. I was tired
    of him.

Manager. Well it seems to me this is all your own affair, and
    that we have to go on with this rehearsal. You, Simon, stand
    over there. That side is the auditorium.

Player Queen. No, no, I am too happy now that I am free of
    him. Who will dance with me?

Player. We have only an hour.

Player Queen. Give us a tune there. Who'll be my partner?
    Come Simon.

Player. Stop the nonsense and go to your places.

Player Queen. Peter, you told me you were in love with me
    only a week [ago]. Come and dance now.

2 Player. No, I won't, for you slapped my face.

Player Queen. Come, if you will dance with me, maybe—I
    do not promise—but maybe I will take a fancy to you.
    What do I care now who lays his head upon my breast?
    (*Player steps out but Stage Manager forces him back.*)

Stage Manager. Back, I tell you. If you stir I'll have you
    dismissed.

Player Queen. Give me a tune. Maybe I'll take a fancy to him
    who plays me music. (*A player begins to play his fiddle.*
    Stage Manager runs after him, but gives it up, saying,
    "but if you don't know your parts you will be all clapped in
    prison." *Player Queen begins to dance by herself. She*
    whirls the scissors about.)

The Friend. O, take those scissors from her. She is only
    pretending. Look how wild she is. She will kill me or herself.

Player Queen. Kill myself—and I free at last—free to choose
    a man where I please? At last. I am full of joy. O, if I were
    not happy now, I could kill someone with these fine sharp
    scissors. (*She dances, waving about the scissors, first before*
    the eyes of the Friend, who cowers back behind the others,
    and then as if to kill herself, and then lets it fall, and holds

out her arms in ecstacy [?] *to the man who plays the fiddle*
and who has mounted on the throne, where he stands.
Martin runs in, still drunk but less so.)

[*Martin.*] The town is roused. The crowds are coming this
way. There is not a moment to lose. They have risen
against us. Our rivals have stirred up the people. They
are coming to murder us. Already I have hardly escaped.

A Player. What, against us?

Martin. They have already tried to murder me, and now they
are coming, shouting through the streets. They know
that but for us nothing would ever happen.

A Player. Tom of the Hundred Tales lives on the seashore,
and he hates our comedies, and Peter of the Love Songs
likes us no better, but murder? That is more than he
has a mind for.

Another Player. I heard some shouting as we were climbing the
hill last night, but it seemed to be against the Queen.

Martin. My friend, do you not understand that the world
cares no longer for queens? It is concerned with more
important matters. There are those will have nothing
described in plays, in poems or stories but what actually
happens. They say here is Yellow Martin and his company,
who have played before Kubla Khan. Where there is a
flood and an Ark, that may be true, for all is in the Bible.
But then there are birds and beasts who talk. That is more
than we can endure. Nobody will listen to us.

Player. Yes, who would listen to Tom of the Hundred Tales
when they can listen to me, a talking nightingale?

Player. You, I like your pride. My performance as the
cat-a-mountain has always been a draw.

Player. Stop this wrangling if you would save your lives.
I am off. (*They go out, all but Player Queen and the*
Friend who stays fastening the heads into a bundle.)

Yellow Martin. The crowd [are] slothful. They are dunces.
They wish to go to sleep. They know that we stir up the
passions of men, and they want to sleep. And so they
say come, let us murder those who will not let us sleep.
(*Player Queen stands before gate.*)

[*Friend.*] Why this gate [is] locked.

Player Queen. I have locked it.

Martin. Open it. Cannot you hear the shouting in the
streets? They may be here at any moment.

Player [Queen]. No, not until I have a promise from you.

Martin. What promise?

Friend. Do not listen to her. Are you a man at all?
Go and take it from her.

Martin. Am I a man indeed? I am a man. A whole town is
trying to have me murdered. I will take the key from
her . (*He puts down animal heads.*)

Player Queen. If you come a foot nearer. I will shove it
through the grating, and then the crowd when they come
will find you here and murder you. I will open the door
when I have a promise that this woman will be driven out
of the company, and that you will never speak to her again.

The Friend. O promise. If you delay we will be murdered.
Promise everything.

Yellow Martin. Yes, I can see your meaning. But you say
to me a promise can be broken, even an oath can be
broken, especially an oath that is made in compulsion. But
no, I say to you no. I am not sober, I am too drunk to be
forsworn. What I promise I perform. Therefore I will
not promise, my little darling.

Player Queen. Ah, now I have got you away from her, for
we shall be killed. In the far air and in the clouds
you belong to me. She will know that only you and
I are fit for the high air. (*Friend snatches key.*)

The Friend. I have it, I have it.

Yellow Martin (*holding Player Queen back*). No, no. Because
I am an unforsworn man I am strong. (*The Friend
runs out, leaving gate open.*) Come now. You are a bad,
bad woman, an unkind woman, beautiful but flighty like
the unicorn, but come too. What, will you not speak?
Well, do as you like. I will go to her, she is my comfort.
But I will take these (*lifting masks*), I will carry these
to safety. I will go slowly, with dignity, an unforsworn man.
(*Goes out.*)

Player Queen. Go slowly, go slowly. But I will run past
you and you will not see me, and if they kill you you

556–57

will not overtake me, for I shall [be] up there and complain
of her and of you. (*Takes up scissors.*) Now, now.
And I shall get myself swift feet. (*Enter Old Man
from house.*)

Old Man. I want straw. My back is itchy. I must lie down
and roll. Where will I get straw? I have been round
to the kitchen, but "go away" they said, and made a
sign of the cross as it were a devil that lies down in
me and rolls. If you will let me whisper it to you, I
will [tell] you who it is that rolls. It is the donkey
that carried Christ into Jerusalem. He always knows from
that hour when there is to be a new king. He comes inside,
and when my back gets itchy I know the time has come to lie
down and roll. I roll, and then I bray like a donkey and
the crown changes. But why do you stare at me not saying
a word?

Player Queen. Are you weary of the world, old man?   604

Old Man. Yes, yes, because when I roll and bray
like a donkey I am
asleep. I know nothing about it and that is a great   606
pity. But I must stop talking. I must find straw
to lie on before my back gets itchy. (*Is going.*)

Player Queen. Old man, I am going to   609
drive this into my heart.   610

Old Man. No, no, don't do that. You do not know   611
what you will be put to do when you are dead, in whose
gullet you will be put to sing or to bray or to
talk. No, no, put that away. I will have no rivals,
and you have a look of a foretelling sort. Who knows
but when they slay you they would put you to foretell
the death of kings. And bear in mind I will have no
rivals. There, there, my back is beginning to itch,
and I have not yet found any straw. (*Goes out.
Player Queen puts scissors against the edge of the
throne and is about to lean upon it when the Queen
comes in and stands behind her.*)

Queen (*taking her shoulders*). No, no. That would be a great sin.   627
Player Queen. Your Majesty.   628

Queen. I thought I would like to die a martyr, but that   629
    is different. That is to die for God's glory.

Player [*Queen*]. I am very unhappy.   632

Queen. I too am very unhappy. When I saw the great   633
    angry crowd I wanted to be a martyr, but I was afraid
    and I have run away.

Player Queen. I would not have run away, O no, but it is   637
    hard to drive a knife into one's own flesh.   638

Queen. In a moment they will come in through that door.
    O where can I go to escape them?

Player Queen. If they would mistake you for me you could
    escape. O, your Majesty, if I could only wear that
    gold brocade and those gold slippers for one moment,
    I would be happy. I would not mind dying.

Queen. They say that those who die for their sovereign
    show great virtue. You would be sure to go to Heaven.

Player Queen. Quick, I can hear them coming. (*They begin
    to change.*)

Queen. Was it love? (*PQ nods.*) O, that is a great   655
    sin. It is the beginning of all sins, I have heard.
    I have never known love. Of all things that is what
    I have most feared. It was my fear of that made me
    shut myself away. I was always afraid it [would]
    come in at the eyes and seize upon me in a moment.   660
    I am not naturally good, and they say people will   661
    do anything for love, there is so much sweetness in   662
    it. That is why it [is] so dangerous to the soul. But you
    will escape from all that, you will go up to God a pure
    virgin. (*The change is now complete.*) Good-bye. I am
    going to pray that you may go straight to God. (*Coming
    back.*) Do not face them like that. If you face them you
    will be afraid. Sit there on the throne and turn your
    face away. (*Goes out.*)
    (*Shouting gets nearer and nearer. Crowd gathers outside
    gates. One sees them through bars. Herald comes in.*)

Herald. Your loyal people, your Majesty, have sent me
    here to say that they have received with gratitude your
    royal will as spoken through the mouth of the Lord

Chamberlain. All misunderstandings between them and
the crown are now over. Your condescension in bestowing
upon him your royal hand has settled all. (*Applause.*)

Chamberlain. I will explain all,   684
   your Majesty. There was nothing else to be done.   685

Crowd. Hurrah! (*They come in. Yellow Martin enters.*)

One. Beautiful, etc.

Another. There is a Queen worth having, etc.

Yellow Martin. But, my lord, that is not the Queen.
   That is my wife.

Chamberlain. Nothing can be done for the present. I am
   their only substitute for a unicorn.
   (*Sound of a donkey braying outside. Crowd drags in Old Man.*)

Crowd. Look at this imposter. He has brayed and there is
   no change in the crown.

Another. Sir, this man was plainly in some conspiracy, to
   put the crown on another head.

Another. Yes, and he thought the conspiracy had succeeded.

Chamberlain. Take him away to prison. (*To Yellow Martin.*)
   That is the sign, curse it. The Devil himself has
   decided the matter.

Commentary

The important thing about this draft bears stating again: Yeats finds here most
of the incidents of the finished play, though many of these are merely shadowed
forth—the Player Queen's choice of another lover, for instance.

The Player Queen has been hiding under the throne (vat and fountain have
finally disappeared); she sings not "The Mask" but the song beginning "My
mother dandled me," composed for Draft 17 and, by the time Yeats wrote this
draft, already in print in *Responsibilities*. Nona and the Player Queen have a
brief exchange during which the Player Queen refuses the part of Noah's wife
and insists she will play only queen roles. When the Friend says that she will
take the part, there is no fight, as there had been earlier and will be later. The
Player Queen merely says "you will be hissed," and the Friend agrees. The
Player Queen states her philosophy of marriage, which is, in good part, to keep
the husband guessing. To show how Septimus feels toward her, she reads a part

of an early version of "A Thought from Propertius" and a quatrain using a Solomon-Sheba allusion. Yeats first used a Solomon-Sheba allusion in "On Women," written in May 1914, and returned to it again in 1918 when he wrote "Solomon to Sheba" and "Solomon and the Witch." This quatrain, which is in a very rough state, was never finished or published so far as I know. Nona tells Decima that Septimus has been sleeping with her and composing his poems in praise of Decima while thumping out their rhythms on her back. The Stage Manager comes in and tries to start a rehearsal, but Decima breaks it up and begins to dance by herself, whirling about the scissors she has taken from Nona. This scene is only a shadow of what it was to become. Decima's notion to take the best dancer among them as her new lover is no more than hinted at: "Give me a tune. Maybe I'll take a fancy to him who plays me music." It is Septimus who now comes in with news of the revolt, a change made necessary by the dropping of Peter and a logical development from Septimus's involvement in the fight between the rival factions in Scene I. Septimus still thinks the whole disturbance is an attack on him and his company: "The crowd are slothful. They are dunces. They wish to go to sleep. They know that we stir up the passions of men, and they want to sleep. And so they say come, let us murder those who will not let us sleep." The locking in of the three principals follows from the old versions, but now Nona snatches the key rather than have Decima give it up when she supposes that Septimus loves Nona. Nona escapes with Septimus. From here on, the scene develops pretty much as it will continue to develop through 1922: the Old Man comes in, looking for straw. His method of foretelling a new occupant of the throne has changed since Draft 18, where he still crowed like a cock. Now he rolls on his back and brays like a donkey. The fleeing Queen enters and Decima takes her place. Yeats no longer shows Decima in the role of Queen, as he had in all the early drafts. Now she becomes Queen all in a moment, and everybody but Septimus accepts her as Queen—she becomes Queen by acclamation, so to speak. Probably the new solution is dramatically safer than the old, since in the theater surprise is often safer than demonstration of the improbable. We conclude with a farcical *gamos* in which the already married Player Queen gets a new husband to go along with her new role.

There are two hints that Yeats is becoming interested in the unicorn that dominates the finished play. Hitherto there has only been a passing allusion to a gift of twenty unicorns from the Great Turk in Draft 6. Here there are two allusions. Septimus compares the Player Queen to a unicorn when he calls her "beautiful but flighty like the unicorn." Then at the end of the play the Prime Minister says in reference to the mob, "I am their only substitute for a unicorn."

I don't feel that the allusion in the description of Decima has any symbolic weight, but the other allusion surely has: there is in it some hint of a hoped-for new dispensation. We will leave it there for the moment.

Drafts 20 and 21

These are so closely related that I have presented them on opposite pages; this is the first time it has been possible to do so in the entire run of surviving drafts. Draft 20, which covers a part of Scene II only, is in Yeats's dramatic blank verse with interspersed prose and lyrics; Draft 21, a draft of the whole play, is in prose throughout. Yeats's usual practice was to write his plays in prose and then turn the prose into verse. He did this with some early versions of *The Player Queen*. Here he worked the other way around, for the verse draft is the earlier. The evidence for this is so overwhelming that citing it would be a waste of time. In short, the shift to prose was part of Yeats's radical new conception of his play; his new conception involved, that is, the complete abandonment of many years of work.

We begin with Draft 21, since Draft 20 is incomplete. When we get to the opening of Act II (Scene II in the finished play) Draft 20 (verse) will be printed on lefthand pages, Draft 21 (prose) on righthand pages. Draft 20 breaks off on page 330 below, and we continue with 21 to the end of the play. Draft 20 has survived in two versions, a manuscript and a typescript dictated from it, which are textually different. For example, the newly invented names (*Septimus, Nona, Decima*) are introduced into the manuscript following line 125; they are used throughout the typescript. Proof of dictation of the typescript is unusually strong, for Yeats's typist wrote "Nona's wife" for "Noah's wife," "cells" for "selves," "hour" for "power," and "died o'er" for "Dido" (this last may say something about Yeats's pronunciation). The manuscript is paged 1 through 24, the typescript 13 through 28. The pagination of the typescript indicates that some version of Scene I preceded it. We will follow the manuscript version of Draft 20 when we get to it, supplying missing passages from the typescript.

[Draft 21]

Act I

An empty street towards dawn. One hears the knockers of various houses going. The sound gets nearer. Enter Septimus drunk.

Septimus. Uncharitable place. Unchristian place.
   (*He knocks at a knocker.*) Open there, open there.   40
   I want to come in to sleep. (*A Man puts his head
   out above.*)
Man. Who are you?
Septimus. I am Septimus. I have a bad wife. I want to   43
   come in and sleep.
Man. You are drunk.   45
Septimus. Drunk! So would you be if you [had] as bad a   46
   wife.   47
Man. Go away. (*Shuts window.*)   48
Septimus. Is there not one Christian in this town? (*Tries another*   49
   knocker.) No one there. All dead or all drunk, maybe.   50
   Bad wives. Well, I'll try another. There must be one
   Christian man. (*Tries another knocker.*)
Man (*at window above*). Who is there? What do   52
   you want? Has something happened?   53
Septimus (*so all through*). Yes, that's it. Something has happened.   54
   My wife has hid herself, has run away, or drowned herself.
Man. What do I care about your wife. You are   57
   drunk.   58
Yellow Martin. Not care about my wife! But I tell you my
   wife's to play by order of the Prime Minister
   before all the people in the great hall of the castle   61
   and now she can't be found.
Man. Go away, I tell you. Go away. (*Shuts window.*)
Yellow Martin. Treat Septimus, who has played before Kubla   64
   Khan, like that? Septimus, dramatist and poet. Septimus.
Man. Go to the Devil.
Yellow Martin. Unchristian town, Must
   sleep in the street. Bad wife. Others have   67
   had bad wives, yes, but others were not left to lie down
   in the open street, under the stars, under the cold
   light of dawn, to be run over, to be trampled
   upon, to be eaten by dogs, and all because their wives   72
   had hidden themselves. Unchristian town. (*Sleeps. Enter
   a knot of men.*)
First Man. There's a man lying here.   107
Second Man. Turn him over.

First Man. Drunk I suppose. He'll be killed or   111
    maimed by the first milk cart.   112

Second Man. Better roll him into the corner. If we   113
    are in for a bloody day's business, there is no need   114
    for him to be killed. An unnecessary death might   115
    bring a curse upon us.   116

First Man. Give me a hand then.

Yellow Martin. Not allowed to sleep. Rolled off   118
    the street. Shoved into a stony place. Unchristian   119
    town.   120

A Man. Are we all friends here, are we all agreed?   121

Another Man. These men are from the country. They   122
    only came in last [night]. They know little of the business.
    They won't be against the people, but they want to   124
    know more.   125

Various Voices. Yes, that's it. We are with the   126
    people. We want to know all, etc.

First Man (*mounting on a stone*). Look down that street.
    There upon the top of the [hill], just showing in the light
    of the dawn is the Queen's Castle. Can you all see it?

A Man. Yes, I can see grey [stone] in the daylight.

First Man. Have you ever seen the Queen? ("No, we [have]
    not, have we, nor anyone else.") Seven years now since her
    old father died she has been shut up in that great black
    house. What is the good of a Queen you have never seen?
    All those seven years the Lord Chamberlain has governed us.
    We have made up our minds to have him for king and to
    pay no more taxes for her, and so this very day we will make
    an end of her.

A Countryman. I always did object to Queen's taxes, but I am
    not a man of blood. I'd let her live.

First Man. Come close about me, who knows what ears are
    listening? It is not for nothing that she lives shut up in that
    dark place where her father and her grandfather and her
    great-grandfather did so many crimes.

Second Man. Yes, did their crimes. But they were right kings
    for all that, and not afraid to show their faces.

First Man. She is a witch, a black witch, and she and those
    women with her give to Satan every night, a little before

the cock crows, three drops of blood apiece, and that
blood gives him strength to walk about in the world. At
this very moment, it may be, he is going from one to
another sucking his drops of blood.

A Countryman. Maybe that's not [true]. In my district she is a
holy woman praying for us all, and that those other women
pray too.

First Man. That's a story is given out. That is all the Lord
Chamberlain's doing.

A Countryman. It's true that they always deceive us
country people. We are not educated like the people   153
of the town.   154

A Countryman. I'd be slow to believe that her father's
daughter is a witch, and I'd want testimony for that,
though I am not against the people.

First Man. Here, Tapster, stand up here and tell what you
know.

Tapster. I live in the quarter where her castle is.   170
The garden of my house, and the gardens of all the   171
houses in my row run right up to the rocky hill that   172
has her castle on the top of it. There is a lad in our
quarter that has a goat in his garden.   174

A Voice. Aye, big Simon, I know him.

Tapster. That goat of his is always going astray. One
morning he got up early meaning to go
snaring birds, and nowhere could he see that goat.   178
He began climbing up the rocks. Up and up he
went till he was close under the wall, and there he   180
found the goat, and it shaking and sweating as though   181
something had come over it. Presently he heard something
neigh like a horse, and after that something like a   183
horse came by, but it was no horse but a uni-
corn. He had his pistol for he had thought to bring   185
down a rabbit, and seeing it rushing at him, as he   186
thought, he fired. It vanished all in a
moment, and there was blood on a great stone.
Seeing what company she has in the small hours
what wonder that she never sets her foot out of doors.

A Man. I would not believe all that night   192

rambler'd say. All we have against
her for certain is that she won't put her foot out of 194
doors. I knew a man once that when he was five and 195
twenty refused to get out of his bed. He wasn't ill, 196
no not he, but he said life was a vale of tears. And 197
for forty and four years till they carried him out to 198
the churchyard he never left that bed. All tried him, 199
parson tried him, priest tried him, doctor tried 200
him, and all that he'd say was "Life is a vale of tears."
It's too snug he was in his bed, and believe me that 202
ever since she has had no father to rout her out in
the morning she has been in her bed, and small blame
to her, maybe. 205
Another Countryman. But that's the very sort that are 206
witches, believe me; they know where to find their own friends
in the lonely hours of the night. There was a witch 208
in my own district that I strangled last Candlemas 209
twelvemonth. Three imps she had that came in the shape
of three hares every night, and sucked the blood from her
poll. It's with their blood they fed them, and till
they get the blood they are but images, but once
they have it drunk they can be for a while
stronger than you or me. 216
Third Countryman. The man I knew was no witch. He 217
was no way active. "Life is a vale of tears," he said. 218
The doctor came and the priest came and the doctor
came, and that is all he'd say.
Another Man. We'd have no man go beyond reason and
evidence, but hear the Tapster out and when you have
you'll say there never was a witch if she's not one.
Tapster. It's not a story I like to be telling, but 225
you're all married men. Another night that boy 226
climbed up after his goat, and it was an hour earlier 227
by his clock, and presently he came right up to the
castle wall and began climbing along the wall
among the rocks and bushes till he saw a light from 230
a little window over his head. It's an old wall full 231
of holes where the mortar's fallen out, and he climbed
up putting his toes into the holes till he could look 233

in through the window, and when he looked in   234
what did he see but the Queen.   235
A Countryman. And did he see what she was like?
Tapster. He saw more than that; he saw her coupling   237
  with a great white unicorn. (*Murmurs among the crowd.*)   238
Countryman. I have strangled to be [?] strangled. I'll
  not have the son of a unicorn reign over us, although
  he'd be but half a unicorn.
Another Man. I'll not go against the people, but   242
  I'd let her live, so that the Chamberlain promises to
  rout her out of bed in the morning and set a guard
  to drive off the unicorn.
First Countryman. I've strangled an old witch with   246
  my two hands, and today I'll strangle a young
  witch.   248
Yellow Martin (*who has slowly got up and staggered over to*   249
  the stone). Did I hear
  someone say that the unicorn is not chaste? It is a
  most noble beast, a most religious beast. It has a   251
  milk-white skin and a milk-white horn and milk-   252
  white hooves, but a mild blue eye and it dances in   253
  the sun. I will [have] no one speak against it, not while   254
  I am still upon the earth. It is written in the great   255
  beastery of Rheims that it is chaste, that it is the
  most chaste of all the beasts of the world.
A Man. Pull him out of that. He is drunk.   258
Yellow Martin. Yes, I am drunk, I am very drunk, but that   259
  is no reason why I should permit anyone to speak   260
  against the unicorn.   261
Another. Let's hear him out; we can do nothing   262
  till the night's gone.
Another. I wish I had half his complaint.
Yellow Martin. No[body] shall speak against the unicorn, no   264
  one, my friends and poets. It is a fine word; it
  rhymes well—"corn," "lorn," "morn"—all fine words rhyme
  to it, and if one likes a bad rhyme one has "forlorn"
  and "shorn," all according to precedent, and one may
  even go on to "dawn" and "lawn" for we must have
  novelty and rhymes wear out; no good thing lasts

forever. A most noble beast. I will hunt it if you
[will], though it is a dangerous and cross-grained beast.   266
Much virtue has made it cross-grained. I will go with   267
[you] to the high tablelands of Africa where it lives,   268
and we will there shoot it through the head, but I   269
will not speak against its character, and if any man   270
declares it is not chaste I will fight him, for I affirm   271
that its chastity is equal to its beauty.   272

A Man. He is most monstrously drunk.   273

Yellow Martin. No, friend, no longer drunk, but inspired.

A Man. Let's hear him out; we'll never hear the like again.

A Man. Come away, I have had enough of this.

Yellow Martin. Hear me, for I am in the full flight of my
inspiration. Ah, but I can see it now. You are bent
upon going away to some deserted market-place, some
lonely spot, where uninterrupted
you can speak against the character of the unicorn,   283
but you shall not, I tell you, [you] shall not. (*He
has got down from stone.*) In the midst of this uncharitable   285
town I will protect that noble, milk-white, flighty   286
beast.   287

Countryman. Let me pass. (*Yellow Martin strikes him and is*   288
knocked down.)

A Countryman. Have you killed him?

Countryman. Maybe I have, maybe I have not.   305
Let him lie there. A witch I strangled last Candlemas   306
twelvemonth, a witch I'll strangle today. What   307
do I care for the like of him?

Another Man. Come round to the east quarter. The tanners
and the carpenters will be all out by this, and it's a
short march from there to the castle gate. (*They go out
at one side, but all come hastily back.*)

A Townsman. Are you sure it is him?

Another. Could I not know? I was standing by the last time.
The Old King was dying. "Get me straw," said the old man,
"my back itches." Then all of a sudden he lay down and
he brayed like a donkey. At that moment the Old [King]
died and his daughter was Queen.

Another Man. They say it is the donkey that carried   333
    Christ into Jerusalem, and that is why he knows
    a rightful sovereign. He hasn't been in the
    town from that day to this. He goes begging about the coun-
    try, and there's no man dare refuse him what he asks.   336
Another. Look, look. There he is, coming over the
    top of the hill and the mad look on him.
Another. Come away. I would not face him for the world.
    Come round by the market-place. We'll be less
    afraid in the moonlight.
Yellow Martin. Unchristian town. First I am so to speak   348
    thrown out into the street, and then I am all but   349
    murdered, and I drunk and therefore in need of   350
    protection. All creatures are in need of protection at   351
    some time or other. Even my wife was once a frail   352
    child in need of milk, of smiles, of love—as if in the   353
    midst of the flood of the world, in danger of drowning
    so to speak.

(An Old Man with ragged hair and beard comes in. Yellow
Martin has rubbed his fingers on to his broken head, and is
now looking at the blood on his fingers.)

Old Man. I want straw.   355
Yellow Martin. Tom of the hundred tales lives near the
    market-place, and Peter, author of "The Purple Pelican,"
    lives close to the cathedral. Yes, they have done it. They have
    stirred the people against me. (*Seeing Old Man.*) There is a
    certain medicine which is made by decocting camphor,
    Peruvian bark, spurge, mandrake and mixing all with
    dissolved pearls and
    four ounces of the oil of gold; and this medicine is   363
    infallible to stop the flow of blood.
Old Man. I want straw.   366
Yellow Martin. Yes, I see you have not got it, but no matter.
    We will be friends.
Old Man. I want straw to lie down on.   369
Yellow Martin. My friend, it is better that I should bleed

to death, for in that way I shall disgrace those poets
who out of despairing jealousy have stirred up the people
against me. But it is necessary I shall die somewhere where
my last
words can be taken down. I am therefore in need of   374
your support.   375

Old Man. Are you not afraid? When my back itches I must
lie down and roll, and then I
bray and the crown changes.   379

Yellow Martin. Ah, you are inspired. Then we are indeed   380
brothers. Come, I will rest upon your shoulders.
We will mount the hill side by side.

Old Man. And will you give me straw to lie upon?   384

Yellow Martin. Asphodels. Yet indeed the asphodel is a   385
flower much overrated by the classic authors. Still if   386
a man has a preference, a preference, I say, for the
asphodel . . . (*They go out.*)

[Draft 20 begins on page 298 and continues on the following
left-hand pages; Draft 21 continues on the facing right-hand
pages.]

[*Chancellor.*] She was to be here by dawn, before the people had
    gone mad, while they had still a night's sleep in their eyes,
    and here is the light streaming in. Will she wait till they
    batter in the door?

Woman. She wants to know . . .
Chancellor. Well, out with it. Are you afraid to speak?
Woman. She wants to know . . .
Chancellor. Well what? What would she know?

Woman. She wants to know if she must wear that dress
    Covered with gilt embroidery, and thinks
    That her own common, straight, everyday clothes
    Better become Christian humility.

[Draft 21 continued]
Act II

The throne room in Queen's castle. At back in center a throne, and on either side openwork iron doors. That to left leads to palace, that to right to open air. In left wall a great window. The dawn is breaking. The Prime Minister is speaking to a waiting woman who stands in door to left. She is dressed almost like a nun.

Prime Minister. She has had my directions and agreed to
    them. She was to have been here at dawn before the people
    have gone mad, while they have still the night's
    sleep in their eyes and are more in the humour to
    yawn than murder. And here we have the light streaming
    in while she waits till the gates are beaten in.

W. Woman. She wants to know. She wants . . .

Prime Minister. Well, out with [it]. What, are you afraid?
    Am I a tyrant that you should stand there dumfounded?
    If I thought you had that notion . . . Well, well, why
    don't you speak?

W. Woman. She wants to know . . .

Prime Minister. Well, well, what will she know? This is
    no moment to waste time by leaving me here guessing.

W. Woman. She wants to know if she must wear that dress
    all gold embroidery, and thinks that her plain everyday
    clothes better become the humility of a Christian.

Prime Minister. Christian humility! When they have seen
    her should they be dissatisfied? Should they say
    this is no queen, this is a little praying woman whose
    like can be seen in the chapel any day? What will
    happen to you, what will happen to me, what will happen

Chancellor. St. Gregory! They may pull down the roof
    Or fling their torches up into the rafters
    Should they when they have had their will and seen her
    Be still dissatisfied. And yet she sighs
    For her straight common everyday clothes. Good God
    A queen is not a woman but a thing
    A block. The embroiderers hang gold thread upon it.
    What, is there more?
Woman.   She would be grateful, sir,
    If she might go bare-footed, for she says
    The cobblestones would be a blessed penance,
    Her bare footsole a homily to her heart,
    That she believes to be most proud and wicked,
    In Christian humility.
Chamberlain.   Barefoot.
    What, barefoot do you say? Well, go and tell her
    That if I do not see her in that door
    Within two minutes, her dress of state upon her,
    Her crown, her gold embroidered slippers upon her
    I will resign. (*Woman goes.*) X Fierce women, treacherous women
  X The dissolute and murderous, every sort
  X Daredevils, blond and blue-eyed devils
  X That are the worst of all have made good queens,
  X But no saint, Well, what is it now?
               O for some wooden mask
    Cut out with an old jackknife and painted vermillion,
    African god, images dressed up in frippery
    Or any savage object stuck with feathers
    So that it is no saint. What now?

to the roof? What will prevent them from flinging
up their torches into the rafters? Her coarse, plain,
everyday clothes. Go, tell her that a queen is not
a woman, a queen is a block for the embroiderers to
hand gold thread upon. Go, tell her that. What, is
there more? Well, go on. I am patient, patient to
the edge of miracle. Go on, go on.

W. Woman. She would be grateful, sir, if she might go
barefooted, for she says the cobble [stones] would be
a blessed penance, and she told me that I must say
that she is idle and careless [?] and in much need
of chastening.

Prime Minister. Barefooted do you say? Well, well, I
must show an example of patience. Please go to her
and say that if I do not see her in that door within
two minutes, her dress of state and her crown upon
her, I will resign. (*W. Woman goes.*)

O for some wooden mask cut with an old jackknife and
painted vermillion, an African god or any like savage object
stuck with feathers, or anything so that it is not a
saint. (*W. Woman returns.*) What now?

Woman.   She asks
    For twenty minutes more to say a rosary.
Chamberlain. For twenty minutes more. For seven years,
    Since she was first made Queen, she has stayed up yonder
    In that old tower at prayer. I have permitted
    Bread and water and a scourge, dried pease,
    All comforts of her church, yet she has asked
    Another twenty minutes. Let her come at once
    Or I shall go [at] once and let the crowds
    Do what they please.
Woman.   Another twenty minutes. (*Queen comes in.*)
Chamberlain. Who made that dress?
Woman. Her majesty will have it that her small wicked body—
    So she has named it—does not deserve new clothes.
    This dress was the late Queen's.
Chamberlain.   It may seem right
    To those upon the edges of the crowd,
    And those that have pressed nearer can be charmed
    If you'll but play your part. But, Majesty,
    Do not hang down your head as 'twere in shame
    Nor hang your arms in that dumfounded way.
    This is no hour for mincing words. Your life,
    The safety of the state, depend it may be

W. Woman. She asks for twenty minutes more to say a rosary.

Prime Minister. Twenty minutes more! For seven years she
has stayed up yonder in that old tower at prayer. I
have permitted bread and water, a hair shirt, a scourge,
and four bushels of dried pease—all the comforts of
her church. And yet she has asked another twenty
minutes. Let her come at once or I shall let the mob
do what they please. (*W. Woman goes.*) Gregory of
Nazianzus, twenty minutes! (*Queen comes in with
waiting women who are all dressed somewhat like
nuns. They remain in the background in the doorway.
The Queen comes down stage. She wears a gold
embroidered dress that does not fit*). Who made that dress?

W. Woman. Her majesty will have it that her body, which
she considers to be most wicked, does not deserve
new clothes. These were the late Queen's.

Prime Minister. Well, we can but hope that they may seem
right to those upon the outer edge of the crowd.
Those who are nearest may perhaps, [if] your majesty but
play your part, he charmed. But do not hang your
head as if in shame, nor hang your arms in that dumfounded
way. Forgive the freedom of my words, this is no time
for mincing words. The safety of the state . . .

Another Version

PM. Who made that dress?

W. Woman. Her majesty is convinced that she does not de-

Upon the springing of your foot, the light
That you can summon up into your eye.
Now walk, your majesty, walk like a queen.
You look the nun that you have always wished to be.
Be more majestic. No no, that is no better
Try and look like some sort of queenly bird
And not a jenny wren.

Queen. But—but . . .

Chamberlain. No no,
There is no need for words. I understand
You would reproach me that I have kept you here
When all your heart was set upon the convent.
Now the event has proved me fool. But madame,
We have to see to it that your life is safe
And the streets clean of blood.

serve new clothes. These were the late Queen's.

Queen. O, sir, I have been a sinful woman, careless and
  indifferent to holy things. I would not seem to
  disguise myself, as though I hoped to deceive God's eye.

PM. Well, we can but hope that it will seem right to those
  upon the outer edge of the crowd. Those who are nearest
  may, if your majesty will but play your part, be charmed.

Queen. No good thing will happen there, and I alone am to
  blame.

PM. Do not hang your head as if in shame, nor hang your
  arms in that dumfounded way. Forgive the freedom
  of my speech. This is no time for mincing words. The
  safety of us all may depend upon the spring of your
  foot or the light in your eye. Walk, your majesty,
  permit me to see you walk like a queen. No no, you
  look the nun you have always wished to be. Be more
  majestic. No, that is no better. Look eagle or vulture,
  anything but the jenny wren.

Friend.   Where are you hidden,
    Where are you, Noah's Wife, where are you? (*Runs in.*)
Chamberlain. Have you no manners that you break in so
    Upon the royal presence?
Friend.   Your Majesty
    Something has happened, a most dreadful thing.
Chamberlain. What, more ill news? Are the gates broken in?

[Draft continues? Gen. Ed.]

Queen. O, it is no use, we will have no luck today. God
will punish us. It is all because of the image.

P. Minister. The image? What image?

Queen. The image of Our Lady in my room. I should have
looked after it myself. I dreamed only last night
that the side that is turned to [the] wall had never
been cleaned for years. I can see that you are as [troubled]
as I am, but you must not blame my women for it.
They all pray a great deal and that makes them sleepy,
so they forgot about it. I should have seen to it myself.

PM. That is indeed a great sin, your majesty, and shows
that you are indeed a most sinful woman.

Queen. Alas.

Prime Minister. But it is certain that when one is a queen,
it does not matter what one is but only what one seems.
Who would fling up his cap if he say any man or woman
as they are, and who would face cannon if [he] did
not seem to himself that he is not? (*Voice
calling* "Decima, where are you Decima?")

Prime Minister (*as Nona enters*). O, here is one who may
perhaps make you understand your duty. Have you no
manners that you break in so upon the royal presence?

Nona. O your Majesty, something has happened, a most tragic
thing.

Prime Minister. What, more ill news, is the hill surrounded?

Friend. Our chief player is lost. She that should play
    The wife of Noah in the Mystery of the Deluge.
    We have spent the whole night searching, and the play
    Begins in an hour.

Chamberlain.   This woman, your Majesty,
    Belongs to a most famed theatrical company
    We have called hither. The best judges hold
    They are the foremost artists in the world.
    I chose [the] play myself—a popular piece,
    "The tragical history [of] Noah's Deluge."
    The wife of Noah is an old crochety woman.
    Her husband has to beat her with a stick
    Before she gives up gossiping with the neighbours
    And swims in the Ark. The common people
    Yell with delight to see her beaten.
    The player's manager was against the piece—
    Thought it beneath their dignity it seems.
    I count upon this piece, some greasy poles
    Bear baitings and the like to keep the crowd
    In tolerable humour.

Nona. Our chief player is lost. We have spent the whole
night searching and the play begins at noon. She was
chosen to play the wife of Noah in the Mystery of the
Deluge.

Prime Minister. Lost, do you say lost? There is a conspiracy.
When I told Septimus, your manager, that I would have
that piece and no other, he wanted some other piece; said
it was against your dignity on so great an occasion, that it
was only fit for cattle farmers and the like. As if the people
were not everywhere the same. Well, if she is not found, I
will hold him responsible. Your Majesty, this woman
belongs to a most famous theatrical company. There are
good judges who hold they are the most famous artists in
the world. I count upon them and certain greasy poles,
bear-baiting and the like to keep the people in good humour.
I saw that piece when I was a boy—just the thing to please
everybody. Noah beats his wife with a great stick because she
won't go into the Ark. She wants to stay at home gossiping
with the neighbours. And now they want to put on their
own choice, some dull tragical thing with long speeches.
O, I know them, but I will clap them all in jail.

        Let her presence
  Remind your majesty that there is a likeness
  Between the business of a queen and a player.
  Scullions may be their natural selves, not we
  That live in public.
Queen.   Have they been unkind?
Chamberlain. Impossible. I have given strict commands
  That all should be well treated and well paid.
The Friend. O no, your majesty. She has hidden herself
  To plague her husband. He is our manager,
  Our poet and dramatist, and much too good
  To be at such mischievous woman's mercy.
  He never has a moment's peace and all
  Because she has no delight but her own power
  She has driven [him] to drink, and at this moment
  He is somewhere drinking his despair away.
Chamberlain. When I was young and went to theatres
  I heard some bitter critic say that always
  It was the best player had the emptiest head
  And the most violent passions.
Friend.   She is our genius
  Because there's nobody to take her place.
  She's a most brazen devil, your majesty.
  There's nothing that she will not do to plague him
  And plague us all, and yet he's mad about her.
  He cries her name out even in his sleep.

Nona. O, sir, we want to be obedient, we have been up
  all night searching. Some of us think she must [have]
  drowned herself, or some other dreadful thing. Septimus, he
  is her husband, is so miserable that he went to the town
  and made himself drunk. We do not know what to do.

PM. I don't believe a word of it, it is a conspiracy.

Queen. O no, sir. I am sure there is no conspiracy. This lady
  looks good and gentle. God has taken away our luck.
  That explains all. I did not dare to tell you all. There
  was a spider and a web and many dead flies, and all the
  folds of Our Lady's dress where it was turned to the wall
  full of old dust.

Nona. She is our best player and a genius, and that is what
  makes her so wicked. I always knew she would go too
  far and get us all in trouble. (*Goes out, calling*
  "Decima, where are you Decima?")

Chamberlain. That is enough. It would be no light matter
  If we should disappoint the common sort
  Upon a day like this, so find your player.
  I have the power to put you all in jail.
The Friend. I always knew that she would go too far
  And get us all in trouble, Merope,
  Where are you, O where is Noah's wife,
  Where are you, Merope.
Chamberlain.   Another moment
  And they will tell us the bears have licked
  The grease from all the poles and run away
  To their own wood again. So let's begone
  Before a certainty that we are accursed
  Dissolves our courage. What are you doing there?
Queen. Praying for those poor players that must leave
  The door of the heart wide open to all passions
  To make our sport. Doubtless when they are alone
  They say their prayers and live before God's eye
  Like you and me. But when the play begins,
  Or when their thoughts run on it, what rivalries,
  What vanities, what pride and jealousy
  Perplex, it seems, their thoughts of one another.
  Besides, the play must put into their heads
  Strange wicked thoughts they never would have thought of
  But for its words. Chamberlain, is it true

Prime Minister. Conspiracy or no conspiracy, let her be
found. It would be no light matter to disappoint the
common people on a day like this. The play must begin
punctually and be well played. When I was young and
went to theatre, I heard some bitter critic say that the
best players had the emptiest heads and the most violent
passions, and here is the whole future of the state
perhaps dependent upon such a creature, upon some brazen
devil whose chief pleasure is to plague her husband and
everyone else she can lay hands upon. Another moment we
shall be told that the bears have licked the grease from
the poles and run away to their own mountains. Come, let
us go before the certainty that we are accursed dissolves
our courage. What are you doing there?

Queen. Praying for players that must admit into their hearts
every passion to make our sport. Doubtless when they
are alone they say their prayers and live before God's eye,
and know what true shape they have and are like any
others, but when their thoughts run on the play, or when it
has begun, what jealousies and rivalries and vanities
trouble their thoughts, and besides the evil that the play
itself must put into their heads, the strange, wicked things
they never could have thought of for themselves.
Prime Minister, is it true that women players let

That women players let themselves be kissed
By men who are not their husbands or their brothers
Because it is in the play?

Chamberlain. Your majesty
Had best continue praying, for they need it.
Pray while we are walking through the corridor,
'Twill be great ease to the mind, but do not pray
Among the people under the eye of day.
There you must seem what you are not, but look
Eagle or vulture, a queen of all birds.
A sacred vulture, but a vulture still.

[Continued from the typescript dictated from the manuscript
we have been following.]

(*They go out. Decima creeps from under the throne, singing.*)

Decima. He went away my mother sang
When I was brought to bed
And all the while her needle pulled
The gold and silver thread

She pulled the thread and bit the thread
And made a golden gown
She wept because she dreamt that I
Was born to wear a crown.

Nona's Voice (*heard outside, crying*). Where are you, where are you
Noah's wife?

(*Decima climbs back under the throne, but Nona comes in, sees her,
and catches her by the leg.*)

themselves be kissed by men who are not their husbands
or their brothers because it is [in] the play?

Prime Minister. Doubtless they need your prayers, your
Majesty, but you can pray as we are walking through
the corridor. It will be a great ease to the mind.
But do not pray among the people, under the eye of
day. There you must look like some sort of an eagle
or vulture, a queen of the birds, that had flown from
far off, as it were, and lit upon the throne. O, sacred
vulture. I would set your mind upon seeming a vulture—
that's what they like. (*They go out.*)

Decima (*creeps from under throne, singing*).

He went away, my mother sang,	94
When I was brought to bed,	95
And all the while her needle pulled	96
The gold and silver thread.	97

She pulled the thread and bit the thread	98
And made a golden gown.	99
She wept because she had dreamed that I	100
Was born to wear a crown.	101

Nona's voice (*outside*). Where are you, where [are] you,
Noah's wife? (*Decima climbs back under throne, but
Nona comes in, catches her by the leg.*)

Nona. Ah, thank God I have found you. We have been
searching for you all night. I thought you had been drowned
in a horsepond with a stone round your neck to keep you
from floating.

Decima. O, I have found out such a wonder. Do you know that
old country ballad that was made by the mad singing
daughter of a harlot?

"When she was got," my mother sang,
"I heard a seamew cry,
And saw a flake of yellow foam
That dropped upon my thigh."

How therefore could she help but braid
The gold into my hair
And dream that I should carry
The golden top of care.

[Back to the manuscript, which now has the final character
names in place.]

Septimus told me once that no one finds their genius but
they have found some role, some image, that gives them a
pose towards life, that liberates something within them that
had before been dumb and numb. Only by images, he said,
do we make the eternal life become a part of our
ephemeral life.

Nona. Perhaps when you are done raving you will put on this
dress and this mask.

Decima. I know now what I want to play, a queen. One was
here just now, and she could not play the part at all. I should
be a little haughty and then when I meet their gaze
I should bend

Nona. Ah, thank God I have found you. We have been
  searching [for] you all night. I thought you had been
  drowned in the horsepond at the bottom of the hill with a
  stone round your neck to keep you from floating.
Decima. O, I have found out such a wonder. Do you know
  the old country ballad that was made by the
  blind singing daughter of the harlot?

"When she was got," my mother sang,	118
"I heard a seamew cry,	119
And saw a flake of yellow foam	120
That dropped upon my thigh."	121
How therefore could she help but braid	122
The gold into my hair,	
And dream that I should carry	124
The golden top of care.	125

  Septimus told me once that nobody finds their genius till
  they have found some role, some image, some pose that
  liberates something within them or beyond them that had
  else been dumb and numb.
Nona. Perhaps when you have done raving you will put on
  this dress and this mask.
Decima. I know what I want to play. A Queen was here just
  now, and she could not play her part at all.
  If I were a queen I would be a little haughty, and
  then when I met their gaze I would bend down to the

Down to the ankles, but shall seem
The dizzy condescension of the skies;
Or I'd look sternly at them and strike the pavement
But yet I would not wear a smooth girl's face.
I would seem young, but have some cobwebby lines
As from the incalculable weight of the crown.
And I'd reshape my nose and give it pride.
But have I that rare gift, can I play pride?
There's scarce a player in the world can play it.

Nona. You let your mind go fly off like the week's washing
in a hurricane. Listen to me, we have only an hour for
rehearsal and we'll never get through unless you get into
these clothes.

Decima. St. Gregory, but I am hungry. I'll go to breakfast.
There was a lobster and a flask of wine on the shelf as I
came through the lobby. (*Tries to go but Nona holds her
back.*)

Nona. I won't let you till you are dressed, ready for the part,
not at all if the bell rings. It's your own fault if you
have had no breakfast.

Decima. Never, never. That I swear. What else had I
Lain hidden for all night on these hard stones.
I'll never wear that dress and mask or play
A character that's more than three and thirty
Or not till I am toothless and begin
To say that I am older than I am.

ankles. Have you not noticed that a bow is no use
that does not go right down to the ankles? Or I
would look stern and I would strike the pavement.
My face is too young. I would put a few cobwebby
lines to show that the crown is heavy, and above all
I would reshape my nose and give it pride. But have
I that rare gift, can I play pride? There is hardly
a player in the world that can play it.

Nona. Your mind runs off like drying clothes in [a] hurricane.
We have only an hour for the rehearsal, and we will never
get through unless you put on this mask and dress
immediately.

Decima. This morning air has made me hungry. I will go
and get my breakfast. There was a lobster and a flask
of wine on the shelf as I came through the lobby.

Nona (*stopping her*). I won't let you go till you have
mask and dress upon you. Who knows when the bell
will ring?

Decima. Do you want to starve me?

Nona. If you will put on these, I will bring the lobster
and the wine.

Decima. That mask and dress? Never in this world, no,
nor any others that make me look more than three
and thirty or not that, and so wrinkled that I
boast that I am older than my years. Look at

I would have hidden till the day was over
And the Old Chancellor's first rage forgotten
If you had not seen me.

Nona. You have played it a hundred times before.
If there's no play, we shall be clapped in prison,
You and I and Septimus and all.

Decima. Prison or not, if anybody dares to take the part
I promise to so work on Septimus
That he will drive her from the company.
Look at that mask, look at the chin and hair
And the old hard cheeks. Half the plays in the world
Are but the brightest history of queens
That had the best men in the world for lovers,
Dido, the woman of Troy, and all the rest.
And why should I be fobbed off with an ancient,
Toothless, peaky-chinned and drop-nosed beldame
That a foul husband beats with a stick
Because she will not clamber among the other beasts
Into his cattle boat?

Nona.   Are you so certain
That Septimus will obey you to his hurt
And drive a woman from the company
That did his will and saved us all from prison?

Decima. If I should bid him burn the properties,
Masks, dresses, stage and all, and wander
A beggar at my side from road to road

that chin and hair. Half the plays of the world
are but the tragical histories of queens, Dido,
the woman of Troy, and all the rest of them. And why
should I be fobbed off with an old, toothless, peaky-chinned,
and drop-nosed harridan that a foul husband
beats with a stick because she won't clamber   144
among the other brutes into his cattle boat?   145

Nona. If there is no play we shall be all clapped in
prison—you, Septimus, me, everybody. So if you
won't play it, we must find someone else that will.
Anybody can play Noah's wife.

Decima. I will never allow another woman to play with
Septimus.

Nona. But only once, and in an old part, and afterwards you
will have the chief parts as always.

Decima. No, that is the way it begins. That is the way
to [?] Septimus. I took the part of Phillis in that old play
of his—the right Phillis was ill—and I made eyes at him
all the while and said things the audience could not hear.

Nona. Somebody must be found to play it.

Decima. If anybody dares to I promise to so work on Septimus
that he will drive her from the company.

Nona. Are you so certain that Septimus will obey you and
drive away a woman that saved us all from prison?

Decima. [If] I should bid him burn masks, dresses, stage,
and all, and wander on the roads a beggar at my side,

He'd have a boisterous night or two at the tavern
Then do it.

Nona.   Why do you make him miserable?
There's not a woman in the world would treat him
As you do that were sworn to him in church.
I've never sworn to any man in church,
But I know church is church, and if I'd sworn
I would not treat him like a tinker's donkey,
I swear to God I would not. I was rightly taught.
My mother always said it's no light thing
To take a man in church. (*She begins to cry.*)

Decima.   Have out your cry,
You are in love with him like all the rest.

Nona. No, more than all the rest, and wherefor not?
And why should I not take him if I can?
I would not make [him] miserable for nothing.

Decima. Well, take him [if] you can. If he were yours
I would not rest till I had taken him
Church or no church.

Nona.   Why do you stand there smiling.

[NOTES FROM THE NEXT PAGE:]

1. Why do you treat him so?
2. You will become like all the rest. You love him and would
   take him from me.
3. No, not as the rest, more. And why should I not take him
   from you, you that torture him?

he'd have a boisterous night or two in a tavern and then
obey me.

Nona (*breaking down*). Why do you make him so miserable?
There is not another woman in the world would do it.
And you were sworn to him in church—O you were, and
there is no good denying it.   183
I've never sworn to a man in church, but if I'd
sworn I would not treat him like a tinker's donkey,
I swear to God I would not. I am rightly taught.
My mother always told me it was no
light thing to take a man in church.   189

Decima. So you are in love with him. You mean to play
that part yourself, and while you have been pretending
to look for me you have been learning it.

Nona. You took him from somebody else and you have made
him miserable.

Decima. And why should you not take him from me? Well,
take him [if] you can.

Nona. Why do [you] stand there laughing?

4. I torture him because I love him, and love is suffering.
5. If one loves, one does not measure to see, and you will
   lose him yet to one who is very kind.
6. Take my part to do? Because you are his confidant you think
   you are safe.

[END OF NOTES.]

Decima. To think how easily I'd take him from you.
  You think I should play the angel for him,
  And all the while, for all that you can know
  He never would have looked my side of [the] table
  But that he saw by something in my looks
  That I'd a devil, and by something else
  That he must win me everyday anew;
  And he'd no fear to pay for every kiss
  So great a price, that love being bought anew
  Day after day, night after night for years
  Would stay forever as when his eyes first looked on mine
  You've known enough of men to know of them
  That only devils keep them. That there is no wine
  Until the boy has trod the grapes.

Nona. There never was right woman but she gave

Decima. To think of your folly. You think that you would
make him happy because you would treat him well. O,
you would play angel all day long. And all the while
for all you know he never would have looked at me but
that he saw by something in my looks that I'd a devil,
and by something else that he must win me every day
over again. O, he was a right man. He was not afraid
to pay so great a price for every kiss that love should
seem a miraculous treasure, that it would stay always
as at the first meeting of our eyes, because it [was]
bought over again day after day, night after night for
years; and yet you should have known enough of men to
know that only devils keep them, I think. There is no
wine until the boy has trod the grapes.

Nona. No, it is you that are ignorant not to know that
all a woman has is that she can make a man or a child
happy, though it is but for a moment. She takes them
both upon her breast.

Decima. So you would give all and lose all.

Nona. Whether it is losing or gaining I do not know, but
I say it into your face that there never was a right

The top of the milk jug to some man and asked
No questions, nor made bargains for herself.
What is love but giving?

Decima.   Why don't you say,
I do not even ask to be loved again?
That is what a young girl thinks, yet all the while
She spins her bait in the stream, and I can see
Plainly enough the bait that you are spinning.
You think to have [them] in your debt forever
If you can play the part I have refused
And make thereby peace with the Chancellor,
And that, because you are his confidant,
He'll pay the debt and never drive you out
For all that I can say or do.

Nona.   And yet
I know of something that would change your tune.
It may be that you pulled the string too tight,
It may be that it's broken, and it may be
That he will never do your bidding again.

Decima (taking paper from her breast).
Then look at what I carry next my heart,
At this—a paper covered up with writing,
A string of verses blaming Father Time
Because a day will come and no man living
Remember me—and there is music for it. (*Sings.*)

woman but she gave without any bargain the top of the
milk jug to some man. That's all I know about it.

Decima. So it's you that are laughing now, so certain you
are that you have got a better secret than mine. You
think that love's all giving. That's what the schoolgirl
thinks who loves her music master: I do not even seek
to be loved again, she thinks.

Nona. I love your husband and I have never sought his love.

Decima. I love my husband. I sought him by every trap and
wile, and by traps and wiles I shall keep him.

Nona. Yet I know something that would change your tune.
Maybe your traps have had too little bait in them,
maybe [he] got tired of your wiles. Maybe he will
never do your bidding again.

Decima. Then look at what I carry here under my bodice,
next my heart, and judge if I have not made myself a
miracle to his eyes. This paper all covered with
writing is a string of verses blaming Father Time
because a day will come when no man living will
remember me. They will not know in their ignorant
happiness, he thinks, how unhappy they [are], and that is
the greatest unhappiness of all. O, I know it is not me he
praises—I am not fool enough for that—it is the dream
I gave him. And there is music to it. (*Sings.*)

"O Time there is one stroke of strokes
An anguish not to be thought upon,
That men may have and live in the sun
No memory of my sweetheart's looks—"

So it begins, a long pitiful poem.
Or look at this—does this that praises me
For being half holy and all desirable
Look like a broken string or a fading love? (*Sings.*)

"She might, so noble from head
To great shapely knees,
The long flowing line
Have walked to the altar
Through the holy images
At Pallas Athene's side
Or been fit spoil for a centaur
Drunk with the unmixed wine."

Nona. O, [I] have known that first long poem to my hurt
Although I never heard a word of it till now.
Four lines a verse, four beats in every line,
And fourteen verses long. My curse upon it.
Decima. Yes, fourteen verses—there are numbers to them.

"O Time there is one stroke of strokes
An anguish not to be thought upon
That men may have and live in the sun
No memory of my sweetheart's looks."

So it begins, a long [?] pitiful poem, and here is another.
But no, I will sing you the one that praises me as if I
were at once holy and desirable. (*She sings.*)

"She might, so noble from head
To great shapely knees,
The long flowing line,
Have walked to the altar
Through the holy images
At Pallas Athene's side,
Or been fit spoil for a centaur
Drunk with the unmixed wine."

Nona. O, I have known that first poem and known it to my
   hurt, though I never heard a word of it till now.
   Four lines a verse, four beats a line, and fourteen
   verses. My curse upon it.   255
Decima. Yes, four-   256
   teen verses—there are numbers to it.
Nona. You have another there besides the one you sang me.
   Ten verses, all fours and threes.
Decima (*counting*). Yes, ten verses and fours and threes.
Nona. And there's another too—long lines, seven beats a
   line, and sung to an old ballad tune.

But how do you know that? I carry them here.
These are a secret between him and me
And no one ever sees them till they have lain
A long while on my heart.

Nona.   They've lain upon your heart
But they were made in the small hours of the morning
Upon my shoulder—so many beats a line
For every beat a tap of the finger.

Decima.   My God.

Nona. That long one kept me from my sleep two hours
And when the lines were finished he lay on his back
Another hour waving one arm in the air
Making the music. You have another
That has ten verses, all fours and threes
[The manuscript ends at this point. The typescript continues
for five more lines.]
I liked him well enough to seem asleep
When he was making them, but the poem you sang
Three beats a line and one short line in the middle
He was so pleased with that he muttered the words.
That made me mad and so I said to him
[Typescript ends. End of Draft 20.]

Decima (*counting*). Yes, seven beats. But how have you
  known all
    this? I carry them here; they are a secret between   262
    him and me, and nobody ever sees them till they have
    lain a long while upon my heart.   264
Nona. They have lain upon your heart, but they were   265
    made upon my shoulder and down along my back in
    the small hours of the morning. So many beats a
    line and for every beat a tap of the finger here.
Decima. My god!   269
Nona. I never thought to tell you, but you vexed me [to] it
    when you gloried in his poems of love [?], and
    I knowing all the time that you had driven him to
    me. That long one kept me from
    my sleep two hours, and when the lines were finished   271
    he lay upon his back another hour waving one arm   272
    in the air making up the music.   273

  I liked him well enough to seem asleep through it all, but
  when he made that second poem that you sang he was so
  pleased that he muttered the words and that made me mad,
  so I said to him "Am I not beautiful; turn round

[Draft 21 continues.]

and look," And so I cut it
short, for even I can please a man when there is but   280
one candle. (*Getting out scissors.*) Now you know
why I can play the part in spite of you and not be driven
out, so work on Septimus if you can, little I now care.
Well, now I will clip this a little here, and re-stitch it
again. I have needle and thread ready. O, I knew how
it would end. (*S. Manager comes in and rings a bell.*
The animals come in with him.)

S. Manager. Put on that mask, get into your clothes.   287
Why are you standing there as if you were in a trance?

Nona. Decima and I have talked the matter over and   289
we have settled that I am to play the part.   290

S. Manager. Well, do as you please. Thank God it is a
part that anybody can play that can copy an old
woman's squeaky voice and has shoulders to be beaten.
We are [all] here now but Septimus. We cannot wait for
him so I will read the part of Noah, and [he] will have come
before we are finished I dare say. This side is the
audience, and we must suppose that the Ark is over
there with a gangway for the beasts to climb, and all you
beasts crowd up on the prompt side. As the first scene is
between Noah and the beasts you go on with your sewing.

Decima. No, I must first be heard. My husband has   303
spent his nights of late with Nona, and that is why
she sits clipping and stitching with the vainglorious   305
air.   306

Nona. I could not help it. She made him miserable, she
knows every trick for breaking a man's heart. He
came to me with his troubles. I seemed to be a
comfort to him. I thought that would content us
both, but we changed. And now—
why should I deny it?—he is my lover.   310

Decima. But now I will take the vainglory out of her.
I drove him away. I denied myself to him, I made
myself a hedgehog to him. But I was dead
sick of him, and now, thank God, she has

him and I am free. I threw away a part and I threw   315
  away a man and she has picked them both up.
S. Manager. Well, it seems to me it concerns you two.
  It is your business and not ours, and I don't see
  why we should delay the rehearsal.
Decima. I will have no rehearsal yet, I am too happy   320
  now that I am free, and I must find somebody who will dance and
  sing with me a while. Come, we must have music. (*She
  picks up a lute.*) You cannot all be claws and hooves.
S. Manager. We have only an hour and the whole play   326
  to go through.   327
Nona. She has taken my scissors. O, take them from—
  hold her hands. She is desperate with killing and maybe
  it will be herself. (*To Stage Manager.*) Why
  don't you interfere? My God, she is going to kill me!   332
Decima (*who has been posturing with the scissors*). Here,
  Peter. I will cut those breast feathers so you can get your
  arms through and play the lute.
Nona. She is doing it all to stop the rehearsal and the
  play itself if she can, and all out of
  vengeance. And you stand there and do nothing.   335
S. Manager. If you had taken her husband you might have
  hidden your news till the play was over. She
  is going to make them all mad now, I can see that   338
  much in her eyes.   339
Decima. Now that I have thrown Septimus into her lap   340
  I shall choose a new man. Shall it be you, Turkey,
  or you, Oxhead, or you, great Turkey Cock?
Turkey Cock. Choose me. I will understand as no one ever
  did before. I have a score of wives.
Decima. I am afraid of you, Turkey Cock, for you might
  expect me to be faithful.
Turkey Cock. No no, neither I nor you.
Nona. You are a disgrace.
Turkey Cock. Be content, you have got a man of your own.
Stage Manager. There is nothing to be done, and it's
  all your fault. If Septimus can't manage his wife,
  it is certain that I can't. (*He sits down helplessly.*)

A Man dressed as a hen. This is no time to be the female
of one's species; I'll go out and rob the cock,
who is not yet dressed [?], of comb and spurs.

Man dressed as doe. And I'll go [for] a pair of antlers.

Bull. Choose me, I am double. A man in the forelegs and
a man in the hindlegs, and so I am double as good as
any other.

Decima. You are too slow on your feet and you would last
too long. Come Sparrow Hawk, can you dance or
[undeciphered]? Maybe I will choose you after all, for in a
day or two you would fly off and I could choose again. But
O, you are all beautiful and it is a hard thing to choose.
Come, we will make up words. I will give myself to
him who sings the best, and I will dance while I sing,
for this is my day of liberation. When I look toward
anyone with amorous looks, he must sing back his answer.

*Decima (dances and then sings, holding out her arms to the
Bull).*

I will not now that I discover
That the dung is to the fly
What my beauty's to a lover
Fall into the dumps and cry,
But rather say I've luck enough
If some strong beast will be my love.

The Bull (sings).

Come live with me and be my love
For of all brutes being most a brute
None other can so plainly prove
That pride and vanity is the root
Of all Love's dreams, and peace can be
But in a brute's humility.

Decima (sings, turning at the end to the Turkey Cock).

I will not have you for my choice
For there's a sort of melancholy
In a slow dull and heavy voice
And I am certain it were folly
Now that love has been disproved
To stretch and yawn as when I loved.

The Turkey Cock (*sings*).
> Come live with me and be my love
> A longdrawn chuckling kind of talk
> A raddled wattle and a ruff,
> The self-complaisance of my walk
> Have shown it plain that wrong or right
> I have a cheerful appetite.

(*Decima turns away dancing, and then seems to hesitate between Bull and Turkey Cock, and then she goes up to the Swan, who is playing the lute, and turns away again. Then she sings.*)

Decima.
> Shall I fancy beast or fowl? 360
> Queen Pasiphae chose a bull 361
> While a passion for a swan 362
> Made Queen Leda stretch and yawn. 363
> Wherefore spin ye, whirl ye, dance ye 364
> Till Queen Decima's found her fancy. 365

(*Septimus comes in, still drunk but less so.*)

B

Septimus (*running in*). Stop, stop, I say. Stand still and
listen, stand still. Is this a moment for dancing,
singing and dancing as we shall be at the last day?
A Player. Look, his head is bleeding. Why what has happened?
Septimus. Will someone bring me a copy of Plutarch's *Lives
of the Noble Greeks and Romans*?
A Player. He is drunk.
Septimus. Why do you delay, why do you not find me a
Plutarch? They are coming to murder us, they have
begun to climb the hill, and we do not yet know
what our dying speeches are to be.
A Player (*who has gone to window*). My God, it is true.
There is a great crowd at the bottom of the hill,
and they are all coming this way, and they have
pikes and dungforks and scythes on poles. (*Almost
all go to window.*)

Septimus. Shall I choose to die as Cato, as Demosthenes,
  as Cicero? Shall I speak with noble and serene eloquence,
  a concise heroic calm? No, I will rather choose the death
  of Petronius Arbiter. That will be finer, more distinguished.
  I will tell stories, witty and scandalous stories. I will go on
  telling them while the doors are battered in, while the bolts
  of the crossbow rattle at the windows.
A Player. Yes, they are all coming this way, but why etc.

B1

Septimus. Stop, I say. In a moment we shall be all dead;
  yes, dead and bloody. And you go on dancing and singing
  as we shall do at the last day.
A Player. You are drunk.
Septimus. Yes, I am drunk, but the wineskin is empty and
  we are all going to be murdered.
Another. His head is bleeding. Look, he is all bloody.
Septimus. Up they are climbing, upon the mountain side,
  to kill us all. The great moment is at hand. Let
  someone bring me a copy of Plutarch.
A Player. My God, it is true. Look, you can see them from
  the window. All climbing the mountain with hay wisps on
  pikes and dung forks. They are going to burn the
  roof over our heads.
Another Player. But why should they quarrel with us, who
  only arrived in the town yesterday?
Another Player. Are there not poets, story tellers, even
  players here? Have we not been chosen before them all
  by the Lord Chancellor because we are the most famous
  players in the world? What could be more simple?
  They have stirred up the mob.
Another Player. When we played at Xanadu my performance
  was so astonishing that all the booths of the story-tellers
  were deserted, and the man who pulled the strings at the
  puppet shows left the puppet lying on its back
  and came to look at me.
Another. Listen to him, his performance indeed—I ask you
  all, speak the truth. If you are honest men you will all
  say that it was my performance as the talking nightingale

that drew the town. Why Kubla Khan himself was
known to have said . . .

Another. Good God, listen to them. Is it not always
the comedies that draw the people? Am I dreaming,
or was it not I who was called six times before the 432
curtain? Answer me that. 433

A Player. But how do we know that it is against us at
all? Maybe it is something against the Queen.

A Player. Then why should Septimus come to us with a
bloody head? He is our manager and poet—everyone
knows that—and so he was attacked.

A Player (*at window*). My God, they have lighted wisps on
their dungforks now. They are pointing at the castle.
They are going to burn the roof over our heads. (*All
go to window again.*)

Septimus (*who has been striking attitudes*). One must at
the very least, not only calmly, not only with a firm voice,
but in a voice that has much sweetness—for after all even
[if] they pull the walls about our ears or blow up the floor
with gunpowder they are merely [?] the mob.

[ALTERNATE VERSION]

A Player (*coming from window*). Well, I don't care what has
made them angry, I will stay here no longer. And you
had better follow before the castle is surrounded if you
would save your lives. (*Goes out.*)

A Player. Must we go dressed like this? 449

A Player. There is no time to change, and besides if
the castle is surrounded we can gather in
some cleft of the rocks where we can be seen only 452
from a distance. They will suppose we are a drove of 453
cattle and a flock of birds. (*All go except Septimus, Decima
and Nona. Nona has begun making a bundle of the angels'
wings and clothes. Decima stands motionless* [?]
watching Septimus.)

Septimus. They are in the right. I deserve their reproof. I
was wrong to think of myself. Of what importance are my
last words? Are we not the last artists? All the others have

surrendered, have given in to the multitude. It is necessary that we remain living for the sake of our art.

[DRAFT CONTINUES.]

Nona (*gathering up angel wings*). Here, take this upon your back. Then we shall have saved everything.

Septimus. That is well thought of. Whatever happens to us the gilded feathers of Saint Michael must not be trampled under the feet of the common people and trodden into the dust. (*He takes up bundle.*)

Decima. Come no nearer. I have locked this gate, and now we shall have a talk. We must understand one another, and do not tell me you are not sober enough to listen, for this is one moment destiny has chosen for a settlement between you and me.

Septimus. Speak, I am very wise today.

Decima. I will not unlock this gate until I have a promise that you will drive her from the company and never see her or speak to her again.

Nona. Do not listen to her. If you are a man at all you will take the key from her.

Septimus. Man [?] I am indeed. I can tell you that I am so much of a man that a whole town is trying to have me murdered. I will take the key. (*He lays down wings.*)

Decima. If you come a step nearer, I will shove this through the grating.

Nona (*pulling him back*). Did you not hear her? She will shove it through the grating of the door and the crowd will find us and murder us.

Decima. I will not unlock this gate until you take a horrible oath to drive her from the company, a terrible oath never to speak with her or look at her again.

Septimus. You are jealous. It [is] very wrong to be jealous. I am only unfaithful when I am sober. Never trust a sober man, all over the world they are unfaithful. I warn you against all sober men from the bottom of my heart.

Nona. O, promise. Take whatever oath she bids you. If we delay we shall be murdered.

Septimus. Yes, I can see your meaning. You would say to
 me a promise can be broken, even an oath can be broken—
 especially an oath made under compulsion. But no, I say
 to you no. I am [not] a rascally sober man, such a man
 as I have warned her against. I am too drunk to be
 forsworn. What I promise I perform. Therefore, my little   544
 darling I will not promise anything at all.   545
Decima. So much the better. We then will wait till the mob
 comes and fires the roof.
Septimus. Yes, that will be well, for here on this earth I
 have become sober. But if I die St. Peter, bowing low,
 will give me a cup of wine. I will drink it off, and it
 will be so made that its effect will stay forever. That
 is the continual intoxication of eternity.
Decima. When we are dead no one will ever triumph over me
 again and take you away, and besides, I shall be
 avenged. (*Nona snatches key.*)
Nona. I have it, I have it. (*Opening gate.*)   557
Septimus (*holding Decima*). No, no. Because I am an
 unforsworn man I am strong.
Decima. Go, I will stay here and be killed.
Nona. Come, follow me. A half hour since she offered herself
 to every member of the company.
Decima. If you will be faithful to me, Septimus, I will not
 let one of them touch me. If you leave I will kill
 myself.
Septimus. Flighty, like the unicorn, but beautiful.
Nona. Come, she is a bad woman. She has driven you to drink.
Septimus. Yes, she is a bad woman. I had forgotten that.
 I have told the whole world that. Because of her I have
 knocked at inhospitable doors and lain down to sleep
 upon the cobblestones. I will come, but I will come
 slowly. I will take this. (*Takes up bundle.*) I will carry
 the golden feathers to safety. But slowly, with dignity, as
 an unforsworn man. (*Goes out.*)
Decima (*alone, striking the wall with her hands*). Betrayed,
 betrayed, and for her, for her, for that woman that was
 molded out of sheep's tallow, that a man can twist and
 shape, that never before got a better man than a prompter

or property man. (*The Old Man enters at other door. She sees him.*)

Decima. Have you come to kill me, Old Man?

Old Man. I am looking for straw, my back is getting itchy.
I must soon lie down and roll, and where will [I]
get straw to roll on?
I went round to the kitchen and "go away" they   588
said, and made the sign of the cross as if it
were a devil that makes me lie down and roll.

Decima. When will the mob come to kill me?   591

Old Man. Kill you? It's not you they are going to   592
kill; it's that itching in my throat that drags them
hither, for when I bray like a donkey the crown   594
changes.   595

Decima. The crown. So then it is the Queen that they are going
to kill.   597
But why should they kill her? Septimus says that it's we
who makes images who are their enemies, and that they
should kill us or adore because he says it is our images that
make anything at all happen but just sleeping and eating.
But the Queen? A poor timid woman who is afraid to
speak when she is spoken to.

Old Man. Heaven settles it all, my dear. But she can't die
till I roll and bray, my dear, and I will whisper to you who
[it] is that rolls. It
is the donkey that carried Christ into Jerusalem, and   600
that is why he is so proud, and that is why he knows
the hour when there is to be a new king or a new   602
queen.   603

Decima. Are you ever weary of the world, Old Man?

Old Man. Yes, yes, because when I roll and bray like a donkey
I am asleep. I know nothing about it and that is a great
pity. I remember nothing but the itching in my back.   607
But I must stop talking and find some straw.   608

Decima (*taking up scissors*). Old Man, I am going to   609
drive this into my heart.

Old Man. No no, don't do that. You don't know   611
what [you] will be put to do when you are dead, into   612
whose gullet you will be put to sing or bray. You

have a look of a foretelling sort. Who knows but you 614
might be put to foretell the death of kings? And bear 615
in mind I will have no rivals. I could not endure a 616
rival. 617

Decima. Do you think, Old Man, that those who are dead
make love? Will I find a better lover there, for
I have been betrayed by a man.

Old Man. You must not reckon on that. I will whisper
you another secret. People talk, but
I have [never] known of anything else to come
from there but an old jackass. Maybe there is no- 623
thing else, that he has all the place to himself. But there,
my back is beginning to itch and I have not yet found
any straw. (*Goes. Decima leans scissors on arm of throne
and is about to press herself upon them when the Queen
comes in from door to left of throne.*)

Queen. No no, that would be a great sin. 627
Decima. Your majesty. 628
Queen. I thought I would like to die a martyr, but that 629
is different. That is to die for God's glory.
Decima. I am very unhappy. 632
Queen. I too am very unhappy. When I saw the great 633
angry crowd and knew that they wished to kill me . . .
Decima. So that is it, it [is] you that they wish to kill.
Queen. I wanted to be a martyr, but I was afraid and ran
away.
Decima. I would not have run away, O no, but it is 637
hard to drive a knife into one's own flesh. 638
Queen. In a moment they will have come, and they will 639
drive in the door, and where shall I go to escape them?
Decima. If they would mistake you for me you would escape,
and O, your majesty, if I could only wear that gold brocade
and those gold slippers for one moment I would be happy.
I would not mind dying.
Queen. They say that those who die for their sovereign
show great virtue. You would be sure of Heaven.
Decima. Quick, I can hear them coming. (*They begin to
change.*)
Queen. Was it love? (*Decima nods.*) O, that is a great 655

sin. It is the beginning of all sin, I have heard.
I have never known love. Of all things that is what
I most feared. It was my fear of that made me shut
myself up. I was always afraid it would
come in at the eye and seize upon me in a moment. 660
I am not naturally good, and they say people will 661
do anything for love there is so much sweetness in 662
it. That is why it is so dangerous to the soul. But you will
escape all that and go up to God as a pure virgin. 664
(*Change now complete.*) Goodbye. I know how I 665
can slip away, and there is a convent that will take me in.
I have long wanted to go there and lose my name and
disappear. Sit there on the throne and turn your face
away. If you do not turn your face away you will be 670
afraid. (*Shouting gets nearer. Crowd gathers outside* 671
iron gates. Herald comes in.)
Herald. Your loyal people, your Majesty, send you greetings
and
homage. I bow before you [in] their name. Your royal 673
will as spoken through the mouth of the Chancellor
has filled them with gratitude. All misunderstand- 675
ing is gone. All has been settled by your condescension
in bestowing your royal hand upon the Chancellor.
(*Applause.*)
Chancellor (*entering with Bishop*). I will explain all, 684
your Majesty. There was nothing else to be done. 685
This holy Bishop will at once unite [us.] Good Lord . . .
(*Great shouting.* "How beautiful, how wise she looks, etc."
Septimus has come in with crowd.)
Septimus (*to Chancellor*). My lord, that is not the Queen.
That is my wife, my bad wife.
Chancellor. Look at the crowd. There's nothing to be
done for the present. The Devil take it.
Decima. So I am not to be killed and I am Queen, and
you will do whatever I like. (*The people kneel.*)
Herald. The people, they are [undeciphered]. All here will
obey you in everything.
Decima. There is a plate of lobster and a flask of wine
on a shelf in the lobby.

Herald. They will be brought, your Majesty.

Decima. Well, I don't [know] how it all happened, and
    I care less. While I am eating I will have a good look
    at my new man over there. (*Plate and flask brought.*
    Braying of donkey outside. The Old Man is dragged in,
    braying, by a soldier. Shouts of the mob.)

Bishop. At last we have found out this imposter who has
    been accepted by the whole nation as the very voice of
    God. He is keeping [at] it even now. Look at his dazed
    eyes, pretending that [he] is in a trance.

Chancellor. Take him to prison. We will hang him in the
    morning. (*Old Man dragged out braying. To Septimus.*)
    The Devil. Nothing to be done now, do you understand
    that? God or the Devil has settled it. He's chosen
    her and I shall have this woman for wife.

Septimus. She is my wife, my bad flighty wife.

Chancellor. Seize this man. He has been whispering slander
    against her majesty in my ear. And cast him beyond the
    border of the kingdom. And find the company of players he
    belongs to. They also are banished, and must not return on
    pain of death. And now, my lord Bishop, I am ready.

Decima. Come, crack that claw.

End

Commentary

Draft 21, Act I. Yeats had not invented the character names he will keep in the finished play when he first wrote this draft, but he had done so before he finished revising it. He changed the name Yellow Martin to Septimus down through line 54, then wrote the note "so all through." I will reserve my comment on the name changes introduced into this and subsequent drafts until the evidence is all in. Here I have printed the speech-tags actually found in the manuscript in order to present them as Yeats indicated them.

    Yeats does not use his two Old Men as a framing or choral device, though he was on the verge of inventing this strategem in Draft 18. There is in Draft 21 no opening fight between the Queen's men and the townsmen as in Draft 18; rather at the outset Septimus enters drunk. I take this to be a farcical representation of the divine afflatus of the artist, an afflatus to which Septimus shortly pretends in the finished play. The scene proceeds much as it will continue to do: countrymen and townsmen discuss the political situation, and the excuse for the revolt; that the Queen is a witch who cohabits with a unicorn, is fully worked out. Again I will reserve any full discussion of Yeats's symbolic intention with the unicorn until the evidence is in, but I will call attention now to the fact that already Yeats conceives of it as an actual beast which can be wounded and bleed. Septimus defends the chastity of the unicorn, as he will continue to do, and his defense brings on a fight with the witch-strangling countryman during which Septimus actually receives the wound he had acquired offstage in Draft 18. The draft continues pretty much as in the finished play down to line 288, where the quarrel with the bloody-minded countryman occurs in a shortened form. Yeats was later to add detail to this scene. The Old Man who foretells a change in the throne enters, and Yeats has him bray like a donkey whenever the crown changes. The change from crowing like a rooster occurred in Draft 19. His encounter with Septimus is a new scene, which Yeats kept. Yeats has made great progress with his first scene. It now has the order of events and the characters that will be kept, and he has finished some 120 lines out of 394.

Drafts 20 and 21, Act II. Since the opening of this act has not survived in Draft 19, this is our earliest example of Yeats's new conception of the scene. Its parallel in Draft 16 was Act I, Scene 2, which began with the rolling in of the money, the overhearing of the Player Queen's song first by the soldiers and then by the Queen, Nona's entering and calling, "Where are you, Noah's wife." All this is swept away. New name tags are in place in Draft 21, but not in Draft 20. At the beginning the Queen's Waiting Woman is on stage with the Prime Minister. She has come in behalf of the Queen, who requests delays in beginning the progress into town. The Prime Minister grows increasingly impatient with the Queen's delay, especially in Draft 21. We will see his anger transferred to the players in later drafts, surely a more appropriate target. Yeats commented in his letter to Brinsley MacNamara of 29 June 1919 that having the Prime Minister get into a "real rage" at the opening of Scene II had proved effective in production [*Letters,* p. 658]. In Draft 20 the Queen's entrance is treated more briefly than in Draft 21, and in 21 an example of her sin of omission is introduced, her forgetting to see to it that the back of the statue of Our Lady, which occupied a shrine in her room, was regularly dusted. Yeats will try several versions of this sin before he gives it up entirely. The Prime Minister's discussion of the company of players is less adroit in the verse than in the prose. He seems particularly heavy handed when he addresses these lines to the Queen:

> Let her presence
> Remind your majesty that there is a likeness
> Between the business of a queen and a player.

The Prime Minister insists that the play be given as planned, though the Queen intervenes on behalf of the players and says a prayer for them as she and the Prime Minister leave for the progress into town.

Then Decima crawls out from under the throne and sings her song "My mother dandled me," as she did in Draft 19, going on soon after to "The Mask," which was not included in Draft 19. The exchange between Nona and Decima follows Draft 19 closely, down to the point where Decima quotes Septimus's poems to her as a proof of his love: "A Thought from Propertius" is now in final form, and the Solomon-Sheba quatrain has been replaced by another, that beginning "O Time there is one stroke of strokes." This, like the Solomon-Sheba quatrain, was never published so far as I can discover. Shortly after this, Draft 20 ends. The play continues in Draft 21, where Yeats expanded the scene in which Decima searches for a new lover among the members of the troupe. In Draft 19 this is no more than sketched. Now the idea of a contest to win Decima is developed, and Yeats wrote several lyrics for the contestants to speak. Though these seem to me quite finished, Yeats never published them. Decima's first song uses excremental and bestial images in a love song in a way that anticipates certain of the Crazy Jane poems and the songs from *A Full Moon in March*. The beasts' replies make use of Marlowe's "The Passionate Shepherd to His Love" by quoting "Come live with me and be my love." Then in "Shall I fancy beast or fowl," which is used in the finished play, occurs the first reference to Leda in Yeats's poetry. Septimus enters drunk, for the first time in Scene II. The scene is more fully developed than in Draft 19; the question of preparing dying speeches is raised here, for example. And so on to the end of the play. The scenes sketched in Draft 19 are all more fully worked out, but there are no fundamental changes. Decima locks the gate; Nona grabs the key, and she and Septimus flee; Decima encounters the prophetic Old Man and then the Queen, with whom she changes roles. The end of the play is changed notably when Yeats remembers Decima's lobster-eating from Draft 16 and reinstates it. He ends the play with a sentence of banishment on the players, followed by Decima's speech to her new husband, "Come, crack that claw," with which the 1922 versions will end.

Notably absent from this draft is any development of the unicorn theme in Scene II to carry on the development in Scene I; indeed only one passing reference occurs here, Septimus's description of Decima as "flighty, like the unicorn." But Yeats has made tremendous progress. He has finished 98 lines, laid out the plan of development for the scene, and established the names he will use for his dramatis personae: Septimus, Nona, Decima. He will complete this tone row, so to speak, when he adds St. Octema in Draft 29. We will speculate then on what he means by it.

CHAPTER THIRTEEN

Drafts 22 through 28

DRAFT 22 is a complete version of Scene I only; Drafts 23 through 28 are all partial versions of Scene II. I discuss Draft 22 before the others, not because I am sure it was written first but only to keep things in some kind of order. Actually I think it probable that it was written at about the time of Drafts 27 and 28, for the handling of the unicorn theme in Draft 22 seems consonant with the development of that theme in those drafts. I have not printed Draft 22 here because it is nearly identical with Scene I in the complete version of the play printed as Draft 29 beginning on page 363: 380 lines of the 394 that make up this scene in the published play are completed in both versions, and the same lines are finished. In short, the two drafts are as alike as separate typings can be. In Draft 22, then, Scene I of the play was almost done.

When Drafts 21 and 22 are compared, we find that Yeats has made the following changes: His initial stage direction is fuller, and it stipulates that the two Old Men who serve as spectator-chorus for the scene are to wear grotesque masks. This I take to mean masks that are obviously masks, masks that could not possibly be mistaken for faces. Yeats has neatly placed at the outset of his play symbolic objects which point to its central theme. The final character names are in place throughout the draft. Yeats uses his two Old Men as a framing device; they open the scene and close it. This works out a strategem that Yeats had almost invented in Draft 18. The two "bad, popular poets" are new characters, though Yeats had Septimus in Draft 18 suspect some "jealous, envious, rancid poet" of stirring up the mob against him and his troupe. Septimus's parting remark to them here, "What do I care for anyone now except Venus and Adonis and the other planets of heaven," comes from life; it uses a saying Yeats recorded in the "First Draft" of his *Autobiographies*:

I remember an intoxicated man coming on Derby Day to apologize for some rudeness by some young men who had not recognized us and his looking at us all, hesitating, and then saying, "No, no, I will not. I care for

nobody now but Venus and Adonis and the other planets of heaven."
(Transcribed from the MS) [Cf. *Memoirs*, p. 111. Gen. Ed.]

As we go on, we notice a good many small changes: the description of the Queen as a witch has been shortened and tightened; the incubus attending the witch that the Big Countryman strangled "last Candlemas twelvemonth" has been changed from three hares to a cat; Septimus's speech working out rhymes on "unicorn" has been cut and the device put into Scene II of the finished play, where Septimus tries to find rhymes for "rail." Septimus's speech about the Countryman's two washings—when he was born and when he will die—has been added, the exposition of the Old Beggar's possession is longer and more detailed, and the Big Countryman imagines his braying as he strangles the Queen. The passages on the unicorn are retained pretty much as in Draft 21, but they are more carefully worked out. (Cf. below, p. 437)

Drafts 23 through 28. These are all parts of Scene II. Most of them show Yeats working on the first half of Scene II, the part of the play he found most troublesome (see his letter to Lady Gregory of 11 May 1916). Draft 23 is a typescript of this scene, which Yeats has carefully corrected. The typed words are nearly identical with the words of Draft 21. Yeats's manuscript revisions include adding the mosaic pictures of the royal line to the setting for use in the scene where Decima appeals to these "ancestors" of hers, a scene that Yeats works up through several drafts and then abandons. The opening dialogue between the Prime Minister and the Queen's waiting woman has been sharpened; the Prime Minister shows greater impatience over the Queen's delay, and he compares her unfavorably with queens he has known: "They had a way with them, and a right appearance. . . . They knew how to play their parts—they were queens." The Queen's sin of neglect has been slightly changed. She now keeps an image of the infant Christ in a cradle in her room, and she has neglected it. The Prime Minister adds to the list of entertainments planned "to keep the people in good humour" a clown who can imitate a cat fight; apparently Yeats found it hard to give up this detail. He also wrote a new speech about the players for the Queen: "I am praying for these players, who must be wicked, and all for our sport. Prime Minister, if a player dies playing some bad part who knows if he is able to get back in his own shape again." The typescript is full of canceled passages for which Yeats does not write revisions; it is, then, a record of his rejections and prepares for the drafts that follow. Nothing, for instance, is made of the mosaic pictures that Yeats had put into the setting. The draft breaks off at line 280 with Nona's "for even I can please a man when there is but one candle."

Draft 24. In this draft, another typescript of part of Scene II, Yeats changes the Queen's attendants to nuns, gives her another sin, stages that sin, and begins to work up the scene in which Decima appeals to the mosaic pictures of her "ancestors." The sin now consists of forgetting to put a hot water bottle at the feet of an image of the infant Jesus lying in his cradle: the cradle is brought in, and the Prime Minister is asked to feel for the hot water bottle himself:

Queen. You can see for yourself if you will put your hand in that
    there is no bottle. Last night I forgot it.
PM. Take it away. (*The nuns carry the cradle out solemnly.*)
Queen. You are ill—you seem faint.
PM. No. I have begun to believe in the unicorn.

This is the only reference to the unicorn in the draft, which, however, ends before Septimus returns from the town talking of the unicorn. The scene where Decima regards the mosaic pictures of past rulers as her ancestors is very brief:

Decima (*looking on the images on the wall*). Kings, you were
    all my fathers and my uncles.
Nona. We have only an hour for rehearsal and we will never
    get through unless you put on this dress and mask
    immediately.
Decima. I must first kiss my father and my grandfather. Savage
    old men, I think I remember sitting upon your knees when I
    was a child—you'll never be fierce with me. But grandfather,
    though we were painted upon the stones and must live among
    rats, you have an air as you had drunk good wine. I will kiss
    you because I know you will not be hard upon me, but will
    sometimes look the other way. Great grandfathers and uncles
    whom I so closely resemble, having the mouth of one and the
    nose of another, later on I will kiss all of you that are
    within reach.

The draft breaks off just before Decima begins to show Nona the poems Septimus has written praising her beauty.

Draft 25. This draft keeps the opening of 24, including the forgotten hot water bottle. Its only importance is that when the Queen and her attendant nuns enter, they carry a banner with a unicorn on it.

The Queen and several nuns enter carrying a gilded cradle and murmuring prayers. They lay the cradle before the Prime Minister. It contains the image of a child. One goes before the cradle with a banner on which is painted or embroidered a unicorn.

Prime Minister (sinking upon seat). Gregory of Nazianzus!

Queen. It is the infant Jesus. Sister Mary's business has always been to boil the kettle, and that of Sister Aloysius to fill the bottle, and mine to lay it at the feet of Our Lord. You can see for yourself if you will put your hand in that there is no bottle. Last night I forgot it, and on a cold night too. You are ill, you seem faint.

Prime Minister. No, I have begun to believe in the unicorn.

Queen. We carry the unicorn upon our banner because of the legend.

Prime Minister. I had thought it was the portrait of someone, of a relation. Forgive, my mind is confused.

Queen. The legend tells how when Christ was being carried upon the ass into Egypt the ass became tired, and [a] unicorn came out of the desert and took its place. From that day the unicorn has been emblematical.

This awkward business, awkward because it has a Christ symbol aid Christ, was dropped after this draft. At about the same place in the finished play the Queen associates her patron saint, Octema, with a unicorn. The draft breaks off at line 35.

Draft 26. This draft is just a scrap, an early version of lines 456–76, but in it Yeats begins seriously to develop the unicorn theme in Scene II. He has Septimus say, "O that the unicorn would engender upon some woman another race; only the unicorn, the griffin, the cockatrice have courage. I am full of sorrow because of the chastity of the unicorn." This presents the essential idea about the unicorn in the finished play, that he become the progenitor of a new race of men.

Drafts 27 and 28. These drafts are separate manuscripts, which do not overlap at any point. Together they provide drafts of lines 1–255 and 380–576 of Scene II. In them Yeats brings Scene II nearly as far along as he had brought

Scene I in Draft 22. They are printed below. The manuscript of Draft 28 has
the notation "Player Queen / late versions / 1919?"

[Draft 27]
Act II

A group of players and the Prime Minister

Prime Minister. You object to the play I have chosen and want
    some dull, poetical thing full of long speeches. I chose the
    Tragical History of Noah's Deluge because when Noah
    beats his wife because she won't go into the Ark everybody
    understands, every-
    body is pleased, everybody recognizes the mulish obstinacy   5
    of their own wives, sweethearts, and sisters. And now
    it can't be given because the leading lady is lost, and
    you give me some unintelligible reason why nobody else
    can take her place. I will have that play and no other. The
    rehearsal must begin at once and the performance   15
    takes place punctually.
Nona. We have searched all night and we cannot find her
    anywhere. She was heard last night to say that she would
    rather drown herself rather than play a woman older than
    thirty. We are afraid she has done it, for Noah's wife
    is a very old woman.
P. Minister. Nonsense, it is all a conspiracy. Your   22
    manager should be here. He is responsible. You can   23
    tell him when he does come that if your leading lady is not
    found and the play performed, I will clap him in jail for a
    year and the rest of you I will pitch over the border.
Nona. O, sir, he could not help it. She does whatever   27
    she likes.   28
P. Minister. A brazen devil—that's what they [are] all
    like. What do I care whether he could help it or not,
    to jail he goes. Somebody   34
    has got to go to jail. Go and cry her name everywhere.   35
    Away with you, let me hear you cry it. (*All go out*
    calling "Where are you Decima?") O Adam, why did you

go asleep? You might have known that the man in the
sky would take the chance to play some trick on you.
(*The Queen enters.*) Ah.   42

The Queen. I will show myself to the angry people as you   43
have bid me. I have prayed all night. I am ready
for martyrdom.

Prime Minister. No no, you will not be martyred. I have a
plan to settle all that. I will stop their anger with
a word. Who made that dress?

Queen. It was my mother's. She wore it at her coronation
I would not have a new one because I do not
deserve new clothes. I am always committing sin.   61

Prime Minister. It is too late now. Nothing can be done. Well,
well, it may appear right to those on
the edge of the crowd. The others must be conquered   69
by charm, dignity, a royal manner. You may put them
in a bad humour—remember they have never seen your
face—if you hang
your head in that dumfounded way.   74

Queen. I wish I could return to my prayers.   75

Prime Minister. Walk, permit me to see you walk like a queen.
No no, be more majestic. Look like an eagle, look like
a vulture. Ah, if you had
known the queens I have known. They had a way   78
with them—morals of a dragoon, but a way, such a way.

Queen. It would be a blessed penance—there are
cobblestones—if I might go barefoot.

P. Minister. Sleep of Adam! Barefoot, barefoot did   85
you say? There is not time to take off your   86
shoes and stockings. Were you to look out of the
window you would see the people crowded at the foot
of the hill and becoming
wickeder every moment. Come. (*Gives Queen his arm.*)   89

Queen. But your plan, what is your plan?

P. Minister. My plan will be disclosed before the   92
face of the people, and there alone. (*They go out.*)   93

Decima (*coming from under throne*).

   He went away, my mother sang,   94

When I was brought to bed   95
And all the while her needle pulled   96
The gold and silver thread.   97

She pulled the thread and bit the thread   98
And made a golden gown   99
She dreamed because she had dreamed that I   100
Was born to wear a crown.   101

Nona (*entering*). Thank God you are found.   102
   Here, get into this mask and dress quickly.
Decima. I found out the one part in the world for me to
   act. Do you remember that old country ballad that was made
   by the mad singing daughter of a harlot? (*Singing.*)

When she was got, my mother sang   118
I heard a seamew cry   119
I saw a flake of yellow foam   120
That dropped upon my thigh.   121

How therefore could she help but braid   122
The gold into my hair   123
And dream that I should carry   124
The golden top of care.   125

Nona. Here, quick. Get in this.
Decima. The Queen was here but now. She cannot play
   her part at all as I could play it. I would know
   how to hold my head up, and would know how to bow with
   all my body down to the ankles, and how to stamp my
   foot and look proud.
Nona. You play the Queen, you that were born
   in a ditch between two towns and wrapped in a sheet   130
   stolen from a hedge. Low comedy, that's what you are
   fit for. Here, put on this—and this.
Decima. What, play an old, toothless, peaky-chinned,
   drop-nosed harridan that a foul
   husband beats with a stick because she won't clamber   144
   among the other brutes into his cattle boat?   145
Nona. If there is no play, Septimus will be clapped in jail.
Decima. Well, give it me. (*Singing.*)

She wept because she dreamed that I
Was born to wear a crown.

Nona. Where are you going?

Decima. To get my breakfast. I saw a bottle [of] wine and
a lobster on a shelf in the passage.

Nona. If you will put on these, I will fetch them for you.
(*Goes out.*)

Decima. My mother dandled me and sang
How young it is, how young
And made a golden cradle
That on a willow swung.

(*She has been putting on dress and mask. Pauses, and looks at
mask. Sings* "How [young] it is, how young!" *She is now
crooked old woman.*)

Decima. O fathers and grandfathers of mine, do you
acknowledge this daughter of your house? Old grandfathers,
though you are painted upon stone and must live among
rats you look as though you had drunk good wine. Would
you let me sit down at your table? I am more a queen than
anybody [in] the world. Will you let me come and kiss you?
No, you say no. You are an old woman out of the markets,
rotten for the grave. And all the rest of you, grandfathers
and great-grandfathers whom I so much resemble, having
the nose of one and the chin of another, you all cry to me to
go out of your house. You look wise. You there, with the
long beard, I am certain that you nursed me on your knees.
(*Nona returns with wine and lobster, which presently she
lays on side of throne.*) You will let me kiss you? No no,
it is plain that there is something about me that you dislike.
Can it be this old face? It hides from you the child that you
knew. (*She begins to take off dress and mask.*) And this
dress too reminds you perhaps of somebody you disliked.
Detestable things. (*She tramples dress underfoot.*)

Nona. What are you doing?

Decima. We have decided that Septimus is to go to prison.

Nona. Why do you treat him so? Why do you make him so
miserable. (*Breaking down.*) And he a great genius
who can't take care of himself. There is not another

woman in the world would do it, and you were sworn to
him in church. O, you were, and there is no use denying
it. I have never sworn to a man in church, but
if I did swear I would not treat him like a tinker's   186
donkey, before God I would not. I am rightly taught.
My mother always told me it was no
light thing to take a man in church.   189

Decima. You are in love with my husband.   190

Nona. Must one be in love with a man not to [want to]
    see [him] sent to jail? But I won't have him sent to
    jail. If you won't play the part, I will.

Decima. I won't have it. I won't let another woman play
    with Septimus.

Nona. Only this once, and in a part nobody can do   199
    anything with.   200

Decima. That is how it begins, and all the time you would
    whisper to him and say things the audience could not hear.

Nona. I have learned the part, every word of it.

Decima. If you dare take it, I will so work upon Septimus
    that he will drive you from the company.

Nona. And will he obey you when I shall have saved him
    from the jail?

Decima. If I told him to burn the stage and all the properties
    and wander with me as a beggar on the roads, he would
    have a boisterous night in a tavern, and obey.

Nona. He will not obey you.

Decima. What are you keeping back?

Nona. May[be] I have my secrets.

Decima. I know what you have been doing. You have been
    sitting in corners giving him sympathy and telling
    him, as you always do, that you are a virgin, and all
    the while he has but stayed there to have the pleasure of
    talking about me.

Nona. You think you have his every thought and all because
    you are a devil.

Decima. Maybe I am no more a devil than you are a virgin, and
    yet his thoughts are full of me wherever he is. (*Sings.*)
        "Put off that mask of burning gold   223
        With emerald eyes."   224

"O no, my dear, you make so bold   226
To find if hearts be wild and wise   227
And yet not cold."   228

Nona. You are not telling the truth.

Decima. Then look what I carry under my bodice. This is   231
a poem praising me: my head and shoulders and praising
me limb after limb. A great many verses. Here is
another that he gave me yesterday
morning. I had turned him out of bed and he had to   236
lie alone by himself, and as he lay there unable to sleep he   237
made it up, wishing that he were blind so as not to   240
be troubled by looking upon my beauty. Hear how it
goes: (*Sings.*)   242

O would that I were an old beggar   243
Without a guide on this earth
But a thieving rascally cur   245
A beggar blind from his birth.   246
Or anything else but a man   247
Lying alone on a bed   248
Remembering a woman's beauty,   249
Alone with a crazy head.   250

Nona. Alone in his bed indeed. I know that long one well,
I know it to my hurt, though I never read a word of it.
Four lines a verse, four beats in every line, and fourteen
verses. My curse upon it.   255

[DRAFT 27 BREAKS OFF. DRAFT 28 BEGINS WITH LINE 380.]

Stage Manager. Stop, stop, here is Septimus.   380

S. Though you are about to beat out my brains, to pierce
my vitals with a pitchfork, to disembowel me, that is
not why I weep. I weep because the unicorn will not
trample you to death, and beget upon some woman a new
mankind. I weep because of the chastity of the unicorn.

Player. What nonsense has he got in his head?

Another Player. It has been broken anyway.

Another Player. He is always quarrelsome when he is drunk.

Stage Manager. Come, come, Septimus. This is not a time to

be making up speeches for a new play. Let us get on
with our rehearsal. If you sit upon the ground you
won't be so unsteady.

Septimus. Open Plutarch, close the book of life. Prepare
the dying speeches. The mob are climbing the hill with
burning wisps to set fire to the roof and pitchforks to
drive into our vitals.

A Player (*at window*). My God, it is true. There is a great
crowd at the bottom of the hill. They have dungforks
and scythes set upon poles. They are coming this way.
(*All but S. go to window.*)

S. Let every man among you consider whether he will speak as
Cato, as Demosthenes, as Cicero—assume an heroic calm
and triumph over death in sonorous eloquence. Perhaps
you may prefer to die like Petronius Arbiter, telling
witty and scandalous stories. To go on telling scandal
while the doors are broken. Yes, that would be more
distinguished. The one thing necessary is to show no
anger, to speak even with a certain sweetness, for after
[all], even if they blow up the floor with gunpowder,
they are no concern of ours. They are
merely the mob.   410
As for me, I shall continue to rail upon the unicorn,
but shall rail sweetly. (*He takes up lute.*) I shall
even put my railing to a tune that even those who murder us
may remember it and tell it to [the] children and the
grandchildren. (*Plays as speaks, walks up and down
trying the strings.*)

[WBY indicates here that no further changes are to be made in
the draft he is following (Draft 21 or a successor of it) down
through line 454, ending "flock of birds." Then the draft
continues down through the exit of Nona and Septimus, pretty
much in final form.]

Septimus. Left to die
alone. I do not blame you. There is courage in red   456
wine, in white wine, in beer—even in thin beer sold   457
by a blear-eyed pot-boy in a bankrupt tavern, but   458

there is none in the human heart. Only the unicorn
and cockatrice and the griffin have courage. I am
full of sorrow because of the chastity of the unicorn.

Nona. I'll tie these upon your back—I can carry the rest myself.
Then we shall have saved everything.

Septimus. You are right. I accept the reproach. It is 466
necessary that we who are the last artists—all the others
have gone over to the mob—shall save, put somewhere in
safety, the symbols and the implements of art. The cloak of
Noah, the high-crowned hat of Noah, the golden face of
the Almighty, the horns of Satan.

Nona. There now, I'll tie these on too. Thank God you can
still stand upright on your legs.

S. Tie them all upon my back. Man is nothing till he is united
to an image. When I have them all I will go to the high
tablelands of Africa and find the cavern of the unicorn. I
will seek my death before that terrible blue eye. We shall
both be killed for I shall carry a knife smeared with the
blood of a serpent that has died from gazing at an emerald.

Decima. Stand back. Do not dare to move a step. 498

Septimus. Beautiful as the unicorn, but fierce. 499

Decima. I have locked the gate that we may have a 500
talk. 501

Septimus. That is well, very well. You would talk with 502
me because today I am extraordinarily wise. 503

Decima. I will not unlock the gate till I have a promise 504
that you will drive her from the company. 505

Nona. Do not listen to her. Take the key from her. 506

Septimus. If I were not her husband I would take the 507
key, but because I am her husband she is terrible.
She is terrible because she loves.

Nona. You are afraid. 510

Septimus. Could not you yourself take it? She does not 511
love you. Therefore she will not be terrible. 512

Nona. If you are a man at all you will take it. 513

Septimus. I am one of Plutarch's people. I am more than
a man. I am extraordinarily
wise. I will take the key. 515

Decima. If you come a step nearer, I will shove the key 516
through the grating of the door. 517

Nona (pulling him back). Don't you hear her? If she shoves
    it through the door we shall not be able to escape.   519
    The crowd will find us and murder us.   520
Decima. I will unlock the gate when you have taken an
    oath to drive her from the company, an oath never   522
    to speak with her or look at her again. A terrible oath.   523
Septimus. You are jealous. It is very wrong to be jealous.   524
    A noble Greek or Roman would not be jealous.
Decima. You have been unfaithful to me.   527
Septimus. I am only unfaithful when I am sober. Never
    trust a sober man. All over the world they are un-   529
    faithful. I warn you against all
    sober men from the bottom of my heart. I am extra-   532
    ordinarily wise.   533
Nona. Promise, promise. It's only an oath she wants. Take
    whatever oath she bids you. If you delay we shall be all
    murdered.
Septimus. I can see your meaning. You would explain to me   537
    that a promise can be broken, more especially
    an oath under compulsion. But no, I say to you no,   539
    I say to you certainly not. Am I a rascally sober man,   540
    such a man as I have warned you against? I am too
    drunk to be forsworn. I am of Plutarch's people, what
    I promise I perform. Therefore, my little darling, I   544
    will not promise anything at all.   545
Decima. Then we three shall wait here. They will come in
    there and there. They will carry dungforks with
    burning wisps. They will put the burning wisps into   548
    the roof and we shall be burned.   549
Septimus. I shall die railing upon that beast because,
    owing to a pedantic scruple or some congenital chill
    of the blood, he will not become the new Adam.
Decima. I shall be avenged.
Nona (who has crept behind Decima and snatches the key). I   556
    have it, I have it.   557
(Decima tries to take it back, but Septimus holds her.)
Septimus. Because I am an unforsworn man I am strong.   558
Decima. Go then. I will stay here and die.
Nona. Let us go. A half hour since she offered herself   562
    to every man in the company.   563

Decima. If you would be faithful to me, Septimus, I   564
    would not let a man of them touch me.   565
Septimus. Flighty, but beautiful.   566
Nona. She is a bad woman. (*Nona runs out.*)   567
Septimus. A beautiful, bad, flighty woman. I will follow   568
    her, but slowly. I will take with me this noble hat.
    (*He picks up with difficulty Noah's hat which Nona has
    let fall.*) I will save the
    noble high-crowned hat of Noah. I will carry it thus   574
    with dignity. I will go slowly that they may see I   575
    am not afraid. (*He goes out.*)   576

[DRAFT BREAKS OFF.]

Commentary

At the beginning of Draft 27 the Prime Minister is angry with the players because the disappearance of Decima threatens his plans for entertaining the people with the Noah play—surely they are more appropriate objects for his wrath than the Queen; Yeats's device for getting the scene under way, the Prime Minister's rage, has been finally worked out. Now there is no attempt to show the Queen as guilty of a sin of omission: Christ child and hot water bottle have been removed, perhaps to avoid any suggestion of blasphemy in making Christ an object of farce. For the first time (at lines 40 and 85) the Prime Minister introduces what was to become his standard oath, "Sleep of Adam," which seems to reflect his distrust of all women—to wish that woman had never been created is to carry misogyny very far. Then the Queen enters, prepared, she says, for martyrdom; martyrdom is not mentioned in Draft 21, so this looks back to earlier drafts of the play, indeed all the way back to Draft 16. We hear for the first time that the Prime Minister has a plan to prevent martyrdom; this, though he will not tell the Queen of it, is his plan to marry her. They go out, and Decima sings her song beginning "My mother dandled me and sang"; Nona finds her, and promises to bring her the lobster and wine if she will dress for the part of Noah's wife. She does dress and goes into her role, appealing to her adopted ancestors in the likeness of an old woman. Her claim that her features resemble theirs and that she has played about their knees as a child uses business previously worked out in Draft 24. Decima's refusal of the role now has added to it the fact that failure to perform the play means Septimus will go to prison. Decima knows this because she has heard the Prime Minister's threats from her hiding place under the throne. Yeats will develop this scene in subsequent drafts. Here her royal "We have decided that Septimus is to go to prison" points toward what is to come. The quarrel between Decima and Nona follows its by now usual pattern with changes in the poems Decima cites. Yeats reintroduces "The Mask" (dropped since Draft 16) in a changed context; Decima now sings it as a proof of Septimus's love. The quatrain "O Time there is one stroke of strokes" and "A Thought from Propertius," which appeared in Draft 21, are dropped, and a new lyric beginning "O would that I were an old beggar" introduced, though it is not yet quite finished. This song will form part of the completed play. Here Draft 27 breaks off.

Draft 28. This draft begins with the entrance of Septimus from the town. He is still drunk, and his mind is still running on unicorns, as it was during his altercation with the townsmen and countrymen. He says, "I weep because the unicorn will not trample you to death, and beget upon some woman a new mankind. I weep because of the chastity of the unicorn." Later, he praises the unicorn along with the griffin and the cockatrice for their courage, and again complains of the unicorn's chastity. This is adapted from Draft 26. Then Septimus's thought takes a new turn. He says, "Man is nothing till he is united to an "image," and he goes on to plan a hunting expedition in Africa, where he will kill the unicorn and the unicorn will kill him. This passage will be extended in later drafts, particularly in the 1922 printed versions of the play. We will ponder Yeats's meaning after we have examined these drafts.

Yeats's progress toward his completed play has been immense in these drafts: Scene I is nearly done; only a few trifles remain to be amended. Scene II is less far along, but it also is taking final form. Some plot elements will be dropped in Draft 29, others worked over and clarified, but many of the lines have reached final, or almost final, form.

CHAPTER FOURTEEN

Draft 29

DRAFT 29 is the first draft of the complete play we have encountered since Draft 21. It is found in two typescripts, which are as nearly alike as different typings can be. The play is now in two scenes, not acts; as in 21, these take place in the town and in the throne room of the castle. Scene I is textually the same as Draft 22; Scene II incorporates the changes made in Drafts 23 through 28 and adds still others. Scene I is nearly done; Scene II still requires further work. One of the two surviving typescripts of this draft is from the papers of Mrs. Patrick Campbell. Revisions are pasted onto eleven of its sheets. These revisions are stylistic only, and the revised text agrees with the other typescript, which is in the National Library of Ireland. Lines that appeared in the 1922 printings but were afterward dropped are marked with the line numbers of the *Variorum* followed by a "v."

The Player Queen
Scene 1.

An open space at the meeting of three streets. One can see for some way down one of these streets and at some little distance it turns, showing a bare piece of wall lighted by a hanging lamp. Against the lighted wall are silhouetted the heads and shoulders of two old men. They are leaning from the upper windows, one on either side of the street. They wear grotesque masks. A little to one side of the stage is a great stone for mounting a horse from. The houses have knockers.

First Old Man. Can you see the Queen's castle? You	1
have better sight than I.	2
Second Old Man. I can just see it rising over the tops of	3
the houses yonder on its great rocky hill.	4
First Old Man. Is the dawn breaking? Is it touching the	5
tower?	6
Second Old Man. It is beginning to break upon the	7
tower, but these narrow streets will be dark for a long	8

while. (*A pause.*) Do you hear anything? You have   9
    better hearing than I.   10
First Old Man. No, all is quiet.   11
Second Old Man. At least fifty passed by an hour since,   12
    a crowd of fifty men walking rapidly.   13
First Old Man. Last night was very quiet, not a sound,   14
    not a breath.   15
Second Old Man. And not a thing to be seen till the   16
    tapster's old dog came down the street upon this   17
    very hour from Cooper Malachi's ashpit.   18
First Old Man. Hush, I hear feet, many feet. Perhaps   19
    they are coming this way. (*Pause.*) No, they are   20
    going the other way, they are gone now.   21
Second Old Man. The young are at some mischief, the   22
    young and the middle-aged.   23
First Old Man. Why can't they stay in their beds, and   24
    they can sleep too—seven hours, eight hours. I mind   25
    the time when I could sleep ten hours. They will   26
    know the value of sleep when they are near upon   27
    ninety years.   28
Second Old Man. They will never live so long. They   29
    have not the health and strength that we had. They   30
    wear themselves out. They are always in a passion   31
    about something or other.   32
First Old Man. Hush! I hear a step now, and it is com-   33
    ing this way. We had best pull in our heads. The   34
    world has grown very wicked and there is no knowing   35
    what they might do to us, or say to us.   36
Second Old Man. Yes, better shut the windows and   37
    pretend to be asleep.

(*They pull in their heads. One hears a knocker being struck in*   38
the distance, then a pause and a knocker is struck close at
hand. Another pause and Septimus, a handsome man of 35,
staggers on to the stage. He is very drunk.)

Septimus. An uncharitable place, an unchristian place.   39
    (*He begins banking at a knocker.*) Open there, open there,   40
    I want to come in and sleep.   41
(*A Third Old Man puts his head from an upper window.*)

Third Old Man. Who are you, what do you want?   42

Septimus. I am Septimus. I have a bad wife. I want   43
    to come in and sleep.   44

Third Old Man. You are drunk.   45

Septimus. Drunk! So would you be if you had as bad a   46
    wife.   47

Third Old Man. Go away. (*He shuts window.*)   48

Septimus. Is there not one Christian in this town? (*He*   49
    begins hammering the knocker at the house of the First
    Old Man but there is no answer.)
    No one there? All dead or drunk maybe   50
    —bad wives. I will try another knocker. There must be
    one Christian man. (*He hammers a knocker at the other*
    side of the stage. An Old Woman puts her head out of
    the window above.)

Old Woman (*in a shrill voice*). Who's there? What do   52
    you want? Has something happened?   53

Septimus. Yes, that's it. Something has happened. My   54
    wife has hid herself, has run away, or has drowned   55
    herself.   56

Old Woman. What do I care about your wife! You are   57
    drunk.   58

Septimus. Not care about my wife! But I tell you that   59
    my wife has to play by order of the Prime Minister   60
    before all the people in the great hall of the castle   61
    precisely at noon, and she cannot be found.   62

Old Woman. Go away, go away! I tell you, go away.   63
    (*She shuts window.*)

Septimus. Treat Septimus who has played before Kubla   64
    Khan, like this. Septimus, dramatist and poet!   65
    (*The Old Woman opens the window again and empties*
    a jug of water over him.) Water! Drenched to the skin—must   66
    sleep in the street (*Lies down.*)—bad wife. Others have   67
    had bad wives, but others were not left to lie down   68
    in the open street under the stars, drenched with cold   69
    water, a whole jug of cold water, shivering in the   70
    pale light of the dawn, to be run over, to be trampled   71
    upon, to be eaten by dogs, and all because their wives   72
    have hidden themselves.   73

(*Enter two men a little older than Septimus. They stand still and gaze into the sky.*)

First Man. Ah my friend, the little fair-haired one is a minx.

Second Man. Never trust fair hair—I will have nothing but brown hair.

First Man. They have kept us too long—brown or fair.

Second Man. What are you staring at?

First Man. At the first streak of the dawn on the castle tower.

Second Man. I would not have my wife find out for the world.

Septimus (*sitting up*). Carry me, support me, drag me, roll me, pull me or sidle me along, but bring me where I may sleep in comfort. Bring me to a stable —my Saviour was content with a stable.

First Man. Who are you? I don't know your face.

Septimus. I am Septimus, a player, a playwright and the most famous poet in the world.

Second Man. That name, sir, is unknown to me.

Septimus. Unknown?

Second Man. But my name will not be unknown to you. I am called Peter of the Purple Pelican, after the best-known of my poems, and this is Tom of the Hundred Tales.

Septimus. Bad, popular poets.

Second Man. You would be a popular poet if you could.

Septimus. Bad, popular poets.

First Man. Lie where you are if you can't be civil.

Septimus. What do I care for anyone now except Venus and Adonis and the other planets of heaven!

Second Man. You can enjoy their company by yourself. (*The two men go out.*)

Septimus. Robbed, so to speak; naked, so to speak— bleeding, so to speak—and they pass by on the other side of the street.

(*A crowd of citizens and countrymen enter. At first only a few and then more and more till the stage is filled by an excited crowd.*)

74
75
76
77
78
79
80
81
82
83
84
85
86
87
88
89
90
91
92
93
94

97
98
99
100
101
102
103

104
105
106

First Citizen. There is a man lying here.   107

Second Citizen. Roll him over.   108

First Citizen. He is one of those players who are housed   109
    at the castle. They arrived yesterday.   110

Second Citizen. Drunk I suppose. He'll be killed or   111
    maimed by the first milk-cart.   112

Third Citizen. Better roll him into the corner. If we   113
    are in for a bloody day's business, there is no need   114
    for him to be killed—an unnecessary death might   115
    bring a curse upon us.   116

First Citizen. Give me a hand here. (*They begin rolling*   117
    Septimus.)

Septimus (*mutters*). Not allowed to sleep! Rolled off   118
    the street. Shoved into a stony place! Unchristian   119
    town! (*He is left lying at the foot of the wall to*   120
    one side of the stage.)

Third Citizen. Are we all friends here, are we all agreed?   121

First Citizen. These men are from the country. They   122
    came in last night. They know little of the business.   123
    They won't be against the people, but they want to   124
    know more.   125

First Countryman. Yes, that is it. We are with the   126
    people, but we want to know more.   127

Second Countryman. We want to know all, but we are   128
    with the people. (*Other voices take up the words:*   129
    "We want to know all, but we are with the people," etc.
    There is a murmur of voices together.)

Third Citizen. Have you ever seen the Queen, country-   130
    man?   131

First Countryman. No.   132

Third Citizen. Our Queen is a witch, a bad evil-living   133
    witch, and we will have her no longer for Queen.   134

Third Countryman. I would be slow to believe her father's   135
    daughter a witch.   136

Third Citizen. Have you ever seen the Queen, country-   137
    man?   138

Third Countryman. No.   139

Third Citizen. Nor has anybody else. Not a man here   140
    has set eyes on her. For seven years she has been shut   141

up in that great black house on the great rocky hill. 142
From the day her father died she has been there with 143
the doors shut on her, but we know now why she 144
has hidden herself. She has no good companions in 145
the dark night. 146

Third Countryman. In my district they say that she is a 147
holy woman and prays for us all. 148

Third Citizen. That story has been spread about by the 149
Prime Minister. He has spies everywhere spreading 150
stories. He is a crafty man. 151

First Countryman. It is true, they always deceive us 152
country people. We are not educated like the people 153
of the town. 154

A Big Countryman. The Bible says, suffer not a witch 155
to live. Last Candlemas twelvemonth I strangled a 156
witch with my own hands. 157

Third Citizen. When she is dead we will make the 158
Prime Minister King. 159

Second Citizen. No, no, he is not a king's son. 160

Second Countryman. I'd send a bellman through the 161
world. There are many king's sons in Arabia, they say. 162

Third Countryman. The people must be talking. If you 163
and I were to hide ourselves, or to be someway hard 164
to understand, maybe they would put some bad 165
name on us. I am not against the people, but I want 166
testimony. 167

Third Citizen. Come, Tapster, stand up there on the 168
stone and tell what you know. (*The Tapster climbs 169
up on to the mounting stone.*)

The Tapster. I live in the quarter where her castle is. 170
The garden of my house and the gardens of all the 171
houses in my row run right up to the rocky hill that 172
has her castle on the top. There is a lad in my 173
quarter that has a goat in his garden. 174

A Voice. That's little Michael—I know him.

The Tapster. That goat is always going astray. One
morning little Michael got out of his bed early to go
snaring birds, and nowhere could he see that goat. 178
So he began climbing up the rock, and up and up he 179

went, till he was close under the wall, and there he 180
found the goat and it shaking and sweating as though 181
something had scared it. Presently he heard a thing 182
neigh like a horse, and after that a something like a 183
white horse ran by, but it was no horse, but a uni- 184
corn. He had his pistol, for he had thought to bring 185
down a rabbit, and seeing it rushing at him as he 186
imagined, he fired at the unicorn. It vanished all in a 187
moment, but there was blood on a great stone. 188
Third Citizen. Seeing what company she keeps in the 189
small hours, what wonder that she never sets foot 190
out of doors. 191
Third Countryman. I wouldn't believe all that night 192
rambler says—boys are liars. All that we have against 193
her for certain is that she won't put her foot out of 194
doors. I knew a man once that when he was five and 195
twenty refused to get out of his bed. He wasn't ill 196
no, not he, but he said life was a vale of tears, and 197
for forty and four years till they carried him out to 198
the churchyard, he never left that bed. All tried him 199
—parson tried him, priest tried him, doctor tried 200
him, and all he'd say was, "Life is a vale of tears." 201
It's too snug he was in his bed, and believe me, that 202
ever since she has had no father to rout her out of a 203
morning she has been in her bed, and small blame 204
to her, maybe. 205
The Big Countryman. But that's the very sort that are 206
witches. They know where to find their own friends 207
in the lonely hours of the night. There was a witch 208
in my own district that I strangled last Candlemas 209
twelvemonth. She had an imp in the shape of a red 210
cat that sucked three drops of blood from her poll 211
every night a little before the cock crew. It's with 212
their blood they feed them; until they have been fed 213
with the blood, they are images and shadows; but 214
when they have it drunk they can be for a while 215
stronger than you or me. 216
Third Countryman. The man I knew was no witch, he 217
was no way active. "Life is a vale of tears," he said. 218

Parson tried him, doctor tried him, priest tried him   219
—but that was all he'd say.   220

First Citizen. We'd have no man go beyond evidence   221
and reason, but hear the Tapster out, and when you   222
have you'll say that we cannot leave her alive this   223
day—no not for one day longer.   224

The Tapster. It is not a story that I like to be telling, but   225
you are all married men. Another night that boy   226
climbed up after his goat and it was an hour earlier   227
by his clock and no light in the sky, and when he   228
came to the castle wall he clambered along the wall   229
among the rocks and bushes till he saw a light from   230
a little window over his head. It was an old wall full   231
of holes, where mortar had fallen out, and he climbed   232
up putting his toes in the holes, till he could look   233
in through the window; and when he looked in,   234
what did he see but the Queen.   235

First Countryman. And did he say what she was like?   236

The Tapster. He saw more than that. He saw her coupling   237
with a great white unicorn. (*Murmurs among the crowd.*)   238

Second Countryman. I will not have the son of the uni-   239
corn to reign over us, although you will tell me he   240
would be no more than half a unicorn.   241

First Countryman. I'll not go against the people, but   242
I'd let her live if the Prime Minister promised to   243
rout her out of bed in the morning and to set a guard   244
to drive off the unicorn.   245

The Big Countryman. I have strangled an old witch with   246
these two hands, and today I will strangle a young   247
witch.   248

Septimus (*who has slowly got up and climbed up on to
the mounting-stone which the Tapster has left.*) Did I hear   249
somebody say that the unicorn is not chaste? It is a   250
most noble beast, a most religious beast. It has a   251
milk-white skin and a milk-white horn, and milk-   252
white hooves, but a mild blue eye, and it dances in   253
the sun. I will have no one speak against it, not while   254
I am still upon the earth. It is written in the great   255
beastery of Paris that it is chaste, that it is the   256
most chaste of all the beasts in the world.   257

The Big Countryman. Pull him out of that, he's drunk.   258

Septimus. Yes, I am drunk. I am very drunk, but that   259
    is no reason why I should permit anyone to speak   260
    against the unicorn.   261

Second Citizen. Let's hear him out. We can do nothing   262
    till the sun's up.   263

Septimus. Nobody shall speak against the unicorn. No,   264
    my friends and poets, nobody. I will hunt it if you   265
    will, though it is a dangerous and cross-grained beast.   266
    Much virtue has made it cross-grained. I will go with   267
    you to the high tablelands of Africa where it lives,   268
    and we will there shoot it through the head, but I   269
    will not speak against its character, and if any man   270
    declares it is not chaste I will fight him, for I affirm   271
    that its chastity is equal to its beauty.   272

The Big Countryman. He is most monstrously drunk.   273

Septimus. No longer drunk but inspired.   274

Second Citizen. Go on, go on, we'll never hear the like   275
    again.   276

The Big Countryman. Come away. I've heard enough of this—   277
    we have work to do.   278

Septimus. Go away, did you say? Leave me in the full tide
    of my inspiration. Ah! but I can see it now—you are bent
    upon going to some deserted market-place,
    some lonely place where uninterrupted
    you can speak against the character of the unicorn,   283
    but you shall not, I tell you you shall not. (*He*   284
    comes down off the stone and squares up at the
    crowd which tries to pass him.) In the midst of this uncharitable   285
    town I will protect that noble milk-white, flighty   286
    beast.   287

The Big Countryman. Let me pass.   288

Septimus. No, I will not let you pass.   289

First Countryman. Leave him alone.   290

Second Countryman. No violence—it might bring ill-   291
    luck upon us. (*They try to hold back the Big Countryman.*)   292

Septimus. I will oppose your passing till the death. For   293
    I will not have it said that there is a smirch or a   294
    blot upon the most milky whiteness of an heroic   295
    brute that bathes by the sound of tabors at the rising   296

of the sun and the rising of the moon and the rising 297
of the Great Bear, and above all, it shall not be said, 298
whispered, or in any wise published abroad by you 299
that stand there, so to speak, between two washings; 300
for you were doubtless washed when you were born, 301
and it may be, shall be washed again after you are 302
dead. (*The Big Countryman knocks him down.*) 303
First Citizen. You have killed him. 304
The Big Countryman. Maybe I have, maybe I have not— 305
let him lie there. A witch I strangled last Candlemas 306
twelvemonth, a witch I will strangle today. What 307
do I care for the likes o' him? 308
Third Citizen. Come round to the east quarter of the 309
town. The basket-makers and the sieve-makers will 310
be out by this. 311
Fourth Citizen. It is a short march from there to the 312
castle gate. (*They go up one of the side streets, but 313
return quickly in confusion and fear.*)
First Citizen. Are you sure that you saw him? 314
Second Citizen. Who could mistake that horrible old 315
man? 316
Third Citizen. I was standing by him when the ghosts 317
spoke out of him seven years ago. 318
First Countryman. I never saw him before. He has never 319
been in my district. I don't rightly know what sort 320
he is, but I have heard of him, many a time I have 321
heard of him. 322
First Citizen. His eyes become glassy, and that is the 323
trance growing upon him, and when he is in the 324
trance his soul goes away and a ghost takes its place 325
and speaks out of him—a strange ghost. 326
Third Citizen. I was standing by him the last time. 327
"Get me straw," said that old man, "my back itches." 328
Then all of a sudden he lay down, with his eyes wide 329
open and glassy, and he brayed like a donkey. At 330
that moment the King died and the King's daughter 331
was Queen. 332
First Countryman. They say it is the donkey that carried 333
Christ into Jerusalem and that is why it knows the
rightful sovereign. I have seen him, many a time I

have seen him. He goes begging about the country, and there is no man dare refuse him what he asks. 336

The Big Countryman. Then it is certain nobody will take 337
my hand off her throat. I will make my grip tighter. 338
He will be lying down on the straw and he will bray, 339
and when he brays she will be dead. 340

First Citizen. Look! There he is coming over the 341
top of the hill, and the mad look upon him. 342

Second Countryman. I wouldn't face him for the world 343
this night. Come round to the market-place, we'll 344
be less afraid in a big space. 345

The Big Countryman. I am not afraid, but I'll go with 346
you till I get my hand on her throat. (*They all go* 347
out but Septimus. Presently Septimus sits up; his
head is bleeding. He rubs his fingers to his
broken head and looks at the blood on his fingers.)

Septimus. Unchristian town! First I am, so to speak, 348
thrown out into the street, and then I am all but 349
murdered; and I drunk, and therefore in need of 350
protection. All creatures are in need of protection at 351
some time or other. Even my wife was once a frail 352
child in need of milk, of smiles, of love, as if in the 353
midst of a flood, in danger of drowning so to speak. 354
(*An Old Beggar with long matted hair and beard and in*
ragged clothes comes in.)

The Old Beggar. I want straw. 355

Septimus. Tom of the Hundred Tales and Peter of the Purple Pelican
have done it all. They are bad, popular poets, and 357
being jealous of my fame, they have stirred up the 358
people. (*He catches sight of the Old Beggar.*) There is a 359
certain medicine which is made by distilling cam- 360
phor, Peruvian bark, spurge and mandrake, and mix- 361
ing all with twelve ounces of dissolved pearls, and 362
four ounces of the oil of gold; and this medicine is 363
infallible to stop the flow of blood. Have you any of 364
it, old man? 365

The Old Beggar. I want straw. 366

Septimus. I can see that you have not got it, but no 367
matter, we shall be friends. 368

The Old Beggar. I want straw to lie down on. 369

Septimus. It is no doubt better that I should bleed to   370
   death, for that way, my friend, I shall disgrace   371
   Peter of the Pelican and Tom of the Hundred Tales; but it
   is necessary that I shall die somewhere where my last   373
   words can be taken down. I am therefore in need of   374
   your support. (*Having got up he now staggers over to*   375
   the old man and leans upon him.)
The Old Beggar. Don't you know who I am, aren't you   376
   afraid? When something comes inside me, my back   377
   itches. Then I must lie down and roll, and then I   378
   bray and the crown changes.   379
Septimus. Ah! you are inspired. Then we are indeed   380
   brothers. Come, I will rest upon your shoulder and   381
   we will mount the hill side by side. I will sleep in   382
   the castle of the Queen.   383
The Old Beggar. You will give me straw to lie upon?   384
Septimus. Asphodels! Yet indeed the asphodel is a   385
   flower much overrated by the classic authors. Still, if   386
   a man has a preference, a preference, I say for the asphodel . . .   387

(*They go out and one hears the voice of Septimus mur-*
muring in the distance about asphodels. The First
Old Man opens his window and taps with his crutch
at the opposite window. The Second Old Man opens
his window.)

First Old Man. It is all right now. They are all gone.   388
   We can have our talk out.   389
Second Old Man. The whole castle is lit up by the dawn   390
   now, and it will soon begin to grow brighter in the streets.   391
First Old Man. It's time for the Tapster's old dog to   392
   come down the street.   393
Second Old Man. Yesterday he had a bone in his mouth.   394

Curtain.

Scene 2.

The throne-room in the Castle. Large pillars on which are
presented in mosaic kings and queens. Between the pillars are

gilded openwork doors, except at one side, where there is a
large window. The morning light is slanting through this
window making dark shadows among the pillars. As the scene
goes on, the light at first feeble becomes strong and suffused,
and the shadows disappear. Through the openwork doors one
can see down long passages, and one of these passages plainly
leads into the open air. One can see daylight at the end of it.
There is a throne in the centre of the room and a flight of steps
that lead to it.

The Prime Minister, an elderly man with an impatient manner
and voice, is talking to a group of players, among whom is
Nona, a fair, comely, comfortable-looking young woman of
perhaps 35; she seems to take the lead.

Prime Minister. I will not be trifled with. I chose the	1
play myself; I chose the tragical history of Noah's	2
deluge because when Noah beats his wife to make	3
her go into the Ark, everybody understands, every-	4
body is pleased, everybody recognizes the mulish	5
obstinacy of their own wives, sweethearts, sisters.	6
And now, when it is of the greatest importance to	7
the State that everybody should be pleased, the play	8
cannot be given. The leading lady is lost, you say,	9
and there is some unintelligible reason why nobody	10
can take her place; but I know what you are all	11
driving at—you object to the play I have chosen.	12
You want some dull, poetical thing, full of long	13
speeches. I will have that play and no other. The	14
rehearsal must begin at once and the performance	15
take place at noon punctually.	16
Nona. We have searched all night, sir, and we cannot	17
find her anywhere. She was heard to say that she	18
would drown rather than play a woman older than	19
thirty. Seeing that Noah's wife is a very old woman,	20
we are afraid that she has drowned herself indeed.	21
(*Decima, a very pretty young woman, puts her head out*	
from under the throne where she has been lying hidden.)	
Prime Minister. Nonsense! It is all a conspiracy. Your	22

manager should be here. He is responsible. You can 23
tell him when he does come that if the play is not 24
performed, I will clap him into jail for a year and 25
pitch the rest of you over the border. 26

Nona. O sir, he couldn't help it. She does whatever 27
she likes. 28

Prime Minister. Does whatever she likes—I know her 29
sort; would pull the world to pieces to spite her 30
husband or her lover. I know her—a bladder full of 31
dried peas for a brain, a brazen, bragging baggage. 32
Of course he couldn't help it, but what do I care. 33
(*Decima pulls in her head.*) To jail he goes—somebody 34
has got to go to jail. Go and cry her name every- 35
where. Away with you! Let me hear you cry it out. 36
Call the baggage. Louder, louder. (*The players go out 37
crying,* "Where are you, Decima?") O Adam! why did 38
you fall asleep in the garden. You might have known 39
that while you were lying there helpless the Old 40
Man in the Sky would play some prank upon you. 41
(*The Queen, who is young, with an ascetic timid face,
enters in a badly fitting state dress.*)
Ah! 42

The Queen. I will show myself to the angry people as you 43
have bidden me. I am almost certain that I am ready 44
for martyrdom. I have prayed all night. Yes, I am 45
almost certain. 46

Prime Minister. Ah! 47

The Queen. I have now attained to the age of my patroness, 48
Holy Saint Octema, when she was martyred at Antioch. 49
You will remember that her unicorn was so pleased 50
at the spectacle of her austerity, that he caracoled in 51
his excitement. Thereupon she dropped out of the 52
saddle and was trampled to death under the feet of 53
the mob. But indeed for the unicorn, the mob would 54
have killed her long before. 55

Prime Minister. No, you will not be martyred. I have a 56
plan to settle that. I will stop their anger with a 57
word. Who made that dress? 58

The Queen. It was my mother's dress. She wore it at her   59
    coronation. I would not have a new one made. I do   60
    not deserve new clothes. I am always committing sin.   61
Prime Minister. Is there sin in an egg that has never   62
    been hatched, that has never been warmed, in a   63
    chalk egg?   64
The Queen. I wish I could resemble Holy Saint Octema in   65
    everything.   66
Prime Minister. What a dress! It is too late now. No-   67
    thing can be done. It may appear right to those on   68
    the edge of the crowd. The others must be con-   69
    quered by charm, dignity, royal manner. As for the   70
    dress, I must think of some excuse, some explana-   71
    tion. Remember that they have never seen your face,   72
    and you will put them in a bad humour if you hang   73
    your head in that dumfounded way.   74
The Queen. I wish I could return to my prayers.   75
Prime Minister. Walk! Permit me to see your Majesty   76
    walk. No, no, no! Be more majestic. Ah! If you had   77
    known the queens I have known—they had a way   78
    with them. Morals of a dragoon, but a way, a way.   79
    Give the people some plain image or they will invent one.   79av
    Put on a kind of eagle look, a vulture look.   80
The Queen. It would be a blessed penance—there are
    cobble-stones—if I might go barefoot. It was especially the
    bleeding feet of Saint Octema that gave pleasure to   83
    the unicorn.   84
Prime Minister. Sleep of Adam! Barefoot—barefoot did   85
    you say? (*A pause.*) There is not time to take off your   86
    shoes and stockings. If you were to look out of the   87
    window there, you would see the crowd becoming   88
    wickeder every minute. Come! (*He gives his arm to*   89
    the Queen.)
The Queen. You have a plan to stop their anger so that I   90
    shall not be martyred?   91
Prime Minister. My plan will be disclosed before the   92
    face of the people, and there alone. (*They go out.*)   93
    Decima (*creeping from under the throne*).

[LINES 94–101 AS IN DRAFTS 21, P. 315, AND 27, P. 352]

Nona (*returns with a mask and dress hanging from one arm
and catches Decima who tries to hide again.*) Thank God, you are found.   102
Get into this mask and dress as quickly as you can.
Decima. I have found the only part in the world that I
am fitted to play. You remember that old country
ballad that was made by the mad singing daughter of a
harlot. (*Singing.*)

[LINES 118–25 AS IN DRAFTS 21, P. 317, AND 27, P. 353]

Nona. Be quick, get into this.
Decima. The Queen cannot play her part at all and I
could play it. I would know how to stamp my foot and
look proud, or how to bow with all my body down to
the ankle.
Nona. You that were born in a ditch between two towns
and wrapped in a sheet stolen from a hedge—you play
the queen! Low comedy is what you are fitted for.
Here, put on this mask.
Decima. What, that old wrinkled mask, when I look beautiful and everybody admires me? Septimus says to himself
"I am married to a phoenix." Every new eye that sees
me is like his eye on the day we met for the first time
and when he hears a murmur run along the benches, he
loves me as well as on that first day. And you would
have me play an old, toothless, peaky-chinned, drop-
nosed harridan that a foul
husband beats with a stick because she won't clamber   144
among the other brutes into his cattle-boat.   145
She wept because she dreamt that I
Was born to wear a crown.
Nona. Where are you going?
Decima. To get my breakfast. I saw a bottle of wine and
a lobster on a shelf in the larder.
Nona. If you will put on that dress, I will fetch them
for you. (*She goes out.*)
Decima (*putting on dress, sings*).

My mother dandled me and sang
How young it is, how young
And made a golden cradle
That on a willow swung.

(*She takes up the mask and holds it out looking at
it, and sings again.*)

How young it is, how young.

(*She puts on the mask and begins to hobble about
as an old crooked woman.*)

O fathers, and grandfathers and great-grandfathers, do you
acknowledge this daughter of your house? (*She walks up to
one of the kings in mosaic.*) Grandfather, though you are
pictured on stone and must live among rats, you have a red
face as if you had drunk good wine; will you let me sit
down at the table? I am more a queen than anybody in the
world. Will you let me come and kiss you? A grandchild
may kiss her grandfather. But no, no, you say; you are an
old woman out of the markets, you say; get you into the
grave, you say; hurry away, hurry away! (*She hobbles to
a distance from the pictured king and stands by another
pillar covered with mosaic, and then turns about from
that. She hobbles about as if driven from pillar after
pillar.*) You have all turned against me—grandfathers and
great-grandfathers. You all call out to the old harridan to
get out of the house, and yet (*She takes off mask.*) I so
resemble you all, having the nose of one and the chin of
another. Ah! you look wise, you there with a long beard. I
am certain that you nursed me on your knee. No, no, (*She
puts on mask again.*) I have to wear this upon my face by
the order of the Prime Minister. You will not let me near
you. It is certain that you also have found something about
me that you dislike. Can it be this old face and this old
dingy dress. They hide from you the child that you have
loved, perhaps remind you of somebody you disliked.
(*She tears off the mask and dress and begins trampling
them under her feet.*)
Nona (*returns with a lobster and bottle of wine and, seeing*

what Decima is doing, lays them upon the ground in the
corner). What are you doing?

Decima. We have all decided that Septimus is to go to prison.

Nona. Why do you always make him so miserable?

Decima. To make him love me better. When he sits down on
the stone floor of the gaol with a jug of water and a bowl
of skilly he will say: "I am doing this for her; she is
fierce, flighty, a dragon," he will say, "but beautiful,
adorable." It is as though one said: "There, remember me
forever" and to help the memory gave him a cuff on the ear.

Nona (beginning to cry). What a way to treat a man and he
a great genius who can't take care of himself. There isn't a
woman in the world would do it, and you were sworn to him
in church—O yes, you were, there is no use denying it. I
have never sworn to a man in church, but

if I did swear I wouldn't treat him like a tinker's   186
donkey. Before God, I would not. I was properly   187
brought up. My mother always told me that it was no   188
light thing to take a man in church.   189

Decima. You are in love with my husband.   190

Nona. Must one be in love with a man if one doesn't want
to have him go to jail, and I won't have him go to
jail; and if you don't play the part I will.

Decima. When I married him I made him swear never   197
to play with anybody but me.

Nona. Only this once and in a part nobody could do   199
anything with.   200

Decima. That is the way it begins, and all the time you   201
would whisper to him and say things the audience couldn't
hear.

Nona. Septimus will break his oath and I have learned   203
the part, every word of it.

Decima. Septimus will not break his oath for anyone in the world.

Nona. There is one person in the world he will break it for.

Decima. No, no.

Nona. He will break it for me.   210

Decima. You have some crazy notion in your head as when
you thought Jeremiah the tumbler was in love with you.

Nona. Maybe I have my secrets.   212

Decima. What are you keeping back? Have you been sit-   213
  ting in a corner giving him sympathy and telling him as
  you always do that you are a virgin? Yes, that's
  it, and he has but stayed in the corner
  to have the pleasure of talking
  about me.   217

Nona. You think you have his every thought, and all be-
  cause you are a devil.   219

Decima. Maybe I am no more a devil than you are a virgin,
  and yet his thoughts are full of me wherever he is.
  (*She sings.*)

[''THE MASK'' AS IN DRAFT 16, P. 249, AND 27, P. 356]

Nona. You are not telling the truth.

Decima. Then look what I carry under my bodice. This   231
  is a poem praising me, all my beauties one after the   232
  other—eyes, hair, complexion, shape, disposition,   233
  mind—everything. And there are a great many verses   234
  to it. And here is a little one he gave me yesterday   235
  morning. I had turned him out of bed and he had to   236
  lie alone by himself.   237

Nona. Alone by himself!   238

Decima. And as he lay there alone, unable to sleep, he   239
  made it up wishing that he were blind so as not to   240
  be troubled by looking at my beauty. Hear how it   241
  goes. (*Sings again.*)   242

[THE SONG ''O WOULD THAT I WERE AN OLD BEGGAR''
FROM DRAFT 27, P. 356]

Nona. Alone in his bed indeed. I know that long poem,   251
  that one with all the verses; I know it to my hurt,   252
  though I haven't read a word of it. Four lines in   253
  every verse, four beats in every line, and fourteen   254
  verses—my curse upon it.   255

Decima (*taking out a manuscript from her bodice*). Yes, four-   256
  teen verses. There are numbers to them.   257

Nona. You have another there—ten verses all in fours   258
    and threes.   259
Decima (*looking at another manuscript*). Yes the verses   260
    are in fours and threes. But how do you know all   261
    this? I carry them here. They are a secret between   262
    him and me, and nobody can see them till they have   263
    lain a long while upon my heart.   264
Nona. They have lain upon your heart, but they were   265
    made upon my shoulder. Ay, and down along my   266
    spine in the small hours of the morning; so many   267
    beats to a line, and for every beat, a tap of the fingers.   268
Decima. My God!   269
Nona. That one with the fourteen verses kept me from   270
    my sleep two hours, and when the lines were finished   271
    he lay upon his back another hour waving one arm   272
    in the air, making up the music. I liked him well   273
    enough to seem to be asleep through it all, and many   274
    another poem too—but when he made up the short   275
    one you sang, he was so pleased that he muttered the   276
    words, all about his lying alone in his bed thinking of   277
    you, and that made me mad. So I said to him, "Am   278
    I not beautiful? Turn round and look." O, I cut it   279
    short, for even I can please a man when there is but   280
    one candle. (*She takes a pair of scissors that are   281
    hanging round her neck and begins clipping at the dress for*
Noah's wife.) And now you know why I can play the part   282
    in spite of you, and not be driven out. Work upon   283
    Septimus if you have a mind for it. Little need I   284
    care. I will clip this a trifle and re-stitch it again—   285
    I have a needle and thread ready.   286

(*The Stage Manager comes in ringing a bell. He is
followed by various players, all dressed up in likeness
of various beasts.*)

Stage Manager. Put on that mask—get into your clothes.   287
    Why are you standing there as if in a trance?   288
Nona. Decima and I have talked the matter over and   289
    we have settled that I am to play the part.   290
Stage Manager. Do as you please. Thank God it's a part   291
    that anybody can play. All you have to do is to   292

copy an old woman's squeaky voice. We are all here	293
now but Septimus and we cannot wait for him. I	294
will read the part of Noah. He will be here before	295
we are finished, I daresay. We will suppose that the	296
audience is upon this side, and that the Ark is over	297
there with a gangway for the beasts to climb. All	298
you beasts are to crowd up on the prompt side. Lay	299
down Noah's hat and cloak there till Septimus	300
comes. As the first scene is between Noah and the	301
beasts, you can go on with your sewing.	302

Decima. No, I must first be heard. My husband has   303
been spending his nights with Nona, and that is why   304
she sits clipping and stitching with that vainglorious   305
air.   306

Nona. She made him miserable, she knows every trick   307
for breaking a man's heart—he came to me with his   308
troubles—I seemed to be a comfort to him, and now   309
—why should I deny it?—he is my lover.   310

Decima. I will take the vainglory out of her. I have   311
been a plague to him. O, I have been a badger and a   312
weasel, and a hedgehog and a pole-cat, and all because   313
I was dead sick of him. And, thank God! she has got   314
him and I am free. I threw away a part and I threw   315
away a man—she has picked them both up.   316

Stage Manager. It seems to me that it all concerns you   317
two. It's your business and not ours. I don't see why   318
we should delay the rehearsal.   319

Decima. I will have no rehearsal yet. I'm too happy   320
now that I am free. I must find somebody who will   321
dance with me for a while. Come, we must have   322
music. (*She picks up a lute which has been laid down*   323
amongst some properties.) You can't all be claws and   324
hoofs.   325

Stage Manager. We've only an hour and the whole play   326
to go through.   327

Nona. O, she has taken my scissors, she is only pre-   328
tending not to care. Look at her! She is mad! Take   329
them away from her! Hold her hand! She is going to   330
kill me or to kill herself. (*To Stage Manager.*) Why   331
don't you interfere? My God! She is going to kill me.   332

Decima. Here Peter, I will cut those breast feathers so that
you can get your arms through and play the lute. (*She
begins cutting through the breast feathers of the swan.*)

Nona. She is doing it all to stop the rehearsal, out of   334
vengeance; and you stand there and do nothing.   335

Stage Manager. If you have taken her husband, why   336
didn't you keep the news till the play was over? She   337
is going to make them all mad now. I can see that   338
much in her eyes.   339

Decima. Now that I have thrown Septimus into her lap,   340
I will choose a new man. Shall it be you, Turkey-   341
cock, or you, Bull-head?   342

Stage Manager. There is nothing to be done. It is all   343
your fault. If Septimus can't manage his wife, it's   344
certain that I can't. (*He sits down helplessly.*)   345

First Player (*who is the forelegs of the Bull*). Choose me.
I am double, one man in the forelegs and another man in
the hindlegs. I am double as good as any other.

Decima. You are too slow on your feet   347v
and there is a sort of melancholy in a heavy, deep
voice; and what a folly it would be now that I have
found love out, to stretch and yawn as if I loved.

Second Player (*who is in the form of Turkey-cock*). Come live with me   351av
and be my love, for as everybody can see by my ruff and my red   351bv
wattle, and my way of strutting and my chuckling speech, I have   351cv
a cheerful appetite.   351dv

Decima. No, Turkey-cock, you might expect me to be faithful.

Second Player. No no, neither I nor you. I have a score of wives.   353bv

Nona. You are a disgrace.   353cv

Second Player. Be content now that you have a man of your own.   353dv
(*They all begin dancing round Decima.*)

[THE SONG BEGINNING "SHALL I FANCY," LINES 360–65
OF DRAFT 21, P. 335]

(*Septimus comes in.*)

Stage Manager. Stop! Stop! Here is Septimus.   380

Septimus. Though you are about to beat out my brains, to
pierce my vitals with a pitchfork, to disembowel me,

that is not why I weep. I weep because the unicorn will not
trample you to death and beget upon some woman a new
mankind. I weep because of the chastity of the unicorn.

Player. What nonsense has he in his head now?

Another Player. His head is broken anyway.

Another Player. He is always quarrelsome when he is drunk.

Stage Manager. Come, come, Septimus. This is not a time
to be making up speeches for the new play. Let us get
on with our rehearsal. If you will sit upon the ground
you won't be so unsteady.

Septimus. Open Plutarch, close the book of life, prepare your
dying speeches. The mob is climbing the hill with burning
wisps to set upon the roof and pitchforks to drive into
our vitals.

A Player (at window). My God! It's   393
true. There is a great crowd at the bottom of the hill.   394
They have dungforks and scythes set upon poles. They
are coming this way. (*All the players go to the window
except Septimus and Decima.*)

Septimus. Let every man among you consider whether he will
speak as Cato, as Demosthenes, as Cicero, assuming an
heroic calm, triumphing over death in sonorous eloquence.
Perhaps you may prefer to die like Petronius Arbiter,
telling witty and scandalous stories, to go on telling
scandalous stories while the doors are being broken in. Yes,
that would be more distinguished. The one thing necessary
is to show no anger, to speak even with a certain sweetness,
for after all even if they blow up the floor with gunpowder
they are no concern of ours; they are merely the mob. As
for me I shall continue to rail upon the unicorn, but I
shall rail sweetly. (*He picks up a lute which lies among
some property.*) I will even put my railing to a tune that
those who murder me may remember the tune and
croon it to their grandchildren.

Upon the round blue eye I rail   411
Damnation on the milk-white horn.   412

Fourth Player. Yes, they are coming this way. But why
should they quarrel with us, who only arrived in the
town yesterday?

First Player. Are there not poets, storytellers, even
    players in this town? Have
    we not been chosen before them all because we are   419
    the most famous players in the world? What can be
    more simple—they have stirred up the mob.

Third Player. When we played at Xanadu, my performance was   422v
    so incomparable that the men who pulled the strings   422av
    of the puppet-show left all the puppets lying on   422bv
    their backs and came to have a look at me.   422cv

Fourth Player. Listen to him! His performance indeed! I ask   423v
    you all to speak the truth. If you are honest men   423av
    you will say that it was my performance that   423bv
    drew the town. Why, Kubla Khan himself gave me   424v
    the name of the Talking Nightingale.   425v

Fifth Player. My God! Listen to him! Is it not always   430
    the comedian who draws the people? Am I dreaming,   431v
    and was it not I who was called six times before the   432v
    curtain? Answer me that.   433

Sixth Player (*at window*). There is somebody making a speech.   442v
    I cannot see who it is.   443v

Second Player. Depend upon it, he is telling them to put   446v
    burning wisps upon dungforks and put them   447v
    into the rafters. That is what they did in the old   447av
    play of the Burning of Troy. Depend upon it, they   447bv
    will burn the whole house.   448v

Fifth Player (*coming from window*). I don't care what has
    made them angry. I will stay here no longer. (*He goes out.*)

First Player. Must we go dressed like this?   449

Second Player. There is no time to change, and besides
    should the hill be surrounded, we can gather in   451
    some cleft of the rocks where we can be seen only   452
    from a distance. They will suppose we are a drove of   453
    cattle or a flock of birds.   454

(*All go out except Septimus, Decima, and Nona. Nona
is making a bundle of Noah's hat and cloak and other
properties. Decima is watching Septimus.*)

Septimus (*while they are going out*). Leave me to die   455
    alone, I do not blame you; there is courage in red   456

wine, in white wine, in beer, even in this beer sold   457
  by a blear-eyed pot-boy in a bankrupt tavern, but   458
  there is none in the human heart. Only the unicorn and
  cockatrice and the griffin have courage. I am full of sorrow
  because of the chastity of the unicorn.
Nona. I'll pile these upon your back. I can carry the
  rest myself, then we shall have saved the rest. (*She
  begins tying a great bundle of properties on to
  Septimus's back.*)
Septimus. You are right, I accept the reproach. It is   466
  necessary that we who are the last artists—all the rest   467
  have gone over to the mob—shall save the symbols and
  implements of our art. We must put somewhere in
  safety the cloak of Noah, the high-crowned hat of   470
  Noah, the golden face of the Almighty, and the horns
  of Satan.
Nona. There now, I have tied them on. Thank God you can
  still stand upright on your legs.
Septimus. Tie them all upon my back. Man is nothing till
  he is united to an image. When I have them all I will
  go to the high tablelands of Africa, I will find the
  cavern where the unicorn is stabled. I will seek my
  death before the terrible blue eye. We shall both
  be killed, for I shall carry a knife smeared with the
  blood of a serpent that has died from gazing at an emerald.
Decima. Stand back, do not dare to move a step.   498
Septimus. Beautiful as the unicorn, but fierce.   499
Decima. I have locked the gate that we may have a
  talk. (*Nona lets the hat of Noah fall in her alarm.*)   501
Septimus. That is well, very well. You would talk with   502
  me because today I am extraordinarily wise.   503
Decima. I will not unlock the gate till I have a promise   504
  that you will drive her from the company.   505
Nona. Do not listen to her, take the key from her.   506
Septimus. If I were not her husband I would take the   507
  key, but because I am her husband she is terrible.   508
  She is terrible because she loves.
Nona. You are afraid.   510
Septimus. Could not you yourself take it? She does not   511
  love you, therefore she will not be terrible.   512

Nona. If you are a man at all you will take it.   513

Septimus. I am one of Plutarch's people, I am more than
    a man. I am extraordinarily wise. I will take the key.

Decima. If you come a step nearer I will shove the key   516
    through the grating of the door.   517

Nona (*pulling him back*). Don't go near her; if she shoves   518
    it through the door we shall not be able to escape.   519
    The crowd will find us and murder us.   520

Decima. I will unlock this gate when you have taken an   521
    oath to drive her from the company, an oath never   522
    to speak with her or look at her again, a terrible oath.   523

Septimus. You are jealous; it is very wrong to be jealous.   524
    A noble Greek or Roman would not be jealous.

Decima. You have been unfaithful to me.   527

Septimus. I am only unfaithful when I am sober, never   528
    trust a sober man. All over the world they are un-   529
    faithful. I warn you against all
    sober men from the bottom of my heart. I am extra-   532
    ordinarily wise.   533

Nona. Promise, promise, if its only an oath she wants. Take   534
    whatever oath she bids you. If you delay we shall be
    all murdered.

Septimus. I can see your meaning, you would explain   537
    to me that an oath can be broken, more especially   538
    an oath under compulsion. But no, I say to you no,   539
    I say to you certainly not. Am I a rascally sober man,   540
    such a man as I have warned you against? I am too
    drunk to be forsworn, I am of Plutarch's people. What
    I promise I perform, therefore, my little darling, I   544
    will not promise anything at all.   545

Demica. Then we shall wait here. They will come in   546
    there and there, they will carry dungforks with
    burning wisps, they will put the burning wisps into   548
    the roof and we shall be burnt.   549

Septimus. I shall die railing upon that beast because,
    owing to a pedantic scruple or some congenital chill
    of the blood he will not become the new
    Adam.   553

Decima. I shall be avenged.

Nona (*who has crept behind Decima and snatched key.*) I   556
   have it, I have it.   557
   (*Decima tries to take the key again, but Septimus holds her.*)
Septimus. Because I am an unforsworn man I am strong.   558
Decima. Go then, I shall stay here and die.   561
Nona. Let us go. A half hour since she offered herself   562
   to every man in the company.   563
Decima. If you would be faithful to me, Septimus, I   564
   would not let a man of them touch me.   565
Septimus. Flighty, but beautiful.   566
Nona. She is a bad woman. (*Nona runs out.*)   567
Septimus. A beautiful, bad, flighty woman. I will follow,   568
   but follow slowly. I will take with me this noble   569
   hat. (*He picks up Noah's hat with difficulty.*) I will save the
   noble high-crowned hat of Noah, I will carry it thus   574
   with dignity. I will go slowly that they may see I   575
   am not afraid. (*Singing.*)   576

   Upon the round blue eye I rail,
   Damnation on the milk-white horn. (*Goes.*)

Decima. Betrayed, betrayed, and for a nobody. For a   581
   woman that a man can shake and twist like so much   582
   tallow. A woman that till now never looked higher   583
   than a prompter or a property man. (*The Old Beggar*   584
   comes in.) Have you come to kill me, old man?   585
Old Beggar. I am looking for straw. I must soon lie   586
   down and roll, and where will I get straw to roll on?   587
   I went round to the kitchen, and "Go away!" they   588
   said. I [they] made the sign of the cross as if it were a
   devil that puts me rolling.   590
Decima. When will the mob come to kill me?   591
Old Beggar. Kill you? It is not you they are going to   592
   kill. It's the itching in my back that drags them   593
   hither, for when I bray like a donkey, the crown   594
   changes.   595
Decima. The crown? So it is the Queen they are going   596
   to kill!   597
Old Beggar. But my dear, she can't die till I roll and   598
   bray, and I will whisper to you what it is that rolls. It   599

is the donkey that carried Christ into Jerusalem, and 600
that is why he is so proud; and that is why he knows 601
the hour when there is to be a new King or a new 602
Queen. 603

Decima. Are you weary of the world, old man? 604

Old Beggar. Yes, yes, because when I roll and bray I am 605
asleep. I know nothing about it, and that is a great 606
pity. I remember nothing but the itching in my back. 607
But I must stop talking and find some straw. 608

Decima (*picking up the scissors*). Old man, I am going to 609
drive this into my heart. 610

Old Beggar. No, no, don't do that. You don't know 611
what you will be put to when you are dead, into 612
whose gullet you will be put to sing or to bray. You 613
have a look of a foretelling sort. Who knows but you 614
might be put to foretell the death of kings; and bear 615
in mind I will have no rivals. I could not endure a 616
rival. 617

Decima. I have been betrayed by a man, I have been 618
made a mockery of. Do those who are dead, old man, 619
make love and do they find good lovers? 620

Old Beggar. I will whisper you another secret. People 621
talk, but I have never known of anything to come 622
from there but an old jackass. Maybe there is no- 623
thing else. Who knows but he has the whole place to 624
himself. But there, my back is beginning to itch, and 625
I have not yet found any straw. 626

(*He goes out. Decima leans the scissors upon the arm
of the throne and is about to press herself upon them
when the Queen enters.*)

The Queen (*stopping her*). No no—that would be a great sin. 627
Decima. Your Majesty! 628
The Queen. I thought I would like to die a martyr, but that 629
would be different, that would be to die for God's 630
glory. The Holy Saint Octema was a martyr. 631
Decima. I am very unhappy. 632
The Queen. I too am very unhappy. When I saw the great 633
angry crowd and knew that they wished to kill me, 634

though I had wanted to be a martyr, I was afraid   635

and ran away.   636

Decima. I would not have run away. O no, but it is   637

hard to drive a knife into one's own flesh.   638

The Queen. In a moment they will have come and they will   639

beat in the door, and how shall I escape them?   640

Decima. If they could mistake me for you, you would   641

escape.   642

The Queen. I could not let another die instead of me. That   643

would be very wrong.   644

Decima. O, your Majesty, I shall die whatever you   645

do, and if I could only wear that gold brocade and   646

those gold slippers for one moment, it would not be   647

so hard to die.   648

The Queen. They say that those who die to save a rightful   649

sovereign show great virtue.   650

Decima. Quick, the dress.   651

The Queen. If you killed yourself your soul would be lost,   652

and now you will be sure of Heaven.   653

Decima. Quick, I can hear them coming.   654

(*Decima puts on the Queen's robe of state and her slippers.*
Underneath her robe of state the Queen wears some kind
of nun-like dress. The following speech is spoken by
the Queen while she is helping Decima to fasten the
dress and the slippers.)

The Queen. Was it love? (*Decima nods.*) O, that is a great   655

sin. I have never known love. Of all things, that is   656

what I have most fear of. Saint Octema shut   657

herself up in a tower on the mountain because she was   658

loved by a beautiful prince. I shut myself up to

be like her in everything. I was afraid it would

come in at the eye and seize upon me in a moment.   660

I am not naturally good, and they say people will   661

do anything for love, there is so much sweetness in   662

it. Even Saint Octema was afraid of it. But you will   663

escape all that and go up to God as a pure virgin.   664

(*The change is now complete.*) Good-bye, I know how I   665

can slip away. There is a convent that will take me   666

in. It is not a tower, it is only a convent, but I have   667
long wanted to go there to lose my name and dis-   668
appear. Sit down upon the throne and turn your face   669
away. If you do not turn your face away, you will be   670
afraid. (*She goes out.*)   671

(*Decima is seated upon the throne. A great crowd
gathers outside the gates. A Bishop enters.*)

Bishop. Your loyal people, your Majesty, offer you their   672
homage. I bow before you in their name. Your royal   673
will as spoken by the mouth of the Prime Minister   674
has filled them with gratitude. All misunderstand-   675
ings are at an end, all has been settled by your con-   676
descension in bestowing your royal hand upon the   677
Prime Minister.   678

Prime Minister (*enters walking backward and speaking to the
crowd who reply at intervals:* "Yes, your honour";
"Quite right, your honour," etc.) You understand,
my men, I must never hear another word of the unicorn.
Banished, exiled, vanished into air. I mean what I
say, not a whisper, not one whisper.
(*Decima has turned round. She looks at the crowd;
there is great shouting. The crowd are impressed.
Septimus forces his way through the crowd and staggers
towards the front of the stage to one side where the
Prime Minister is standing.*)

Septimus. My lord, that is not the Queen, that is my   701
wife, my bad wife.

Prime Minister. Look at that crowd, they believe that she
is Queen. They will have nobody else now that they have
set their hearts upon it. They wouldn't believe a word
I'd say. O, I know them. Sleep of Adam. There is
nothing to be done at the present.

Bishop. We are all your faithful servants.

Decima (*looking at the Prime Minister*). All?   709

Prime Minister. All, your Majesty.   710

Decima (*singing*).

    She pulled the thread, and bit the thread   711
    And made a golden gown.   712

Hand me that plate of lobster and that bottle of	713
wine. While I am eating I will have a	
good look at my new man. (*The plate and bottle of*	714
wine are handed to her. The bray of a donkey is	
heard, and the Old Beggar is dragged in amid the hoots	
of the mob.)	
Bishop. At last we have found this imposter out. He	715
has been accepted by the whole nation as if he were	716
the voice of God. As if the crown could not be	717
settled firmly on any head without his help. It's plain	718
that he has been in league with the conspirators, and	719
believed that your Majesty had been killed. He is	720
keeping it up still, look at his glassy eye. But his	721
madman airs won't help him now.	722
Prime Minister. Carry him to prison. We will hang him	723
in the morning. (*The Old Beggar is dragged out. The*	724
Prime Minister takes Septimus by the arm.) Do you	
understand that God or some fiend has settled it—	
that the crown is on her head for good—that I shall	
have this woman for wife? Do you understand that the	
crown has changed, changed—and there's no help for it.	
Sleep of Adam!	
Septimus. She is my wife—she is my bad, flighty wife.	733
Prime Minister. Seize this man. He has been whispering	734
slanders against Her Majesty. Cast him beyond the	735
border of the kingdom, and find the	736v
company of players he belongs to. They also are banished, and must not	736av
return on pain of death. Now, my Lord Bishop, I am ready.	736bv
Decima (*singing*).	
She wept because she dreamt that I	736cv
Was born to wear a crown. (*She flings the lobster's*	736dv
claw at the Prime Minister.) Come—crack that claw.	736ev

The end.

Commentary

Scene I has here the form it had in Draft 22, so very little comment needs to be made. We should note that this scene is nearly finished; Yeats revised only 14 lines of it before he printed his play. Only one change is substantial, the addition of the swan image to one of Septimus's speeches on the unicorn (lines 279–82), an image which, as he tells us, describes his inspiration.

Scene II was considerably revised over its counterpart in Draft 21. Yeats works into it most of the changes made in Drafts 23 through 28 and adds some new ones. A summary view of these revisions may help us to understand the details that follows: Draft 29 adds the mosaic pictures of the royal line to the preliminary description of the setting. At the beginning of the scene the Prime Minister is angry with the players (because Decima cannot be found and the play cannot be given without her) rather than with the dilatory Queen. In 21, after Nona finds Decima, she doesn't leave the stage, although she offers to go fetch the lobster and wine. In 29 she does fetch them, leaving Decima alone on stage for the scene with her imagined ancestors. The scene in which Decima says she will choose a new lover from the troupe is both more elaborate and more lyric in 21. In 29 it has been cut back, although Yeats was to build it up again before the play was printed. There are no references in 21 to the unicorn, and the Prime Minister's oath, "Sleep of Adam," does not occur. The properties that Septimus and Nona save when they escape are not specifically related to Noah as they are in 29. The end of the play in 29 is more carefully worked out; it was scarcely more than an outline in 21.

Lines 1–101. These achieve nearly their final form in Draft 29. Only 23 lines had been completed in early drafts, but the general plan of development was worked out in Draft 27. In addition to finding the expression he will keep, Yeats does make a few important changes. The Queen's patron is now St. Octema, to whom Yeats here has her allude three times (lines 49, 65, 83), and St. Octema is associated with a unicorn, the sign or emblem of her chastity. With the addition of St. Octema, Yeats completes the tone row, so to speak, which he began in Drafts 20 and 21, where he introduced the names Septimus, Nona, and Decima to replace Yellow Martin, the Friend, and the Player Queen. Our principal players are now numbers 7, 9, and 10, and the addition of 8 to this series calls our certain attention to it. At the end of this commentary I will speculate on the meaning of this row. The Prime Minister's allusion to Adam's sleep and his favorite oath "Sleep of Adam" are taken over from Draft 27.

Lines 102–219. This portion of the play, from the discovery of Decima to the beginning of the contest between Nona and Decima concerning which of them Septimus loves best, is much less far along. Fewer lines have final form. The biggest changes to occur will involve the lobster and the wine, and the entire deletion of the scene in which Decima, dressed and masked as Noah's wife, claims kinship with the royal portraits. Lobster and wine become bait for the trap Nona sets to catch Decima; the scene with the royal portraits is excised entirely along with the portraits themselves. Here Yeats builds on Draft 27 and has clearly improved his language. He begins to work on the passage where Decima imagines Septimus in prison, but this will have another form in Draft 30. Yeats still had much to do with this part of the play.

Lines 220–345. This scene, which includes Decima's claim that Septimus loves her and that his poems written to her prove it, together with Nona's counter claim, is nearly finished in Draft 29. Draft 27 contains a version of lines 220–55; we have to go back to Draft 21 for an earlier version of lines 256–345. Draft 27 is close to Draft 29, Draft 21 less close. Yeats's revisions are of language rather than matter, for this part of Scene II follows the action of the earlier drafts closely.

Lines 346–79. This scene, where the players stage a kind of contest to win Decima, is a special case, since Yeats revised it after the 1922 printings of the play. Here it is shorter and less lyrical than the corresponding passage in Draft 21. Yeats kept only the song beginning "Shall I fancy beast or fowl" in the final version of the play. He wrote eight other lines that appeared in the 1922 printings.

Lines 380–584. These lines cover Septimus's return from the town with news of the revolution, the players reaction and flight, the scene where Decima locks Nona and Septimus in, and the flight of Septimus and Nona. Versions of lines 380–417 and 455–576 are found in Draft 28; for the rest we must again go back to Draft 21. Yeats will radically revise parts of these scenes in Draft 30. Here lines 380–410 follow Draft 28 almost word for word down to "Upon the round blue eye I rail," which is new; lines 412–33 are an adaptation of Draft 21; the eight following lines are new, then we return to the last of the alternate versions in Draft 21 and follow it down to line 455. (Yeats revised lines 418–49 after the 1922 printings; this explains the many lines marked "v" in this section of the play.) At line 456 Yeats returns to Draft 28, which he follows very closely except for lines 469–97, which he will revise further in Draft 30. Lines 498–584 follow Draft 28 and here reach nearly final form. In summary, these scenes follow either 21 or 28; some of them will be revised further.

Lines 595–736. Yeats has not worked on the end of the play since Draft 21. Lines 585–678 are very close to what Yeats wrote in 21; at no point is the revision more than stylistic. Lines 618–20 illustrate the kind of changes Yeats made. In 21 these went:

Decima. Do you think, Old Man, that those who are dead make
love? Will I find a better lover there, for I have been
betrayed by a man.

This becomes:

Decima. I have been betrayed by a man, I have been made a
mockery of. Do those who are dead, old man, make love and
do they find good lovers?

Lines 679–736ev were rewritten almost completely. Only four of these lines
have the form they had in Draft 21. Still, the incidents are much the same as
the incidents in the earlier version. The Player Queen is Queen all in a moment, the Prime Minister and Septimus know she is not the real Queen but
cannot do anything about it. The Prime Minister has in any event accomplished his objective of becoming King in name as well as fact. Septimus does
not have the power to act, and the Player Queen is Queen indeed.

The question of what Yeats means by his use of the series Septimus, Octema,
Nona, and Decima has been largely ignored by commentators on the play with
the exception of William Becker, "The Mask Mocked: or, Farce and the
Dialectic of Self" (*Sewanee Review,* Winter 1953, p. 102), and though Becker
tried all the approaches he could think of to discover Yeats's meaning, including asking Mrs. Yeats, he admitted defeat. I am not sure I can do any better.

To begin with the facts: Yeats introduced the names Septimus, Nona, and
Decima into his text late in 1915, while working on Drafts 20 and 21. [Yeats
mentions Septimus in a letter misdated 1 May [1909] in *Correspondence,* p. 15,
but the actual date is probably 1917. Cf. p. 467. Gen. Ed.] Folio 24 of Draft
20 has on its back the inscription "Player Queen rejected. Nov 1915 partly
verse," and on its front part of Decima's proof that Septimus loves her. She is
about to read "A Thought from Propertius" and says "Or look on this, does this
not praise me" (p. 328). The speech-tag "Decima" does not occur on the
page, but the tag "Nona" does, and "Decima" occurs on both the preceding and the following pages. This seems to me sure proof that Yeats had made
the change in names by November 1915, especially since there is other evidence,
cited in my commentary on Draft 20, pp. 344–46, which confirms this date.
He changed the name of the Queen's patron saint from Winifred to Octema in
Draft 29, just discussed, which I think he completed in the spring of 1917.

This early date excludes all possibility that Yeats named his characters after his own descriptions of human personality according to the phases of the moon in *A Vision,* which, given the late publication of *The Player Queen* (1922) and the date of the first *Vision* (1925), seems at first sight a promising hypothesis. The automatic writing and trance-speaking of Mrs. Yeats on which *A Vision* are based began late in 1917 after Draft 29 of *The Player Queen* had been written. And besides this, the descriptions in *A Vision* of the personalities associated with phases 7, 8, 9, and 10 do not fit the characters in the play. Phase 7 goes fairly well for Septimus: the historical examples include Alexandre Dumas and James Macpherson, writers of a sort but not, after all, Septimus's kind of writers. Yeats does not characterize Octema beyond designating her a saint, but saintliness is no attribute of phase 8, for which Yeats finds no historical examples and suggests "the Idiot of Dostoieffsky perhaps." The unnamed artist of phase 9 was Augustus John (the incident Yeats describes in *A Vision* was recorded with names in his Journal, 1908–1914 [Cf. *Memoirs,* pp. 214–15. Gen. Ed.]). The character Nona is in no respect like Augustus John, as far as I can discover. The example used for phase 10 is Parnell. Decima is certainly no Parnell.

William Becker asked Mrs. Yeats about the meaning of the names, and so did I. She apparently told him that Septimus "was a good Irish name," and it may be that the whole series grew out of Yeats's adopting this new name in place of "Yellow Martin" which had persisted for so long. She told me, and my question was about the whole sequence, that Yeats "wanted to call them that." I took this hardly informative reply to mean either that Mrs. Yeats did not know why Yeats had named his characters as he did, or that she did not wish to say. She was always very reticent about matters concerning the Golden Dawn or Stella Matutina (she always used the second name), a society of modern cabbalists which Yeats had joined in 1890 and which Mrs. Yeats had joined before her marriage, Yeats acting as her sponsor. If the answer to my question involved the Golden Dawn, Mrs. Yeats probably would have parried it. But apparently it did not. I have examined Israel Regardie's *The History of the Golden Dawn* volumes and found no evidence that Yeats derived his names from the rituals of that order. These rituals do use both numbers and simple equations, but I found no explanation of the series 7, 8, 9, and 10.

If we look next to traditional numerology as that is presented in such a work as V. F. Hopper's *Medieval Number Symbolism* (New York, 1938), from which I have extracted most of the lore that follows, we find a good deal that is suggestive, but again no certain explanation of Yeats's series. On page 141 Hopper makes the point concerning Dante that "magic of any sort" is usually accompanied by "complex numerology," and this was certainly true of

Yeats's studies in magic. He knew something, though perhaps in a debased form, of both astrological and Pythagorean numerology. These lie back of the almost insane numerology of the Middle Ages, and Yeats knew something of this as well.

In astrological numerology we encounter one series of numbers that is suggestive, the 12 signs of the zodiac. Personality types were assigned to each of these in casting horoscopes, and the descriptions of the types associated with the seventh, ninth, and tenth signs fit Septimus, Nona, and Decima well enough. The appropriate signs would be Libra (7), Sagittarius (9), and Capricorn (10). I quote the description of the personality traits attached to these signs from *The Guide to Astrology* by "Raphael" (pseud. of R. C. Smith). Libra: "Ambitious, talkative; fond of the other sex." Sagittarius: "Bold, active, and generous; free and good-hearted; . . . laudable in actions, and generally to be depended upon." Capricorn: "Sharp, subtle, and capricious; covetous, envious, jealous, crafty, selfish, and unstable." These descriptions, which apply to Septimus, Nona, and Decima without any forcing and which are much the same in all manuals of astrology, would certainly have occurred to Yeats, who was constantly casting his own and other horoscopes, sometimes on the manuscripts of *The Player Queen*. However, the description of the eighth sign, Scorpio, will not fit a saint; quite the opposite: "a malicious, deceitful, cunning person." We know that Yeats added the name Octema to complete his series after Septimus, Nona, and Decima had been established, and it is possible that this completion was all he had in mind: that in order to accomplish it he simply ignored the personality characteristics assigned to Scorpio, which he would certainly have known. I do feel, however, that the fact that Octema does not fit her zodiacal sign weakens the whole argument.

Actually a more probable explanation of the name "Octema" comes from Pythagorean numerology, as that was extrapolated by St. Augustine and the other Church Fathers. In their writings 8 became the number of salvation, of eternity after the mutability of this life. And Pythagorean numerology is at least suggestive for 7, 9, and 10 as well. To return again to Hopper for a description of the Pythagorean theory, we find that all four numbers lie with the "decad," the first ten numbers to which all other numbers can be reduced. Seven is the "universal number . . . the number of harmony"; 10 is emblematic of completeness, while 9 is trying to be 10 and shares something of this completeness. But I cannot establish that Yeats knew much about Pythagorean numbers in 1915–1917, when he sets this series: in his poetry he first alludes to Pythagoras in 1926 when he wrote "Among School Children."

After thinking about this series for a very long while, I have concluded that seeking an explanation of it outside Yeats's play involves us in the intentional fallacy. It is impossible, in this way, to establish what Yeats's intention was. I do not think he was sending us to any external source to determine the meaning of his series; there is no dark conceit.

We are left, therefore, with a row of ascending numbers, which is unique in Yeats's work and which seems to say that the poet is below the saintly woman (St. Octema), the domestic woman (Nona), and the fatal woman (Decima). It also ranges these types of women in an order: Yeats admired saintliness in an abstract sort of way, but seems not to have greatly cared for it. He tended always to put the domestic woman below the fatal woman, emblematically, for instance, in "Two Songs of a Fool." In putting Septimus on the bottom, Yeats, I suspect, is being gallant and also indulging in a small irony. The emblem of the artist as "workman" (in early drafts of "The Gyres") and as "servant" ("The Municipal Gallery Revisited") pleased Yeats, but of course he didn't really believe this; to the contrary he believed that the artist was the most important human type. The whole of his work shows this belief, but if an instance is needed, "Coole Park and Ballylee" will serve.

And of course the place of 7 in the magic of numbers is widely known; indeed it is the only number of the series with which Yeats could be sure his audience would have associations: the seven planets, the seven days of the week, the quartiles of the lunar month each made up of seven days, the seven deadly sins, the seven cardinal virtues, the seven liberal arts, the seven ages of man, and so on.

Yet if Yeats intends to call our attention to his series, and I think he does, this will only register with readers of the play. On any program where the players are named in order of appearance, the characters Septimus, Nona, and Decima will appear widely separated (see, for instance, the program Lennox Robinson reproduced in *Ireland's Abbey Theatre,* p. 130). Yeats did put them together in the order Decima, Septimus, and Nona in all his own printings of the list of persons in the play, an order that suggests their triangular relation. St. Octema's name, of course, will not appear on the program at all. In the dialogue of the play Septimus is named 15 times (I, lines 43, 64, 65, and 89; II, lines 111, 148, 176, 214, 284, 294, 300, 340, 344, 380, and 564), Decima and St. Octema six times (Decima II, lines 38, 289, 365, 367, 373, and 379; St. Octema II, lines 49, 65, 83, 631, 657, and 663), but Nona only once (II, line 304). I do not see, therefore, how persons merely hearing the play could be expected to notice the sequence. Perhaps it is legitimate for a playwright to make some things apparent to his readers that his hearers will not notice, though I have my doubts about such a procedure. It strikes me as akin to those harp flourishes Wagner sometimes put into double forte passages, which no one but the harpist ever hears, if indeed he hears them.

CHAPTER FIFTEEN

Drafts 30 and 31

DRAFTS 30 and 31 are the last we have before the play was printed in 1922. When 30 is added to the record, we still do not recover the copy Yeats sent to the press; this was derived from the Abbey prompt book. Draft 30 is a revision of parts of Scene II: lines 94–230, the discovery of Decima and her exchange with Nona in which each claims Septimus's love; lines 345a–417, the scene in which Decima stages a kind of contest to help her choose a new lover and the return of Septimus with a report of the rebellion; and lines 455–501, the scene between Septimus, Nona, and Decima following the exit of the rest of the troupe down to the locking of the gate.

(They go out. Nona comes in with a bottle of wine and a
lobster on a plate and puts them in middle of floor. Lays her
finger on her lips and stands in doorway at back, watching.
Decima comes cautiously out of her hiding place.

[Decima] (*singing*).

[THE SONG BEGINNING "HE WENT AWAY" AND ENDING "WEAR A CROWN" AS IN DRAFT 21, P. 315]

(She is reaching out her hand for the lobster when Nona
comes in holding out the dress and mask for Noah's wife.)

Nona. Thank God you are found. (*Getting between her*	102
and lobster.) No, not till you put on this	
dress and mask. I have caught you now and you are	104
not going to hide again.	105
Decima. Very well, when I have had my breakfast.	106
Nona. Not a mouthful till you are dressed ready for	107
the rehearsal.	108
Decima. Do you know that song I was singing just	109
now?	110

Nona. It is that song you are always singing. Septimus   111
made it up.   112
Decima. It is the song of the mad singing daughter of   113
a harlot, the only song she had. Her father was a   114
drunken sailor waiting for the full tide, and yet she   115
thought her mother had fortold that she would   116
marry a prince and become a great queen. (*Sings.*)   117

[THE SONG BEGINNING "WHEN SHE WAS GOT" AND ENDING "TOP OF CARE"
FROM DRAFT 21, P. 317]

A moment ago as I lay here I too thought "I could play
a queen's part, a great queen's part, the only part   127
in the world I can play is a great queen's part."   128
Nona. You play a queen's part. You that were born   129
in a ditch between two towns and wrapped in a sheet   130
that was stolen from the hedge.
Decima. The Queen cannot play at all, but I could play   132
it so well. I would bow with my whole body down to
my ankles, and could [be] stern when hard looks were   134
in season. And I would know how to put all summer
in a look and after that all winter in a voice.   136
Nona. Low comedy is what you are fit for.   137
Decima. I understood all this in a wink of the eye, and   138
then just when I am saying to myself I was
born to sit up there with soldiers and courtiers to do my will, you
come in shaking in front of me that mask and that
dress. I am not to eat my breakfast unless I play an   142
old, peaky-chinned, drop-nosed harridan that a foul   143
husband beats with a stick because she won't clamber   144
among the other brutes into his cattle-boat. (*She*   145
makes a dart at the lobster.)
Nona. No, not a drop, not a mouthful till you have   146
put these on. Remember that if there is no play,   147
Septimus must go to prison.   148
Decima. Would they give him dry bread to eat?   149
Nona. They would.   150
Decima. And water to drink, and nothing in the water?   151
Nona. They would.   152
Decima. And a straw bed?   153

Nona. They would, and only a little straw maybe.   154

Decima. And iron chains that clanked?   155

Nona. They would.   156

Decima. And keep him there for a whole week?   157

Nona. A month maybe.   158

Decima. And he would [say] to the turnkey "I am here   159
because of my beautiful cruel wife, my beautiful   160
flighty wife"?   161

Nona. He might not, he'd be sober.   162

Decima. But he would think it, and every time he was hungry,   163
every time he was thirsty, every time he felt the   164
hardness of the stone floor, every time he heard the   165
chains clank he would think it, and every time he   166
thought it I would become more beautiful in his   167
eyes.   168

Nona. No, he would hate you.   169

Decima. Little do you know about the love of a man. If
that holy man in the church where you put all
those candles at Easter was pleasant and affable, why   172
did you come home with the skin worn off your   173
two knees?   174

Nona (*in tears*). I understand, you cruel, bad woman.   175
You won't play the part at all, and all that Septimus   176
may go to prison, and he a great genius that can't   177
take care of himself. (*Seeing Nona distracted with*   178
tears, Decima makes a dart, almost gets the lobster.)
No, no, not a mouthful, not a drop. I'll break   179
the bottle if you go near it. There is not another   180
woman in the world would treat a man like that, and   181
you were sworn to him in church. O yes you were,
there is no good denying it. (*Decima darts at the*   183
food, but Nona, who is still in tears, puts the lobster in her
pocket.) Leave the food alone, not a mouthful will   184
you get. I have never sworn to a man in church, but   185
if I did swear I would not treat him like a tinker's   186
donkey, before God I would not. I was properly   187
brought up. My mother always told me it was no   188
light thing to take a man in church.   189

Decima. You are in love with my husband.   190

Nona. Because I don't want to see him jailed, you [say]   191
   I am in love with him. Only a woman with no heart   192
   would think one can't be sorry for a man without   193
   being in love with him—a woman who has never   194
   been sorry for anybody. But I won't have him jailed,   195
   and if you won't play the part I'll play it myself.   196
Decima. When I married him I made him swear never   197
   to play with anybody but me, and well you know it.   198
Nona. Only this once, and in a part nobody can do   199
   anything with.   200
Decima. That is the way it begins; and all the time you   201
   would be saying things the audience could not hear.   202
Nona. Septimus will break his oath, and I have learned   203
   the part, every word of it.
Decima. Septimus will not break his oath for any-   205
   body in the world.   206
Nona. There is one person in the world for whom [he]   207
   will break his oath.   208
Decima. What have you got in your head now?   209
Nona. He will break it for me.   210
Decima. You are crazy.   211
Nona. Maybe I have my secrets.   212
Decima. What are you keeping back? Have you been   213
   sitting in corner with Septimus giving sym-
   pathy because of the bad wife he has? And all the   215
   while he has sat there to have the pleasure of talking   216
   about me.   217
Nona. You think you have his every thought be-   218
   cause you are a devil.   219
Decima. Because I am a devil I have his every thought.   220
   You know how [his] own song runs:

["THE MASK" FROM DRAFTS 16, P. 249, AND 27, P. 356]

Nona. His every thought. That is a lie. He forgets   229
   all about you the moment you are out of his sight.   230

[The draft breaks off. The omitted lines, 231 through 345 were
virtually completed in Draft 29]

First Player (*who is forelegs of bull*). Come   345av
   live with me and be my love.   345bv

Decima. Dance, Bullhead, dance. (*The Bull dances.*)   346^v

     You are too slow on your feet.   347^v

First Player. But though I am slow I am twice as good as any other, for

     I am double. One in the forelegs and one behind.   347b^v

Decima. You are heavy of build and that means jealousy, and   348^v

     there is a sort of melancholy in your voice.   349^v

     And what a folly now that I have found out

     love to stretch and yawn as if I loved.   351^v

Turkey Cock. Come live with me   351a^v

     and be my love, for as everybody can see from my ruff and my red   351b^v

     wattle and my way of strutting and my chuckling speech, I have   351c^v

     a cheerful appetite.   351d^v

Decima. Dance, dance. (*Turkey Cock dances.*) Ah, Turkey Cock, you   352^v

     are lively on your feet, and I would find it hard to hide if   353^v

     you followed. Would you expect me to be faithful?   353a^v

Second Player. No, neither I nor you. I have a score of wives.   353b^v

Nona. You are [a] disgrace.   353c^v

Second Player. Be content, now that you have a man of your own.   353d^v

Decima. You are quick of mind, Turkey Cock,   354^v

     I see that by your bright eyes, but I want to let   354a^v

     my mind go asleep.   355^v

     Yes, all dance, all, all, and I will choose

     the best dancer among you.   358^v

First Player. No, let us toss for it. I understand that better.   358a^v

Decima. Quick, quick, begin to dance. (*All dance around Decima.*)   359^v

Decima.   360

     Shall I fancy beast or fowl?

     Queen Pasiphae chose a bull   361

     While a passion for a swan   362

     Made Queen Leda stretch and yawn   363

     Wherefore spin ye, whirl ye, dance ye,   364

     Till Queen Decima's found her fancy.   365

     Chorus

     Wherefore spin ye, whirl ye, dance ye,   366

     Till Queen Decima's found her fancy.   367

Decima.

     Spring and straddle, stride and strut   368

     Shall I choose a bird or brute?   369

Name the feather or the fur   370
For my single comforter?   371

Chorus

Wherefore spin ye, whirl ye, dance ye,   372
Till Queen Decima's found her fancy.   373
Decima.
None has found that found out love   374
Single bird or brute enough   375
Any bird or brute may rest   376
An empty head upon my breast.   377

Chorus

Wherefore spin ye, whirl ye, dance ye,   378
Till Queen Decima's found her fancy.   379
Stage Manager. Stop, stop, here is Septimus.   380
Septimus. Prepare to die.   381v
Consider whether you will speak as Cato or Demosthenes or Cicero,
triumphing over death in sonorous eloquence, or like Petronius   381bv
Arbiter, telling witty, scandalous tales.   381cv
Stage Manager. Come, Septimus, this is not a time for the making up 385v
speeches for the new play. Let us go on with the play.
Septimus. Look at my wounds, and now the mob is climb-   390v
ing up the hill with pitchforks to stick into our vitals,   391
and burning wisps to set the roof on fire.   392
Player (*who is at window*). My God, it is   393
true. There is a great crowd at the bottom of the hill.   394
Another Player. But why shold they attack us?   395
Septimus. Tom of the Hundred Tales and Peter of the Purple Pelican have
stirred up the mob.   395bv
Another Player (*who has run to window*). My God, they have dung- 397
forks and scythes set on poles. They are coming   398
this way. (*Many players gather round window.*)   399
Septimus (*who has found bottle and is drinking from it*). I
shall not copy Cicero or Cato or Demosthenes or even
Petronius Arbiter. I will be more original.
I will die railing   400v
upon the unicorn because he will   405v
not trample mankind to death under his hooves and beget
upon some woman

a new race. But I will rail sweetly. We must not allow
our murderers to discompose us, for after all, even   408v
if they blow up the floor with gunpowder, they are   409
merely the mob. I will even put my railing into rhyme   410v
that it may linger in the ear:
Upon the round blue eye I rail   411
Damnation on the milk-white horn.   412
A telling sound, a sound to linger in the ear—hale,   413
tale, bale, gale. My God, I am too sober even to   414
find a rhyme. (*Another drink.*) A   415
tune, that even my murderers may remember my last   416
words and croon them to their grandchildren.   417

[There is a break in the manuscript, which picks up again at line 455.
Again Yeats had nearly completed these lines in Draft 29.]

Septimus. Leave me to die   455
    alone. I do not blame you. There is courage in red   456
    wine, in white wine, in beer, even in thin beer sold   457
    by a blear-eyed pot-boy in a bankrupt tavern, but   458
    there is none in the human heart. O, who will journey
    to a cavern in Africa and sing into the ear of the
    Unicorn epithalamions until he, unable to endure
    any longer his desirous heart, becomes the new Adam.
Nona. I'll pile them upon your back. I shall carry the
    rest myself, and so we shall save all.   465
Septimus. You are right. I accept the reproach. It is   466
    necessary that we who are the last artists—all the rest   467
    have gone over to the mob—shall save the symbols
    and implements of our art. We must carry into   469
    safety the cloak of Noah, the high-crowned hat of   470
    Noah, and the golden face of the Almighty, and the horns of Satan   471v
Nona. Thank God you can still stand upright on your legs.   475–76
Septimus. Tie all upon my back, and I will tell you a
    great secret that came to me at the second mouthful
    of the bottle: man is nothing till he is united to an   479
    image. Now the Unicorn is both an image and a beast.   480
    That is why he alone can be the new Adam. When   481
    we have put all in safety we will to the high   482
    table lands of Africa and find where the Unicorn is   483

stabled. I will stand before
the terrible blue eye.   485
Nona. There, now I have tied them all on. (*She begins
making another bundle for herself.*)
Septimus. You will make Ionian music—music with its   487
eyes upon voluptuous Asia. The Dorian scale   488
would but confirm him in his chastity, one Dorian   489
note might undo us. And above all we must be careful   490
not to speak of Delphi.
Nona. Come, let us go.   492
Septimus. If we fail he will deserve death, and it is not
true that the unicorn cannot be killed. What they
dread most in the world is a blow from a knife that   495
has been dipped in the blood of a serpent that died   496
gazing on an emerald.
Decima. Stand back. Do not dare to move a step.   498
Septimus. Beautiful as the Unicorn, but fierce.   499
[*Decima*]. I have locked the gates that we may have a   500
talk. (*Nona lets the hat of Noah fall in her alarm.*)   501

[THE DRAFT BREAKS OFF.]

Commentary on Draft 30

Lines 94–230. Nona now brings the lobster and wine with her, and uses them as bait for a trap to catch Decima. Decima takes the bait, and her attempts to grab the food during her talk with Nona help the farce. Before she sings the song of the harlot's daughter Decima says "her mother had foretold that she would marry a prince and become a great queen"; this looks forward to the end of the play. Nona's comment on Decima's claim to queenly roles is made more acid. Decima replies by asserting more strongly than ever her longing for such roles and the disparity between what she longs for and the reality of playing Noah's wife. The dialogue in which Decima and Nona work out Septimus's life in prison is new; the question and answer passage is more vivid than Decima's descriptive speech in Draft 29. The scene between Decima and her imagined ancestors is cut entirely. Decima's recollection of Nona's asceticism at Easter is new, shrewd, and vivid. From this point to the break in the draft, the revisions are stylistic, though Nona's speeches at 175–79 and 191–96 are expanded.

Lines 345–417. Here Yeats writes a version of the ballet scene between Decima and the masked and costumed players that is much fuller than the corresponding scene in 29. It now has the dimensions it had in Draft 21, though Yeats does not keep all the songs he wrote for that draft. The echo of Marlowe's "The Passionate Shepherd to His Love" is back, and there are two new quatrains, that beginning "Spring and straddle, stride and strut," and that beginning "None has found, that found out love." The last two lines of "Shall I fancy" are now used as a chorus. Lines 360–80 are in final form. The scene following Septimus's return shows stylistic revision, a rearrangement of items previously used, and important additions. In Draft 29 Septimus in his first speech following line 380 says: "I weep because the unicorn will not trample you to death and beget upon some woman a new mankind." This is now dropped down into the speech that begins at line 400.

After the break in the manuscript at lines 417–54 Septimus expands his scheme for hunting the unicorn. Now he says: "Who will journey to a cavern in Africa and sing into the ear of the Unicorn epithalamions until he, unable to endure any longer his desirous heart, becomes the new Adam." A little later Septimus introduces the passage that, in my reading, is the key to the play. Part of it goes back as far as Draft 21, where Decima talks of the necessity of union with an image (p. 317), but part of it is new: "Man is nothing till he is united to an image. Now the Unicorn is both an image and a beast. That is why he alone can be the new Adam." Lines 487–91, in which Septimus says "You will make Ionian music" and continues with a caution against the Dorian scale and the influence of Delphi, are new.

Description of Draft 31

This typescript of the whole play is from the files of the Abbey Theatre. It is a mosaic text, consisting for the most part of typed sheets from one copy of Draft 29 (that in the National Library of Ireland) into which additional typed sheets have been inserted. These include all of the changes made in Draft 30 (discussed above) and a few further changes that have been written into the text. I believe that this text was the one produced at the Abbey in December 1919. As we shall see, Yeats based the copy he made for Macmillan in 1922 on this Abbey version.

The revisions made in Draft 31 go as follows:

Scene I. All changes have been written into the text; the typed sheets are identical with Draft 29, copy 2.

Line 87 deleted ("my Saviour was content with a stable").

Lines 95 and 96. "and this is Tom of the Hundred Tales" becomes "and my friend is called Happy Tom. He also is a poet."

Line 237. The word "coupling" deleted.

Line 356. "Tom of the Hundred Tales" becomes "Happy Tom."

Line 372. "and Tom of the Hundred Tales" becomes "Happy Tom."

Scene II.

Initial s.d. "Large pillars on which are presented in mosaic Kings and Queens" deleted.

Lines 94–230 inserted on typed sheets. The text is that of Draft 30 except for lines 221–22 and 225, where the staging of "The Mask," so to speak, has been added ("The man speaks first—" "and the woman answers").

Lines 346–501 inserted on typed sheets with manuscript corrections. The text is that of Draft 30 through line 417 except for a few words. Yeats did not revise lines 418–54 in Draft 30; the text used for these lines is essentially that found in Draft 29. Lines 454–501 follow Draft 30. Two stage directions were added, and the phrase "and the gold face of the Almighty" cut from line 471v.

Lines 502–27 are found on a type sheet of Draft 29, copy 2. The following changes were written in:

Line 514. "I am one of Plutarch's people" cancelled.

Lines 524–26. "An ordinary man would be lost—even I am not yet wise enough. (*Drinks again.*) Now all is plain. You are jealous. It is very wrong to be jealous."

New copy was typed for lines 528–80. Yeats made the following changes:

Lines 542–43. "Shall I be foresworn before the very eyes of that cold rocky oracle."

Lines 551–52. After "chill of the blood" the phrase "or the machinations of Delphi" added.

Lines 554–55. "She starved me, but I shall have killed her" added.

Lines 579–80. "But not one word of Delphi. I am extraordinarily wise" added.

Beginning with line 581 and continuing to the end of the play, the sheets of Draft 29, copy 2, were used. No changes were written into the text.

Commentary

I feel quite certain that this was the version performed at the Abbey in December 1919, which served as the basis for the text Macmillan printed in 1922. In an unpublished letter dated 8 March 1922, Yeats requested Lennox Robinson to send him a copy of the Abbey script. He speaks of this script as the "later version" and says he has no copy of it. He needs one "for a new edition of my plays Macmillan is bringing out." This clearly refers to *Plays in Prose and Verse,* which Macmillan published in November. (Letter No. 37, folder 146 B, Lennox Robinson Collection, Southern Illinois University, Carbondale.) The phrase "later version" may indicate that Yeats revised the play after its London production and that Drafts 30 and 31 are a record of this revision. But since the prompt book of the London production seems not to have survived, there is no certain proof of this. It was, however, Yeats's usual practice to revise the texts of his plays after their first production.

Enough has been said above in the commentary on Draft 30 about the changes made there. The additional changes made in Draft 31 are of two kinds: further revisions that Yeats was to keep in the printed versions of his play (the staging of "The Mask" in II, lines 221–22 and 225 is such a revision); and the toning down of certain passages that might have offended a Dublin audience (the deletion of "coupling" at I, line 237, for example).

CHAPTER SIXTEEN

The 1919 Productions
and the 1922 Printings

The London Production

The Player Queen was first produced by the Incorporated Stage Society at the King's Hall, Covent Garden, on Sunday and Tuesday, 25 and 27 May 1919. Yeats's note to the play, written in 1922, says that he was present at this production and found himself applauding the second scene, having forgotten for the moment that it was his own work. The Stage Society produced *The Player Queen* along with Swinburne's *The Duke of Gandia,* which came first on the bill. The cast of *The Player Queen* included Nicholas Hannen as Septimus, Maire O'Neill as Decima, and Edith Evans as Nona. Yeats was surely fortunate in his leading ladies: Maire O'Neill was a veteran of the Abbey company, which she had joined in 1906. She appeared regularly in play after play into the spring of 1911. She returned to the Abbey in 1916–1917. She had been the original Pegeen Mike in Synge's *A Playboy of the Western World,* and would have married Synge if it had not been for his untimely death. Dame Edith Evans was in the early years of her astonishing career, having made her debut in 1912. Several critics noted that Maire O'Neill did not know her lines, and that the prompter virtually took over her part in the marvelous exchange between Decima and Nona in Scene II. Reviews of the production appeared next day (26 May) in the *Morning Post* and *Daily News;* on 28 May in the *Times;* on 1 June in the *Sunday Times* and the *Observer;* and, finally, *The New Age* carried a long notice on 12 June.

Sydney W. Carroll, writing in the *Sunday Times,* expressed the attitude of the professional drama critics toward the experimental productions of the Stage Society. This attitude, one of disfavor, perhaps accounts for the emptiness of all the reviews; no reviewer had the least idea what Yeats was up to.

These unpleasant Sunday afternoons in the theatre remind me of the Holy Cross days on which Jews were formerly forced to attend Christian sermons in Rome. Everybody seems to be present from a sense of enforced duty. Shakespearean actresses roughly handled by the critics of late may consider themselves amply avenged. Having recently assigned their contemners to a place where the temperature is somewhat warmer than it is on earth, they can have the satisfaction of knowing that critics are this glorious summertime condemned to these sultry purgatories compared to which Ruhleben must have been a paradise.

An unsigned review in the *Morning Post* on 26 May was among the most perceptive Yeats received. After summarizing the action accurately, the reviewer comments that much of this is crowded into the last minutes and that the "converse," which makes up the bulk of the play, "though frequently entertaining and suggestive" is "far from clear." He then goes on to speculate about the meaning of the unicorn but gives this up, concluding that it is "suggestive of troubled slumbers after a debauch of lobster-salad and Swedenborg." He notes that the names of the three principals are seven, nine, and ten (the only reviewer to do so), and wonders if this has some special meaning. His last sentence reads: "Is it possible that we are in the presence of another Great Cryptogram?"

The *Daily News* that same day carried a review signed with the initials "E. A. B." (I doubt if this was E. A. Boyd, who surely would have been more perceptive, since he was well acquainted with Yeats's earlier work.) After a brief summary of the action, the review concludes

> . . . what it all means I do not know, unless it be the simple thing that a people admire a Queen who is not a would-be martyr like the real princess, but a woman of themselves who can throw a lobster's claw at her Prime Minister. Mr. Yeats has a vein of wit of his own, and its occasional flashes were welcome.

The *Times* reviewer seems to have enjoyed the play but to have made no effort to understand it. He alone comments on Yeats's style, finding Septimus's rhetoric reminiscent of "Shakespeare the mock Euphuist." He gives a brief summary of the plot and concludes: "All in the fantastic key, as you see, and revealing a new gift in Mr. Yeats, the gift of writing thoroughly enjoyable nonsense."

The review in the *Sunday Times* damns by faint praise: Both Yeats's and Swinburne's plays are "tremendous trifles . . . both written by true poets, both essentially unsound dramatically." The reviewer's final comment is as follows:

> Yeats has an exquisite whimsicality and a sense of humour all his own. I will not pretend that I understood what he is driving at in "The Player Queen." I was chiefly interested in the study of a drunken poet who wrote verses to his wife on the back of his mistress.

The account in the *Observer* is the most sympathetic, so I quote from it at length:

. . . "The Player Queen," a comedy in two scenes, is a delicious piece of nonsense—shrewd underneath as all good nonsense is, but on the surface irresponsible and wayward. Only once did we feel a little bored—when that drunken rogue of a poet-player and his alluring baggage of a wife, the Player Queen, and the dull, peevish wench with whom he has been consoling" himself for his wife's cruelty, got to arguing. They seemed earthy and "real" in the middle of all this fantasy, lacking the light of poetry in them. But when Septimus, royally, poetically drunk, was declaiming to the rebellious townsmen on the chastity of the unicorns (how came they not to know for themselves that in mediaeval lore the unicorn was the very symbol of chastity?); or when we saw at last that poor little Queen against whom her subjects were rebelling and found her to be no witch but an awkward gawk of a *Backfisch* with a passion for dowdy clothes and martyrdom; or when that delicious rogue of a Player Queen sat comfortably on the real throne, eating lobster and throwing claws at the Prime Minister (who had publicly stated his intention of marrying "the Queen," and must now keep his word or the new "Queen" will know the reason why); or when two old, old men at their bedroom window piped us in silvery, faded voices the futility of all this fuss of heady youth and love and striving, when one might sleep and chatter and watch for the butcher's dog coming down the street with or without a bone in his mouth—all of this was full of light and laughing beauty.

This reviewer has grasped something of the tone of the play and perceived the importance of the unicorn, though his boredom with the Molièresque exchanges in Scene II is hard to understand.

John Franic Hope, writing in *The New Age,* had the longest time to ponder *The Player Queen* but spent it to little purpose. He seems to have understood nothing of Yeats's meaning:

. . . We are tired of [Yeats's] old men, his Queens in castles, his unicorns and prophetic asses; they mean nothing, they are mere padding, and they produce the bewildering effect of a medley of styles. The poet and his two doxies afforded examples of creation nearer to the dramatic tradition; and the quarrel of the two women concerning the poet would have been quite effective if Miss Maire O'Neill had not allowed the prompter to play so much of the part . . . Miss Edith Evans had to struggle along in her altercation as best she could retorting on Miss Maire O'Neill the defamation of her character made by the man behind the scenes. There was an under-vein of satire running throughout the play which was not effectively ren-dered, and the play itself established no mood consonant with these touches. The discussion of the other world, for example, between the beggar and the player-Queen, wherein he declares that, so far as he knows, nothing but a jackass has ever returned to give tidings of it, is more comical in intention than in realization; points of that kind cannot be effectively made unless the contrasting mood has been created. The general impression left by the play was that it was full of jokes that did not make people laugh, of satirical touches (such as the player-Queen eating lobsters on the throne) that were indeterminate in direction, of an almost Elizabethan frankness in speech that produced the opposite effect of vigorous mascu-linity, so anaemic was the spirit animating the play. The Stage Society is to be commiserated.

In short, it is difficult to imagine incomprehension carried further than it is carried in these reviews. Surely the central point that an actress born in a ditch between two towns can, if she is a good actress, make a better queen than one born to the purple is not difficult to grasp. Perhaps the only conclusion to be drawn is that theatrical reviewing is perennially poor.

The Abbey Production

The Player Queen was next produced by Lennox Robinson at the Abbey Theatre on 9 December 1919. Arthur Shields played Septimus; Christine Hayden, Decima; May Craig, Nona; Eric Gorman, the Prime Minister; Shena Tyrecon-nell, the Queen; and Michael Dolan, the Old Beggar. The present Secretary of the Abbey Theatre reports that no prompt copy from that production exists in the Theatre's files; it is thought to have burned in the fire that destroyed the original Abbey in 1951. Draft 31 does exist in the Abbey files, as we have seen, and I have concluded above that it was probably this draft which was produced. It would give a text for Scene II, in which Septimus does not announce the end of the Christian Era. I will give further reasons for this conclusion after describ-ing the notices of this production, since these notices bear on the problem.

I have found five notices: W. A. Henderson wrote a long account of it into his "Diary"; then there were four reviews in the 10 December issues of the *Irish Times* (p. 6), the *Freeman's Journal* (p. 2), the *Evening Telegraph* (p. 2), and the *Irish Independent* (p. 4). All five notices show considerable be-wilderment over the meaning of the play, and several are patronizing of Yeats.

Henderson's account is the longest: he first names various persons who attended, describing them as "all the highbrows." He does not name Yeats himself or Mrs. Yeats; indeed the whole tone of his entry indicates that Yeats was not present. (A letter from Yeats to A. H. Bullen on 15 November is dated from Broad Street, Oxford. Yeats and Mrs. Yeats were to leave for the United States on 6 January 1920.) The audience included Jack Yeats and his wife, Dr. and Mrs. Oliver Gogarty, F. R. Higgins, Walter Starkie, and Brinsley MacNamara. Here is Henderson's description of the play:

> Yeats's play was looked forward to with interest and modified excitement owing to rumours of its nature. Its strange story baffles one, while its unfolding is put in so picturesque an environment that it charmed the eye if it didn't satisfy the mind. A young Queen lives in a big castle and never shows herself to her people. Stories of evil doing come to their ears, and they determine to storm her castle and put an end to her. The real Queen happens to be a weak, religious little person, and resigns her position to a Player Queen who brazens it with the people and intends to continue to reign with the Prime Minister as her husband, she having relinquished her player-husband, Septimus, to another player of the troupe, Nona. There is a lot of talk in Act I about the chastity of a unicorn, and in Act II marriage is made very light of.
>
> [MS 1850, fols. 1261–62, National Library of Ireland]

Henderson continues with comments on the reactions of the audience: "Neither Starkie nor Higgins had a good word to say of it. It baffled all, but the beauty of setting pleased most." He comments on the acting of the various players, particularly May Craig and Arthur Shields, and goes on to say that the Abbey Company has "lost the art of peasant acting, but certainly the Company can play out-of-the-way plays like *The Dragon* [by Lady Gregory, produced 21 April 1919], *Androcles* [produced 4 November 1919], and then here and now *The Player Queen*." After describing the setting, Henderson concludes:

> The play was followed with intense interest, and loud applause followed its conclusion. Though its purport is wrapped in mystery, its beauty comes home. You can admire a thing of beauty you can't wholly understand.
>
> [Folio 1263]

The reviewer for the *Irish Times* was clearly puzzled, so he said very little about the play but exuded a murky cloud of allusions that included Swift, Shakespeare, Alice in Wonderland, and Gilbert's *Patience*! According to him the play "met with a reception from a fairly large house which might be described as mildly appreciative. The mildness of the appreciation was probably attributable to the fact that the majority of the audience, if not the entire house, were not a little perplexed as to the author's meaning." After demonstrating his own lack of understanding, he praises Yeats's "keen and bright and flexible and poetic English," and goes on to comment on the setting and the acting.

The reviewer for the *Freeman's Journal* was likewise bewildered, and added to the mélange of literary allusions one to Victor Hugo:

What is "The Player Queen"? Is it a play, or a poem, a tragedy, a phantasy, a comedy, an extravaganza, a satire? Quite possibly the last most, though there are elements of all the others. "The whole of summer in a look" [Scene II, lines 135–36] is Yeats in his own realm. But in the first of the two scenes into which the work is divided the shaft of satire may be discerned in the horrible whispered gossip of the mob who attribute ghastly sin to the fair young Queen in the castle on the rock in the fashion of mediaeval superstition. There is certainly comedy on the Victor Hugo model in the dissolute actor Septimus . . . and so on with the other elements.

The review goes on to praise the acting of the players and to sketch the plot, then comments: "The puzzled audience admired the poetry, applauded the occasional flashes of humour, and whole-heartedly demonstrated its admiration of the players." The review ends with this question, which I do not understand: "Is the statement in the programme that the scenery was designed by Lennox Robinson and painted by Seaghan Barlow a subtle touch of humour?"

The notice in the *Irish Independent* is brief and unfriendly. The reviewer, like Henderson, comments on Yeats's apparent attitude toward marriage:

A good deal of cleverness is displayed in the construction of one or two dramatic incidents, but an atmosphere is occasionally created in which it seems natural enough to hear expressions loosely and indiscriminately flung around which suggest strange ideas as to the sanctity of marriage. This is not the only thing that will grate on many to be found among Dublin audiences.

A longer review in the *Evening Telegraph,* signed with the initials J.A.P. (Henderson lists a J. A. Power among the members of the audience), is the least friendly of all. He repeats the allusion to Alice and adds a new comparison of Septimus to Villon, which he elaborates. His title is indicative of the tone of his review: "Mr. W. B. Yeats Out with Muck Rake." J.A.P. begins by saying that *The Player Queen* is a riddle that Yeats has intentionally concocted: "he gave us a Unicorn to parallel Lady Gregory's Dragon [Lady Gregory's *The Dragon* had been first produced at the Abbey 21 April 1919] and threw in a party of strolling players, masked as a section of the Ark's population, to make weight."

He goes on to say that Yeats "glimpsed Ruritania in the Celtic Twilight and resurrected François Villon and sent him reeling drunk through the lantern lit streets of its capital." Septimus's morals are no better than Villon's, but "Mr. Yeats has a whim [for] stark portraiture when he thinks it will annoy commonplace respectability." We should be grateful that Yeats concentrates on Septimus's drunkenness rather than his amours, wherein he seems to equal Villon. The present Yeats is then contrasted with the former:

> It is indeed a far cry from the Yeats of "Cathleen Ni Houlihan" to the Yeats of "The Player Queen." Scant trace is there in this affair of the mystic poet of bygone days or of the skilled playwright of the earlier Abbey.

J.A.P. then discusses the acting and is friendly toward the actors, whom he regards as struggling with impossible roles. He says of the wonderful exchange between Nona and Decima as to which of them Septimus loves: "One did not envy these ladies the 'big scene' which gave them most chance. The unsavouriness of the dialogue was unredeemed by any scintilla of style or any flash of genuine poetry. It grated, tighten one's nerves how one would." Comments on various technical aspects of the production follow, such as the settings and the handling of the crowd scenes. He liked the setting of Scene I but not of Scene II and thought the crowds poorly handled, perhaps because of the smallness of the Abbey stage. Here is his conclusion:

> When it was all over there was some applause. I think it would have been less were it not that the audience wished to show their appreciation of the players. But there were large areas of silence in every section of the house. A great many people, it was clear, were conscious of an unpleasant taste in the mouth.
>
> I wonder what the next freak play at the Abbey will be like. And if they will offer a prize of a season ticket for the best solution.

Given the conventionality of these responses to *The Player Queen,* it seems to me almost certain that, if Septimus's lines announcing the end of the Christian Era had been in the text of the play, some or perhaps all of the reviewers would have commented on them. That they make no such comment is for me good evidence that the text used in this production was Draft 31 and that Yeats made the additions discussed in the next section of this chapter before having the play printed in 1922. The year 1919 is not too early a date for the expression in Yeats's work of the concept that the Christian Era was ending, for he had completed "The Second Coming" in January; but, since none of the reviewers of *The Player Queen* mentions what would have been to them a shocking idea, I feel as sure as one can in the absence of a prompt book that Yeats had not yet added those speeches by Septimus to his text.

Yeats printed *The Player Queen* in three separate places in November 1922: Macmillan published the play in *Plays in Prose and Verse* and also as a separate volume, and it appeared in the November issue of *The Dial* (along with Eliot's *The Waste Land*). The two Macmillan texts are identical, and they may even have been printed from the same plates with changed page numbers. The *Dial* text represents a slightly earlier version of the play: after making the *Dial* text Yeats revised Scene II at lines 381–416 and 459–63 and dropped lines 484, 551, and 559–60. Since these variants have been printed in Russell Alspach's *Variorum Edition* of the plays, they are ignored here, and the discussion that follows compares the latest draft versions with the Macmillan texts.

Scene I. Lines 51, 175–77, 279–82, and 334–35 were changed from the form they have in Draft 31. At lines 279–82 Yeats added a swan image to express Sepitmus's inspiration: "and my breast feathers thrust out and my white wings buoyed up with divinity." All other changes are of wording only. Scene I reaches final form in the 1922 Macmillan texts.

Scene II. Yeats made a great many changes in Scene II, though only a few of them alter his meaning in any important way. The textual problem is further complicated by the fact that Yeats made additional changes for *Collected Plays,* 1934. These will be considered by themselves. The present discussion is concerned only with changes made in the 1922 text after Draft 31 had been finished.

1. Changes in style occur at lines 81–82, 103, 126, 131, 133, 135, 139–41, 170–71, 182, 204, 214, 406–8, 410a, 418–21, 464, 475–77, 486, 497, 535–36, 589, and 659. These changes, most of which are slight, do not seem to me to affect the meaning. The other changes do.

2. I group here changes which make Yeats's meaning clearer or slightly change it but which could not be called radical alterations: At lines 468–69 Yeats changes "shall save the *symbols* and implements of our art" to "shall save the *images* . . ." [Editor's italics]. Yeats in Draft 29 has Septimus make a number of references to Plutarch's *Lives* in the scene following his entry from the town at line 380: "Open Plutarch, close the book of life, prepare your dying speeches" and so on. He took some of these out when preparing Draft 31 and revised lines 400–404 and 541–43 again before the 1922 printings. I don't know why he made this change, unless the allusions seemed to him to make the passage too dense. It is very dense as it stands.

3. Yeats made a number of changes which fit the play more tightly into his emerging "system." This was his own term for his personal myth, which was nearing completion by 1922. He had added the principle of Unity of Being in *If I were Four-and-twenty* in 1919 and at the time of publication was at work elaborating his own cyclic view of history, printed in "Dove or Swan" in the first edition of *A Vision,* in 1925. Yeats added to the 1922 *Player Queen* passages that relate it to Unity of Being and to the cycles. What he does is to enlarge the myth of the Unicorn so that it will include these elements. Here are the more important additions.

Lines 381–84:

Gather about me, for I announce the end of the Christian Era, the coming of a New Dispensation, that of the New Adam, that of the Unicorn; but alas, he is chaste, he hesitates, he hesitates.

Lines 387–88:

His unborn children are but images; we merely play with images.

Line 396: "Because we are the servants of the Unicorn."

Lines 405–7:

I will rail upon the Unicorn for his chastity. I will bid him trample mankind to death and beget a new race.

Lines 459–64:

When my master the Unicorn bathes by the light of the Great Bear, and to the sound of tabors, even the sweet river water makes him drunk; but it is cold, it is cold, alas! it is cold.

Though lines 479–84 were nearly finished in Draft 31, I record the 1922 version here for the sake of completeness. The phrase I have italicized is new:

Man is nothing till he is united to an image. Now the Unicorn is both an image and beast; that is why he alone can be the new Adam. When we have put all in safety we will go to the high tablelands of Africa and find where the Unicorn is stabled *and sing a marriage song.* I will stand before the terrible blue eye.

Then Yeats adds to line 491 "The oracle is chaste" and rounds out the earlier version of Lines 493–94 by writing: "If we cannot fill him with desire he will

Figure 1. Endpapers of The Dome *in the years 1898–1899. From Giorgio Melchiori,* The Whole Mystery of Art *(New York: The Macmillan Company, 1961).*

1. End-papers of *The*

in the years 1898–9.

deserve death." Line 509 becomes "The Unicorn will be terrible when it loves."
In lines 530–31 and 541–43 Septimus associates himself with what he has said
about the Unicorn:

> Never trust a man who has not bathed by the light of the Great Bear. . . .
> Shall I be forsworn before the very eyes of Delphi, so to speak, before
> the very eyes of that cold, rocky oracle?

And, a little later, in lines 550–53, the added phrases which I have italicized
announce again that the Christian Era has come to an end:

> I shall die railing upon that beast. *The Christian era has come to an end,*
> *but* because of the machinations of Delphi he will not become the new
> Adam.

Yeats added lines 559–60; I do not know whether they refer to Septimus, to
the Unicorn, or to both:

> a violent virginal creature, that is how it is put in 'The Great Beastery of
> Paris.'

Finally, just before his exit at lines 579–80, Septimus says, and I italicize the
added words:

> *But not one word of Delphi.* I am extraordinarily wise.

4. I reproduce the 1922 version of the end of the play here to get the whole
of that text before us. It has been considerably revised since Drafts 29 and 31.

Her Majesty, who has	678
hitherto shut herself away from all men's eyes that	679
she might pray for this kingdom undisturbed, will	680
henceforth show herself to her people. (*To Player*	681
Queen.) So beautiful a queen need never fear the	682
disobedience of her people (*Shouts from crowd of*	683
'*never*'.)	
Prime Minister (*entering hurriedly*). I will explain all,	684
your Majesty—there was nothing else to be done	685
—This Bishop has been summoned to unite us (*seeing*	686
the Queen); but, sleep of Adam!—this—who is this?	687
Decima. Your emotion is too great for words. Do not	688
try to speak.	689
Prime Minister. This—this!	690
Decima (*standing up*). I am queen. I know what it is to	691

be queen. If I were to say to you I had an enemy you 692
would kill him—you would tear him in pieces.
(*Shouts 'we would kill him,' 'we would*
tear him in pieces,' etc.) But I do not bid you kill 695
any one—I bid you obey my husband when I have 696
raised him to the throne. He is not of royal blood, 697
but I choose to raise him to the throne. That is my 698
will. Show me that you will obey him so long as I 699
bid you to obey.   (*Great cheering.*) 700

(*Septimus, who has been standing among the crowd, comes*
forward and takes the Prime Minister by the sleeve. Various
persons kiss the hand of the supposed Queen.)

Septimus. My lord, that is not the queen; that is my 701
    bad wife. (*Decima looks at them.*) 702
Prime Minister. Did you see that? Did you see the devil 703
    in her eye. They are mad after her pretty face, and 704
    she knows it. They would not believe a word I say; 705
    there is nothing to be done till they cool. 706
Decima. Are all here my faithful servants? 707
Bishop. All, your Majesty. 708
Decima. All? 709
Prime Minister (*bowing low*). All, your Majesty. 710
Decima (*singing*).

    She pulled the thread, and bit the thread 711
    And made a golden gown. 712

Hand me that plate of lobster and that bottle of wine.
While I am eating I will have a good look at my new man.

(*The plate and bottle of wine are handed to her. The*
bray of a donkey is heard and the Old Beggar is
dragged in.)

Bishop. At last we have found this imposter out. He 715
    has been accepted by the whole nation as if he were 716
    the Voice of God. As if the crown could not be 717
    settled firmly on any head without his help. (*Shouts* 718
    from the mob of 'imposter,' 'rogue,' etc.) It's plain
    that he has been in league with the conspirators, and 719

Figure 2. Robert Gregory's unicorn in a circle. From Discoveries; A Volume
of Essays *by William Butler Yeats (Dundrum: Dun Emer Press, 1907).*

DISCOVERIES; A VOLUME OF ESSAYS BY WILLIAM BUTLER YEATS.

DUN EMER PRESS
DUNDRUM
MCMVII

Figure 3. Sturge Moore's panel with a leaping unicorn and the words "Monoceros de Astris." From Reveries over Childhood and Youth *by William Butler Yeats (Churchtown, Dundrum: The Cuala Press, 1915).*

**REVERIES OVER CHILDHOOD AND
YOUTH BY WILLIAM BUTLER YEATS**

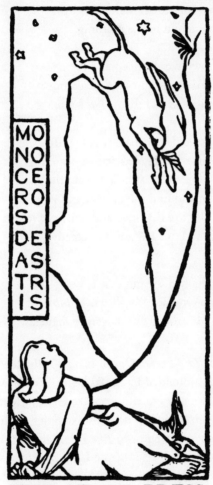

**THE CUALA PRESS
CHURCHTOWN
DUNDRUM
MCMXV**

believed that your Majesty had been killed. He is   720
keeping it up still. Look at his glassy eye. But his   721
madman airs won't help him now.   722
Prime Minister (*shaking Septimus*). Do you under-   724
stand that there has been a miracle, that God or the   725
Fiend has spoken, and that the crown is on her head   726
for good, that fate has brayed on that man's lips.   727
(*Aloud.*) We will hang him in the morning.   728
Septimus. She is my wife.   729
Prime Minister. The crown has changed and there is no   730
help for it. Sleep of Adam, I must have that woman   731
for wife. The Oracle has settled that. (*Take him   732
away to prison.*)
Septimus. She is my wife, she is my bad, flighty wife.   733
Prime Minister. Seize this man. He has been whispering   734
slanders against her Majesty. Cast him beyond the   735
borders of the kingom and find the company of players
he belongs to. They also are banished and must not return on
pain of death. Now, my Lord Bishop, I am ready.
Decima (*singing*).

> She wept because she had dreamt that I
> Was born to wear a crown. (*She flings the lobster's
> claw at the Prime Minister.*) Come—crack that claw.

The unicorn motif in *The Player Queen* is now fully developed, and we must
ask ourselves what Yeats intended by it. To begin, Yeats lived among unicorns,
so to speak; that is, with many unicorn icons, as Giorgio Melchiori has told us in
The Whole Mystery of Art. I will repeat his examples, adding a few he did not
cite. Yeats was a frequent contributor to *The Dome* during the years 1897–1900;
the unicorn was the badge or symbol of the Unicorn Press, which published this
magazine. It appeared there in two forms, one of which Melchiori prints (cf.
Fig. 1). Later the Cuala Press used three unicorn badges—Robert Gregory's
unicorn in a circle, first used in *Discoveries* (cf. Fig. 2); Sturge Moore's panel
with a leaping unicorn and the words "Monoceros de Astris," first used in
Reveries over Childhood and Youth (cf. Fig. 3); and Edmund Dulac's unicorn
in a rectangle commissioned for *A Vision* but used by the Press beginning with
Stories of Michael Robartes and His Friends (cf. Fig. 4). The bookplate that
Sturge Moore designed for George Yeats in 1918 (cf. Fig. 5) shows a unicorn

Figure 4. Edmund Dulac's unicorn in a rectangle. From Stories of Michael Robartes and His Friends: An Extract from a Record Made by His Pupils: And a Play in Prose *by W. B. Yeats (Dublin, Ireland: The Cuala Press, 1931).*

STORIES OF MICHAEL ROBARTES AND HIS FRIENDS: AN EXTRACT FROM A RECORD MADE BY HIS PUPILS: AND A PLAY IN PROSE BY W. B. YEATS.

THE CUALA PRESS
DUBLIN, IRELAND
MCMXXXI

Figure 5. Bookplate designed by Sturge Moore in 1918 for George Yeats. From Giorgio Melchiori, The Whole Mystery of Art *(New York: The Macmillan Company, 1961).*

Figure 6. Gustave Moreau, "Licornes."

leaping out of the ruins of a tower that has been struck by a bolt of lightning, a design Yeats greatly admired (See *Correspondence,* p. 35). A print of Gustave Moreau's "Licornes" (cf. Fig. 6) hung on the wall of Yeats's bedroom at Riversdale; presumably he had lived with it for years (cf. letter, 8 November 1936, in *Letters on Poetry,* p. 110).

In addition to these homely occurrences of the unicorn badge or emblem, Yeats must have frequently encountered it in art galleries, art books, and architectural monuments, for it is a common icon in European painting, illuminations, and tapestries from the Middle Ages down through the nineteenth century and is everywhere present in the decoration of medieval churches where the unicorn was carved in wood and stone and pictured in stained glass. Thomas Henn's view in *The Lonely Tower*—and it is elaborated by Melchiori—is that Yeats's favorite icons often came to him through the eye. I wholly agree. After all, he was son, brother, and father of painters and had thought of becoming a painter himself.

In Yeats's works, to turn to them, the unicorn is not as common as gyres or towers, but it does occur rather frequently. Here again I follow Melchiori, adding a few items: Its earliest *apparent* use occurs in "The Adoration of the Magi" (1897); in fact, this is the *latest,* for Yeats inserted the unicorn passage along with much else into the 1925 version of this story, printed in *Early Poems and Stories.* Actually the unicorn first appeared in Yeats's works in a charm he put into the 1906 version of *On Baile's Strand*:

> . . . for they anoint
> All their bodies joint by joint
> With a miracle-working juice
> That is made out of the grease
> Of the ungoverned unicorn.   [*Variorum Plays,* p. 497]

This seems little more than magic pharmacology, though "ungoverned" is suggestive. The unicorn does have a symbolic meaning in *The Unicorn from the Stars.* The words of the play as Yeats often said were largely by Lady Gregory, but he supplied its title from one of the grades in the Order of the Golden Dawn and apparently planned its symbolism. Martin dreams that the unicorn is a means used by God to destroy the world in order that a new dispensation may dawn. Yeats explained the symbol, something he rarely did, in a letter written to his sister Lolly while *Michael Robartes and the Dancer* was in press (1920): "The truth is that it is a private symbol belonging to my mystical order and nobody knows what it comes from. It is the soul" (*Letters,* p. 662), meaning thereby, I take it, the soul as destructive of mundane things. This takes us

Figure 7. Illustration to "The Book of Lambspring" in The Hermetic Museum Restored and Enlarged, *trans. A. E. Waite (London: Elliott and Company, 1893).*

Figure 8. The chariot of chastity. From Hypnerotomachia Poliphili *(Venice, 1499. Westmead, Farnborough, Hants: Gregg International Publishers, 1969).*

TRIVMPHVS

TERTIVS

to rituals of the Golden Dawn, and Israel Regardie tells us that the title *monoceros de astris* was given a novice of the order when he was admitted to its third grade, that of Practicus (*Golden Dawn,* II, 118). As far as I can discover, this constitutes the sole reference to the unicorn in the rituals of the Golden Dawn, and the order apparently never used it as an icon; at least it does not appear in any of Regardie's illustrations.

Yeats used a unicorn simile in "The Two Kings," which Richard Ellmann dates October 1912 (*Identity,* p. 294):

> They tugged and struggled there
> As though a stag and unicorn were met
> In Africa on Mountain of the moon.
> [Lines 18–20, early version. *Variorum Poems,* p. 277]

This confrontation recalls the plate from The Hermetic Museum which Melchiori prints (cf. Fig. 7), and follows standard unicorn lore in making its haunts the Mountains of the Moon in Abyssinia, where Septimus imagines them still to be. Then, in the seventh poem from "Meditations in Time of Civil War," under way while *The Player Queen* was going through the press in 1922, Yeats wrote

> Their legs long, delicate and slender, acquamarine their eyes
> Magical unicorns bear ladies on their backs. . . .
> The cloud-pale unicorns, the eyes of aquamarine . . .
> [Lines 17–18, 25. *Variorum Poems,* pp. 426–27]

This recalls Septimus's description of the unicorn's blue eye, but it is, I think, pictorial rather than symbolic, the uttermost contrast Yeats can think of to the "rage-hungry troop" of line 11. Yeats's description recalls the *Hypnerotomachia Poliphili,* one of the glories of the Aldine Press, wherein the chariot of Diana (chastity) is shown drawn by unicorns with ladies on their backs (cf. Fig. 8). Melchiori (pp. 113–14, 133–37) has written in detail of Yeats's knowledge of the *Hypnerotomachia,* from which he appears to have drawn part of his imagery for "Leda and the Swan."

All of this is something to go on, particularly the symbolic unicorn in *The Unicorn from the Stars,* but we must find the meaning of Yeats's myth within the developing text of *The Player Queen.*

It started back in Draft 6 with an allusion. In his prologue to the Noah play Septimus speaks of a gift from Kubla Khan and the Great Turk of twenty unicorns:

> But they die when their feet touch Ireland
> Because of St. Patrick's curse on all unchaste things.

Yeats was then thinking of the unicorn in terms exactly the opposite of the chastity symbol it becomes; indeed the successive allusions to the unicorn in the drafts of *The Player Queen* show a steadily increasing knowledge of unicorn lore. We then skip all the way to Draft 19, where Septimus describes Decima as "beautiful but flighty like the unicorn," and where the Prime Minister says rather cryptically at the end of the play, "I am their only substitute for a unicorn." This at least hints at the people's desire for a new revelation. In Draft 21 Yeats begins to develop his myth in Scene I: the Tapster repeats at second hand the story told by Strolling Michael that he has encountered and shot a unicorn in the environs of the Queen's castle and that it left blood upon a stone, that on another day he saw the Queen coupling with a unicorn. Septimus rises to defend the unicorn's chastity. This defense is elaborated in Draft 22, where Septimus's long speech beginning at line 293 first occurs to the effect that the unicorn is a "heroic brute" without a "smirch or a blot." Scene II in Draft 21 does not carry on the unicorn theme, though it occurs in the same manuscript as Scene I. There is only a repetition of Septimus's description of Decima from Draft 19 as quoted above, nothing more. The result is that the two parts of the play are decidedly out of balance; Yeats does not pursue in Scene II the unicorns that he starts in Scene I.

In drafts of Scene II, which I have placed after Draft 22, Yeats slowly expands the unicorn theme. In Draft 24 the Prime Minister, when confronted by evidence of the Queen's "sin," says, "I have begun to believe in the unicorn." Then in Draft 25 the Queen and her attendants enter carrying a banner with a unicorn upon it. They explain the relation of the unicorn to Christ by inventing a fable that has the unicorn take the place of the tired ass on the flight into Egypt. This is quickly dropped, perhaps because it is confusing on the symbolic level—it has a common Christ-symbol aiding Christ's escape from Herod. Then in Draft 26 Yeats for the first time suggests Septimus's drunken idea that the unicorn may become progenitor of a new age: Septimus says: "O that the unicorn would engender upon some woman another race. . . . I am full of sorrow because of the chastity of the unicorn." In Draft 28 Yeats elaborates the sentences just quoted. Septimus says he will "continue to rail upon the unicorn" because he will not engender a new mankind. He goes on to state the central theme of the play in the words, "Man is nothing till he is united to an image," presumably with such an image as the unicorn. Septimus will hunt the unicorn in Africa, where they will both be killed; later, while expecting the arrival of the mob, he says: "I shall die railing upon that beast because, owing to a pedantic scruple or some congenital chill of the blood, he will not become the new Adam."

In Draft 29, the final surviving draft of the full play before its publication, Yeats copies out Draft 22 of Scene I exactly, but in Scene II he makes several additions to the unicorn myth: He has the Queen speak of the unicorn as associated with her patron, St. Octema. Septimus says all the things he has said in Draft 28, and Yeats begins to elaborate them. His railing is given these words:

> Upon the round blue eye I rail
> Damnation on the milk-white horn.

He repeats his plan to hunt the unicorn in Africa, and also his speech while expecting the mob. He leaves the stage with Nona while repeating the lines above. All this was completed in the published version of the play, where Yeats added the material quoted under 3 above (cf. pp. 421–24): to summarize it, when Septimus enters at line 380, he announces the end of the Christian Era and hopes for the coming of a new dispensation wherein the unicorn will be the New Adam. He fears the new age will not dawn because the unicorn hesitates out of his love of chastity, hence his unborn children are but images. But, says Septimus, we artists are servants of the unicorn, we must persuade him to abandon his chastity by singing him marriage songs and playing him Ionian music, trying by these means to overcome the chaste influence of the Delphic oracle. We must do this because only the unicorn, who is both image and beast, "can be the new Adam." When Septimus leaves the stage with Nona, he leaves, half hoping, half despairing: though the Christian Era has come to an end, the unicorn will not, he fears, become the new Adam because of the machinations of Delphi; still his last words are, "But not one word of Delphi." He has said earlier, "The unicorn will be terrible when he loves."

We have here the earliest use by Yeats of the myth of the beast-god who impregnates a mortal woman and begets a new age. The myth is fully stated in "Leda and the Swan," which Yeats wrote in 1923, the year after publication of *The Player Queen*. Yeats returned to the theme with tantalizing vagueness in "What Magic Drum" (published 1935) from "Supernatural Songs." Indeed the theme of the mortal woman with god in her womb fascinated Yeats, as "The Mother of God" shows. For Yeats an age began with the birth of its god, and Septimus, the artist, wants the age that will follow the Christian Era to be begotten by the unicorn. From the 1890s Yeats had been announcing the birth of new ages. Poems such as "The Secret Rose" and stories such as "Rosa Alchemica" and "The Adoration of the Magi" are full of apocalyptic feeling.

Figure 9. "Santa Giustina of the Belvedere" by Alessandro Buonvicino, called Moretto.

The theme is carried forward in *The Unicorn from the Stars,* where already the unicorn is thought of as an apocalyptic beast who will trample the old order to pieces under his hooves. The very image of trampling to pieces is carried over into *The Player Queen.* If the unicorn should become the god of the new era, it would be an age characterized by Unity of Being, for the unicorn is both beast and image; that is, both face and mask. If we regard "The Second Coming," in which Yeats tells of the sphinx coming to life in the desert and slouching "towards Bethlehem to be born" as an expression of his fears for the age that was aborning, then we may say that *The Player Queen* expresses what Yeats, part of the time at least, extravagantly hoped. Surely an age whose presiding deity is a unicorn, emblem of Unity of Being, will be different from and better than an age whose presiding deity is a sphinx.

Trouble comes from the fact that unicorn lore is no longer widespread: whereas every schoolboy knows that Zeus took the form of a swan when he begot on Leda a new age, few schoolboys or even schoolmasters know that the unicorn haunted the imagination of Europe from Ctesias, who wrote in the fifth century B.C., to the end of the nineteenth century. Through the ages there developed around this central symbolic meaning a congeries of related meanings, many of which Yeats explores. What follows depends wholly on C. G. Jung's "The Paradigm of the Unicorn" (Jung, *Psychology and Alchemy,* pp. 415–51) and Odell Shepard's *The Lore of the Unicorn.*

In following Yeats's spreading circle from the image of the god-beast who might start a new cycle, we begin as Yeats began with the unicorn as a symbol of chastity. This was a late development but iconographically a very widespread one. From it grew the association of the unicorn with saintly and chaste women. Yeats invented St. Octema, but he did not invent showing a saintly woman accompanied by a unicorn; it is always shown in pictures of St. Justina, for example (cf. Fig. 9; Shepard, Plate VIII). I agree with William Becker (pp. 95–96) that what the goatboy saw through the castle window was the Queen and her unicorn, perhaps with its head on her lap as in so many medieval pictures (cf. Fig. 10). The unicorn is the emblem of her saintly life, or, if we look back to the central meaning of the symbol, the unicorn is Christ (cf. Fig. 11), and the Queen who has always wanted to be a nun is bride of Christ. The goatboy's misinterpretation is a sign of his brutal nature, of his goatishness. But Yeats's readers must supply the proper traditional icon, as Septimus instantly does.

Other elements in the play can be related to the unicorn. Curiously enough the Talmud relates it to the story of the Deluge: the problem it treats is how the unicorn was saved from the flood, since it was far too large to enter the

Figure 10. The virgin capture, from Fabro's translation of Catelan's Histoire de la Licorne. *Reproduced from Odell Shepard,* The Lore of the Unicorn *(Boston and New York: Houghton Mifflin Company, 1930).*

Figure 11. Woodcut representing the Holy Hunt from Der beschlossen gart des rosenkrantz Marie, *1505, on folio x of* Das sechst buch. *Reproduced from Odell Shepard,* The Lore of the Unicorn *(Boston and New York: Houghton Mifflin Company, 1930).*

ark. The right answer is "They tied its horn to the ark" (cited by Jung, pp. 438–40). Now a Noah play has been present in *The Player Queen* from the very beginning, and we may well wonder if the late arrival of the unicorn is related to that fact. I do not surely know the answer, but such a bringing together of related elements is a very Yeatsian procedure.

Yet more curious is the fact that the unicorn as a Christ symbol was at times, though so far as I can discover very rarely, related to the creation of Eve during Adam's sleep. Jung in his Figure 248 (cf. our Fig. 12) prints an illumination from a fifteenth-century manuscript "Trésor de sapience" in the Bibliothèque de l'Arsenal, whose subject is the creation of Eve. God is in the center of the picture; Adam is asleep in the foreground; the figure of Eve rises from his side. Behind Eve is a figure of a unicorn, and at either side are birds, which I cannot interpret symbolically. Jung's caption reads, "The Creation of Eve, prefiguring the story of salvation; hence the presence of the unicorn." Now the Prime Minister's favorite oath, repeated several times, is "Sleep of Adam," and at the opening of Scene II, when he hears of Decima's trick, he recapitulates the story of Eve's creation: "O, Adam! why did you fall asleep in the garden? You might have known that, while you were lying there helpless, the Old Man in the Sky would play some prank upon you." One would give a great deal to know whether Yeats had ever seen a reproduction of this illumination.

In short, we find in *The Player Queen* a congeries of symbolic elements all of which are traditional and which are interrelated in tradition. As F. A. C. Wilson has shown in *W. B. Yeats and Tradition,* this frequent practice by Yeats makes his symbolism richer and hence more moving than any idiosyncratic, personally invented symbolism can ever be, even when his readers are not familiar with the traditional associations. What the mind of man has put together over the centuries somehow belongs together. Yeats could never have written Arnold's line "The unplumb'd, salt, estranging sea" ("To Marguerite—Continued"), for to Yeats the sea always stands for the sensual life, as it has stood for millennia.

Yeats last used the unicorn symbol when he rewrote "The Adoration of the Magi" for *Early Poems and Stories,* published in 1925. I cannot certainly date this revision, though clearly it was done after the Leda sonnet was written in 1923. Yeats violently reshaped his story, and, I think, spoiled it by thrusting into early Yeats many emblems from his later work. Along with the unicorn we find Leda and the swan. This disruption has caused difficulties for many Yeats scholars. In the original story there is no unicorn, nor any Leda, nor any

Figure 12. The creation of Eve, prefiguring the story of salvation: hence the presence of the unicorn. Trésor de sapience MS 5076 *(15th cent.), Paris Bibliothéque de l'Arsenal. Reproduced from C. G. Jung,* Psychology and Alchemy, *second edition, trans. R. F. C. Hull, Bollingen Series* XX *(Princeton University Press, 1968).*

swan. It is full of *fin de siècle* bilge and is very much in the mood of the poem "The Secret Rose." Yeats's late nineteenth-century magi receive a revelation from a dying harlot in Paris who prophesies the imminent arrival of a new age, an age wherein art has wholly displaced religion. The passage into which Yeats put the unicorn comes just after the "second eldest" of the magi has gone into trance and crowed like a cock, an incident Yeats seems to be remembering in the many drafts of *The Player Queen* where the Old Beggar crows like a cock whenever the throne changes. The magus speaks while entranced, as follows in the 1904 version:

> "Bow down before her from whose lips the secret names of the immortals, and of things near their hearts, are about to come, that the immortals may come again into the world. Bow down, and understand that when they are about to overthrow the things that are to-day and bring the things that were yesterday . . ." [*Tables of the Law*, p. 52]

In changing the scene Yeats has the harlot-goddess simulate birth pangs. Then the magus crows and goes into trance as before, but now he speaks these words:

> "The woman who lies there has given birth, and that which she bore has the likeness of a unicorn and is most unlike man of all living things, being cold, hard and virginal. It seemed to be born dancing; and was gone from the room wellnigh upon the instant, for it is of the nature of the unicorn to understand the shortness of life. She does not know it has gone for she fell into a stupor while it danced, but bend down your ears that you may learn the names that it must obey." Neither of the other two old men spoke, but doubtless looked at the speaker with perplexity, for the voice began again: "When the Immortals would overthrow the things that are to-day and bring the things that were yesterday . . ."
> [*Early Poems and Stories*, pp. 522–23]

This passage has caused all sorts of trouble in the interpretation of *The Player Queen,* since it introduces a harlot-goddess who miraculously gives birth to a unicorn, accompanied by the crowing of a cock. It surely explains, for instance, why Wilson finds in Decima such a harlot-goddess who may or will give birth to a new age of which the unicorn is sire, and so on (*W. B. Yeats and Tradition,* pp. 180–85). It has led critics, in Peter Ure's words, into "collating [*The Player Queen*] with Yeats's story" (*Yeats the Playwright,* p. 139).

My own conclusion is that this cannot profitably be done. The passage throws no light that I can see on the meaning of *The Player Queen.* It is merely another, for me, pinched and unhappy use of the unicorn as a traditional symbol of coldness and virginity. This is the only time in Yeats's writings that the unicorn seems to have pejorative associations. Differences between this story and *The Player Queen* are great: In the play all the associations with the unicorn are pleasant, even charming. In the story the Mary figure gives birth to a unicorn; in the play Septimus hopes that the unicorn will sire a new race of men on some unnamed woman and become the New Adam. He does not indicate in any way that he has picked Decima for this role; indeed, although she has been a bad wife, he wants her back.

CHAPTER SEVENTEEN

Draft 32

IN HIS RAPALLO NOTEBOOK labeled "D" on the cover and "A" on the flyleaf, Yeats wrote out a series of revisions of Scene II of *The Player Queen*. He included the substance of these but not too many of the actual words in the text of the play printed in *Collected Plays*, 1934. He may have made these changes, which he labeled "corrections for sake of dancers," for the revival of his play by the Cambridge Festival Theatre in the week beginning 16 May 1927. I cannot discover whether the dance elements in the play were enhanced in this production or not, but Ninette de Valois devised and staged the third part of the program, "A fourth series of dance-cameos." The page numbers to which Yeats refers in Draft 32 do not correspond to any printing of *The Player Queen*. They come closest to the numbers in the text of the play in *Collected Plays*, 1934, where the play is found on pages 387–430. I have no certain explanation of these facts. Perhaps Yeats's numbers refer to a set of page proofs of *Collected Plays;* Yeats often worked on page proofs, for he hated galley proof and his publishers frequently supplied page proof instead. If this explanation is correct, Yeats copied the changes into his manuscript book in order to have a record of them. That was a frequent practice.

Player Queen
corrections for sake of dancers

page 403

Delete from "Come live with me" to "understand that better"
on page 404 and insert following

Decima. Dance Bullhead—no, no, he is slow on the feet and heavy
in build and that means jealousy, and there is a sort
of melancholy in his voice. What a folly now that I
have found out love to stretch and yawn as if I loved.
Stop. I will not have you for my man. Dance, Turkey-cock,

dance. He is lively on his feet and he has a quick
eye, and that goes with a ready mind. But no, no,
stop, I will [not] have you [for] my man. I will not
have those round eyes fixed on me now that I will have
my mind go to sleep. Yet what do I care who it is, so
that I choose and am done with it. Dance all, dance,
and I will choose the best dancer among you.

page 407

Delete from "when we played" down to "nor I" page 408.

1 P. It is of me that they are jealous. They know
what happened at Xanadu. They know that when, after
[I] had played Agenor [?] in the old
play "The Fall of Troy," Kubla Khan sent [for] me and
said that he would give his kingdom for such a voice
and such a presence. It's where I reproach Helen
with all the deaths and misery she
had wrought.

2 P. My God, listen to him. Is [it] not always
the comedian who draws the crowd? Am I dreaming
or was it not I that was called six times before the
curtain. Answer me that.

1 P. What of that?
The players of this town are not jealous because of
the applause of crowds, that they have themselves, the
uneducated thought. What wrings them with agony is
that neither they nor any other player forever will
look as an equal into the eyes of Kubla Khan.

Stage Manager. Stop quarrelling with one another and
listen to what's happening out there. There is a
man making a speech and the crowd is getting
angrier, and which of you they are jealous of
I don't know, but they are looking this way and maybe
in a little they will all be coming up here with
wisps set upon dungforks to set fire to the place,
as this were Troy. And if you will do as I tell you, you will all
get out of this.

422
424
425
429
430
433
435
441
442
443
448

First Player. Must we go dressed like this?
   Then as before.

   page 409

Delete "cloak of Noah" insert "hat of"
Delete "and the golden face of the
Almighty" and "the horns of Satan"

Insert the following:

   and the mask of the sister of Noah. She was   471
   drowned because she thought her brother was telling   472
   lies, and yet we [undeciphered] the rosy cheeks and rosy mouth. I
   say that above all we must save that mask, that drowned,
   wicked, rosy mouth."

   page 410

Mask of Noah's Sister falls when hat of Noah does.

   page 413

after "he picks up Noah's hat with difficulty" insert "he tries to
pick up mask of Noah's sister but fails" and then insert in his speech
                 No, it may   570
   lie there. What have [I] to do with that drowned   571
   wicked mouth—beautiful, drowned, flighty mouth,   572
   I will not have anything to do with it, but I have saved
   the noble, high-crowned, etc.
[*Prime Minister.*] Cast him beyond the
   borders of the kingdom, and his players with him.
PQ. Let him be banished. He must not return upon pain
   of death, and his company of players are banished [with]
   him. He has wronged me; I will never look upon his
   face. What have I but my good name? But I will see
   the players before they go, and reward and praise them.
PM. Sleep of Adam! What is [she] going to do? Fetch the players.
PQ. Let them [be] well rewarded.
PM. They shall be well rewarded.
PQ. Not one of them must be poorer because he is banished.
   (*Players enter.*) Dance for me. You are all banished,
   but dance for me, and though you must not return on

pain of death you shall suffer [no] loss because of that.
One loss I would not remedy if I could, a woman player that
has left you. Do not mourn her. She was a bad, headstrong, cruel woman. Put her out of your minds forever.
I am told she was such a woman that this mask I wear
would well become her, this foolish, smiling face.
(*They dance, and at certain moments in the dance she
cries* "Good-bye, good-bye.")

759

Commentary

These changes provide a mask for Decima to wear while a final dance is given
by the company of players she has deserted. Presumably Yeats had been asked
to make an opportunity for a second dance, and perhaps it seemed better to
have Decima masked while in the company of her former companions. Or he
may simply have wished to round out his play with a symbolic object pointing
to the meaning: at the outset his two Old Men wear grotesque masks; at the
end Decima is masked. Since there is no Biblical authority for providing Noah
with a sister, doing so seems a little awkward. I cannot see that Yeats's other
changes, particularly those when the members of the troupe speak their past
successes in somewhat changed words, do anything to increase the opportunities
for the dancers, and I prefer the play with its 1922 ending. The dropping of
the stage direction that Yeats intended at line 570, "he tries to pick up mask
of Noah's sister but fails," obscures his intention to have the mask lying on
the stage for Decima's use at the end of the play.

When Yeats revised these additions before printing them in *Collected Plays*,
he did add one thing that slightly changes our conception of Decima's character. At lines 759–61 he has her say, "She . . . seeks destruction somewhere and
with some man she knows nothing of." This expression of uncertainty, perhaps
even of fear, about her new role makes her seem more human at the end, though
I am not sure that this is a good thing.

Yeats made a few other changes in his text when he revised the play for
Collected Plays: He dropped the line from the Prime Minister's speech to the
Queen which begins at line 76: "Give the people some plain image or they
will invent one." I wonder if this was an accident; I can see no reason for it.
At line 333, Scene II, he dropped the words "Play the lute" from "Here, Peter,

Play the lute." A slight revision at lines 546–47 makes things clearer: "They will come in there and there" becomes "They will come in through this door." At line 693 the phrase "would you not" was added to Decima's appeal to the crowd, and at 713–14 Decima's "Hand me that plate of lobster and that bottle of wine" is shortened to "Hand me that plate." In its original form it prepared for the curtain-line, now abolished, "Come—crack that claw." It was a good curtain line.

CHAPTER EIGHTEEN

Conclusion

THREE TASKS remain: (1) to look back over the long road we have traveled with Yeats in order to chart his movement down it precisely; (2) to speculate on why the play took so long; and (3) to ask whether the result was worth the effort expended. I propose to deal with the first task by categories: the protagonists and the evolution of their characters, the development of major incidents, the shift in style from high-flown verse to biting farce, and the evolution of the theme. I shall trace this evolution while performing the second task, citing certain aspects of Yeats's personal and intellectual biography to explain both the developing theme and why it took so long to write the play. The third task will involve an analysis of the play and an evaluation.

I.

The central triad of characters, two actresses and an actor-manager who were eventually to become Nona, Decima, and Septimus, are present from the outset; and along with them a Queen who wishes to be a nun, and her first minister. Yeats's conception of the Prime Minister was clear from the beginning, and the long process of his development does not show so much a change in his conceptions as a refinement of his ideas. The Prime Minister has—through all this process of refinement—been a hearty, bluff, no-nonsense kind of person, at once loyal to his Queen and personally ambitious. He has had no time for love or other aspects of the personal life, and at first he seems to regret what he has missed. For a long time Yeats involves him in an affair with Nona; later, the Minister plans to marry the Queen and is at once dismayed and pleased when he finds her metamorphosed into Decima. Yeats conceives of him as the total man of action, able and willing to deal with any and all events and not given to speculation. Yeats seems as impressed by the practical abilities he gives him as he was in fact with the practical abilities of his fellow senators in the 1920s.

The Queen whom the Prime Minister serves goes through a more complex evolution. Yeats always conceived of her as an ascetic, but for a long time could not decide whether to make her a militant saint bent on reforming the world according to her own notions of what is right, or a timid girl afraid of the world and its ways. This later conception is the one he finally chose.

The central triangle of characters did not always have that dramatically conventional conformation: though Nona always loved Septimus, he did not always love her. Eventually Septimus is shown in love with both fatal Decima and domestic Nona—a common enough configuration, though having the "other woman" be the one whose nature is domestic does ring a change. For a long time Yeats conceived of Nona as a woman who has to have a man and who, when she cannot have the man she wants, consoles herself with others; but in the end he makes her totally loyal to Septimus. Decima is conceived of initially as a hyperromantic, a would-be Iseult or Deirdre, anxious to cast Septimus as Tristram or Naoise, but above all a believer with Yeats that life should somehow partake of the enhancement of art. At first she thinks she would be content to play a traditional romantic role, but in time she comes to want only power and opportunities to show her power. These ends she pursues implacably—indeed implacability is perhaps finally her principal characteristic. Septimus, too, undergoes great change: at first he is brother to Aleel in *The Countess Cathleen,* blindly loyal to the woman he serves. He also shares with Decima something of Forgael's longing (*The Shadowy Waters*) for some impossibly exciting way of life. In the end he emerges as a conservator of traditional values and as a prophet who knows what is wrong with the world and would like to change it—in short, as an embodiment of Yeats's concept of the poet.

Only a few of the incidents that Yeats invented at the outset to embody his belief that the mask has greater force than the face beneath it survived in the finished play. Back in 1907 or 1908 Yeats thought to embody this theme by having a gifted actress who longed to play traditional romantic heroines become queen for a day during the course of a revolution in the state to which her troupe of strolling players has come. She makes an excellent queen, though the question of what to do with her once the revolution collapses and she doffs her mask, Yeats never answered satisfactorily. Should she be executed by the rebels, take her own life, or be content to return to her role as Noah's wife? Yeats found that only the third solution worked; he discovered, in short, that what he had written was technically a comedy. He then turned with relief to the Comic Muse and wrote the play we know. He achieved this by abandoning entirely the end in which Decima returns to her previous existence: at the end of the play she is totally in role; she is Queen indeed, and she has a new husband to go with her new life. She has made the mask prevail.

This change in concept demanded a wholly new style. Yeats first wrote a play in highly-charged verse; he then wrote the play we have, one of the best pieces of prose he was ever to achieve. He found that the events of the play as they worked out during actual composition resisted first a tragic and then even a serious tone. Through many drafts he wrote on the verge of bathos, then saw the implications of the fact that his play threatened to collapse into melodrama, and so shifted to prose and the comic mode. The final language of the play was achieved by writing many drafts marked by an increasing refinement of style, until he reached one kind of verbal perfection.

The evolution of the subject of the play through the proper wearing of the mask to the doctrine of the self and the anti-self and finally to a fable about Unity of Being can be dealt with in the next section while we speculate on why *The Player Queen* took so long.

2.

The play started out with what was at the beginning a rather simple concept, that of the mask. We have already quoted Yeats's 1909 statement on the mask, written in March when he was at work on the early drafts of the play, but it is worth quoting again:

> I think all happiness depends on having the energy to assume the mask of some other self; that all joyous or creative life is a rebirth as something not oneself, something created in a moment and perpetually renewed; in playing a game like that of a child where one loses the infinite pain of self-realization, a grotesque or solemn face put on that one may hide from the terrors of judgment, an imaginative Saturnalia that makes one forget reality.
>
> (From the MS. Yeats revised this for Section VI of "The Death of Synge") [Cf. *Memoirs*, p. 191. Gen. Ed.]

This states an idea, in other words an abstraction: turning it into a play was sure to be difficult, as Yeats knew from his earlier experience as a playwright.

He had described the difficulty in an entry written in the same Journal in January:

> In Christianity what was philosophy in Eastern Asia became life—biography, drama. A play passes through the same process in being written. At first, if it has psychological depth, there is a bundle of ideas, something that can be stated in philosophical terms; my *Countess Cathleen,* for instance, was once the moral question, may a soul sacrifice itself for a good end? But gradually philosophy is eliminated more and more until at last the only philosophy audible, if there is even that, is the mere expression of one character or another.
>
> (From the MS. Revised for "Estrangement," Section XVIII)
>
> [Cf. *Memoirs,* p. 150. Gen. Ed.]

To bring to dramatic life the notion that an actress might make a better queen than a queen born to the purple constituted Yeats's initial problem.

Yeats's interest in the mask had its origin in his own life experience. He was by temperament an artist and recluse; he wrote in the "First Draft of *Autobiographies"* that had it not been for Maud Gonne, he would perhaps never have left his desk. Maud Gonne entered his life, as he put it, with the clang of a gong, and he set about at least half-consciously to make himself into the kind of man that would interest her. He assumed the mask of a man of action. He became the great founder—O'Casey's nasty phrase—founding societies whose longevity troubled his own last years. He entered Nationalist politics and developed the ideal of "the movement," which was, to put it simply, that Ireland should emerge before the world, once independence had been won, with both a nation and a culture. From about 1898 on, most of his energies went into developing a national theater. The Abbey Theatre was founded in 1904. From 1904 to 1909 he found himself involved increasingly in the practical affairs of the Abbey. He had then, as later, to raise money; he was what we would now call the Abbey's public relations man; but after the trouble with the Fays he had to stage and rehearse plays as well. He thought, and often expressed the thought, that the heterogeneous activities of those years might forever dry up his well of poetry. Such writing as he found time for was largely dramatic, an effort to create an heroic drama using Irish themes and legends. Yeats often wrote—he says it three times in *Per Amica Silentia Lunae*—that in choosing a mask one should pick from those not impossible the mask most difficult to achieve. This he had surely done.

His personal situation when he began *The Player Queen* was, in short, not unlike the situation of Decima in the early drafts. Decima, born in a ditch between two towns, wrapped in a sheet stolen from a hedge, chooses to be queen. She succeeds, but only at the risk of her life. Perhaps her assumption of this mask will destroy her, as Yeats feared that becoming a successful man of the theater had destroyed his own poetic talent.

Once Yeats was relieved of the day to day running of the Abbey, it became clear that this had not happened. Indeed, the decade 1910–1920, during which *The Player Queen* was in process, was perhaps the most astonishingly productive in Yeats's long and always productive career. I do not know whether he was aware that his long immersion in "theatre business" had been good for his poetry, as Thomas Parkinson (*W. B. Yeats Self-Critic*) has clearly demonstrated that it was, but he must have realized how rich these years were. In addition to many magnificent poems—all of *Responsibilities, The Wild Swans at Coole,* and much of *Michael Robartes and the Dancer* were written in these years— Yeats began his *Autobiographies* and *A Vision*, wrote *At the Hawk's Well, The Dreaming of the Bones, Calvary;* all this and *The Player Queen.*

Once these fecund years had begun it became possible to think of the mask in a more relaxed way, as perhaps no more than an amusing plaything. Such a view would seem to explain those middle versions of *The Player Queen* in which Decima is quite content to doff the mask of queen once she has assured herself she can play the part, and return to playing Noah's wife. But I think Yeats was quite right when he claimed in his note to the play that the obstructive thing was the onset and slow development of the ideas expressed in "Ego Dominus Tuus" and *Per Amica Silentia Lunae:* the concept of the anti-self. The anti-self is more than a mask. It is your opposite, and not merely your temporal opposite, but your eternal opposite—your daimon, tutelary spirit, or guardian angel.

> I call to the mysterious one who yet
> Shall walk the wet sands by the edge of the stream
> And look most like me, being indeed my double,
> And prove of all imaginable things
> The most unlike, being my anti-self.
>
> [*Variorum Poems,* p. 371]

During these years Yeats was actively engaged in forming or discovering his own daimon or anti-self. He preferred one Petre the Malachite, a spirit of great dignity and power about whom Yeats has left only a fragmentary record in his esoteric journals, but another spirit claiming to be Leo Africanus moved in on him, so to speak, in 1912 and claimed quite bluntly to be his anti-self. Yeats never really took to Leo Africanus or his claims; on this occasion as on others the esoteric world didn't produce exactly what Yeats wanted. But, to return from the esoteric to the mundane text of the play, Decima, whether she knows it or not, expresses the concept of the anti-self when in many late versions of the play she says something like this: "Septimus told me once that nobody finds their genius till they have found some role, some image, some pose that liberates something within them or beyond them that had else been dumb and numb" (Draft 21).

Yeats's thought culminates in the ideal of Unity of Being, which grows out of the concept of the anti-self. We achieve Unity of Being when there is a complete coherence between the self and the anti-self, when face and mask wholly conform to each other. The concept emerged late in Yeats's thought, though Decima's speech quoted above clearly points toward it. But it had fully emerged by 1919, the year of the production of *The Player Queen*, in his noble essay *If I were Four-and-twenty*. He expresses the concept of Unity of Being everywhere in his later work, but perhaps most memorably in the final stanza of "Among School Children":

> O chestnut-tree, great-rooted blossomer,
> Are you the leaf, the blossom or the bole?
> O body swayed to music, O brightening glance,
> How can we know the dancer from the dance?
> [*Variorum Poems,* p. 446]

It is a very ancient ideal, of course, eventually Greek. Its value comes not from its originality but from the beauty and force of Yeats's many expressions of it. Surely Decima achieves at least tentative Unity of Being when she becomes the queen she has pretended to be. In his latest revision of the play Yeats lets us know that she is uncertain of her fate in her new role: "She . . . seeks destruction somewhere and with some man she knows nothing of." But for the moment she is queen, and we leave her queening it to the top of her bent.

So the answer to the second question is Yeats's own answer: *The Player Queen* took so long because it embodies many aspects of what Yeats came to call his "system," his personal philosophy expressed in *Per Amica Silentia Lunae, Autobiographies,* and *A Vision:* the mask, the self and the anti-self, Unity of Being. He could not finish the play until he had worked out these aspects of his system. During the years he was at work on it the concepts he was expressing were changing and deepening, refusing to remain static. No wonder Yeats had so hard a time transfusing them into life and drama. His situation was like the one his father had experienced many years before when painting the pond near Farnham Royal:

> He began it in spring and painted all through the year, the picture changing with the seasons, and gave it up unfinished when he had painted the snow upon the heath-covered banks.
>
> ["Reveries over Childhood and Youth," v, *Autobiography*, p. 17]

But the younger Yeats was able, as he nearly always was, to finish his picture.

3.

A considerable body of criticism has developed around *The Player Queen* since William Becker's pioneer discussion of it in "The Mask Mocked: Or, Farce and the Dialectic of Self," *Sewanee Review* 61, 1 (Winter 1953): 82–108. Becker's is still one of the best essays, though I am glad I did not see the production he describes. Five years later appeared Norman Newton's "Yeats the Dramatist," in *Essays in Criticism* 8 (1958): 269–84, and F. A. C. Wilson's *W. B. Yeats and Tradition* (London, 1958, pp. 180–85). Giorgio Melchiori included his study of the unicorn symbol in Yeats's total work in *The Whole Mystery of Art,* published in England in 1960 and in the United States in 1961 (pp. 35–72). In 1963 Peter Ure and Helen Vendler discussed the play, Ure in *Yeats the Playwright* (New York, 1936, pp. 134–45) and Vendler in *Yeats's "Vision" and the Later Plays* (Cambridge, Mass., 1963, pp. 124–38). As I write, John Rees Moore has just published his essay "The Janus Face" in the Winter 1968 issue of the *Sewanee Review* (pp. 608–30). [Included in Moore's *Masks of Love and Death* (Ithaca and London, 1971), pp. 164–92. Gen. Ed.] Critical opinion has been divided rather sharply, ranging from enthusiastic praise to the expression of serious reservations. Though I shall not attempt to restate the arguments of these critics, I cite them to show what lies behind my own considerations. I have learned from all of them, not least when I thought them wrong.

I greatly admire Yeats's plays, and among them would place *The Player Queen* high. I think Yeats is at his very best as a dramatist in short plays such as *The Dreaming of the Bones, A Full Moon in March,* and *Purgatory,* plays in which the traditional theater is pared to the bone. The casts have been reduced to two or three persons, the action to some single intense situation; they might almost be called anti-dramas, if we accept as drama what generally passes for it.

In such plays Yeats's tremendous lyric power is seen at its most intense. But among his plays which use large casts and exploit more of the traditional resources of the theater, plays like *The Green Helmet* and *The Herne's Egg,* we must, I think, place *The Player Queen* in the first rank. I think so first of all because, if we consider it for a moment just as a work of style, it is a triumphant success. Of the play's critics only Becker has made any objections to its style, and he only to the speeches of the Citizens and Countrymen in Scene I. Becker is simply wrong in his objections to these speeches; indeed, his own text shows that Yeats has accomplished exactly what he wanted to accomplish—that is, to convey to us by the most economical means the simple-mindedness and brutality of these folk. If one thinks for a moment of how rarely in literature the rhetorical mode that farce demands has been achieved and sustained (one can only think of such giants as Aristophanes and Molière), we must say that the style of *The Player Queen* is almost a miracle. It ranges all the way from the brutal speech of the Big Countryman, through the Molièresque exchange between Nona and Decima in Scene II, to Septimus's extravagant rhetoric, and it never flags. Style is the surest hallmark that a work of art has been achieved, the made thing totally made, and *The Player Queen* has this hallmark on every page.

Its genre is one that Yeats largely invented, the heroic farce, and only he has practiced it. Its brothers are *The Green Helmet* and *The Herne's Egg.* Yeats never said much about the heroic farce compared, say, with his discussion of the play for dancers. For me it is one of his most original and happy achievements. An heroic farce is first of all farce; it shares with other varieties of farce extravagant characters involved in impossible events, but to this it adds the spoofing of elements from the tradition of heroic poetry. Here the aspects of heroic poetry which have been reduced to the dimensions of farce are less obvious than in the other plays in this mode; we have, for instance, no characters drawn from Ireland's heroic legends. But the plot elements used are of heroic size: revolution, a change of rulers, and so on. Another element found in Yeats's heroic farces is a tangential relevance to contemporary events: in one of its dimensions *The Green Helmet* is about the *Playboy* crisis, about an Ireland where everybody was trying to outshout everybody else; *The Herne's Egg* is about the desperate moral and political climate of the 1930s, *The Player Queen* about the European situation following the first World War: after all, it appeared the same year as *The Waste Land* and *Ulysses.* Therefore, all three of Yeats's plays in this genre are concerned with very serious matters which the author has decided for the moment to laugh at rather than to cry over. He has chosen another way of speaking, put on another mask; in his own words, quoted earlier, he has assumed the "grotesque" in place of the "solemn face" of prophet-poet, which he usually wore when speaking his great poems. Or, to change the metaphor, he uses another stick to beat the donkey—that is to say, the intellectually unwashed—in all times and all places.

As for the text of the finished play, the first thing we notice is that Becker was absolutely right about its double plot: By the end of 1915 Yeats had achieved a play about the mask. Decima, born in a ditch and wrapped in a sheet stolen from the hedge, is behaving in a proper Yeatsian way when she chooses the opposite or anti-self hardest for her to achieve—that of Queen. First she gets a chance to play Queen, and she plays it very well; then all in a moment she is Queen, and we have no doubt she will do that very well too. Late in the process of making his play, Yeats superimposed on this plot one of his myths of the birth of a new age, wrote of another second coming, that of the unicorn. The critical problem this fact poses is the problem of fit—can Yeats bring the two themes together in a single play successfully? I think he can and does. If Decima is ever to have the chance of wearing the mask of Queen, some disturbance of the political order must provide it. What can provide it so well as a revolution? Indeed revolution has been present since the first scenario. Modern revolutions, notably the French and the Russian, have in fact been interpreted by some of their protagonists and observers as the dawns of new ages; once the inevitable disillusion sets in, these are seen to be false dawns, but that is a morning-after effect. Several observers have noted that the revolution in *The Player Queen* is of the comic-opera kind. At the outset the Prime Minister has power, at the end he keeps power. But no other kind of revolution would fit Yeats's rhetorical mode, and, if we think of the play as a paradigm of events going on in the world, the putting together of a peculiar concern of Yeats, the achieving of the anti-self, with something of wider concern, this seems a happy solution. One trouble with the early versions of the play is a sheer lack of weight; it hardly seems that the theme of achieving the mask can sustain a play.

What is going on beneath the frivolous surface is deadly serious, a play of ideas. All the play's critics note this, and it is usually the cause of their quarrel with it, when they quarrel. They do not find it self-contained; members of its audience would, they insist, have to go outside the play to other works of Yeats's in order to grasp what he is saying. Of course the spectator who knows his Yeats will get more out of the play than one who does not, but I think this is inevitable with any artist; for the full enjoyment of any work of art, the context of the total work of the artist is essential. It seems to me that the ideas Yeats explores are not difficult. The achieving of the anti-self is no doubt Yeatsian, though ideas similar to it have been common in Western thought from the Greeks through the Renaissance and into modern times. It is one form of the search for the rich, many-faceted personality that has been the goal of so many thinkers from Plato through Mann. As for the apocalypse for which Septimus longs, surely this is in no sense peculiarly Yeatsian; surely it has been one of the commonest themes in European literature from the 1890s on. Everywhere we turn we find the theme of the destruction of the old order handled either in realistic terms or in paradigm, followed by hopes for a new and better order. The noise in the street, the crashing glass and toppling masonry of Stephen Dedalus's nightmare, has haunted the European mind.

Let me sustain the argument by noting very briefly what I think the play says; I do not exactly agree with any of the readings made by other critics, who in my opinion tend to push the text too hard. The scene opens at night, though soon the first streaks of dawn light up the castle tower. The Old Men are commenting on some still not defined disturbance of the social order when a drunk poet staggers onto the stage looking for his wife. She has hidden herself, although she is to play Noah's wife in "The Tragical History of Noah's Deluge" in the castle at noon. Two poets come in from a night at a brothel. Septimus asks them for help. They exchange credentials, so to speak; Septimus insults them by calling them "bad, popular poets" while he claims to be the most famous poet in the world, and they go out without helping him. A group of would-be revolutionaries comes in; they see Septimus, and one of them rolls him off the street. Then the townsmen in the group explain the cause of their revolt to the countrymen. Their Queen has for seven years lived a recluse life; rumors have circulated that she is a witch who copulates with a great white unicorn. The crowd plans the Queen's death. Septimus, who as poet is inheritor of traditional images, rises from his gutter to defend the unicorn's chastity with extravagant rhetoric. In short, Yeats tells us immediately after introducing the unicorn symbol that it stands for chastity, one of its central meanings in tradition. This embroils Septimus with the crowd, and he gets knocked down by the Big Countryman, whom he has insulted. The crowd goes off to storm the Queen's castle, but returns in a moment because it has encountered an Old Beggar with prophetic powers—he rolls on his back and brays like a donkey whenever the crown changes. The crowd leaves, and Septimus sits up and is rubbing his broken head when the Old Beggar enters. He knows that the crown is about to change and is on his way to the castle where he expects to perform his prophetic function. At the end of the scene, he and Septimus, supporting each other, stagger off toward the castle. A poet does not fear a prophet, since prophets are merely another vehicle for the divine afflatus. Surely this fills the Aristotelean prescription for a beginning; it does not require anything to precede it; something else must naturally follow it. And Yeats has established his fairy tale atmosphere of far away and long ago, replete with reports of recluse queens, witchcraft, unicorns, and so on.

Scene II opens with the Prime Minister in a rage at the hidden Decima, a tight link back to Scene I. Her disappearance will prevent the giving of the play, and to the Prime Minister even the least change of plan seems at the moment dangerous to the state. The actors leave, and the Queen enters in a badly-fitting robe of state which has belonged to her mother. She at once fears and is eager for martyrdom at the hands of her rebellious subjects. We hear more of the unicorn, who was associated with the Queen patroness, holy St. Octema; again such an association is traditional. The Queen is by nature a recluse and ascetic, quite unfitted for the role into which she has been born. She and the Prime Minister leave for a progress into town after he has told her twice that he has a plan to save her from martyrdom. Nona comes in and baits a trap for Decima by laying a plate of lobster and a bottle of wine on the floor. During the scenes with the players and with the Queen, Decima has been sticking her head out from under the throne where she has hidden. Now she comes out, singing verses of the song beginning "My mother dandled me and sang." She is just about to grab the lobster when Nona catches her and says she is not to have her breakfast till she is dressed for her part. Nona never succeeds in getting Decima into costume, but she does prevent her from eating, so that Decima is still hungry at the end of the play. Decima expresses her longing for an anti-self, that is for queen roles, and criticizes the performance of the actual Queen. She hates the part of Noah's wife, and rather than play it is quite content to have Septimus go to jail, where he will come to love her more than ever. Nona attacks Decima for her lack of feeling, and says she will take the part herself. She dares to take this strong line because Septimus is her lover. In the quarrel that follows between the two women, Decima cites poems Septimus has written in praise of her beauty as proof that he loves her, only to learn that he has composed the poems while in bed with Nona, who is altering the Noah's wife costume to fit herself when the Stage Manager comes in with the other players dressed as birds and beasts. Decima claims she was sick of Septimus, and stages an impromptu ballet of the costumed players, saying she will choose for her new lover the player who dances best. The songs that they sing while dancing are full of allusions to women who took brute lovers, a theme that anticipates the Leda sonnet. Septimus comes in and stops the ballet.

Septimus announces the end of the Christian Era; with the traditional enthusiasm of the poet, he had mistaken a revolution that will shortly abort for the end of the old order and the birth of a new and better order. He hopes the new age will be the age of the unicorn, for the unicorn, who is both an image and a beast, would preside over an age whose ideal would be Unity of Being. But this is all poetry, as they say, and even in his inspired condition Septimus knows it. Still, he has no doubt about his duty as an artist; he longs for a new age, although he knows that its dawn is unlikely, and meanwhile he saves the "images and implements" of traditional art. He leaves, hoping still to persuade the unicorn to become the new Adam, for as he leaves with Nona he says, "But not one word of Delphi." Delphi, surely representative of the classical age that was displaced by Christianity, does not want the new age to dawn.

The plot goes on its extravagant way in a series of mad reversals. Thwarted Decima meets the Old Beggar, who predicts a change of ruler and the death of the Queen. She is thinking of taking her own life when the Queen enters, fleeing from the mob. Decima offers to take her place, puts on the Queen's robe, and seats herself on the throne as the real Queen escapes to a convent. A Bishop enters to tell the "Queen" that the revolution is over: "All has been settled by your condescension in bestowing your royal hand on the Prime Minister." This was the Prime Minister's plan for saving the Queen's life and, though he has not mentioned it, fufilling his own ambition. He enters. He has never seen Decima before and knows she is not the Queen. The crowd is wildly enthusiastic about her, however, and she makes the Prime Minister aware that since the crowd is wholly with her, he can only gain his ends by agreeing to a marriage to which he hardly seems averse. The end is a masterpiece of cruelty and wild event. Decima is still hungry, so she asks for and gets the lobster and wine Nona had denied her. The Old Beggar brays to mark the change of throne, but is dragged in and accused of conspiracy. The Prime Minister says, "Carry him to prison, we will hang him in the morning." And, when Septimus insists on iden-tifying Decima as his bad wife, the Prime Minister orders him cast out of the kingdom. Decima seems firmly on the throne; she has become what she once hoped only to play at being, a Queen—this whether one takes the 1922 or 1934 ending. The play ends with the *gamos* as loved by Aristophanes. There is an element of cruelty in all farce; it is to be doubted whether Socrates found *The Clouds* funny. There does seem to be one inconsistency, however. Yeats appears to say that Decima has achieved Unity of Being, that face now wholly conforms with mask. Yet Septimus's hopes for a new age dominated by the unicorn—an emblem of Unity of Being, since the unicorn is both an image (a mask) and a beast (a face)—have been totally frustrated. Perhaps this was why when Yeats provided the play with a new ending, he had Decima, speaking of herself in her final speech, say: "She was a bad, headstrong, cruel woman, and seeks destruc-tion somewhere and with some man she knows nothing of." Yeats came to feel that true Unity of Being was not possible to twentieth-century man, that it was possible only in an age like that of Justinian or the imagined age of the unicorn, but that nonetheless it was an ideal worth striving for. Decima has achieved her ambition, but perhaps only for the moment.

In its characterization, *The Player Queen* is unlike the typical farce. The protagonists in most farces can hardly be said to be characters at all, merely grotesque masks. I do not mean that Yeats seeks to present character in three dimensions here, an achievement nearly impossible in drama, but rather that he does brilliantly succeed in making his type-characters individuals, and largely, I think, by the modes of speech he invents for them. This is true whether the role is small or large: the Third Countryman with his tale of the man who went to bed for forty-four years and who was "no way active" is as sharply limned as Septimus. The two Old Men who open and close Scene I seem old age itself; their fear and distrust of the world is so great that they withdraw even from the onset of a traumatic event to concentrate on a dog going by with a bone. The rebels are harshly treated: Yeats loved the mob no more than Shakespeare. They are superstitious and brutal, easily aroused, and, at the end, easily assuaged. As for Septimus's mode of speech, no praise is too great. It is so highfalutin as to be irresistibly funny, and yet it is truly poetic if extravagant. And Septimus is indeed a poet, not a *poète maudit* as some critics have found him. He knows his bestiaries, which is to say that he is a conservator of traditions, and he espouses the highest ideals: he too

> chose for theme
> Traditional sanctity and loveliness.
> [*Variorum Poems*, p. 491]

Yeats develops him with loving care, and there can be no doubt that in the play he stands for Yeats's own views. That he is made ridiculous in no way alters the equation, for with little or no forcing, his role can be seen as a paradigm of Yeats's own role. Even the Old Beggar does more than serve a function: his prophetic role has given him a philosophic turn of mind; he can talk to Decima about eternity.

New characters crowd Scene II. The Prime Minister is the eternal man of action, Septimus's opposite, who understands nothing except affairs but understands these wholly, who is able to deal with events however unexpected. The Queen, about whom the critics have said unkind things, emerges for me as pathetic, totally unsuited for the role into which she has been born, but seen by her creator with kind eyes. Yeats allows her at the end to escape to the convent, where she has always wanted to go. The leading ladies, Decima and Nona, present a brilliant contrast. Surely Decima is Yeats's best Lilith: venereal as a sparrow, totally self-centered, unscrupulous, hungry, yet capable of playing any role demanded of her. Her debate with Nona about which one of them Septimus loves is one of the deftest scenes in modern comedy. As for Nona, I deplore those critics who see in her Bunthorne's Bride. She is the other aspect of essential woman, domestic in spite of every frustration, practical, earthy, the loyal supporter of the artist. All together they are a marvelous crew.

I have nothing to add to what has been said by others on the relation of this play to Yeats's other work. Both Peter Ure and John Rees Moore have dealt with this subject fully. Yeats himself in his note to the play written in 1922 observed that *The Player Queen* was his only play not set in Ireland, although there was to be another, *A Full Moon in March*. Both deal with subjects that are timeless and placeless, and both have, I think, great power. They share a concern with the brutal aspect of human love but aside from that are quite unlike. *A Full Moon in March* presents a terrible myth starkly. *The Player Queen* is a romp of the mind among topics all of which are ultimately serious: the problem of identity, the nature of art, the question of what kind of culture was to rise from the ruins of the World War I. But the mask of comedy never slips, which is but another way of saying that the play of the mind never ceases to be that. It is a highly intellectual work. Whether or not it can be successfully produced in any theater we know I cannot say. Two of its producers, Lennox Robinson and William Becker, have had reservations. In a theater I can imagine, it is a triumphant success.

The Dates of Letters

The letter written to John Butler Yeats on 17 July (*Letters*, pp. 532–33) should be dated 1908, not 1909. Yeats went to Paris in June 1908 to see Maud Gonne (entries in an unpublished manuscript book given to Yeats by Maud Gonne establish this date), and he worked on the new series of "Discoveries" in 1908 (see *Massachusetts Review* 5, no. 2 [Winter 1964]: 297). Robert Gregory had taken a house on the Burren coast, and the party from Coole was staying there (Elizabeth Coxhead, *Lady Gregory*, p. 153n.). The letter of 7 August, which follows in Wade (pp. 533–34), should be dated 1910, not 1909. Yeats had again been staying at Burren. This stay is mentioned in several entries in his *Journal* 1908–1914 [Cf. *Memoirs*, pp. 252–56. Gen. Ed.]; the 1910 date is confirmed by the fact that Yeats dated his essay "The Tragic Theatre," August 1910, "Synge and the Ireland of His Time," 14 September 1910. Both are referred to in the letter. Also, the Abbey Players first toured the United States in 1911, and 1909 seems too early even for preliminary plans. Finally, the letter dated 12 September (*Letters*, p. 588) was written in 1915, not 1914. Various events referred to in the letter can be dated. Sir Ian Hamilton left England in charge of the Gallipoli Expedition in March 1915; the first zeppelin raid on London occurred 31 May 1915, and there was a spectacular raid, to which Robert Gregory's letter no doubt referred, on 8 September 1915 (*Encyclopaedia Britannica*, 12th Edition, "Sir Ian Hamilton" and "Air Raids"). [I think that Yeats's letter to T. Sturge Moore dated 1 May (1909) in *Correspondence*, p. 15, and mentioned by Bradford on p. 4 above, probably should be dated later, and I suggest 1917. Cf. *Letters*, p. 625, where Yeats writes to his father on 12 May 1917, that "I have just made a revision of my *Player Queen*, a prose comedy, and Mrs. Campbell talks of playing [it] for the Stage Society." In the 1 May letter he is about to have such a revision—for Mrs. Campbell and the Stage Society—typed. (Both letters were written at Coole.) The implication that this is a two-act version—as the final *Player Queen* is a two-scene version—is consistent with the later date. Finally, Septimus is mentioned in the 1 May letter, yet according to Bradford (p. 396), the names Septimus, Nona, and Decima came into the play in 1915. Gen. Ed.]

Description of Manuscripts

ALL MANUSCRIPTS with the exception of one version of Draft 29 are in the National Library of Ireland.

1. Scenarios, TS, loose sheets of quarto-size paper, 22 folios.
2. Draft 1. Notebook, MS, 6½″ × 8″; green deckled cover with label "A", 20 folios.
3. Drafts 2, 3, 4, 7, 11. Notebook, MS, 7½″ × 9¼″; purple cover with label "A2", 115 folios.
4. Draft 5. Notebook, MS, 6″ × 8⅓″; red cover, 62 folios. At the end of the draft is a trial plan for the *Collected Works* of 1908.
5. Draft 6. Tablet, MS, 8⅛″ × 10⅝″, 81 folios. Contains list of appointments, astrological reckonings, as well as Draft 6.
6. Draft 8. Two manuscripts: (1) Notebook, MS, 6⅞″ × 8¼″; blue cover with label "B. Act I continued", 20 folios. (2) Same notebook as Draft 5, with label "Player Queen B. Act III." Has note "Act III should play 30 minutes as it is here."
7. Draft 9. Notebook, MS, 6½″ × 8⅛″; blue cover with printed label "Sapphire Series No. 463," 28 folios.
8. Draft 10. Notebook, MS, 6⅛″ × 8¼″; blue cover with printed label "Sapphire Series No. 360," 18 folios.
9. Draft 12. Notebook, MS 6⅞″ × 8⅞″; deckled green cover, 36 folios. This MS is not in Yeats's hand; it was dictated to an amanuensis. Mrs. Yeats did not recognize the hand. The writing is not that of Lady Gregory or Ezra Pound.
10. Drafts 13 and 14. Bound looseleaf notebook sheets, MS, 7⅛″ × 9¼″; buff cover sheets with inscription "Player Queen IV", 51 folios.
11. Draft 15. Three MS notebooks, numbered; TS loose sheets. (1) 8¼″ × 6⅝″; reddish tan covers, printed label "Browne and Nolan's Exercise Books," 25 folios. (2) 6⅜″ × 8″; printed label "The Russet Series No. 604", 20 folios. (3) 6½″ × 8⅜″; blue cover with printed label "Sapphire

Series, No. 360", 24 folios. TS pinned 8"× 10½" sheets, at top title with list of characters, 24 folios.

12. Draft 16. Looseleaf binder with MS and TS, 7⅜" × 9⅜"; inside cover has printed label "Walker's Manuscript Transfer Case" and inscription "Please return to W B Yeats / 18 Woburn Buildings / Euston Road," 118 folios.

13. Draft 17. Looseleaf notebook sheets, MS, 5" × 8", 73 folios.

14. Draft 18. Looseleaf notebook sheets, MS, 6⅞₆" ×8¼₆", 16 folios.

15. Draft 19. Looseleaf notebook sheets, MS, 7⅛" ×9", 23 folios, numbered.

16. Draft 20. Looseleaf notebook sheets, MS, 7" × 9"; labeled "B"; sheets numbered with inscription on verso of folio 24 "Player Queen rejected. Nov 1915 partly verse", 24 folios. TS dictated from this MS, loose sheets, 8" × 10⅜", 16 folios.

17. Draft 21. Loose sheets, MS, 7" × 9"; labeled "A", 73 folios.

18. Draft 22. Loose sheets bound in brown cover, TS, 8" × 10⁵₁₆", 25 folios.

19. Draft 23. Loose sheets, corrected TS, 8" × 10", 18 folios.

20. Draft 24. Loose sheets, TS, 8⅛" × 10½", 14 folios.

21. Draft 25. Loose sheets, MS and TS, 8"× 10⅜", 7 folios and a slip.

22. Draft 26. Notebook, MS, 6½" × 8⅛"; cover has printed label "Eason's Terra Cotta Series No. 9256", 4 folios.

23. Draft 27. Loose sheets, MS, 8" × 10", sheets numbered, 16 folios.

24. Draft 28. Notebook, MS, 6½" × 8¼"; blue cover. On first leaf this note: "Player Queen / late versions / 1919?", 39 folios.

25. Draft 29. Two versions: (1) Loose sheets, TS, 58 folios; from the Mrs. Patrick Campbell papers at the Princeton University Library. (2) Loose sheets, tied, TS, 8" × 10¼", notation "2nd Carbon" on cover, 40 folios. Two typings of the same version.

26. Draft 30. Loose sheets, MS, 6½" × 8⅛", 22 folios.

27. Draft 31. Loose sheets, TS, 8" × 10¼", 42 folios. Another copy of the play as typed in Draft 29, copy 2, with the changes made in Draft 30 inserted on additional typed sheets. Other textual changes inserted in MS. From the files of the Abbey Theatre.

28. Draft 32. From the Rapallo Notebook labeled "D" on the cover and "A" on the flyleaf.

Curtis Bradford

CURTIS BAKER BRADFORD (1911–1969) received a good share of appreciation in his lifetime, and he was publicly honored. Grinnell College, Grinnell, Iowa, where he taught from 1946 until his death, soon made him Chairman of the Department of English and of the Division of Language and Literature, and in 1961 honored him with the Oakes Ames Professorship in Literature. He was privately revered by friends and students, as a letter from R. J. Kaufmann, printed below, beautifully attests. He was considered by scholars to be an impressive scholar. But the true dimensions of the man's achievement have not been realized. This is only partly because of the breadth of his interests.

Yeats scholars know Bradford as the author of important essays, beginning with his piece on the late Yeats and T. S. Eliot, "Journeys to Byzantium," in the Spring 1949 *Virginia Quarterly Review*. He was certainly the leading scholar in transcribing, editing, and interpreting Yeats's manuscripts. While on a Ford fellowship in 1954–1955, and while simultaneously lecturing on American literature at Trinity College, Dublin, Bradford met Mrs. Yeats and worked all year on the manuscripts in her home on Palmerston Road. (He wrote about his impressions of the poet's wife in the Summer 1969 *Sewanee Review*.) Until very recently the only published knowledge of Yeats's novel *The Speckled Bird*, of which a section appeared in the Summer 1955 *Irish Writing*, was due to Bradford's efforts. His study of the development of the Byzantium poems in the March 1960 *PMLA* is, along with Jon Stallworthy's study of about the same time, essential for Yeats scholars—thorough, profound, and illuminating. Based on manuscript sources, his piece on "Yeats and Maude Gonne" in the Winter 1962 *Texas Studies of Literature and Language* seems the definitive study of that relationship and of its importance to Yeats's poetry. The Winter 1964 *Massachusetts Review* contained Yeats's "Discoveries: Second Series" and his "Modern Ireland," both transcribed and edited by Bradford. Bradford's *Yeats at Work* (Southern Illinois University Press, Carbondale and Edwardsville, 1965) shows us Yeats's methods of composition in a variety of contexts by presenting the manuscripts of selected poems, plays, and prose. His pieces on the order of Yeats's *Last Poems* in the June 1961 *Modern Language Notes* and in number 8 of the *Yeats Centenary*

Papers (Dublin: The Dolmen Press, 1966) are based on manuscript evidence and demonstrate the superior meaningfulness of the order in *Last Poems and Two Plays* (Dublin: The Cuala Press, 1939) to the order in the collected editions. Even his reviews of Yeats's *Letters* (*Virginia Quarterly Review,* Winter 1956) and of *The Variorum Edition of the Poems of W. B. Yeats* (*Sewanee Review,* Autumn 1958) are themselves permanently valuable pieces of Yeats scholarship. When Senator Michael Yeats reinstituted the Cuala Press he asked Bradford to do the first volume, *Reflections*, by W. B. Yeats, *Transcribed and Edited from the Journals.* This appeared in 1970 after Bradford's death.

But Yeats scholars may have missed Bradford's essays and reviews on other authors: John Dos Passos, T. S. Eliot, Ernest Hemingway, Willa Cather, William Wordsworth, and Samuel Johnson. Professor Albrecht B. Strauss wrote to me to say:

> Curtis Bradford did some very fundamental work on Johnson in his fine 1937 Yale doctoral dissertation dealing with *The Rambler.* He was the first, for example, to analyze in detail Johnson's heavy revisions for the second and fourth editions, and the report on his findings, "Johnson's Revision of *The Rambler,*" *Review of English Studies,* XV (1939) continues to be authoritative. Thus, Professor William K. Wimsatt leans heavily on the dissertation in *The Prose Style of Samuel Johnson* (see especially pp. 152–53), and in my textual introduction to *The Rambler* volumes in The Yale Edition of the Works of Samuel Johnson I could do little more than repeat some of the things that Bradford had already said thirty years earlier. It's true, I disagreed with Bradford concerning the significance of the Edinburgh *Ramblers;* but this is a small matter. When Mr. Bradford graciously let me consult his *collation* of the various editions, what awed me most of all perhaps was the meticulous care with which he had done a job at which I myself had labored for years and which for him was after all only a small part of his dissertation. I remember telling him the only time I saw him that he must be an enormously fast worker—and the winning smile with which he acknowledged this compliment. He was an impressive man all right.

Bradford also published essays on Johnson in *The Modern Language Review, The Philological Quarterly,* and in *College English.*

But the extent of Bradford's achievement in Yeats studies alone is still unknown because much of his most important work is unpublished. James Ludovic Allen and M. M. Liberman tell the poignant story in their valuable essay "Transcriptions of Yeats's Unpublished Prose in the Bradford Papers at Grinnell

College," *The Serif: Quarterly of the Kent State University Libraries* 10, 1 (Spring 1973): 13–27.

[A major product of Bradford's work in Dublin during 1954–1955] has unfortunately remained almost entirely unknown to the community of Yeats scholars because of the unusual circumstances surrounding it. Along with his other work, Bradford had patiently and meticulously transcribed from almost undecipherable manuscripts and sometimes difficult typescripts what he considered to be the major items of Yeats's unpublished prose. This dedicated labor was done with Mrs. Yeats's permission and presumably with the expectation on Bradford's part that publication of the material under his editorship might be the eventual product. However, after the work was almost complete, Mrs. Yeats changed her mind about publication.

After George Yeats's death, the poet's son, Michael, became chief proprietor of the literary estate. A little more than a year later, Professor Bradford also died, late in 1969. His widow appointed a former colleague, M. M. Liberman, as Bradford's executor. When Liberman sought Senator Michael Yeats's permission to publish the Bradford papers in 1970, the son sustained his mother's decision to keep the materials out of print. However, more recently Senator Yeats has authorized other scholars to study and transcribe some of the same manuscripts for publication (Allen and Liberman, pp. 13–14).

The materials edited for publication by other scholars "duplicate slightly less than half of the material in the Bradford typescripts." Since "Michael Yeats has indicated that he does not anticipate granting permission for publication of these remaining materials in the foreseeable future . . . about four hundred and fifty typewritten pages of transcribed and edited prose by Yeats will remain unpublished on the library shelves at Grinnell" (Allen and Liberman, p. 15). Senator Yeats has "granted James L. Allen permission to study and quote, within reasonable limits, the Bradford papers at Grinnell" (Allen and Liberman, p. 14).

I have some letters from Bradford that deal with this matter. On 6 May 1957, he wrote me, "My edition of the unpublished prose is done and in the hands of Rupert Hart-Davis. You can imagine how eagerly I go for the mail each day hoping to hear from Mr. Hart-Davis." But he was doomed to disappointment. On 28 July 1963, he wrote me that "Yeats's unpublished prose is very extensive. I have collected all? of it and transcribed it, but was unable to get Mrs. Yeats's permission to publish the book." Earlier, in a *vita* dated 27 April 1960, Bradford had listed the *Unpublished Prose of W. B. Yeats* and had commented, "This, my principal scholarly work, has not been cleared for publication by Mrs. W. B. Yeats." That he felt it a more important accomplishment than *Yeats at Work* is shown by the fact that the latter, finished in June 1959, is also listed in the *vita*.

In his memoir of Mrs. Yeats, Bradford describes her impatience· with the subject of the automatic writing which she did under Yeats's influence, and the inclusion of such material as the Leo Africanus letters may in part have caused her unwillingness to have the prose appear. Bradford suggests another reason for that unwillingness, which must certainly be wrong: "It is also a fact that many unpublished portions of Yeats's papers deal with Maud Gonne. George Yeats witheld them from publication because 'W B would not have wished it.' " If there is an implication here that Mrs. Yeats herself "would not have wished it," I can only say that Mrs. Yeats was in no way a petty person—quite the opposite. On the other hand, I have heard her say that while she had no objection to publishing manuscript versions of already published titles, she did object to publishing today works which Yeats in his lifetime had not chosen to publish. The attitude has logic and reveals loyalty. Senator Michael Yeats, too, must think primarily of Yeats's literary reputation in deciding what may or may not be published. Nevertheless, Yeats scholars may be forgiven for hoping that we may ultimately have all of the *Unpublished Prose* in print.

Bradford's final achievement was *W. B. Yeats: The Writing of The Player Queen*. On 29 June 1969, weeks before his death, Bradford wrote to me: "The book has been considerably revised since the copy I sent you, and, I hope, improved. I have still retained my interest now after three years of little else, and that may be a good sign or merely an indication of fatigue. I shall be glad to get on to other work."

General Editor

The University of Texas at Austin
Austin, Texas 78712
25 February 1970

Prof. David R. Clark
Dept. of English
University of Massachusetts
Amherst, Mass. 01002

Dear Prof. Clark:

I received your letter of the 17th only yesterday. Naturally, I am eager to do anything within my power to assist you in the making of your statement of appreciation. Curtis Bradford was a man about whom I cared deeply.

I will not try to construct a shaped statement. My aim will be to provide a few pieces of information about our relationship and my perceptions of him as a man. You are more than welcome to quarry, quote, assimilate anything you choose. My endeavor is a pragmatic one: to help you deliver the truest, most attractive statement possible.

I returned to Grinnell after the War in 1946. I was then twenty-two and I imagine Curtis was around thirty-four. He had just joined the English Dept. after his own War stint. He was tall, very slender, faintly ascetic but without harshness, aristocratic in bearing with a subdued elegance of movement and manner conferred by a sense of style and his fine taste, for he was as poor and shabby as the proverbial garret poet. He loved his wife—a wonderful, spiritually resilient but suffering refugee, Maria. They had a very young family started. They lived across the street from the campus in a large, under-furnished second floor apartment of a rambling old house. I dwell briefly on these physical aspects, because they introduced me (I do not mean recruited me) to a way of inflecting and ordering life which I had not encountered. It was a way of life that pressed upon my imagination, for it had a kind of wholeness; it was authentic. This was despite the most unremitting sequence of bad luck, mishap, and even tragedy, when Maria's sole surviving close relative, her nephew, was killed in a motor-cycle accident in North Carolina and his body was sent to Grinnell in high Springtime for burial in the little, village-like graveyard on the hill outside the town. I had come from the War; so had all the other pallbearers. Death was very familiar to me, but this was the first time I ever really felt its full force. Curtis himself organized the beautiful little ceremony. I shall not forget, ever, his sweet and firm reading of Collins's "How sleep the dead . . ." at the graveside, but even more than this his magnificent goodness, his almost circumambient solicitude for his bereaved wife, for whom the death completed the Nazis' violation of her family and her past. I simply tell you the truth when I say that his behavior at that moment—at that period—taught me (and I have never forgotten it) that there are dimensions to manhood I had not previously suspected. There is more to being a teacher than explicating texts.

He did this well too. I studied modern poetry with him for a year. I had been a mathematician before returning from the War. I came from a wholly scientific family. In his class I first encountered Yeats and Eliot and Pound. At his house and working together in the large vegetable garden we had together to supply extra food, since we were both poor, I heard for the first time about Kafka and Proust and Joyce and a dozen others whom I read with the voracious endurance of the young man whose true vocation has been found. He had and we read through a complete file of *Horizon* which he had paid for and let accumulate during his service years—it was a kind of half symbolic, half practical umbilicus to keep him, however tenuously, connected to the life of the mind he hoped to resume. You see, simply put, Curtis Bradford was the first disinterested, dedicated intellectual I had ever seen. No one since has seemed more perfectly to capture the authentic core of his role—a role I now try to play myself.

Curtis Bradford had his foibles. I saw them then, but they did not put me off as they surely would have done in a man less genuine inwardly. He was much harassed, he was worried about money and family matters, but these were never uppermost. In manner he expressed an almost gallant cheerfulness. His speech was a little finicky, his manner in class until he found his postwar stride was alternately almost reverentially severe in his priestly dedication to the texts or a little too sophisticated and artful in his use of language. I now see—and I did fairly soon at that time—that he was a shy man who was talking in public about something he loved, truly loved, and he needed to find a *persona* which could at once protect his sensitivity and preserve his sincerity. He gradually evolved this right in our presence; by the end of the year his classes were among the best I have ever attended. Beyond a doubt they sealed my conviction that this was the way I wanted to spend my own life.

I cried when Edward Foster (one of my own Ph.D. students at Rochester who had gone to Grinnell as a new Ph.D. and done so well that he was the Chairman of the Humanities Division at the time of Curtis's death) called me to give the news. This was at first a profound surprise, for I haven't cried more than a couple times in 25 years. But as I dwelt on my memories of Curtis, I came to understand that the love for his work, his family, his students, his friends, which was the core of Curtis's nature, had been so nonacquisitive, so unsentimentalized, so unselfish and constant that I had partly forgotten it— *assumed* it you might say. But there it *had* been; and now it was gone. Curtis was a profoundly genuine man. He went the extra mile; he cut no corners in human or professional relationships; he cared and he taught others to care. I am not myself a believer, not even a Christian at all; I think he wasn't really one himself despite his childhood indoctrination, but still for me he stands as an index of an almost vanished Christian goodness—firm rather than soft, quiet rather than assertive, a kind of luminous witness to a way of life that none of his wearying cares, his worn suits, his ravaged, eager face can ever dim. I loved the man, the teacher, the mind. If I knew how, I would bless his memory as I thank him for his life.

Sincerely,

R. J. Kaufman
Prof. of English

CURTIS BRADFORD 1911–1969

PERSONAL LIFE, EDUCATION, AND EXPERIENCE

1911 June 2, born in Mattituck, New York. Son of Lewis Addison and Ella Grace (Baker) Bradford.

1929 Graduated from Olean High School, Olean, New York.

1933 B.A. in English, College of Wooster, Wooster, Ohio.

1937 Ph.D. in English, Yale University. Dissertation on Johnson's *The Rambler.*

1937–1941 Instructor in English, University of Wisconsin, Madison.

1941 August 15, married to Maria Gerson. Her education: Certificate, Pestalozzi Froebel Haus, Berlin, Germany.

1941–1943 Assistant Professor, Rockford College, Rockford, Illinois.

1943 April 23, daughter Maria Ann born.

1943–1946 U.S. Army Air Force.

1944 December 25, son Lewis Addison II born.

1946 August 30, son Walter Gerson born.

1946–1950 Moved to Grinnell College, Grinnell, Iowa, as Associate Professor. Became Chairman of Department of English and Chairman of Division of Language and Literature.

1950 Professor of English, Grinnell College.

1951 Summer. Studied fine arts and history, University of Wisconsin.

1953 September 2, daughter Nancy Ellen born.

1954–1955 Ford Fellowship. Visiting Lecturer in American literature, Trinity College, Dublin. Worked on manuscripts of W. B. Yeats at Mrs. Yeats's home and the National Library, Dublin. Traveled in Holland and Germany, 1954.

1960 Summer in Ireland.

1961 Honored with Oakes Ames Professorship in Literature, Grinnell College.

1962–1963 Mexico.

1968–1969 Sabbatical leave in Ireland to work on manuscripts of *The Player Queen.*

1969 October 2, death in University Hospital, Iowa City, Iowa, after a summer's serious illness.

CURTIS BRADFORD—Publications

BOOKS

The Communication of Ideas (Boston: D. C. Heath, 1951). (A textbook for the first course in communication skills.)

Yeats at Work (Carbondale and Edwardsville: Southern Illinois University Press, 1965). (A study of representative manuscripts of Yeats: poems, plays, and prose.)

Reflections by W. B. Yeats, transcribed and edited by Curtis Bradford from the Journals (Dublin: The Cuala Press, 1970).

W. B. Yeats: The Writing of *The Player Queen* (DeKalb: Northern Illinois University Press, 1976).

ARTICLES

"Wordsworth's White Doe of Rylestone and Related Poems," *Modern Philology*, 36: 59–70.

"The Edinburgh Ramblers," *Modern Language Review*, 34: 241–44.

"Arthur Murphy's Meeting with Johnson," *Philological Quarterly*, 18: 318–20.

"Johnson's Revision of *The Rambler*," *Review of English Studies*, 15 (1939): 302–14.

"On Teaching the Age of Johnson," *College English*, 3: 650–59. With S. G. Brown.

"John Dos Passos—a Defense," *University Review*, 7: 267–72.

"Footnotes to East Coker: a Reading," *Sewanee Review*, 52: 169–75.

"The Short Stories of Ernest Hemingway," *Tanager* (December 1946): 3–7.

"Journeys to Byzantium," *Virginia Quarterly Review*, 25, 2 (Spring 1949): 205–25.

"Willa Cather's Uncollected Short Stories," *American Literature*, 26: 537–51.

"*The Speckled Bird:* A Novel by W. B. Yeats. A Selection from the Novel, with a Note," *Irish Writing*, 31 (Summer 1955): 9–18.

"Yeats's Letters," *Virginia Quarterly Review*, 32, 1 (Winter 1956): 157–60.

"*The Variorum Edition of Yeats's Poems*," *Sewanee Review*, 66, 4 (Autumn 1958): 668–78.

"Yeats's Byzantium Poems: A Study of Their Development," *PMLA*, 75, 1: (March 1960): 110–25. Reprinted in *Yeats: A Collection of Critical Essays*, ed. John Unterecker (Englewood Cliffs, N. J.: Prentice-Hall, 1963), pp. 93–130, and in *Aspects of Poetry*, ed. Mark Linenthal (Boston and Toronto: Little, Brown, 1963), pp. 64–103.

"The Order of Yeats's Last Poems," *Modern Language Notes*, 76, 6 (June 1961): 515–16.

"Yeats and Maude Gonne," *Texas Studies in Language and Literature*, 3, 4 (Winter 1962): 452–74.

"Modern Ireland: An Address to American Audiences, 1932–1933" by W. B. Yeats, transcribed from the MS and edited by Curtis Bradford, *Massachusetts*

Review, 5, 2 (Winter 1964): 256–68. Reprinted in *Irish Renaissance,* ed. Robin Skelton and David R. Clark (Dublin: The Dolmen Press, 1965), pp. 13–25.

"Discoveries: Second Series," by W. B. Yeats, transcribed from the MS and edited by Curtis Bradford, *Massachusetts Review,* 5, 2 (Winter 1964): 297–306. Reprinted in *Irish Renaissance,* ed. Robin Skelton and David R. Clark (Dublin: The Dolmen Press, 1965), pp. 80–89.

"Yeats's 'Last Poems' Again" by Curtis Bradford, Being No. VIII of the Dolmen Press Centenary Papers MCMLXV [Dublin: The Dolmen Press, 1966], pp. 259–88.

"George Yeats: Poet's Wife," *Sewanee Review,* 67 (1969): 388–404.

List of
Works Cited

Becker, William. "The Mask Mocked: Or, Farce and the Dialectic of Self (Notes on Yeats's *The Player Queen*)," *Sewanee Review*, 61, 1 (Winter 1953): 82–108.

Bradford, Curtis B. *Yeats at Work*. Carbondale and Edwardsville: Southern Illinois University Press, 1965.

[Colonna, Francesco.] *Hypnerotomachia. The Strife of Love in a Dream*. London, 1592 [Ann Arbor, Mich.: University Microfilms, 1967].

Colonna, Francesco. *The Strife of Love in a Dream, Being the Elizabethan Version of the First Book of the Hypnerotomachia of Francesco Colonna*, ed. Andrew Lang. London: David Nutt, 1890.

———. *Hypnerotomachia: The Strife of Love in a Dream*. Farnborough, Hants: Gregg International Publishers, 1969.

Coxhead, Elizabeth. *Lady Gregory: A Literary Portrait*. London: Macmillan and Company, 1961.

Ellmann, Richard. *The Identity of Yeats*. New York: Oxford University Press, 1954.

———. *Yeats the Man and the Masks*. London: Macmillan and Company, 1949.

Henn, T. R. *The Lonely Tower: Studies in the Poetry of W. B. Yeats*. London: Methuen and Company, 1950.

Jung, C. G. "The Paradigm of the Unicorn," *Psychology and Alchemy*, trans. R. F. C. Hull, *Collected Works*, XII. Princeton, N.J.: Princeton University Press, 1953, pp. 415–51.

Melchiori, Giorgio. *The Whole Mystery of Art: Pattern into Poetry in the Work of W. B. Yeats*. New York: The Macmillan Company, 1961.

Moore, John Rees. "The Janus Face: Yeats's *Player Queen*," *Sewanee Review*, 76, 4 (Autumn 1968): 608–30.

———. *Masks of Love and Death: Yeats as Dramatist*. Ithaca and London: Cornell University Press, 1971.

Newton, Norman. "Yeats the Dramatist," *Essays in Criticism,* 8 (1958) : 269–84.

Parkinson, Thomas. *W. B. Yeats Self Critic: A Study of His Early Verse.* Berkeley: University of California Press, 1951.

Regardie, Israel. *The Golden Dawn: An Account of the Teachings, Rites, and Ceremonies of the Order of the Golden Dawn.* 4 vols. Chicago: The Aries Press, 1937—; reissued (4 vols. in 2), St. Paul, Minn.: Llewellyn Publishers, 1969.

Robinson, Lennox. *Ireland's Abbey Theatre: A History, 1899–1951.* London: Sidgwick and Jackson, 1951.

Saul, George Brandon. *Prolegomena to the Study of Yeats's Plays.* Philadelphia: University of Pennsylvania Press, 1958.

Shepard, Odell. *The Lore of the Unicorn.* Boston and New York: Houghton Mifflin Company, 1930.

Synge, John M. *Deirdre of the Sorrows: A Play.* ["Preface" by W. B. Yeats] Churchtown: Cuala Press, 1910.

Ure, Peter. *Yeats the Playwright: A Commentary on Character and Design in the Major Plays.* New York: Barnes and Noble, 1963, pp. 134–45.

Vendler, Helen H. *Yeats's "Vision" and the Later Plays.* Cambridge, Mass.: Harvard University Press, 1963.

Wilson, F. A. C. *W. B. Yeats and Tradition.* London: Victor Gollancz, 1958.

Yeats, J. B. *Letters to His Son W. B. Yeats and Others, 1869–1922,* ed. Joseph Hone, pref. Oliver Elton. New York: E. P. Dutton and Company, 1946.

Yeats, W. B. *The Autobiography of William Butler Yeats.* New York: The Macmillan Company, 1953.

———. *The Collected Plays of W. B. Yeats.* London: Macmillan and Company, 1934.

———. *The Collected Works in Verse and Prose of William Butler Yeats.* 8 vols. Stratford-on-Avon: Shakespeare Head Press, 1908.

———. *Discoveries: A Volume of Essays.* Dundrum: Dun Emer Press, 1907.

———. "Discoveries: Second Series," *Massachusetts Review,* 5, 2 (Winter 1964) : 297–306.

———. *Early Poems and Stories.* New York: The Macmillan Company, 1925.

———. *If I were Four-and-Twenty.* Dublin: The Cuala Press, 1940.

———. *The Letters of W. B. Yeats,* ed. Allen Wade. London: Rupert Hart-Davis, 1954.

———. *Letters on Poetry from W. B. Yeats to Dorothy Wellesley.* London, New York, Toronto: Oxford University Press, 1940.

———. *Michael Robartes and the Dancer.* Churchtown, Dundrum: The Cuala Press, 1920.